DOMESTICATING THE EMPIRE

*Race, Gender, and Family Life in French
and Dutch Colonialism*

DOMESTICATING THE EMPIRE §*Race, Gender, and Family Life in French and Dutch Colonialism ⁊*

Edited by JULIA CLANCY-SMITH
and FRANCES GOUDA

UNIVERSITY PRESS OF VIRGINIA
Charlottesville and London

For notice of previous publication, see chapter 7, note 1, chapter 8, note 1, and chapter 12, note 1.

THE UNIVERSITY PRESS OF VIRGINIA
© 1998 by the Rector and Visitors of the University of Virginia
All rights reserved
Printed in the United States of America

First published 1998

∞ The paper used in this publication meets the minimum requirements of the American National Standard for Information Sciences—
Permanence of Paper for Printed Library Materials, ANSI Z39.48-1984.

Library of Congress Cataloging-in-Publication Data
Domesticating the empire : race, gender, and family life in French and
   Dutch colonialism / edited by Julia Clancy-Smith and Frances Gouda.
      p.   cm.
   Includes index.
   ISBN 0-8139-1780-8 (cloth : alk. paper). — ISBN 0-8139-1781-6
(pbk. : alk. paper)
      1. Women—France—Colonies—History—19th century.   2. Women—
   France—Colonies—History—20th century.   3. Women—Netherlands—
   Colonies—History—19th century.   4. Women—Netherlands—Colonies—
   History—20th century.   I. Clancy-Smith, Julia Ann.   II. Gouda,
   Frances, 1950–   .
   HQ1613.D62   1998
   305.3'0944—dc21   97-39064
                                                                    CIP

Frontispiece: French postcard of an Algerian Arab Muslim woman writing in ungrammatical French: "If you lift my skirt, you can see the arts of the colonies." This card and others like it were sold at the Colonial Exposition held in Paris in 1931. The depiction of a Muslim woman writing in French is particularly ironic since the colonial state in Algeria discouraged Arab women from gaining a modern French education. (Photograph KIT, Amsterdam)

FOR OUR *Mothers*

CONTENTS

ILLUSTRATIONS

ACKNOWLEDGMENTS

The editors have incurred a large number of intellectual debts which reach distant corners of the globe. First of all, our contributors, some of whom were located in faraway places, deserve our gratitude for their prompt attention to the interminable requests for revisions and diskettes. We also wish to thank our editor at the University Press of Virginia, Richard Holway, whose patience helped us not to lose heart in the face of the usual delays and other problems. In addition, the anonymous readers of the manuscript in its various guises merit our recognition. The University of Arizona provided financial support: the Provost's Authors Fund awarded this collection of essays a grant, while the Department of Near Eastern Studies generously assisted as well, particularly Professor Charles D. Smith and Elizabeth Dyckman. Bethany Fitch, Beth Kangas, and Maureen Moynihan, graduate students at the University of Arizona, carefully read the introduction and made insightful comments. At the end, when we faced the complicated task of producing a master diskette that could incorporate texts produced on twelve different, often incompatible, computers, Gary L. Kabakoff saved the day with his technological expertise. Finally, all of us as authors of chapters have benefited over the past several years from the intellectual comradery of friends, colleagues, and many others who have pored over drafts, discussed ideas, and offered critiques of work-in-progress.

DOMESTICATING THE EMPIRE
Race, Gender, and Family Life in French and Dutch Colonialism

1. INTRODUCTION

Frances Gouda and Julia Clancy-Smith

THEORETICAL CONSIDERATIONS

Until quite recently scholars of empire seemed to resemble the objects of their own inquiry. Empire was imagined as a global chess game whose players were almost exclusively European men, often hailing from elite backgrounds. The official agendas, secret strategies, and back-room deals of empire builders in European or colonial capitals represented the sum total of historical problems judged as significant. Millions of different ethnic peoples populating colonized societies were virtually absent from conventional political or diplomatic narratives. Also ignored were marginal Europeans who forged the social fabric of many of the makeshift expatriate communities in Asia or Africa. These uprooted Westerners consisted of poor shopkeepers, petty traders, dirt farmers, and eccentrics who had settled down in colonial outposts with native partners; their descendants were designated as "mixed bloods" or described by a wide range of other, often derogatory, terms.

Women, whether European or non-European, were rarely singled out as deserving special scrutiny in this older scholarly tradition. The historical narratives detailing international politics or the global dissemination of European culture, written before decolonization altered the map of the world, were regarded as immune to gender analysis. The primary sources recording the history of European expansion consisted of written decrees, treaties, and the policy proposals of statesmen.[1] When scholars utilized oral data, they tended to privilege the statements of ministers, colonial civil servants, or European "merchant princes" in overseas territories.[2] Hence, historians investigating the nature and mechanisms of colonial rule from this earlier position could be considered just as imperial in their approach as the military officers, administrators, and adventurers who, by force or guile, expanded Europe's overseas possessions so that by 1914 roughly four-fifths of the world's inhabited surface was controlled in one way or another by the Great Powers.

A new generation of scholars in the 1960s, when the world had become a tentatively postcolonial place, evinced a critical concern with international political economy. With a new set of questions in mind, historians began to recalculate the balance sheets of imperial ventures in order to assess profits and losses to the mother countries.[3] Yet some within this next cohort of students of Western imperialism, propelled by a sense of guilt or moral outrage, have represented European colonialism as a faceless Behemoth of political and economic subjugation that was unilaterally imposed upon vulnerable, if anonymous, native victims. These more recent interpretations, even if inspired by high-minded motivations, have produced a curious irony. Many among these second-wave scholars in the Western world have also been somewhat Eurocentric in their approach.[4] Because few analyzed the arts of resistance deployed by indigenous peoples under Western colonial rule, they often replicated the visions of earlier imperial historians as well as those of local colonial officials. Not infrequently, these civil servants viewed the natives as little more than a potential source of agricultural labor that might expedite the economic profitability (*mise en valeur*) of colonized lands, a perception that resurfaced in the 1960s in many chronicles concerning European rule in Asia or Africa.

In recent years, however, the imperial theater as a site for research and debate has become both more crowded and more contentious. While historians have not entirely lost their grip on the subject, they have been forced to share the intellectual stage with scholars from other disciplines; what is currently known as colonial studies, an unruly offshoot of cultural studies, has burgeoned during the past decade or so.[5] Because of this transformation new voices and social groups from the colonial past are now listened to and acknowledged. Women settlers, female and male native servants, missionaries, and mixed-blood children have emerged as legitimate objects of inquiry. Their stories, which historians have begun to uncover in a piecemeal fashion, convey the poignant realities of semiconcealed lives. Such narratives now function either as counterpoints or subtexts to the classic narratives about self-disciplined European men and their intrepid actions in foreign lands. In the process current scholars now mine unorthodox historical evidence, which ranges from manuals for colonial housewives and novels for young girls to photographic depictions of quaint ethnic groups or prurient descriptions of the marital practices of the colonized.

This new multidisciplinary lens trained upon Western imperialism and its intrusions into the world beyond Europe has profoundly altered our thinking about the colonial encounter.[6] These most recent perspectives have produced a realization that colonial societies were eclectic communities deeply divided by local political frictions, class antagonisms, or competing cultural claims. As a result a simple dyadic model, representing colonial mastery as a monolithic Western world that inflicted its materialistic greed upon innocent native captives, no longer suffices. More flexible definitions of what constitutes historical evidence about the imperial enterprise have placed issues of gender and race or identity and status on center stage; such new perspectives, in turn, have further nuanced the true nature of white men's political agency in the colonies. At the same time these novel modes of engaging colonial histories have provoked a wide-ranging scholarly conversation on the nature of legitimate texts, the relationship between knowledge and power, and the politics of representation.[7]

During the past two decades or so, a growing number of historians, political scientists, anthropologists, and literary critics have focused attention on the diverse peoples and regional cultures subsumed under the unsatisfactory rubric of the "colonized." They have emphasized that imperial policies and practices were formulated not only in Paris, The Hague, or London. Instead, the significance of complex negotiations between European administrators and indigenous actors in particular locales has been recognized. Native elites, wives and children, priests and village chiefs, or peasant elders influenced the ground rules of European domination; apparent complicity or accommodation might also include resistance.[8] At the same time scholars of women's history in non-European regions began to ponder the oft-repeated bromide that the colonies were "no place for a white woman." Out of this questioning came the 1992 collection of essays edited by Nupur Chaudhuri and Margaret Strobel, *Western Women and Imperialism: Complicity and*

Resistance, which argued against casting white women in a simplistic role, as either heroic opponents of worldwide imperialism or complicit agents in it.[9] In many ways Chaudhuri and Strobel's important volume provided the inspiration for our present endeavor.

In this collection of essays, however, we have deliberately chosen to focus exclusively upon the two European powers that were the runners-up in the global seizure of land—France and the Netherlands. Despite the fact that France came close to Great Britain in terms of Asian and African real estate holdings and the number of peoples subject to France's imperial embrace, the lion's share of theoretical and empirical scholarship on colonial history has revolved around the British Empire, especially in India. Not far behind France and Great Britain was the Netherlands, whose domains in Southeast Asia constituted the third largest, yet by far the most lucrative, colonial treasure trove in the world.[10] Curiously, the followers of the subaltern studies movement, although offering powerful critiques of British imperialism in recent years, have not subverted the primacy of the British imperial model.[11] While bringing into the scholarly limelight indigenous perspectives on European mastery and listening to the insurgent voices of Indian men and women, the subaltern approach may have reinforced the paradigmatic stature of British colonialism rather than dismantling it.[12]

This continuing emphasis was one factor in our decision to restrict attention to the empires of France and the Netherlands, domains that have not been investigated as thoroughly in English-language scholarship as the British case. But there is a more compelling reason. These two competing yet intersecting empires in Asia and Africa force us to revisit a body of theoretical literature that has been inscribed to a great extent with the uniqueness of British India. A detailed examination of French and Dutch colonial cultures enhances our understanding of the differences and similarities in national styles and in the particular sensibilities that infused almost every colonial state, above all, as a "nexus of projects and arrangements."[13] Most forms of colonial mastery encompassed much more than a homogeneous ideology conjured up merely to disguise or vindicate Western modes of domination. Instead, colonial cultures were also expressive and constitutive of local imperial relationships themselves.[14] Indeed, European colonialism on the ground tended to be partially shaped by indigenous traditions, while conversely attempting to recast native customs and practices in its own image.[15]

In addition, imperial administrators worldwide carefully studied each other's strengths and weaknesses. French and Dutch orientalists exchanged scholarly findings about Eastern religious traditions or about the nature of Islam. Thus, scholars were directly implicated in the imperial project; their research greatly increased Europeans' collective knowledge of, and power over, Asians and Africans. Of particular concern to Dutch and French colonial authorities and to the orientalist scholars associated with them were the diverse Muslim peoples in such disparate regions as Indonesia and Morocco.[16]

In many academic discussions and transactions, issues of Muslim sexuality and Islamic marriage practices, customs, and laws were placed at the forefront of imperial agendas. To provide but one example among many others: by the early twentieth century, colonial authorities in the Dutch East Indies and French North Africa viewed Islam as a political force that could destabilize colonial regimes. At the same time orientalist scholars became deeply interested in Islam as an intrinsically different form of sociosexual organization due, in large part, to Europeans' growing obsession with the status of women in Islamic cultures. Although the women were relegated to a position of subservience within marriage, customs and traditions on the overwhelmingly Muslim island of Java in colonial Indonesia, for instance, granted them a variety of legal rights including inheritance and control of their own property in the case of divorce. Many of these same rights were still denied to European women during the first half of the twentieth century.[17]

By juxtaposing France and the Netherlands—while making use of the theoretical insights of scholars of British India, such as Homi Bhabha, Gyatri Chakravorty Spivak, and Nicholas Dirks—we can test a range of hypotheses regarding metropolitan ideas about gender relations, race, and class alignments and their translation into highly specific social settings worldwide. This collection of essays highlights the distinct social and political practices embedded in either Dutch or French national culture and the ways in which ingrained national conventions were exported overseas, only to journey back to Europe again. By tracking these processes, the essays in this collection chronicle how and why national values underwent subtle changes or, in some cases, were warped beyond recognition when transplanted in the colonial periphery, taking root in alien or hybrid cultural soil.

Indeed, European metropoles and their Asian or African colonies were subjected to a reciprocal, if convoluted, flow of ideologies and social processes. The current, if belated, scholarly recognition of this has produced an analogous reconfiguration of history as an academic discipline. Historical turfs, until now quite distinct, have been nudged closer together by the simultaneous interest in imperialism, gender, and the cultures of formerly colonized peoples. Until very recently, historians and social scientists of modern France or the Netherlands remained largely within the confines of national borders. Events in Southeast Asia or just across the Mediterranean were only explicitly woven into nation-state narratives when extraordinary upheavals, such as the trauma of Indonesian decolonization in the post–World War II period or the Algerian War (1954–62), brought colonial crises home to the mother countries. The Eurocentric orientation of the historical profession also stemmed from the fact that those scholars placing the colonized at the center of their research often were relegated to distant outposts within many academic institutions.

The chapters in the volume demonstrate that definitions of the proper domain of historical inquiry are changing and that history can be "rescued from the nation-state," to use Prasenjit Duara's apt phrase.[18] French or Dutch colonialism, which many scholars previously viewed as largely irrelevant to the transformations of politics and civil society within the European heartland, are now seen as intrinsically related to the unfolding of those histories. Scholars trained primarily in French or Dutch history are reaching beyond the confines of Europe. Several of the authors of chapters in this collection were not initially schooled in the study of European imperialism. All of the contributors, however, combine a profound understanding of the histories of France or the Netherlands with explorations of how European and colonized women and men forged new political and cultural identities or attempted to cling to older ones in the course of lopsided and at times brutal colonial encounters.[19] In short, the historiographical task here is to transcend not only the intellectual dominance of "First World" logic but also to rise above the notion of "Third World" reactivity.[20]

The chapters in this book deal with French and Dutch engagements with civilizations and cultures, stretching from Africa to Indochina and the Indonesian archipelago. By fusing an analysis of relations between the sexes or gendered rhetoric with colonial ideologies across a wide geographical expanse, the essays in this collection show that feminist scholars can steer the discussion about the multiple meanings of colonial legacies in as yet unplotted directions. Not only have our contributors read the standard archival records; they have also ransacked imperial attics in search of more unusual chronicles, documents, or literary texts. The imaginative use of these neglected sources from the past preserves the integrity of the historian's craft, with its abiding respect for sources—both their limitations and possibilities.

THE ESSAYS

Since the Renaissance and the early modern era, travel journals, composed by European explorers or settlers about their encounters with unfamiliar peoples in distant lands, have proliferated. Initially portraying non-Europeans as heathen barbarians who belonged to the realm of demonology, chroniclers during the Enlightenment depicted them above all as naive and unenlightened. The so-called primitive mind represented the infancy of the human spirit, while rational Europeans personified its highest form, because native people everywhere failed to recognize the primacy of reason and logic by invoking spirits or appealing to magic.[21]

These eighteenth-century depictions of non-Europeans as untutored children eventually gave birth to a more wide-ranging set of tropes. When later European travelers observed the Dutch East Indies, for example, they glorified the islands of Java and Sumatra and their "golden-bronze" inhabitants in rhapsodic language. But the Occident and the Orient, a Dutch journalist named Charles Boissevain proclaimed in 1909, belonged together as man and woman. The West was strong, energetic, and logical, while the East was weak, languorous, and emotional. Hence, the European husband should take his fragile Asian bride by the hand and escort her through life: because of her inherent frailty, she would always need powerful masculine guidance from the West.[22]

Boissevain's reliance upon images of masculinity and femininity in depictions of the relationship between robust, rational Dutch colonizers and the supposedly delicate populations of the Indonesian archipelago was far from unique. Virtually all residents of European settler societies attempted to legitimize their presence in Asia or Africa through historically specific languages of politics and culture. These frequently were informed by familiar notions of masculinity and femininity or motherhood and fatherhood.[23] Whether they wrote in French, Dutch, English, Spanish, Portuguese, German, or Italian, whenever Europeans talked about the nature of their rights and responsibilities vis-à-vis colonized subjects, they frequently employed gendered metaphors. Gender-based figures of speech concealed, while also revealing, unequal social positions unrelated to female versus male identity per se. In addition, these analogies constituted widely recognizable symbols that gave concrete expression to perceived differences in power, intellectual ability, and cultural or moral refinement.

Through elaborate figures of speech, the idea of gender was often dislodged from the tangible realm of physiological distinctions between men and women. It became a narrative tool or an epistemological device designed not only to illuminate but also to affirm social hierarchies. However, metaphor, metonymy, or analogy, whether they created allusions that were earthy or sublime, did not merely serve a descriptive purpose; they also operated as constitutive elements in cognitive processes and influenced the development of human understanding.[24] Most people relied upon particular tropes because they expressed "a pre-existing and culturally shared model" through verbal imagery that was both graphic and readily comprehensible.[25] This is illustrated by Janet Horne's essay, "In Pursuit of Greater France: Visions of Empire among Musée Social Reformers in France, 1894–1931." Horne argues that "culturally forged paradigms" articulated an understanding, shared by a particular group of French social reformers, as to how the world worked at the end of the nineteenth century. These paradigms also encompassed a diffuse set of cultural ideals regarding how the world ought to function and might unfold in the future. Knowledge and power, their interpretations and representations, are "inextricably connected to the specific rhetorical envelope in which they are conveyed." Or to put it another way, the meanings of formal imperial domination or of the ebb and flow of daily life as lived and experienced by colonizer and colonized "derived in part from the way in which they are narrated."[26]

Europeans' use of a language of the family in Asia or Africa, trying to accentuate the necessity and normalcy of colonial rule, registered a consensus—albeit a highly malleable and self-serving one—about the parental nature of their obligations toward their non-European proté-gés. This vocabulary, in turn, intermingled with cultural practices and political concerns in the European heartland. Such interactions pro-duced a flexible repertoire of rhetorical constructions that verbalized Europeans' visions of imperial relationships and helped to convert ideas into practice. At times colonial discussions in some arenas shifted from maternal to paternal models or represented native peoples as either re-bellious young boys or defenseless little girls. This allowed European guardians to endow their middle-class hegemony with an organic co-herence, whether at home or abroad.

Obviously a single fund of rhetorical devices characterizing relations of power between Europeans and indigenous "others" did not exist. In-deed, as the history of French Algeria demonstrates, several discourses flourished simultaneously. One was the official colonial ideology for-mulated in France, which tended to celebrate France's "civilizing mis-sion" and drew upon a ready-made stock of parental images by the end of the nineteenth century. The *pieds-noirs* or Mediterranean settlers in Algeria, however, rarely used a language of family or kinship to describe their day-to-day encounters with the Arab and Berber populations. In contrast, their vocabulary defined Algerian Muslims as the "enemy" and asserted the irreconcilable differences between Islam and the West.[27] In the face of these multiple idioms and stories, the historian's task is to read between the lines in order to describe the unequal, at times violent, yet intimate entanglements of colonizers and colonized. By uncovering shifts in the ways in which colonizers talked about the colonized, im-perceptible to those who employed such language, it is possible to chart changing forms of oppression, control, and contestation.

By no means the first to point out the interplay between colony and mother country, Michel Foucault systematically linked the knowledge acquired by Europeans in their search for remunerative dominions in Asia, the Americas, or Africa to the formation of economic divisions and class identities within the nations of modern Europe.[28] While the notion of internal colonialism was hardly new—it has an older pedi-gree among world historians, macro sociologists, and scholars of the modern world system—Foucault's contribution was to make us think about semantics. He emphasized that the practice of gathering cultural information on colonized societies constituted, above all, a particular form of knowledge which simultaneously obscured yet revealed the realities of Europeans' political and economic might. By translating the complexity of colonial relationships into a domestic, kin-centered language that summoned the ubiquitous, if diverse, phenomenon of family life, the social control exerted by white-skinned foreigners—or their native retainers—could be rendered "recognizable, habitable, intelligible, and natural." [29]

Foucault's work has spawned a new academic cottage industry of colonial-discourse analysis during the past two decades, incorporating both postmodern textual criticism and subaltern studies. One of the best-known books in this Foucault-inspired genre is Edward Said's much-debated *Orientalism*, which in its own right provoked yet another wave of critical scholarship. [30] Collectively Foucault, Said, and a variety of disciples and detractors have made us realize that the language of European colonial mastery was rarely "transparent and ahistorical" or merely "instrumental." [31] Even the most innocent narrative representation of colonized peoples and cultures unwittingly justified or tried to prolong a system that made Europeans' power appear inescapable and normal.

It must be remembered that the topography of colonial domination was at all times and in all places uneven. What Foucault, Said, and many of their imitators or critics have ignored is how this vocabulary of domesticity and parenthood—or other forms of imperial language—was admitted or contested by those designated as its apparent consumers: the colonized. But the issue of audiences is inherently complex, since colonial rhetoric often was tailored for the consumption of fellow Europeans, both at home or abroad, who also required a set of images that could render frequently unsavory colonial projects palatable. Finally, the anxious affirmation of the bonds of brotherhood between European nations also hinged on the ways in which colonial administrators understood and, above all, co-opted "nationalist and traditionalist patriarchal policies," which deeply affected women and men among both the colonizers and the colonized. [32]

Again the issue is whether, or to what degree, theoretical formulations inspired by Great Britain's imperial experience are useful to the study of other colonial cultures. The national identities of both France and the Netherlands were also deeply invested in their stature as global powers. Governing an empire was just as much a "protracted, almost metaphysical obligation" for France and Holland as it was for Great Britain.[33] As Antoinette Burton has recently observed, "Imperial and national identities were co-dependent." Hence, Dutch or French colonial styles constituted a "moral yardstick" with which to measure discrete differences in national identity.[34] The centrality of India in the theoretical literature has prompted Robert J. C. Young to observe that a "homogenization" in scholarship on European colonialism has arisen. As he recently posed the question, "Does the fact that modern colonialism was effected by European or European-driven powers mean that the discourse of colonialism operated everywhere in a similar enough way for the theoretical paradigms of colonial-discourse analysis to work equally well for all of them?"[35]

It is surprising that Young fails to mention the Dutch Empire, which a French colonial scholar, Pierre Leroy-Beaulieu, described in 1872 with barely suppressed envy as "a prolific Frisian dairy cow which the Dutch milked with great care."[36] Be that as it may, Young's point is well taken: the ideologies and practices of Dutch, French, or British — or German and Portuguese — men and women overseas rested upon crucial internal differences. Accordingly, colonial-discourse analyses must be situated squarely in their historical contexts. In doing so, we can investigate more effectively the linkages between political trends and social tensions within a specific European nation and unravel the ways in which they played out in a particular colonial arena.

These are the questions that our contributors explore in the following chapters, which, it should be pointed out, are not arranged according to empire but rather in thematic and chronological order. The central problem, which unifies the twelve essays, revolves around the many ways in which Europeans, both male and female, conceived of gender differences and verbalized them in their daily encounters with Asian and African subordinates. In addition, the authors probe the imagery of paternalism and maternalism, decoding the vocabulary of femininity and masculinity to evaluate the ways in which such tropes permeated political rhetoric at home and shaped visions of empire abroad.[37] Many

Europeans implicated in imperial ventures overseas manipulated the notion that they were in charge of educating colonized peoples for eventual adulthood, though this maturity was expected to occur only in some future golden age. But European civil servants in the colonies maintained different attitudes toward the education of African or Asian males and females. Native girls were often viewed as needing more protection but less intellectual instruction than boys, since their principal purpose in life was to become supportive wives to husbands and good mothers to children.

Invariably, the cultural and political grammar of the European metropole included a similar assortment of gendered and parental figures of speech. In Europe itself bourgeois politicians and social elites also characterized "dumb" peasants or "disorderly" wage laborers as intractable children in need of civic education before they could become full-fledged adult citizens in the body politic. Hence, colonial elites' euphemistic, hyperbolic, or allegorical language, routinely designed to justify mastery of overseas subjects, had a resonance with the vocabulary of national elites who sought to rationalize the great social divide between bourgeois respectability, on the one hand, and the abject condition of rural folk or proletarian workers, on the other.[38]

Jean Pederson in her essay on "'Special Customs': Paternity Suits and Citizenship in France and the Colonies, 1870–1912" confronts these connections directly. She employs the parliamentary debates preceding the passage of a law in 1912 legalizing paternity suits in France and its colonies as a prism to illuminate a variety of middle-class politicians' anxieties. Although the men who framed the law on paternity characterized both working-class women in urban France and colonized women as "manipulative" and "unscrupulous," the end result was that the 1912 law allowed native women in the colonies to sue French partners for paternity only at the discretion of colonial governors.

Pederson's essay indirectly highlights a subtle difference in metropolitan attitudes toward the unruly working classes or backward peasants at home and colonized peoples abroad. Political leaders and social reformers in most European countries presumed that their peasants and laboring classes were speakers of the same national language, however deficient their understanding of the nation's cultural vocabulary may have been.[39] In contrast, many Europeans, particularly in Africa south of the Sahara, tended to view their colonial subordinates as preliterate; many clung to the opinion that indigenous people were congenitally incapable of mastering the "civilized" human speech of the West. Whether Europeans sought to endow native people with the potential to learn to employ a proper Western lexicon constituted yet another marker of difference between colonial cultures. The volume's frontispiece illustration portrays this is in unambiguous terms. The postcard's deliberate use of *petit negre*—a pejorative term meaning incorrect or unintelligible French, as in *ti* instead of *tu* for "you"—implied that even literate Africans or other colonized peoples could never hope to completely master the French language, the matrix of civilization and the key to citizenship. And the crude sexual innuendo suggested a link between semiliteracy and sexual exploitation.

In the Islamic regions of Africa or on the island of Java in the Indonesian archipelago, most orientalists and administrators conceded that their subjects were heirs to a classic, literate tradition. Dutch scholars in central Java lavished their intellectual attention on the shadow puppet theater (*wayang*), but they exalted the ancient Indic-Hindu origins of Javanese culture, contained in the *wayang*'s transcription of the many stories from the *Ramayana* and *Mahabharata*, in an effort to frustrate the potentially disruptive influence of expanding, populist Islam.[40] European scholars harbored a similar begrudging admiration for the architectural sophistication and artistic beauty of Hindu culture on the Southeast Asian island of Bali or Khmer Buddhist civilization in Cambodia.

From this recognition, in part, emerged the renewed debate in colonial circles in the late nineteenth century about the policy of assimilation versus the program of association between the cultures of West and East. Due to an abiding faith in the superiority of French civilization, the advocates of assimilation appeared victorious in the French Empire, even though the logic and effectiveness of the assimilationist project came under attack after the turn of the century. Then powerful intellectuals in Paris, among them Emile Durkheim, or highly placed colonial civil servants such as Louis-Hubert-Gonzalve Lyautey and Joost van Vollenhoven, criticized assimilationist policies for reducing native traditions to "social dust" and replacing the "rigorous [native] hierarchy of yesterday with a well-intentioned but emasculated [French] one today."[41]

In the Dutch East Indies, on the other hand, scrupulous association became the celebrated mode of administration. Dutch civil servants' ideal of synthesis entailed strategically adjusting Dutch colonial measures to each ethnic group in the vast Indonesian archipelago to avoid stifling the uniqueness of local cultures. Regardless of these ideological differences, both French and Dutch colonial officials increasingly employed the position of women among particular indigenous groups as a criterion for measuring the relative backwardness of native cultures. In doing so, Europeans attempted to impose essentialist Western ideas about women's weakness, women's maternal destiny, or the undesirability of women's work upon native societies. By gazing through a Western lens, European analysts distorted the meaning of local traditions, sometimes for conscious political purposes.

Rita Smith Kipp's essay, "Emancipating Each Other: Dutch Missionaries' Encounter with Karo Women in Sumatra, 1900–1942," demonstrates that deeply entrenched Western views of women's subordinate role within the family caused Protestant missionaries to misjudge the highly respected position of women within Karo Batak culture. This gross misinterpretation undermined the very objectives the missionaries sought to achieve. Or, to cite a different example: if European settlers represented themselves as the embodiment of manly vigor, rationality, and emotional self-control, then it was but a small step to portray their subjects—or at least, some of them—as undisciplined, effeminate creatures who were their sexual opposites.[42]

As Yaël Simpson Fletcher and Danilyn Rutherford explore in their chapters, not only colonized peoples but also the landscapes they inhabited were inscribed with feminine characteristics. "'Irresistible Seductions': Gendered Representations of Colonial Algeria around 1930" (Simpson Fletcher) and "Trekking to New Guinea: Dutch Colonial Fantasies of a Virgin Land, 1900–1942" (Rutherford) survey the representation of indigenous peoples within their physical environment in Algeria and in New Guinea. Europeans frequently depicted those landscapes as pristine, albeit barren or undeveloped, prior to the arrival of settlers from the West; the tacit message they conveyed was that the inhabitants of precolonial lands had allowed the resources of potentially fruitful deserts or prolific jungles to lie fallow. These opinions, however, gradually evolved into a sense of mission: only the natural virility of Western men could transform virginal plains or primeval rain forests into fertile and productive lands.

In short, these essays trace the ways in which settlers in the colonies or policymakers in the European metropole projected both their illusions and delusions—"their ambivalent protocols of fantasy and desire"—upon the colonized and their natural environment.[43] Frequently, these aspirations were couched in an erotic language that conflated Europeans' yearning for the possession of land with other sorts of desires. Yet there was an oddly androgynous quality to these fictions and projections. In certain instances European colonizers endowed Cambodians in Indochina, the Javanese in Indonesia, or Arabs in North Africa with an indolence or passivity that was presumably feminine in character. In other contexts they portrayed native people as dominated by an insatiable libido, often defined as a quintessential male attribute, which could prompt them, under unpredictable circumstances, to disrupt European residents' peace of mind, or worse, to threaten their bodies and livelihoods.

Hence, some of the contributors to this volume are also preoccupied, both implicitly and explicitly, with the political construction and expression of sexual desire in Europe as well as in overseas settlements. By analyzing the relationship between modern European ideas about sexuality and their permutations in a colonial setting, these authors reveal the ways in which middle-class conceptions of propriety shaped European men's daily interactions with female others, whether indigenous women in the colonies or working-class women at home. In other words, they explore how "race and the colonial order of things" were imbricated in Europeans' definition of self and their ideas about both legitimate and illicit sexual behaviors, either within Europe or in "out-of-the-way places" across the globe.[44]

In some regions of Africa south of the Sahara or in Indochina and the Dutch East Indies, male explorers, settlers, or local administrators established households with native spouses or concubines as normal practice. Since these arrangements routinely produced mixed-blood children, hybridity was one of the more prominent features of many

settler communities. Historically constructed, hybridity created identities and meanings that transcended the physical reality of large groups
of mixed-blood people in colonial societies. In fact, it was one of the
most tangible products of the European presence. Hybridity constituted
a liminal cultural and racial terrain located halfway between East and
West, which gave birth to ambivalence, "mighty mimicry," and contestation.[45] Nevertheless, in French Algeria, concubinage involving Arab
(or Berber) Muslim women and European men was not a common
practice, and equally rare were children of mixed blood. However, cultural as well as biological hybridity undergirded the unique identity of
the pieds-noirs. Europeans of Maltese, Spanish, Italian, or Provençal
origins who by 1900 called Algeria home saw themselves as racially different from French women and men in the metropole. Their disparate
Mediterranean origins supposedly had disappeared through intermarriage among themselves; the newly constructed hybrid "Latin" identity
of pieds-noirs marked them, in their own imagination, as distinct from
both Algerian Muslims and ordinary French citizens.[46]

In a different setting Elsbeth Locher-Scholten's essay, "So Close and
Yet So Far: The Ambivalence of Dutch Colonial Rhetoric on Javanese
Servants in Indonesia, 1900–1942," probes one of the more critical in-
between spaces of settler colonialism: the European household on Java
in the Dutch East Indies. Her examination of Indies residents' ambivalence about their intimate interactions with their Javanese domestic servants discloses how these processes of "overlap and displacement" shaped the daily lives of European housewives and their
subordinates. Penny Edwards's chapter, "Womanizing Indochina: Fiction, Nation, and Cohabitation in Colonial Cambodia, 1890–1930," operates in the same hybrid realm—in between Frenchmen's romanti-
cized stories about "authentic" Cambodian culture and the real world
of native concubines, who allegedly served as cultural tutors to their
sexual partners from the West. But Edwards adds a significant third
angle to what she labels "the trigonometry of gender," consisting of
white men's distaste for European feminism. This disapproval prompted
many Frenchmen in Indochina to concoct a counterideal of gentle, pliable Cambodian women, who embodied a true femininity most liber-
ated women in France had long since lost.

Frequently lurking behind men's overt dislike of feminist movements in the European heartland was their more fundamental ambivalence about modernity—about its discontents and disruptions. By 1900 some Europeans reimagined African or Asian people in overseas possessions around 1900 as endangered species that sheltered the remnants of a pure, primordial culture imperiled everywhere by the inroads of progress. Native women were assigned the task of preserving tradition against the assaults of the modern era. However, the identification of women with cultural authenticity was rife with contradictions. Around the turn of the century, as Janet Horne shows in her essay on "Musée Social Reformers," women in France were routinely depicted as a bulwark against "the dissolution of traditional social bonds"; at the same time, however, they were cast in the role of bearers of modern social reformism in the colonies.

Across the Mediterranean, as we discover in Jeanne Bowlan's chapter on "Civilizing Gender Relations in Algeria: The Paradoxical Case of Marie Bugéja, 1919–1939" and in Julia Clancy-Smith's "Islam, Gender, and Identities in the Making of French Algeria, 1830–1962," the emerging debates concerning tradition and modernity also placed North African Muslim women in a central, if paradoxical, position. Some colonial administrators saw them as obstacles to the civilizing mission; others celebrated Muslim women as vehicles for social experimentation or as agents who could uplift Arab society through Western instruction. As Bowlan and Clancy-Smith reveal, underlying the arguments of advocates in favor of French education for Algerian girls was the fear of marriages between Westernized Muslim men and European women. The threat of intermarriage—which in French eyes raised the specter of expanded political rights—would be reduced if Algerian men could marry properly educated Muslim females who spoke French and had absorbed the bourgeois domestic culture of the West. In addition, these authors show that polemics about women's education were intimately linked to sexuality. However oblique colonial discussions may have been, sexuality, both within and outside marriage, constituted a subliminal element of European racism, even though Ronald Hyam's assertion in 1990 that "sex was at the very heart of racism" may be an overstatement.[47] Nonetheless, toward the end of the nineteenth century, Europeans began to make the management of sexuality an increasingly important pillar of enduring colonial mastery.

This was particularly true in French Algeria and in French colonial possessions with large Muslim communities; Islamic sexual practices were continually invoked in Paris, Algiers, or Dakar to argue against citizenship.

Initially the language of sex was articulated in either titillating descriptions or bureaucratic prescriptions that sought to normalize intimate relations between men and women across the colonial divide. Early writings on the sexual traffic between Europeans and indigenous partners were somewhat haphazard in character because authorities were reluctant to interfere in existing patterns of cohabitation and miscegenation, inherited from preceding eras of informal colonialism. In other cases they simply lacked the means to force changes upon wealthy European merchants and planters who defined the status quo and maintained multiracial households. Moreover, European men established interracial unions simply because white women in most colonial societies were relatively scarce, at least until the beginning of the twentieth century. Until then many traders, planters, and government officials may have approached the colonies as sensual playing fields, unrestrained by the stultifying mores and Victorian conventions of the metropole. Imperial rule was grounded in asymmetries and thus fostered transgressive desire or, in some places, a sense of masculine impunity in matters of sexuality.[48]

In the late nineteenth century, however, European regimes in Asia and Africa began to devise and implement detailed legislation to limit or prohibit interracial unions. Alice Conklin's essay, "Redefining Frenchness: Citizenship, Race Regeneration, and Imperial Motherhood in France and West Africa, 1914–1940," traces the complicated processes whereby French officials developed "a specific kind of gendered imperial rhetoric" in the colonial capital of Dakar in West Africa, not only to clarify and entrench racial differences but to enable them to define Frenchness more conclusively. This is also an issue that Pamela Pattynama engages in her treatment of Louis Couperus's *The Hidden Force*, a novel published in Dutch in 1900 and translated into English in 1922.[49] She argues that Couperus's work registered a turning point in the carefree attitudes of the Dutch East Indies community toward the interracial sexuality that had characterized Dutch colonial rule until then. Thus, *The Hidden Force* recorded the emerging—and self-consciously modern—anxieties about miscegenation that produced demands for more clearly defined racial boundaries.

Europeans' growing misgivings about hybridity eventually fused with their fears of nationalist movements. In the early twentieth century, the most vocal demands for a coequal voice in the colonial body politic came from those Asian or African social groups—or individuals such as Ferhat Abbas in Algeria, Blaise Diagne of Senegal, or Tjipto Mangoenkoesoemo in the Dutch East Indies—who were born and raised in the interstices of colonial cultures. Often they were intellectuals who had mastered the language of their colonial overlords in order to employ it for their own subversive political purposes. As Frances Gouda explores in her essay on "Good Mothers, Medeas, or Jezebels: Feminine Imagery in Colonial and Anticolonial Rhetoric in the Dutch East Indies, 1900–1942," the Indonesian nationalist Tjipto Mangoenkoesoemo parodied the wide range of complementary metaphors about the strict paternal instruction of native sons and daughters, on the one hand, and the maternal nurturance of vulnerable indigenous people, on the other hand, which permeated the rationale behind Dutch social welfare efforts (the Ethical Policy) in Indonesia since the turn of the century. By learning to navigate effectively these in-between spaces of colonial societies, the colonial "progeny" formulated a sophisticated yet seditious language of national identity and independence due to or in spite of Europeans' civilizing mission with its parental language of mothering and fathering.

The contributors to this collection suggest that since the Enlightenment many of these parental or gendered tropes have appeared timeless, even if their meanings and uses have changed over time. No doubt other sets of symbols or models existed in the rhetoric of colonial rule—imagery that deviated from invocations of the organic unit of the family with its stern or gentle parents and its obedient or rebellious children. The structural conditions of colonial mastery in Asia and Africa produced a noisy concert of discourses designed to perpetuate white-skinned rule over native people in order to garner profit or to enhance international prestige for the mother country.

By concentrating on one particular strand of imperial rhetoric—the ways in which notions of parenthood or emblems of masculinity and femininity undergirded French and Dutch efforts to normalize their subjugation of native peoples—the essays in this collection both refine and expand our general understanding of the history of European imperialism. Compelling evidence of the continued importance of gendered language to express the colonial relationship was provided recently by the French Jesuit Henri Sanson, who has lived in independent Algeria for the past thirty years. Attempting to explain the violence wracking today's Algeria, he observed in 1996 that "the Algeria of now is the product of many cultures . . . she [Algeria] is the fruit of a rape. Until now, [Algeria] has defined herself solely through the gaze of others." [50]

2. IN PURSUIT OF GREATER FRANCE: Visions of Empire among Musée Social Reformers, 1894–1931

⅁ *Janet R. Horne*

"If France were not in Algiers, in Dakar, in Hanoi, one might wonder if she would [still] be in Paris." This intriguing query was posed by Maurice Reclus on the occasion of the 1931 Colonial Exhibition held in Paris. Resonant with self-doubt, his comment captures the high level of national anxiety in France during the interwar years and points to the intricate web of forces that linked the metropole, or *la mère patrie*, to its colonial empire. Yet, what was this idea of France to which Reclus referred? By harkening back from the year 1931 to the turn of the century, it becomes clear that many French republicans, in the liberal tradition defended by Reclus, sought to avert the specter of national decline by embarking on a quest to secure a Greater France. Understood in both moral and territorial terms, the notion of a Greater France—whether grounded in research, experience, or pure imagination—was commonly invoked to promote "the renaissance of the colonial idea." A figurative geography, this notion also implied that the campaigns for domestic reform and colonial expansion were part of the same overarching quest for the national renewal of France.[1]

In the devastating aftermath of the Franco-Prussian war of 1870, liberal republicans hoped to rejuvenate France through programs of economic, moral, and social reform. At the Musée Social (Social Museum), a republican think tank created in Paris in 1894, reformers believed that their legislative proposals and private efforts at social reform would help build a Greater France at home and abroad. Although not part of their formal agenda, the goals of colonial expansion were actively pursued by individual Musée Social reformers. Some had worked in the colonies, others had not; but a careful reading of their writings and statements on social reform and colonialism reveals that in their minds there was often no fixed divide between empire and metropole. All the world appeared as a potential laboratory for the application of their programs of reform.[2]

Gender relations frequently structured this quest for the national renewal of France. They contributed as much to the design and discourse of republican social reform as they did to the construction of empire.[3] This chapter demonstrates how the visions of empire prevalent among Musée Social reformers between 1894 and 1931 were articulated as gendered paradigms on three distinct, yet overlapping, levels: discourse, representation, and policy. Gendered discourse, for instance, operated as a common metaphor of territorial possession, as illustrated by the term *la mère patrie* wherein France and its colonial empire are discursively linked in a naturalized mother and child relationship. Reformers and colonizers alike used gendered discourse to achieve cultural and political domination and to exert rhetorical control over a social reality that resisted or defied colonial rule and social regulation.[4] Representations of empire, such as those seen at the 1889 Universal Exposition, invoked gender to communicate a broader message about the hegemonic social order of republican France. Finally, in the interest of consolidating a Greater France, reformers incorporated gendered strategies into the policies they designed for the colonial empire. In each case the organizational forms and the sources of intellectual inspiration marshaled to promote change in metropolitan France were strikingly similar to those used to ensure imperial domination. Metropole and empire, therefore, like a pair of communicating vessels, formed a more intricate whole. The issues relevant to the historical construction of a Greater France are illuminated by recent scholarship that suggests the conceptual interrelatedness of gender, colonialism, nationalism, social reform, and modernity and that argues for a reformulation of the political and intellectual history of this period, which gave rise to both the welfare state and the imperial nation-state.[5]

THE MUSÉE SOCIAL AND REPUBLICAN SOCIAL REFORM

A cursory presentation of the Musée Social itself is in order before exploring the interaction of some of its members with France's colonizing mission. An independent research and advisory group on social policy, the Musée Social proclaimed that its mission was to work toward "the moral and material betterment of workers." It brought together politicians, philanthropists, and experts in the nascent social sciences, financed research projects and study missions abroad, and influenced social legislation. In short, the Musée Social was a private foundation devoted to the public interest. Its leadership featured liberal republicans, such as President Jules Siegfried, Vice President Emile Cheysson, and Honorary President Jules Simon. Until 1916 the Musée Social was an exclusively male club. Fearing that suffrage campaigns would destroy the institution's vocation to remain above partisan politics, the Musée Social banned women from official membership. Women did participate, however, in several ad hoc research efforts sponsored by the institution. Before admitting them as members, therefore, Musée Social reformers attributed an increasingly important role to women in their public efforts to promote social peace.[6]

THE 1889 UNIVERSAL EXPOSITION:
REPRESENTING REFORM AND EMPIRE

Although privately endowed in 1894, the Musée Social's origins date back to the 1889 Universal Exposition held in Paris. That grandiose international showcase of industrial production featured two smaller exhibits: the social economy section and the colonial section. The first was devoted primarily to representations of labor within the industrial republic, and the second, to representations of the colonial world. The exhibits presented the public with mirror views of two separate but related paths to achieving a Greater France: social reform and colonial dominion. Their studied representations of national grandeur also attributed a remarkably similar role to gender relations. Here, too, begins our story of metropolitan and colonial encounters.

In the carefully ordered fairgrounds on the Esplanade des Invalides, the social economy exhibit was assigned a spot directly across from the colonial exhibit where, significantly, they both adorned the main display of the French Ministry of War. The social economy exhibit, however, was officially promoted by the government as the Exposition's monument to social peace, since its primary goal was to suggest ways to regulate and reduce social conflict within the Republic. A handful of conservative republican reformers had designed the social economy exhibit to proffer the social wares of enlightened industrialists. Theirs was the only exhibit at the 1889 Universal Exposition to address the social question directly. On display were employer-owned day-care centers, housing and old-age pension plans, and a variety of organizations promoting mutual aid and self-help among the working classes. The social economy exhibit gave rise, five years later, to the creation of the Musée Social, whose founders hoped to showcase similar reform initiatives on a more permanent basis.[7]

The theme of France's national and military grandeur, however, prompted Exhibition organizers to situate the social economy and colonial exhibits together on the Esplanade des Invalides. Commenting upon this curious spatial juxtaposition, Cheysson remarked, "By a contrast which, although not planned, is nevertheless striking, the social economy exhibit was installed directly across from Annam, Cambodia, and Tonkin. Along one axis of the Esplanade, there was the Orient, frozen in the immobility of forty thousand years; whereas, along the other, there was the West, burgeoning with the problems of the modern world." By characterizing social reform as inherently modernist and progressive, in sharp contrast to the ancient, immobile world of the Orient, Cheysson interpreted the physical positioning of these exhibits as "object lessons of evolutionary theory." The nascent anthropological discourse implicit in Cheysson's comment asserted that human societies, in a manner analogous to human biological evolution, evolved according to a hierarchical order of complexity. Such rhetorical mirroring of metropole and empire became a common feature of a discursive strategy to define the concept of civilization itself as an evolutionary hierarchy placing complex Western industrial societies at its pinnacle.[8]

To a more prescient observer, however, the proximity of the colonial and social economy exhibits might have suggested yet another implicit ethnographic logic: the observation and comparison of cultures so distinct from the dominant model of the French bourgeoisie that they both seemed to warrant the status of curiosities. The analogy between the two exhibits was further reinforced by their similar physical layouts. Covering half of the total space of the Esplanade, the displays of the colonial exhibit included ornate national-style palaces representing Algeria, Tunisia, Annam, Tonkin, Cochin China, and India, an entire re-constructed African village, a *souk* (marketplace) replete with indige-nous merchants, and a life-size simulation of a typical animated Arab street, lined with palm and coconut trees. Women appeared alongside men merely as secondary actors in simulated displays of street life, tra-ditional dance, and the material culture of domestic life. The official catalog even concluded that "the illusion was complete, visitors could imagine themselves on the other side of the Mediterranean." Here, the imagined empire was construed as more true to life, more perfectly rep-resented, than the imperfect reality it sought to emulate. At the 1889 Exposition the public encountered an idealized version of imperial rule, one which had a lasting impact on French popular representations of the colonial world.[9]

In mirrored fashion, on display as part of the social economy exhibit was the Workers' Housing Street, composed of four full-scale models of low-cost housing, some of which were decorated with domestic fur-nishings typical of a working-class household and, in one case, adorned with workers themselves, accompanied by their "courageous families."[10] Visitors who strolled down the exhibit alleys could participate in a con-tinuum of displays that spatially and discursively linked clean workers in model housing to the exotica of African dancers and the amusement of donkey rides across the street. Both the social economy and the co-lonial exhibits provided commentaries on the hegemonic bourgeois re-publican order by offering the public carefully planned visual demon-strations of the moral and material progress of industrialism, on the one hand, and of colonialism, on the other.

Gendered categories of thought and expression provided a rich cul-tural idiom for communicating these reform ideas to the public. Thus, the message of social harmony promoted by the social economy exhibit was subtly underscored by a series of gendered suppositions intended to infuse the exhibit's central idea with a more general, even universal, value. Designed, in part, to reconcile the working classes with the Third Republic, the social economy exhibit carefully avoided any potential image of conflict that might tarnish its representation of the Republic as an organic industrial family and a harmonious model of industrial relations. Familial metaphors were used repeatedly throughout the ex-hibit, thereby underscoring a basic idiom of the republican language of social peace. Invoking the family as a metaphor of social relations shrouded the brutal reality of class conflict and industrial strife in fin de siècle France in the discursive cloak of social cohesion. The social world presented to the public was one in which harmony reigned and discord had been vanquished by the mutual discovery of the identity of interest between labor and capital. This representation had been achieved primarily through references to the gendered world of bourgeois social relations, with the family as the basic, stabilizing unit, without which the entire social order itself might crumble.

The 1889 Universal Exposition also served as a catalyst for a vast network of reform efforts that sought to have an impact upon both metropolitan France and its colonial empire. Congresses devoted to colonial sociology and anthropology explored new directions for imperial expansion under the auspices of the Third Republic. These new directions, moreover, would be decidedly modern, informed by the social sciences, pursued under the guise of a republican civilizing mission, and given buoyancy by the optimistic belief that only economic expansion could truly consolidate the social goals of the Republic. The 1889 Universal Exposition, therefore, made a statement to the world that republican France was strong and prosperous and that the new regime fully intended to merge the republican tradition with that of a unified industrial and imperial nation. In the spirit of the 1889 Universal Exposition, the Musée Social invited professionals and experts to act in the public interest and contribute to the social, moral, and material rearmament of the nation.

MUSÉE SOCIAL REFORMERS AND THE COLONIES, 1894–1931

The goal of colonial domination reinforced the domestic concerns of reformers at the Musée Social. Their critique of France's excessive administrative centralization, for instance, was directed at the colonial empire as well as the metropole. The same was true of their preoccupation with projecting an aura of political neutrality. In each case the colonial empire served as both a laboratory and a mirror for the social reformers of metropolitan France.

Like the colonial lobby itself, Musée Social members interested in the colonies were a diverse lot. Some with political influence had been instrumental in establishing the colonial party: Musée Social President Jules Siegfried led the colonial group in the Senate; Prince Auguste d'Arenberg founded the Comité de l'Afrique Française; and the textile manufacturer Edouard Aynard sent a team of colonial prospectors out to China. Others were colonial theorists, such as Paul Leroy-Beaulieu, or members of the colonial administration, such as Charles Jonnart, governor-general of Algeria. Still others expressed a more professional interest in the colonies: Émile Levasseur served as president of the Society of Commercial Geography and wrote geography textbooks that he hoped would stimulate an early interest in the overseas empire and encourage emigration. Abel and Jacques Ballif headed the Touring Club de France, a burgeoning travel association which published and circulated maps and encouraged colonial tourism.

In 1908 the Musée Social's newly founded Section on Urban and Rural Hygiene attracted, among others, doctors and architects who turned to the colonial laboratory when urban reform in prewar France appeared more and more elusive. These men sought to consolidate their professional identities and elaborate strategies for urban reform, including long-range planning and public hygiene. Architect-urbanists, such as Henri Prost (who teamed up with Resident-General Lyautey in Morocco from 1913 until 1930 and redesigned the administrative center of Rabat), increasingly focused much of their work on the colonies where they often were given freer rein than in the metropole to accomplish large-scale plans for urban development. Prost and his colleagues aimed primarily, however, at gaining professional recognition at home and therefore kept an eye on the metropolitan mirror. The colonies thus frequently served as a professional springboard for achieving acclaim in metropolitan France.[11]

CRITICIZING FRENCH ADMINISTRATIVE CENTRALIZATION

Liberal reformers at the Musée Social commonly believed that France suffered from excessive administrative centralization. They directed their criticisms on this subject to both the metropole and the colonial empire. Paul Leroy-Beaulieu even argued that the fewer civil servants in the colonies the better.[12]

The liberal critique of state centralization was frequently expressed in gendered terms and revealed a crisis of masculine identity linked both to the ideal of national grandeur and to the expansionist colonial imagination. In 1895 Musée Social member Georges Picot concurred with Leroy-Beaulieu that no ideas of lasting value had ever been generated by civil servants. "Sterility," he concluded, "is the effect of this system." In a discursive sense Picot's comment drew upon nationalist rhetoric used to promote natalism and colonialism, two revanchist stratagems whereby the French were called upon to avenge the loss of Alsace-Lorraine to Germany. References to vital energy—in a Barrèsian sense of the term—were common in this masculinist procolonial and pronatalist discourse. Energetic, intrepid young men, not passive, neurasthenic civil servants, were needed to expand imperial territory. They were also needed in the metropole to reverse the trend of a declining birthrate. The Anglophilia of these same liberal reformers also helps explain their repeated references to the benefits of indirect rule, individual initiative, self-help, and even physical exercise. Anglophilia and references to vital energy should be interpreted within the context of gender anxieties and in relation with the humiliating defeat of 1870, the loss of Alsace-Lorraine, and the subsequent push to reconstruct national and masculine honor in the overseas territories. A call went out for industrious, dynamic young men in the service of metropolitan France and the colonies. Such real men would provide a new elite for modern France: they would one day supplant the docile, ineffectual civil servants in the colonies and rejuvenate a vital liberal republic at home.[13]

Just before the First World War, Musée Social reformers once again returned to the theme of male identity when discussing how to promote public parks, playing fields, and physical exercise as part of a global strategy to improve public health standards and strengthen the nation. A pervasive nationalist discourse underscored each of these discussions. In 1910 Georges Benoît-Lévy extolled the benefits of physical exercise for young men by quoting Disraeli: "A people that does not play will always be defeated by a people that plays." In addition to the reference to physical exercise, the type of play in question here was the race for imperial domination over England. Underlying this national and imperial construction of play—and, by extension, of playgrounds as training fields—was Benoît-Lévy's gendered proposition that France needed to champion a new, more vigorous type of manhood to produce a strong and brawny nation. Moreover, Benoît-Lévy suggested that if many French men had reached adulthood without having learned to enjoy sports and physical exercise, it was largely the fault of the country's educational system, which instead revered "sonorous words" and rhetoric. "It is not with such a system of education," he intoned, "that we create explorers and colonizers!"[14]

Continuing this prewar debate on urban renewal and public hygiene, other Musée Social members, such as André Lichtenberger, Lucien March, and Georges Blondel, couched their support for sports and playgrounds in nationalistic terms that stressed eugenics, the preservation of the French race, and the reversal of the falling birthrate, which was often perceived in terms of physical degeneration. Public hygiene and the concept of national interest were conflated into a pseudobiological discourse of physical revival that barely disguised other prevalent anxieties in prewar France concerning gender identities and the uncertain reaches of imperial rule.[15]

CULTIVATING AN AURA OF POLITICAL NEUTRALITY

The colonies also were frequently construed as providing a common terrain where political discord would dissipate. At the Musée Social and, by projection, in the colonies as well, reformers would be shielded from the changing tides of political passions, policy pressures, and historical polemics.[16] One way to supersede politics was to develop new cognitive tools with which to study society. The nascent social sciences were to generate impartial, objective criteria needed for social regulation and new standards and techniques for social intervention. By the late nineteenth century, the writings of Frédéric Le Play had already had a crucial impact on the rise of a sociological method in France and abroad. Although Le Play's vocabulary was infused with Christian moralism, he approached social problems primarily from an inductive standpoint and therefore laid the groundwork for "a secular mode of social action" widely adopted at Musée Social.[17]

The particular attention Le Play paid to customs and the family formed the basis of a culturally based sociology in fin de siècle France. In turn, emergent theories of social and cultural development would increasingly have an impact on both republican social reform and colonial practice. Le Play insisted on the centrality of the family as the basic social unit and on the importance of reinforcing ties between the generations. An understanding of, and respect for, family life, he argued, would provide the key to attaining social harmony, whether in the workplace or in public life generally. There was, he contended, an essential link between the private behavior and the public action of individuals. His ideas and writings on social economy provided many late nineteenth-century republican reformers with an empirically based language and a model of social reform that they could adapt to their own political designs.[18]

Le Play's vision of gender roles was also very similar to that espoused by liberal republican reformers. According to Le Play, women, and particularly mothers, were responsible for creating the mores of a nation; thus, they were considered to be "the primary agent(s) of social progress." "A woman's true function," he argued, "is the government of the home," or "the domestic ministry," where traditions and the "cult of ancestors" were preserved. It was also, he claimed, the basis of national stability. In Le Play's view, therefore, the home occupied a critical social and political function. Le Play concluded that "a woman's affection, virtue and intelligence have a most direct effect upon civic and political life." Accordingly, Emile Cheysson promoted women as the guardians of social peace and mothers as the essential agents of reform within the family. "Everything depends on the quality of the woman," he professed, "she is the good angel and the evil genie of the family." Thus, Cheysson promoted training courses for women in home economics and infant care so that they might ensure the solidity of the family unit and future generations of citizens, workers, and soldiers. In the discourse of republican reformers, women were consistently linked to their social roles within the private sphere of family life.[19]

At the turn of the century, the social theories generated in metropolitan France also shaped colonial practices. The combined input of reformers, sociologists, geographers, economists, architects, and historians encouraged colonial administrators to think about new ways of intervening in, and exerting control upon, the colonial context: living and health standards, social structure, family life, and working conditions all became objects of potential intervention. The underlying premise of colonial sociology, however, was that social science would help further the goals of French colonization. Understanding local customs would help avoid cultural conflicts, thereby lessening the resistance of the colonized. The logical conclusion of such reasoning was that knowledge about indigenous cultures and societies could ultimately be used to subvert them.

The combined effect of the political neutrality attributed to nascent social science and the liberal critique of administrative centralization had an even more far-reaching impact on reformers at the Musée Social. It led them to promote the ideal of association at home and in the colonial empire.[20] On the one hand, association referred to a new colonial policy expected to replace the traditional approach of assimilation. On the other, the model of republican association was championed by liberal reformers in numerous ways. Two examples are examined: the first briefly highlights the role of mutual aid societies in France and the colonies; the second analyzes in more detail the active association of French women with the colonial effort as moral, cultural, and social intermediaries.

ASSOCIATION IN METROPOLITAN AND COLONIAL CONTEXTS

Musée Social reformers actively promoted mutualism as a model of republican association. In their view mutual aid societies furthered the goals of the Third Republic, since they promoted an association of the weak and the strong, the rich and the poor, and often attempted to preserve an apolitical facade. They combined self-help and private initiative with a social mission. Mutual aid societies—as decentralized, voluntary associations—would provide a necessary counterbalance to the centralized state in the area of social welfare. A strong state, yet one stimulated by private initiative, was the ideal of Musée Social reformers, whether in France or in the colonies.[21]

Following their blueprint for metropolitan France, Musée Social reformers decided in 1904 to launch a concerted effort to promote mutualism in the colonies. Siegfried, Cheysson, Victor Lourties, and Musée Social director Léopold Mabilleau created a committee to organize the first Congress on Colonial Mutualism held in Algiers and Tunis the following year.[22] Octave Depont, the general secretary of the organizing committee, explained that mutualism was all the more important as a moral force since the public was cognizant of the bloody repression by the French military in the Congo, the Sudan, and Indochina. He vehemently denounced this behavior, declaring that these "monstrous proceedings of our colonial administrators are the work of demented, neurasthenic, and unbalanced individuals." Mutualism thus would help achieve the goal of a more modern, less violent form of colonial domination and would act as a moral force upon both the colonizers and the colonized. Mutual societies would also help consolidate a settler community in Algeria by helping European farmers obtain credit. Depont added that the health benefits afforded by mutual societies hopefully would attract Muslims as well.[23] Accordingly, in 1905 the Musée Social sent the comte de Rocquigny to Algeria on an official study mission with instructions to obtain statistical information on the impact of mutual aid societies upon the Algerian population.[24] Despite his findings that mutualism in Algeria had only meager results—particularly among the Muslim population—Musée Social reformers continued to sing the praises of mutualism as a form of social mediation for the metropole and the colonies.[25]

In France these same reformers believed that bourgeois women had an essential role in promoting thrift and mutualism among the working classes. Housewives were widely assumed to control the family purse strings; women therefore were targeted as determinant agents in a family's decision to join a mutual aid society.[26] Women were also considered to possess the moral qualities and generosity of spirit necessary to bridge the gap between social classes. Augusta Moll-Weiss, one of the few female reformers commissioned to do studies by the Musée Social during the prewar period, agreed that women were well suited to the republican task of class reconciliation and social peace since, as she argued, "social solidarity exists naturally in [women]."[27] But even Moll-Weiss felt that women needed more than a good heart to accomplish their social mission: they needed training. Consequently, she and other reformers vigorously launched campaigns to promote courses in home economics.

Beyond assigning responsibility to women for the material upkeep and moral virtues of the home, reformers increasingly recognized the potential role of women as agents of social reform within the community. Inspired by the Anglo-American model of the friendly visitor, a prototypical social worker, Cheysson proposed the creation of a special diploma in social nursing for bourgeois women to help them learn how to heal "the wounds from the battlefields of life," such as alcoholism, tuberculosis, and infant mortality. "The wounded are not only in the battlefields of Morocco," he admonished his primarily female audience at a meeting in 1900 of a new voluntary organization of Parisian day-care centers. According to Cheysson, only women could easily penetrate within working-class families and "dissipate their instinctive distrust" of outsiders, particularly of bourgeois men who were often suspected of concealing a political agenda. Women, on the other hand, were perceived as being inherently apolitical—because of their lack of full civic equality—and thus more altruistic. Moreover, a woman would automatically be perceived as a mother, and Cheysson added that "the magic charm of the child" would forge a bond between the working-class woman and the friendly visitor: "Nothing is more powerful than a child's cradle to draw together and reconcile the social classes." Within this imaginary bond of social mediation, two women of radically different social backgrounds would successfully overcome the prejudices and distance of class and forge the basis for social peace within the Republic.[28]

Fin de siècle debates on the role of women formed a fundamental, recurring trope for metropole reformers as well as for colonialists throughout France's empire. Through their discourse on women, both social reformers and colonizers expressed broader views on the world and the specific gender and political order they sought to uphold. How they articulated their views on women said much about how they viewed the proper organization of society as a whole. These views, moreover, were often extended to more sharply delineate the contours of a Greater France.[29]

The Musée Social's approach to the woman question was rife with the same sort of contradictions found in liberal bourgeois thinking throughout the Third Republic. On the one hand, the Musée Social had been innovative by creating a section devoted to feminism in its library and by gathering extensive documentation on the workplace conditions of female laborers. On the other hand, the Musée's administration resisted integrating women within its organization for both political and social reasons. As was the case of many reform-oriented clubs and parapolitical associations, the Musée Social had long been a male preserve. Of course, this exclusion of women did not prevent gender from being a central structuring vector of reform discourse and practice. In fact, reformers regularly acknowledged that women played important roles as social intermediaries. Housing reformers, mutualists—indeed all republican reformers—sought the active association of women in order to have access to the inner sanctum of the home—to have an in-house missionary invoking the benefits of savings and the dangers of the cabaret.

Finally a special Feminine Section was created at the Musée Social in 1916, and nearly one hundred women were invited to join. The catalyst for this unprecedented event came from Eliska Vincent, a friend of Louise Michel and the founder of Equality, one of France's oldest feminist organizations. Vincent also had been the president of the French Union for Women's Suffrage until her death in 1914. Known as "the archivist of the feminist movement," Vincent had designated the Musée Social as the primary beneficiary of her personal estate. In her home Vincent and her sister had compiled an impressive feminist library, "an entire arsenal of old and new arguments" with which she hoped the Musée Social would found the Feminist Institute of her dreams. The Vincent endowment (although not accepted in the end due to outstanding tax debts) is what finally prompted the men at the Musée Social to sanction a Feminine Section. A far cry from her dream, however, this new section was strictly regulated. Most notably, its members were forbidden from explicitly addressing political matters, such as citizenship rights and suffrage, an interdiction which can be interpreted both as an extension of the Musée's general policy "of leaving politics in the cloakroom" and as a continuing deep-seated resistance to women's participation in political life. Although women clearly had a social and familial duty to fulfill, their path to full political participation remained obstructed at the Musée Social.[30]

Despite their initial barring from this exclusive club of republican social reformers, women often were viewed by these men as reformers in their own right. The Musée Social, for instance, acknowledged and promoted women's expertise as social investigators, hiring Kaëte Schirmacher, Augusta Moll-Weiss, and Claire Gérard to report on domestic economy, child care, and women's work. Male investigators at the Musée Social studied women's labor and founded groups for the defense of women's rights in both the French Chamber of Deputies and the Senate. The Musée Social also sponsored a course in public speaking for women at the behest of Mme Marcelle Kraemer-Bach. Therefore, in a variety of ways, the Musée Social as an institution and several of its members independently promoted women's rights and the betterment of women's working conditions.[31]

In a more general sense, women occupied the discursive space of reformer par excellence since, above all, they were entrusted with the mission of moral and cultural betterment. This was true in France as well as in the colonies. Both liberal reformers and colonialists perceived gender roles as being distinct and complimentary. Even those who supported women's rights did so from the position of equality in difference and based their views on some concept of a nature-based, reproductive, and familial function for women in society. Karen Offen has characterized this general outlook, which predominated in the women's rights circles of fin de siècle France, as "familial feminism." Familial feminists shared the fundamental perception of women as the guarantors of a stable social order, a vision which, in turn, was based upon the idealization of motherhood and a harmonious domestic sphere.[32]

Liberal republicans further argued that universal rights should be extended only gradually, preferably after a period of apprenticeship, whether with regard to social reform, suffrage, or colonial rule. Education and experience, therefore, were considered to be necessary preludes to full citizenship. In this strategic and incremental approach to civic equality for French women, however, bourgeois feminists led the way. Women needed to demonstrate their capacities, they argued, and express their devotion to the French nation within the accepted terms of public debate. Consequently, bourgeois and familial feminists molded their demands within the "male idiom" that dominated French political life.[33] National sentiment, the gradual apprenticeship of civic rights, and reverence for the fatherland—*la patrie*—became common features of prewar feminist rhetoric in France.[34]

The patriotic pragmatism of bourgeois feminists only increased with the onset of the First World War. Women such as Julie Siegfried, although challenging accepted gender norms at home, increasingly expressed their commitment to the nation's active defense. In a public call to arms at the Musée Social in 1915, Siegfried declared, "We have finally understood that the first thing to do . . . is to work jointly and form one single and unique family, the family of the fatherland." Abundantly sprinkled with Christian references to devotion, her appeal promoted motherhood as a service to the nation and called upon women to work the plowshares and "contribute to building a new France" once the war had ended.[35] A familial feminist, Julie Siegfried accepted maternity, particularly the ideal of republican motherhood, as a social duty. The extension of republican political rights, she felt, would be linked to the responsible exercise of civic duties. Bourgeois feminists thus strategically chose to cast their own demands for political and civic reform within the larger framework of national interests. Reasoning such as this also helps explain why feminists espoused the cause of the French Colonial Union (FCU), as early as 1897, in its attempts to encourage female emigration to the colonies.

When the Society for the Emigration of Women to the Colonies was created by the FCU in 1897, nearly five hundred emigration requests were submitted by French women, although certainly not for reasons of feminist strategy. Sometimes submitting a photograph, which was requested in the application, schoolteachers, governesses, office workers, midwives, seamstresses, stylists, cooks, a doctor, and a dentist were among those who initially expressed an interest in emigrating to the colonies. A thinly disguised matrimonial agency, the society was actively promoted by the comte d'Haussonville, a Musée Social member who was hardly a feminist or even an active colonialist. A moralist concerned primarily with preserving the family and improving the national birthrate, he lent hearty support to the idea of sending women to the colonies to establish a more firmly rooted domestic order there. "Without marriages, without families, there will be no future colonies." His proposition, moreover, potentially served a multiplicity of purposes. For one thing, he hoped it might reduce the number of problematic single women in the metropole, especially those with advanced educational degrees but no jobs, who faced the moral constraints of nineteenth-century bourgeois society. D'Haussonville considered these women to be more mobile since, by virtue of their education, they had already broken with traditional bourgeois roles and could be persuaded more easily to reside in the colonies where they might find a new mission in life: to form domestic unions, procreate, and thereby further the goals of colonial settlement. Considered to be more virtuous due to their education and thus fit to represent France overseas to the natives, these women, d'Haussonville argued, would be entrusted with bringing "decency and dignity" back to colonial life. In both a discursive and real sense, these women were entrusted with key roles in a social utopian drama to be enacted on the African continent, one which set the stage for both the physical and moral regeneration of France.[36]

Women considered problematic in metropolitan France were suddenly transformed into energetic and healthy forces in the colonies where, in d'Haussonville's words, they would replace the "bored wives of civil servants," the café-concert singers, or the Catholic nuns, none of whom would contribute to establishing a domestic and maternal order in the French Empire. Motherhood and domesticity, therefore, were considered to be women's essential contribution to France's national welfare, whether in the metropole or the colonies. Furthermore, these educated women would help foster the Republic's civilizing mission abroad merely by virtue of being designated emissaries of French culture. By this period the French language had already been invested with a much larger cultural and imperial project: that of prevailing against the domination of English. Thanks to French women and families abroad, d'Haussonville argued, "our French language will spread throughout the world," and "we will be able to struggle . . . against the great invasion of English."[37]

Again with regard to the colonies, Musée Social reformers repeatedly invoked Le Play's dictum that the extent of a culture's social perfection could be measured in terms of its cult of women, specifically young women and mothers. Not only did this view fit perfectly with metropolitan natalist discourse, but it also provided its logical extension: that women and children were essential to the overseas civilizing mission of the Third Republic. Just as Emile Cheysson had argued that women were essential to the promotion of domestic and hygienic sciences in metropolitan France, his colonial counterparts felt that women should adopt a similar mission in the empire. French women were thus entrusted with a double mission: although they were to respect and uphold traditional gender roles, bourgeois women were also increasingly viewed as messengers of modernity in French overseas territories. Reformers claimed that women could gain access to native homes easier than men through their natural contact with other mothers. In much the same way that the family had been identified by reformers as the primary site for producing republican citizenship, loyalty to the colonial project of pacification and modernization needed to be rooted in the family as well. Championed as the pillars of a traditionally gendered domestic order, women also became the bearers of a modern ideology, one that was based nonetheless upon an essentialist, maternalist discourse. Although French women may have been invested with a modernizing mission abroad, this mission remained rooted in the general cult of domesticity and motherhood long established as a nineteenth-century archetype.[38]

Since French women served as conduits to the working-class family in the metropole, they were also seen as potential vectors of influence in the Muslim families of Algeria and Tunisia. If Muslim women could be reached with the lessons of French modernity, the family and the very constitution of Muslim society could be altered. At the Musée Social in 1913, Georges Vabran explained that only women could unravel the cultural construction of the veil which separated Muslim women from public life. The Islamic veil was perceived as a form of female dissimulation as well as a covert challenge to colonial rule. Accordingly, Vabran argued that only French women could penetrate the mysterious intimacy of these private domestic spaces: "Only the hand of a woman can lift the veil which protects Muslim women." Vabran also proposed that French women organize home economics classes for Muslim girls and visit families to spread lessons of hygiene: "It is true that the child and the mother can help us accomplish and continue our educational and civilizing mission in the Islamic world." Western medicine, therefore, seemed to offer an important means of influence to French women in the colonies. Confronted with smallpox epidemics, French women could pay home visits to the sick and help organize vaccination services; they could persuade Muslim women to allow their children to be cared for by French doctors. French women would perform a new kind of volunteerism or social work for the empire. The dilemma, according to Vabran, was how to do this without repeating the previous errors of assimilation in Algeria and without portraying French customs as threats to Islam or as harbingers of cultural dislocation.[39]

The importance reformers paid to domestic arrangements also extended to the physical layout of Muslim homes. Reformers remarked upon the problematic structure of the typical Muslim home, which they felt was not in conformity with modern hygienic standards as defined in the metropole. The relative absence of windows, they complained, did not allow for ventilation or sunlight to penetrate the Arab house and created conditions for the spread of infectious disease. Moreover, these traditional homes did not open onto a public thoroughfare but instead onto an inner maze of courtyards and back alleyways. While reformers described their dissatisfaction with these physical arrangements in terms of hygienic standards, they were also bothered by a more pervasive concern. The physical layout of the traditional Muslim house seemed to incarnate yet another form of the obtuse cultural veil that defied and eluded colonial understanding and control. It designated a spatial separation of domestic and public functions that was quite unlike the bourgeois model promoted in republican France. Whereas in the metropole the workers' home had been identified as an incubator of social discontent and strikes, in the colonial context the Muslim interior was marked as a core of resistance to modernization and change. Reformers created a discursive link between these two interior spaces, both of which were represented as possible seedbeds for sedition. In each case, with regard to these interior spaces of domestic life, women were identified as having the power to intervene most effectively as intermediaries. Although denying women full political rights, many republican reformers and colonial sympathizers gradually recognized the salubrious influence women could have upon civil society, be it in the metropole or the colonies.[40]

Vabran also invoked the value of marriage, viewed as another form of association, that could actually reinforce France's protectorate over Tunisia. According to this idea, Tunisian women needed modern education in order to be better wives. Vabran described how modernized Tunisian men often suffered because they had been unable to merge what he referred to as their "two inner men"—one modern, the other traditional. These two inner men, he claimed, remained juxtaposed in an unstable psychological alliance. Modernized Tunisian men, he argued, needed native female partners able to understand them. In turn, companionate marriages would wed the Tunisian bourgeoisie to the protectorate and, more importantly, discourage unions between Tunisian Muslim males and European women. These arguments are reminiscent of those invoked by republicans who advocated education for French women so that they might accompany male citizens in harmonious, if not equal, marriages. As Philip Nord has pointed out, instead of the authoritarian model of marriage enshrined in the Civil Code (which Louis Blanc characterized as a form of "domestic despotism"), the republican ideal of marriage was a "free association of individuals."[41] Both in the metropole and the empire, a certain typology of marriage was invoked not only as a symbol of gender relations but also as a microcosm of public life generally. Whether in a colonial or a metropolitan context, women were most often portrayed in reform discourse as emissaries of moral reform, but in a political universe defined and circumscribed principally by men.

Following the First World War, however, women, such as Julie Siegfried, who had supported the patriotic efforts of national defense and colonial expansion were not rewarded for their efforts; the Senate denied French women suffrage in 1922. That same year, when the city of Marseilles inaugurated its colonial exhibit under the banner of a Greater France, the term had acquired new meaning. During a postwar surge of interest in France's colonial empire, the exhibit's fanfare offered the public a kind of symbolic exchange linking imperial preeminence to national strength, yet one that also underscored the blow to national prestige dealt by a victorious but devastating war.[42] Although sometimes referred to as "the apotheosis of Greater France," the interwar years also revealed the depth of renewed anxiety in France concerning national decline, depopulation, and loss of international stature.[43] When the grandiose 1931 Colonial Exhibition was inaugurated in Paris, the first rumblings of anticolonial sentiment in the metropole were clearly audible.

Albert Sarraut, the former resident-general of Indochina, explicitly linked the colonial empire's future to the survival or decline of Europe. His book *Grandeur et servitude coloniales* (Colonial grandeur and servitude), published in 1931 to coincide with the Colonial Exhibition, suggested that after the First World War "Europe lost, along with its unity, the authority of its moral command, with which it once dominated and regulated the universe." Poised on the threshold of a decade that announced increasing social and political division and that led eventually to the collapse of the Third Republic, the 1931 Colonial Exhibition was entrusted with a difficult and ultimately impossible mission: to orchestrate a last-gasp effort to revive the colonial ideal in the service of national renewal. Despite these obvious difficulties, optimism dominated the tone of official discourse at the fair. General Lyautey, the legendary seigneur of Morocco, presided over the Exhibition with great assurance, proclaiming that France's colonial empire was a source of modernity. Lyautey even imagined that the Colonial Exhibition, situated in the Bois de Vincennes, could serve as a springboard for the total redevelopment of that area of the city. While calling for a new urban plan, Lyautey nevertheless recognized that mounting social problems plagued France: "I am persuaded that the Exhibition can be a great factor of social peace in this region." In this instance the rhetorical mirroring of metropole and empire portrayed mainland France as a laboratory for colonial experimentation.[44]

Musée Social reformers also helped organize a display for the Colonial Exhibition on what a "Greater France [was] capable of doing in the areas of hygiene, philanthropy and thrift."[45] These themes were avoided, however, by the women of the Musée Social who joined in the spirit of colonial celebration. To mark the 1931 Colonial Exhibition, the Estates General of Feminism decided to organize a banquet and congress devoted to the theme of women's activities in the colonies. Present at this meeting were many women from the Musée's Feminine Section, some of whom, such as Avril de Sainte-Croix, had taken on a high international profile within the League of Nations. Only Maria Vérone refused to collaborate with these colonial festivities, turning instead to journalism and to a denunciation of violence and forced labor in the colonies.[46]

A total of 150 individual members, representing eighty associations, attended the Estates General of Feminism. These women used the Colonial Exhibition as a public platform to promote colonial nursing and social work and to seek greater professional guarantees for women who had embarked upon colonial careers. As was the case during the prewar years, bourgeois feminists continued to stress the social responsibilities incumbent upon women in the colonies and the need to propagate notions of public hygiene and infant care. Embedded within this pro-colonial message, however, was an even stronger call to defend the professional rights of working women including guaranteed salary levels, improved educational opportunities, state accredited diplomas for social assistants and colonial nurses, and vacation and retirement benefits. As expressed at the 1931 Estates General of Feminism, many French women sought and eventually found places in public life as volunteer home nurses or social workers long before they were granted full political and civil rights within the republican polity.[47]

From the 1889 International Exposition to the 1931 Colonial Exhibition, the varied examples explored in this chapter demonstrate how France's empire formed a pervasive subtext of the reform discourse of the Musée Social and, by extension, of the metropole. Practical efforts to promote both colonial expansion and metropolitan reform were also linked in fundamental ways. Republican campaigns for social betterment and the impulse to consolidate the empire constituted two primary and recurrent vectors of the national renewal of France, expressed in a variety of guises. Both reformers and colonialists used gendered discourse to justify their policies by grounding them in broad, essentialist norms that portrayed women primarily as mothers but also as messengers of social mediation and modernity. Conversely, bourgeois feminists, hoping to improve the lot of French women, referred increasingly to the fatherland in their efforts to attain full civic rights.

In each case the colonies were represented as laboratories, virgin territories for testing the new empiricism of reform, lands "with endless perspectives on a future with no past." In these idealized territories, women would promote a less violent, more enlightened form of colonization, private initiative would develop unhampered, and excessive state intervention and political partisanship would be circumvented. A Greater France, a more self-assured, far-reaching, vigorous, regenerated France, was the desired goal. But the ideal of Greater France was itself a geographical metaphor that sought to capture a more secure sense of national identity at home. Although the colonial empire was vaunted as a new measure of modernity, mounting domestic turmoil had begun to suggest otherwise. The vision of Greater France could not protect the country from its internal problems, nor could it withstand the forces that would ultimately undermine France's self-proclaimed role as a moral leader of the colonial world.[48]

3. "SPECIAL CUSTOMS": Paternity Suits and Citizenship in France and the Colonies, 1870–1912

Jean Elisabeth Pedersen

In 1912 the French Senate and Chamber of Deputies legalized paternity suits in France for the first time in over a hundred years. The new law allowed an unmarried mother to pursue the father of her child in court. If the court allowed her claim, the man in question could be required to acknowledge the child as his own, fulfill his paternal obligation of support, and accept the child among his heirs. The law was originally discussed as an option for women in continental France, but the last clause, added just before the law was passed, specified that it should also apply in the colonies if both parties were French citizens, or, at each colonial governor's discretion, if only one was French.

The debate over the legalization of paternity suits, at least as old as the French Revolution, had emerged as a central issue in the first decades of the Third Republic. The passage of the 1912 law ended almost forty years of parliamentary debate in response to demands from an unlikely combination of feminists, socialists, doctors, and conservative moral reformers. Although instituting paternity suits in the colonies, first proposed in the Senate in 1910, seemed like an afterthought, the idea that colonized women might sue French men for paternity was immediately controversial. Before the Chamber of Deputies could examine the Senate's proposal, the ministry of colonies questioned colonial governors on the consequences of such a provision. My desire to understand the responses to this questionnaire and the implications of the controversy that surrounded it provided one of the major incentives for this essay.

Feminist theorists and women's historians have urged us to consider the ways in which people are defined and define themselves not only in terms of gender but also in terms of other identities including race, class, ethnicity, religion, and sexual orientation.[1] As a result, race, class, and gender have become a familiar list of analytical categories. These categories seem parallel to the extent that a focus on any one of them can reveal the ways in which cultures and their historians have rendered some people central and highly visible, others marginal and obscure.

However, these categories are also interconnected. The French debate over paternity suits provides a particularly good case for examining the implications of intersecting gender, class, and race identities in the definition of nationality and citizenship. French law distinguished between male and female citizens both in public, where only men could vote, and in private, where husbands and fathers enjoyed different rights and responsibilities from wives and mothers. Although class was not a legal category like sex, men and women in different social circumstances had different degrees of access to the law. Finally, the indigenous peoples of French colonies, who rarely became French citizens, faced their own legal challenges depending on how French administrators responded to local practices of politics, kinship, and economics.

Supporters of legal paternity suits presented single mothers as innocent women who deserved support or as fallen women who could redeem themselves through motherhood. Those who opposed them presented the same single mothers as calculating women whose words were untrustworthy. Politicians on both sides revealed their anxieties over class and race as well as gender by focusing attention on relations between middle-class French men and working-class or colonized women. This suggests not only that sexual relationships were particularly controversial if they threatened to cross class or race lines, but also that both class and race distinctions were understood in gendered terms.

Feminists demanded paternity suits as an extension of women's rights, but republican men were more interested in defining their family responsibilities. The law of 1912 marginalized women based on sex, class, and race, not through a series of parallel maneuvers but through three interconnected strategies that were rhetorically similar but structurally distinct. The text of the law suggested that all women were potentially untrustworthy by promising to punish women who brought suits in "bad faith." However, the full significance of labeling a woman unreliable differed depending on her class position and citizenship status. In the metropole the law implicitly excluded working-class women, setting standards of proof which servants and factory workers were unlikely to meet. In the colonies, by contrast, the law explicitly excluded native women, granting them access to the law only at colonial governors' discretion. Although supporters of the law usually contrasted moral women with immoral men, the law also distinguished among women by coding morality as the property of those who approached the ideal of monogamous marriage among middle-class French citizens.

Analyzing debates over paternity suits in their historical context explains how a plan to help all women became a law which extended only to some. Paternity suits had been legal in the eighteenth century, restricted during the French Revolution, and eliminated by Napoleon in his Civil Code of 1804.[2] The Code provided for abandoned children by allowing maternity suits through which a child could claim a woman as its mother and demand her support in court.[3] However, it explicitly forbade paternity suits which would compel fathers to take similar responsibility except in the rare case where conception followed kidnapping and rape.

The Civil Code became one of the most enduring legacies of the French Revolution, surviving the Restoration of 1815, the Revolution of 1830, the July Monarchy, the Revolution of 1848, the Second Empire, and the Paris Commune to become the basis for the laws of the Third Republic. In the 1870s and 1880s, demands for the legalization of paternity suits appeared in the Paris papers, at the meetings of prestigious organizations such as the Academy of Medicine, at feminist congresses, and in the Senate and Chamber of Deputies.[4] These demands continued debates over the woman question which had reappeared in the liberalized political atmosphere of the late Second Empire.[5] They took on new urgency in the early Third Republic when republicans were struggling to establish a new government and concern over depopulation, provoked by French defeat in the Franco-Prussian war, made the fate of every child a matter of national security.[6]

Those who demanded the legalization of paternity suits promised that this revision of the Civil Code would create moral, social, and political order by realigning relationships between women and men. Depopulation, urban poverty, and political unrest could all be controlled by providing a father and mother for every child. These arguments said less about racial tensions in the colonies than they did about class tensions in metropolitan French cities. However, they may be understood as expressions of racial anxiety as well, for French fears of national decline were often linked to fears of racial degeneration.[7]

Doctors and other social reformers pointed to statistics showing that single mothers were more likely to resort to prostitution, abortion, and infanticide, and that infant mortality was dramatically higher among illegitimate children. Hoping to combat death and disease by encouraging marriage and legitimate births, they wanted to discourage men from illicit sexual relationships by forcing fathers to provide economic support even for their illegitimate children. In a special meeting of the Academy of Medicine in 1878, doctor and anthropologist Gustave Lagneau called for the legalization of paternity suits without delay.[8]

Social reformers promised that paternity suits would not only lower infant mortality but also eliminate the social injustice, sexual disorder, and political unrest that resulted from urban poverty. For example, Jules Simon, a republican senator, supported paternity suits because they would protect "the woman who works and suffers" from the unwanted attention of factory owners and their sons.[9] M. Bry, professor of law at the University of Aix, warned the Congress of Learned Societies in 1897 that unrecognized illegitimate children who survived to adulthood constituted a grave social danger, an "army that above all . . . recruited the authors of crimes, [and] the soldiers of riot, as well as the victims of prostitution."[10]

Feminists also demanded moral reform and sought social peace. In 1878 the first feminist congress in France, the International Congress on Women's Rights, included paternity suits in its list of legal demands because "both morality and social order require that the parentage of every human being should be a matter of record."[11] However, feminists differed from other social reformers by combining demands for moral reform with demands for women's rights. Women in the early Third Republic could not vote or serve on juries. Married women could not even control their own incomes without their husbands' permission. Republican feminists argued that the French Revolution had freed men but done nothing for women. In the words of Maria Deraismes, who founded some of the most important feminist organizations and publications: "We want to reclaim our revolutionary tradition, continue the work of enfranchisement. The eighteenth century stopped at men. It made them citizens. The nineteenth century must move on to women and proclaim their citizenship."[12] Legalizing paternity suits would be a way of creating equality between women and men by forcing men to assume equal responsibility for raising all their children.

Opponents of the reform, mostly lawyers and judges, tended to stress the difficulty of proving paternity, the danger of scandal if prominent men were brought to trial, and the impossibility of legislating morality. Larombière, the former president of the Court of Appeals, argued that women needed no special protection since they were just as likely to seduce men.[13] The question of whether women were active seducers or innocent victims would become one of the key issues when parliamentary politicians defined the conditions for bringing paternity suits.

Anxiety over depopulation reached new heights in the last decades of the nineteenth century, a period when the pace of French colonial expansion increased, debates over gender roles became particularly intense, and the Civil Code approached its centennial.[14] Sociologist Abel Pouzol, whose book on paternity suits won a prize from the Academy of Moral and Political Sciences in 1900, complained that "there is no Book of Revelation, Bible, Gospel, or Koran, whose word is more obeyed than the letter of the Napoleonic Code." He reminded his readers that France had changed since 1804 and expressed his hope that the new century would see a "truly liberal code, with equality for all."[15]

From 1878 to 1900 a range of conservative, radical, and socialist senators and deputies had submitted over half a dozen proposals to legalize paternity suits. In general, conservatives stressed help for innocent women who had been raped or seduced; radicals were more likely to advocate help for any child whose mother could prove paternity, and socialists advocated paternity suits as the first step in eliminating all legal distinctions between legitimate and illegitimate children.[16]

The proposal that finally passed was submitted to the Senate in 1905 by two unlikely partners, Gustave Rivet and René Bérenger, politicians who had been sponsoring separate proposals for the legalization of paternity suits since 1878. Rivet, who became the primary speaker for the bill, was a senator on the democratic Left and editor of a progressive republican journal, the *Radical*.[17] René Bérenger, by contrast, was a

Catholic social reformer whose other causes included the regulation of obscene posters and pamphlets, the censorship of information about birth control, and the regulation of prostitution. The joint proposal and the parliamentary debates that culminated in the law of 1912 opened with the radical assertion that paternity suits were a woman's right but ended by reaffirming women's domestic role.

Rivet argued for the legalization of paternity suits as a way of adjusting the Napoleonic Code "to give the woman . . . the rights which the egoism of man has refused her up to now." He protested French women's current "state of servitude and inferiority," which he characterized as a "violation of equity." Although he admitted that diamond-covered courtesans and wealthy women of leisure might not need the protection of such a law, he urged his colleagues to disregard such exceptions and focus instead on "the truer, more general picture" of the "woman of the people," whether peasant or factory worker.[18]

However, Rivet immediately qualified his apparent support for women's rights by limiting their extent, distinguishing between a woman's necessary "human rights" and her less obvious "political rights." According to Rivet, the "natural conditions" of a woman's life, "pregnancy, delivery, nursing, [and] child care," were the "fatal causes" that would prevent her from ever having "a regular, active, exterior life." He reassured his colleagues, "We do not dream of a woman freed from the laws of nature; we hope on the contrary that [gender] roles will remain well-determined, perfectly fixed."[19] Here, the legalization of paternity suits became a means of improving women's legal situation while simultaneously reaffirming their sexual, social, and political differences from men.

Other senators, who rose to defend the general proposal, echoed Rivet in stressing the importance of sexual difference as the basis of family unity. Even radical socialist Senator Louis Martin, a parliamentary supporter of women's suffrage after the First World War, assured his audience that he was reluctant to give women political rights which might interfere with their family obligations. Women could not replace men "in the legislative palaces" because men could never replace women "in our children's rooms."[20]

Rivet, Martin, and their colleagues were less interested in women's political rights, or even in their rights to child support, than they were in making sure that women had husbands and children had fathers. For example, Louis Martin argued that paternity suits were important because they would create new families, serving the "social interest" of seeing "every child surrounded by a family which raises it honestly and feels itself responsible for all its acts." Although Martin glorified maternity, explaining that a fallen woman could redeem herself by caring for her child, he stressed the importance of having a father in every family. The senators clearly agreed because they applauded Martin when he named the father as the most important figure in "the care of feeding the child, of raising it, of making it a good citizen for the French fatherland."[21]

For paternity suits to create new families instead of troubling old ones, both partners had to be unmarried. Politicians were unwilling to give rights to single women if they challenged married men. When socialist Maurice Viollette defended the Senate proposal to the Chamber of Deputies, he stressed that paternity suits would not be allowed for adulterous relationships, whose discussion in court could threaten established families with scandal and financial hardship. Where both parents were single, however, the law could restore social order by converting the illegitimate child from a potential danger to "the hyphen which brings the parents together." He insisted, "Far from being directed against marriage, the new law intends nothing less than to develop it and to generalize it."[22]

In his initial proposal Rivet had promised his colleagues that paternity suits would not threaten honest men and their families because "a disorderly woman would never be able to bring a suit." He suggested that a woman could only bring suit if she had lived in what he characterized as an "illegal household . . . where the woman, although in an irregular situation, played the role of the wife." In other words, women could only use paternity suits if they had been living in a situation that almost perfectly duplicated the ideal of the legitimate family.[23]

The debates that followed made it clear that although any woman was potentially disorderly, politicians were particularly likely to suspect her if she was a working-class French woman or a colonized woman of whatever social standing. One of the major senatorial debates focused on what proof a woman needed to supply to begin a suit. Pierre-Ernest Guillier, the republican lawyer who had reviewed Rivet and Bérenger's proposal for the Senate, was sympathetic to the ways in which women were disadvantaged in French law. In 1906, for example, he had worked on a law which allowed widowed and divorced women to remarry without forfeiting their control of their children's property to their new husbands. In his Senate report on paternity suits, he recommended that women who gave birth after kidnap or rape should be able to sue if their attacker was convicted of the crime. Women who became pregnant after seduction based on abuse of authority or "fraudulent schemes" should be able to bring suit based on the word of witnesses. Written proof in the form of correspondence, notes, or other private papers would be necessary only if the woman had been seduced by a promise of marriage.

Guillier's provisions on seduction were challenged by another republican lawyer, Théodore Girard, who argued that written proof was always necessary to prevent devious women from conspiring to blackmail innocent men. Girard showed his class anxiety in his assertion that Guillier's loose standards of proof would endanger any man with servants. If oral testimony was allowed, any maid might convince her lover to witness that she actually had been seduced by her master, forcing this innocent man to bear the shame and pay the expenses of another's illegitimate child.

When Guillier defended the committee's decision to trust witnesses, he stressed its desire to give "effective protection" to as many women as possible by allowing them to "prove the deceit, the fraud, and the violence which they have had to suffer by all the means in their power."[24] Independent Senator Félix Martin, who had often studied female and child labor, stressed the class implications of requiring written proof when he asked pointedly: "[What about] the patron who commits an abuse of authority? What beginning of proof in writing will he give his servant? . . . [I]f one wants to abuse his servant, one is not going to tell her so in a letter."[25] Louis Martin expanded on this theme later when he argued that raising the standard of evidence would eliminate all women who suffered from "the most common form of corruption: the abuse of authority exercised by the boss or the foreman over a woman working in his shop, by the master over his servant, in a word, domestic seduction or employee seduction."[26] In this conflict the interests of male employers won out over those of their female employees when the higher standard of proof became part of the law. The words of working-class women and their male coworkers were devalued in favor of written testimony from literate masters. In this way working-class women whose relationships crossed class lines could be effectively silenced by a law which ostensibly helped all women.

A similar conflation of working-class status with dishonesty occurred in the debate over cohabitation. Guillier's Senate committee had suggested that a woman could sue for paternity based on "notorious cohabitation" if she and the alleged father had been living together. Opponents as diverse as the ultraconservative lawyer Gustave de Lamarzelle and the moderate jurist Jean Richard complained that this would allow any servant to sue her master if she got pregnant while living under his roof. Richard asked his colleagues, "What if a very honorable person had a somewhat frivolous servant?" He protested, "Truly, if the woman is a feeble creature, as she has been represented to us, meriting the solicitude of public powers and Parliament, it still has to be recognized that, in the reality of things, this weak woman is excessively sly and cunning." [27]

This description of the female servant as "excessively sly and cunning" echoed the generalized distrust of women evident from the beginning of the debate. However, Richard revealed the class bias of this distrust when he stressed not only the gender difference between men and women but also the social difference between "a very honorable person" and his "somewhat frivolous servant." The Senate responded to this contrast by changing the phrase from "notorious cohabitation" to "notorious concubinage," thus letting masters off the hook for a second time. The Chamber of Deputies accepted this modification, and it, too, became part of the law.

These examples show that although politicians claimed to be intent on protecting all deserving women, the law on paternity suits excluded many working-class women through clauses that, although ostensibly included for uniformity and clarity, served to deny these women's particular needs and experiences. The politicians ignored the case in which a working-class woman tried to sue her working-class partner instead of her employer, but even such same-class suits would have been made harder by the high standards of evidence that the law imposed.

Like women in the metropole, especially working-class women, indigenous women in French colonies were stereotyped as manipulative and untrustworthy. The same clauses that excluded working-class women would have prevented many colonized women's claims as well. However, although the language used to describe them was similar, the mechanism used to exclude them was different. While working-class women in France were only implicitly excluded by the imposition of high standards of proof, native women in the colonies were explicitly excluded in a special clause whereby they could only sue for paternity at the discretion of colonial governors.

The final clause of the proposal that the Senate sent to the Chamber of Deputies in 1910 extended the law to Algeria and the other French colonies. Unlike the clauses raising class issues, the senators passed this colonial clause easily, with no discussion. However, before the deputies could consider the proposal, the ministry of colonies intervened to survey its colonial governors for their response. Maurice Viollette complained that the Colonial Ministry's intervention had been unnecessary but compiled the results, nonetheless, and modified the colonial clause accordingly.

Historians have noted that at the turn of the century colonial administrators moved from a position of assimilation, which stressed the application of French law to colonized peoples, to a position of association, which stressed respect for local customs. This policy shift responded both to the difficulties of combining colonial control with Muslim assimilation in Algeria and to the expansion of French territory in Africa.[28] After 1900 socialists and feminists criticized French colonial policy for denying the benefits of French law to colonized peoples.[29] Viollette's response to the ministry of colonies reveals the tensions between socialist anticolonialism, with its demands for assimilation, and the government's new policy of association. However, it also shows the tension within socialism itself between a desire to improve the treatment of colonial peoples and a desire to maintain French control of colonial territories.

Since the turn of the century, colonial administrators had tried to guarantee peaceful relationships with colonial subjects less by proclaiming the benefits of French law than by promising to leave local traditions intact. So, for example, the governor and the officers of the French courts in India justified their approval of the proposal by remarking that "paternity suits are authorized in Hindu law." Similarly, the interim governor-general of Indochina concluded that the law should apply there because the "Annamite code" already provided for paternity suits under "about the same conditions" as the French proposal.[30]

Even under the policy of association, respect for local tradition had its limits, especially regarding familial and sexual relationships. Governors in the old colonies, still following a policy of assimilation, wanted to apply the law precisely because it would change local custom. The governor of Martinique observed that applying the law there "could only be advantageous" because it would "encourage people who live in an irregular fashion to regularize their situations." Guadeloupe's governor agreed that "it would only present advantages because it would increase the number of marriages, unhappily very restricted in Guadeloupe." The governor of Guyana reported that in his colony "free unions are frequent and appear to be allowed by tradition. Natural children are numerous." Although he recommended implementing the law gradually to avoid shocking local customs, he also reported that the courts, the colonial commission, and the department of agriculture agreed that legalizing paternity suits should change behavior among Guyana's indigenous peoples.[31]

The prevailing support for paternity suits among colonial governors makes it all the more intriguing to consider the minority of cases, all African, in which colonial governors spoke against the law's application. On the Somalian coast the governor agreed to accept the law only if it did not include followers of "Koranic law." In Madagascar the governor argued both that the law would be unnecessary and that it might be abused. Viollette further noted that the administrators of "the [other] two African governments," French West Africa and Equatorial French Africa, probably would reject the proposed law.[32]

Viollette's report said little about why African governors opposed the proposal, and their reasons are difficult to reconstruct. French African colonies were home to hundreds of different peoples and groups, each with distinctive laws and combinations of animist and Muslim religious observances.[33] Customary law developed through oral tradition and could vary dramatically from people to people. Codified Islamic law may have appeared more uniform, but its application changed over time and varied from place to place as African Muslims modified its provisions according to their own local understandings of what was appropriate. Furthermore, French administrators' positions could have as much to do with their own political concerns as with the social practices of the peoples they governed.

Early twentieth-century French observers, administrators, and anthropologists often focused on the ways in which African customary law and Islamic law regulated family life and inheritance in strikingly different ways from French practices. Concepts of paternity, illegitimacy, and property had radically different meanings in many African societies. For example, later administrative surveys of African customary law reported that African peoples, reckoning descent through the mother's family, gave her brother more authority over her children than her husband. Among some peoples adoption might be forbidden, while among others single women might adopt children to raise their social status. Even groups that used the more familiar formula of paternal descent were likely to think of property and inheritance in collective, rather than individual, terms.[34] Paternity suits would have disrupted such systems by assigning each child to a biological father.

Islamic law established more familiar forms of paternal authority and property transmission. Although it allowed men to recognize their sons under certain conditions, it did not permit women and children to claim paternity that was not offered voluntarily.[35] As a result, legalized paternity suits probably would have contradicted Muslim practices along the Somalian coast and among some peoples of French West and Equatorial Africa.

The governor of Madagascar's objections to the proposal presented a particularly interesting case. Unlike other colonial governors, he saw both good and bad in his colony. On the one hand, he reported that such a law was unnecessary because among the indigenous peoples of Madagascar, natural children were always welcome, fathers usually acknowledged their children, adoption was unlimited, and there was no moral or material difference between legitimate and illegitimate children. On the other, he and other officials feared the law would be abused if it extended to relationships between "Europeans" and "indigenous peoples."[36]

A decree of 1909 had already specified that French citizens in Madagascar would be governed by French law. Although indigenous peoples would be ruled by native courts following the laws of the Merina people who had controlled the island before the French conquest, the decree of 1909 also held that "judges could apply French law wherever Malagasy law appeared to be insufficient or non-existent."[37] These provisions could have opened a way to legalize paternity suits in Madagascar if the colonial governor found it desirable.

It is hard to know what customs or local political conditions led the governor to feel that paternity suits were unnecessary in Madagascar and that, if implemented, they would be abused. The dominant Merina had produced a series of their own legal codes in the nineteenth century, but the local customs of other peoples had continued seemingly unchanged and unchallenged in many parts of the island.[38] Contemporary anthropologists have continued the debates begun by earlier colonial observers over whether the admitted linguistic unity of the islanders indicated a cultural unity or rather masked considerable ethnic differences.[39] Nineteenth- and early twentieth-century British and American observers reported that Malagasy women often had children before getting married; that among some peoples, the women were polyandrous, taking more than one husband; and that some peoples were matrilineal instead of patrilineal. Later administrators and anthropologists have argued that like other African peoples, Malagasy peoples under either system of descent believed that children belonged to the entire extended tribal family. Similarly, they recognized collective property rights rather than individual inheritance.[40] These dramatic differences between local and French practices of marriage and inheritance may have been at the root of the governor of Madagascar's worry about abuse in his colony.

Acknowledging these differences between French, African customary, and Islamic family law cannot alone explain how French administrators decided whether or not to replace African systems with French ones. French observers identified Islam with resistance both to colonial rule and to the processes of French civilization.[41] Respect for Islamic law could be a way of minimizing colonial unrest by allowing Muslims a sense of autonomy as long as they kept to themselves.[42] Respect for non-Islamic customary law could also be a way of limiting the spread of Islam by supporting the practices of African peoples with other beliefs. In 1935 colonial administrator Georges Bruel suggested that in Equatorial Africa "our duty is to establish peace among all [animists and Muslims], to maintain an equal balance, in making use of both [peoples] without ever giving to either of them the preeminence which should belong only to us and our direct agents."[43] French colonial policy changed over time; Bruel's considerations in 1930 may not have been those of colonial administrators at the time of the 1910 survey on paternity suits. However, his interest in maintaining French control suggests that administrators could apply laws for political reasons having little to do with the content of the laws themselves. Even when the French respected local practices, they changed them by centralizing Muslim courts and codifying fluid oral traditions.[44]

Viollette dealt with the colonial governors' conflicting reports by proposing that the law on paternity suits be applied in the colonies wherever at least one of the parties involved was a French citizen by birth or had achieved naturalized French citizenship. However, he suggested that colonial governors hold discretionary power to limit the law to cases where both parties were born or naturalized French citizens.

The Chamber of Deputies approved this modification with no deliberation, but the modified colonial clause provoked new controversy when the proposal was returned to the Senate for final approval. Pierre-Ernest Guillier reported that the clause raised objections both from those who feared that it would do too little and from those who feared that it would do too much. Some "found excessive the right given to local powers to deprive indigenous women and the children they might have with French colonists from the benefits of the law." Others feared "the dangers which Frenchmen returning from the colonies could be forced to endure from claims formulated by children who will pretend to issue from relations which they could have had with indigenous women."[45]

The controversy continued not only in the metropole but also in the colonies. Guillier reported that "colonists hostile to the reform" worried about lawsuits from "women of color" and feared suits based on "the testimony of suspicious and unscrupulous indigenous women." The image of the "suspicious and unscrupulous" native woman recalls the image of the "excessively sly and cunning" servant that already excluded many metropolitan working-class women from the law's benefits.

Guillier supported the modified clause, arguing, like other associationists, that French law was simply not appropriate in every situation.

He explained that although his commission had "no intention of proclaiming racial inferiority" and fully supported "the principle of equality of all the French before the law," it was "indispensable to take account of . . . local laws and customs." However, his claims that the clause made no reference to "racial inferiority" were clearly unfounded. Although he reassured his colleagues that "suspicious and unscrupulous" native women would be prevented from abusing the law by the courts' high standards of evidence, he did not deny that such women existed. Furthermore, he acknowledged that the law was least likely to be applied in "the countries most recently submitted to our domination," the French colonies of Africa.[46]

When the clause came up for its last discussion in the Senate, radical socialist Louis Martin, radical Paul Strauss, and several French senators representing the colonies all objected to Viollette's modification, although for different reasons. Martin and Strauss, who represented departments in the metropole, objected particularly to the exclusion of native women. Marcel Saint-Germain, Amédée Knight, and Maurice Colin, who represented departments in the colonies, objected more generally to the admission that colonial governors might modify French law.

Paul Strauss was a radical republican who specialized in public assistance, especially measures to improve the health of mothers and their children.[47] He reported that the possibility of ignoring colonized women who had given birth to children with French fathers had "provoked extremely lively protest and pressing resolutions in feminist circles, at the League for the Rights of Man, and elsewhere." He acknowledged that indigenous peoples should be allowed to regulate their own lives but argued that if an indigenous woman had become involved with a French man, this "indigenous mother" and her "métis child" deserved consideration under French law. He warned his colleagues, "We must not give the impression—happily untrue—that we make distinctions among races, [or] that we [ourselves] have the prejudices of inferior races."[48] Here Strauss used racial difference to describe French superiority to other European countries, while minimizing racial differences between French citizens and their colonial subjects. The French could prove that they were better than other colonial powers by insisting on better treatment for their subjects.

Guillier, speaking for the Senate commission that had reviewed the clause, responded to Strauss's charges that it was an "abnormal disposition" by stressing again the need to "respect the usages, statutes, habitudes, laws—if one can speak of laws for certain of these countries—at least the customs under which the indigenous peoples are placed." Guillier's distinction between laws and customs here suggests that he was thinking of African customary law, but later he also reminded his colleagues that some of "our [French] possessions" also had "a great number of Muslims" with special laws. He reiterated the associationist point that the colonies could not all be treated the same way because they were not all the same, and he reminded his senatorial colleagues that no French law applied in the colonies, anyway, until announced by a governor's decree. Strauss and Martin responded to the commission's opposition by withdrawing their amendment.[49]

Where Strauss and Martin raised objections against the racism of the new clause, French senators representing Algeria and the old colonies objected that the modified clause gave colonial governors too much authority over French law. Marcel Saint-Germain, republican senator from Oran, complained that Algeria and the old colonies had already accepted the Civil Code and should institute its changes automatically. When Guillier dismissed this concern, Maurice Colin, a lawyer from Lyons who represented Algiers, reiterated, "One of the greatest difficulties in Algeria is knowing what laws are applicable. It is precisely with vicious texts like these that you complicate the problem."[50]

Algeria's legal situation was indeed complex in 1912, as the relationships among French and Muslim courts had been continually contested and reorganized since the 1850s. However, Saint-Germain and Colin's complaints may have sprung more from a desire to contest their colonial governor's power than from any interest in applying the new law. In 1870 the colonists' successful implementation of the Civil Code in Algeria had granted them the same rights as French citizens at home, while limiting the rights of the indigenous Muslim population. In the 1890s French politicians, trying to facilitate colonial rule by mitigating the tensions between colonists and Muslims, intervened in Algerian affairs by appointing colonial governors who represented the interests of the metropole. French citizens who became Algerian senators and deputies in Paris objected to this practice both as an infringement of their right to self-determination and as a threat to their advantages over their colonized subjects.[51] In this context Colin and Saint-Germain's objections to the clause may have been provoked both by the way it might validate Muslim claims against colonists, if the governor did not restrict the clause, and by the way it might enhance the governor's power over the colonists' legal behavior, if he did.

Saint-Germain and Colin found support from Amédée Knight, a senator from the radical socialist party of Martinique, who also complained that colonial governors were not supposed to have discretion over the application of the law in Algeria and the old colonies. The peoples of the West Indies had all been French citizens since the extension of the suffrage to free blacks in the 1830s and manumission in 1848. Male inhabitants of these colonies had elected predominantly radical republican and socialist deputies to the National Assembly since 1875. West Indian representatives were assimilationists who wanted French laws to be applied equally and immediately in their territories. Knight reminded the senators that his people had "been French for a long time" and expected the benefits of French law.[52]

The colonial clause, with its dubious provision for colonized women, remained part of the final law, which included what one legal analyst has called "eight of the most detailed dispositions of the Code."[53] A woman could bring suit within two years of her child's birth if she could establish either that she had been raped, kidnapped, or seduced under false pretenses or that the man in question had lived with her in a monogamous relationship, declared paternity in writing, or supported the child as his own. A separate section of the Civil Code prevented suits for the children of adulterous or incestuous relationships, but a woman could sue a man who, though single at the time of her relationship with him, had subsequently married someone else. In such a case, the child would receive the father's name and the right to financial support but could only inherit under very restricted conditions. If a woman failed in her suit, and the court determined that she had acted in bad faith, she could be fined or imprisoned.[54]

The most conservative members of the Senate objected to the law despite its limits. Adrien Gaudin de Villaine cried out in an early debate, "It's a law against the family, like all your [republican] laws, you're always seeking to destroy something."[55] In a later debate Charles Rieu interrupted, "You never stop damaging the family."[56] They linked the legalization of paternity suits to republican redefinitions of family life that included the loosening of marriage ties through the legalization of divorce and the loosening of a father's control over his children through mandatory secular public education.

Roman Catholic politicians accused republicans of damaging the family, but they overlooked the ways in which secular republican politicians themselves had valorized the family. One justification for divorce was that it would allow separated couples to contract new marriages rather than living in illicit unions. One assumption behind anticlerical lay morality was that secular schools would teach French children to be good citizens by teaching them to be good fathers and mothers.[57] The paternity suit law of 1912 was similarly respectful of the family. Extending benefits to women, it maintained both the identification of women with children and the superiority of families with fathers over families with mothers alone.

Feminists had mixed reactions to the law. In 1914 lawyer Jeanne Deflou interpreted the new law as the most recent addition to numerous laws that republicans had already passed to help women. Looking at this "balance of feminism" gave her hope that republican politicians were sympathetic to feminist arguments.[58] Maria Vérone, general secretary of the French League for the Rights of Women, also pointed out that the parliamentary discussion over the bill had included references not only to feminist ideas but to feminists themselves, showing that politicians were taking the women's movement seriously. The willingness of male politicians to acknowledge feminist women's opinions in public debate is particularly noteworthy because these same politicians had decided the fate of colonized women without seeking any opinions beyond those of their colonial administrators.

Nevertheless, Vérone also felt that the 1912 law left much to be desired. The "appalling" penalties for failure if a judge decided that a woman had acted in bad faith violated a defendant's civil rights and made the law "impossible to put into effect." Furthermore, in the colonies the law would apply only if at least one and preferably both of the parties were French citizens, making it difficult for colonized women to proceed against French men. In a formulation which admitted racial difference, while denying its importance in legal situations, Vérone announced the beginning of a new campaign "to proclaim the fact that there are no inferior races and that human creatures, black, yellow, and white alike, have a right to the same legal protection." She concluded, "The clumsy gesture of the Parliament serves the suffragist cause because it shows that women will always be sacrificed as long as their rights as citizens are not recognized."[59]

Although feminists levied the most comprehensive critique of the new law, the only one which championed the cause of colonized women as well as French women, others protested as well. Groups such as the Freemasons, the Republican Youth, and the League for the Rights of Man attacked the bad faith clause for its addition of criminal penalties to civil law, while socialists focused on the unreasonably high standard of proof. In Lyons these groups sponsored an outdoor meeting where they met together with feminist groups in the region. Louis Martin criticized the law as one which "protects seducing sons of good families against the just claims of seduced and abandoned working women."[60] A male lawyer named Bosquet added that "such iniquitous laws could not be passed if women were represented in Parliament."[61] The protestors moved as a body to pass a resolution that "women obtain the vote as soon as possible, for it is the only guarantee that they will be permitted to examine and to modify the laws which concern them."[62]

These changes did not come fast. In 1931 Juliette Akar, looking back in La Française, commented, "Eighteen years have passed since the passage of this law, which was welcome at the time . . . now we see all its shortcomings."[63] She reported that the National Council of French Women was trying to change the law, but without success. French women and colonial peoples finally gained the right to vote after the Second World War, but the law on paternity suits remained untouched until 1955.[64]

Contemporary feminist scholars such as Carol Pateman, Joan Landes, and Joan Scott have shown the ways in which eighteenth-century debates culminating in the French Revolution produced an ostensibly universal subject who was a gendered male.[65] The Constitution of 1791 divided free men into active and passive citizens but denied women the vote altogether, the Jacobins denied women the right to attend political meetings, and Napoleon restricted women's rights even within the family. The Revolution of 1848 freed slaves and instituted universal manhood suffrage but reiterated the exclusion of women from politics, citing the French Revolution as precedent.[66] Throughout the nineteenth and early twentieth centuries, feminists and their republican and socialist allies demanded social and political advancement in the name of "the rights of woman," a universal female subject who had been excluded from full French citizenship. The demand for the legalization of paternity suits was one manifestation of this concern, and when the law of 1912 left them dissatisfied, they again demanded the vote.

However, if the debate over paternity suits shows that social understandings of sexual difference were a crucial category of French political thought, they also show that this was not the only such category. The 1912 law mainly protected women whose personal lives lived up to the ideal of the middle-class family in all respects except the recitation of marriage vows. On these grounds, it implicitly excluded many working-class women and explicitly excluded many indigenous women in French colonies.

The feminist demand for the vote as a guarantee that the law would respond to women's needs would have enabled working-class women to make their voices heard but might not have reached colonized women. French men in 1912 voted regardless of class, but most colonized men could vote only if they passed highly restrictive tests for admission to French citizenship, and even then only in some colonies. Except in the old colonies, it was easier for another European to gain French citizenship than for a French colonial subject to do so. The most systematic encounters between more recently colonized peoples and French law were not through the Civil Code but through the *indigénat* or "indigenous code" which allowed French administrators to fine or jail their colonial subjects for resisting the colonial enterprise.[67] In this context women's suffrage would have given French women a voice in the legislature regardless of their class position but would still have required indigenous women to rely on the goodwill of their colonial rulers.

When the law on paternity suits was passed, French law made crucial distinctions between French citizens and their colonized French subjects. On a structural level citizens, regardless of class or gender, had access to the law in a way that subjects did not. As Rogers Brubaker has recently pointed out, citizenship is exclusive by its nature, "a distinctively modern institution through which every state constitutes and perpetually reconstitutes itself as an association of citizens, publicly identifies a set of persons as its members, and residually classifies everyone else in the world as a noncitizen, an alien."[68] However, the denial of citizenship to colonial subjects was particularly exclusionary because unlike the citizens of independent countries, colonial subjects had no alternate citizenship status to call their own.

Considering the intersecting images of gender, class, and race in the debate over paternity suits suggests that as long as France had an empire, the structural difference between French citizens and their colonial subjects may have been the most basic difference of all. However, this is not a completely satisfactory conclusion for several reasons. First of all, by making a binary opposition between colonial citizen and colonial subject, it flattens out the variety of ways in which imperialism was enacted in different colonies. For example, French law in all the colonies was mediated by the colonial governor, but in old colonies such as Martinique, all the inhabitants were citizens, while in the African and Asian colonies, most inhabitants were not. Even French policy toward Muslim subjects, one of the most controversial aspects of colonial rule, varied from colony to colony. In Algeria, Muslim men could vote only if they became naturalized citizens by renouncing Islamic law in favor of French law. In Senegal, by contrast, although Muslim men also had to renounce Islamic law to become citizens, they could act as electors even if they did not take this step.[69]

A focus on citizenship and formal access to law also reveals little about who could actually use a law. Working-class French women had legal rights as citizens that colonized women lacked, but the way in which they were marginalized by the provisions of the law on paternity suits shows that even laws that officially included them could still effectively exclude them.[70] On the other side of the colonial divide, colonized women may have been uniformly excluded from the automatic reach of the law, but they were no more likely to be socioeconomically homogeneous than French women. Their circumstances varied from colony to colony and from people to people. Focusing on exclusion reveals little about the various ways in which they mobilized their resources to deal with that exclusion.

Furthermore, stressing access to French citizenship and to French law implies that colonized people would have wanted this citizenship and this law. Sally Engle Merry's work suggests that women may have benefited from colonial legal systems which offered new legal options but may also have suffered if those options consolidated male control of the legal process.[71] Without further evidence both of native women's beliefs about paternity and politics and of their experiences with French colonial courts, we do not know whether they found the law on paternity suits a help or a hindrance.

Finally, although gender is not the only important category of analysis in this study, stressing the structural difference between colonizer and colonized could lead us to forget the ways in which gender was important on both sides of the divide and sometimes across it as well. Martin Chanock's work on the British in Rhodesia has suggested that British imperial administrators and African tribal chiefs collaborated to produce codification of customary law that devalued female autonomy in order to consolidate male control.[72] While this analysis cannot erase the asymmetries in power between the colonial administrators and the tribal chiefs, it shows how men on both sides of the divide manipulated beliefs about masculine superiority in order to shape the terms of the colonial encounter to their own purposes. Neither British nor colonized women were parties to this exchange.

Similarly, although French women were citizens regardless of class, even the citizenship of middle-class women was limited by their inability to vote in national elections. French women had more access to French law than colonized women, but even French women were excluded from complete participation in republican political life. French politicians, even those who supported women's rights, valued women chiefly for their capacity as mothers of new French people. The law of 1912 granted a woman the right to sue a man for paternity not for herself but for the sake of her child. This was true whether she was the French mother of a French child or, in Strauss's words, the "indigenous mother" of a "mixed-blood child." The other side of this glorification of motherhood was the vilification of dishonest women who might use the law to sue men who were not really their partners. Although this fear was particularly attached to working-class and colonized women, the "bad-faith" clause could theoretically be levied against any woman who brought a losing suit. This categorization of women into worthy mothers and unworthy liars must have had different implications for middle-class, working-class, and colonized women, but the fact that these were the only two images available demonstrates the ways in which race and class differences were understood in gendered terms.

4. REDEFINING "FRENCHNESS": Citizenship, Race Regeneration, and Imperial Motherhood in France and West Africa, 1914–40

Alice L. Conklin

On July 22, 1993, the newly elected conservative government in France amended laws (Code de la Nationalité) to make the acquisition of French citizenship more difficult for children of foreigners born in France. Chirac's cohabitation government had considered similar legislation in the mid-1980s, but the outcry from the Left managed to kill the measure before Parliament could vote on it. The conservative government was more successful. According to the new legislation, children born on French soil to immigrant parents no longer automatically become French citizens. Instead, they must apply for citizenship between the ages of sixteen and nineteen, and applications may be rejected on any of the grounds listed in the new law. A subsequent opinion poll revealed that three out of four French citizens supported the government in this matter.[1]

Increased racial tensions in France over the last ten to fifteen years explain the recent legislation. The immigrants targeted are primarily from France's former colonies, who stand out by virtue of different skin color, religion, and language. But the debate over citizenship—and, more specifically, over who is French and who is not—has a much longer pedigree. The same debate erupted, for example, in the late 1930s when France felt overwhelmed by refugees from Hitler's Germany and Franco's Spain. The citizenship of colonial subjects within the French Empire in Africa and Asia was also often a contested issue. This was never more true than in the 1920s and 1930s, when new challenges to France's authority overseas and a more conservative climate in the metropole after World War I fostered a reconsideration of what it meant to be French. This essay examines the interwar debate over French identity with reference to French West Africa.[2] I devote special attention to the intersection of race, culture, and gender in this debate and to the ways that simultaneous developments at home and overseas helped to reconfigure relations between the French and Africans.

When France began expanding its West African holdings in the 1890s, the republicans in power made it clear that certain colonized subjects would have the opportunity to become French citizens if they proved themselves worthy. Having embraced this principle, colonial policymakers soon began to have second thoughts about the wisdom of granting citizenship to any of their subjects. The politics of inclusion and exclusion in the colonial context, these officials discovered, were much more complicated than initially thought. The principle of granting citizenship was predicated on the notion that the colonizer and the colonized made up two distinct groups, and that the boundaries between them were easily drawn but also permeable.[3] According to a 1912 decree, an African subject who learned French, served the French administration loyally, and agreed to be bound by the precepts of French law and the Civil Code had become French and could be included in the French family of citizens with a full complement of rights—regardless of skin color. Conversely, those who failed to meet any or all of these criteria deserved to be excluded from the family of French citizens; they would remain subjects, with duties rather than rights.

A straightforward dichotomy between colonizer and colonized, between citizen and subject, failed, however, to reflect colonial realities as they evolved over time. By the early 1920s colonization had produced a new French-speaking elite eager for a share of power and willing to contest French rule in order to achieve a say in their own administration. Perceiving these actions as disloyal, the French government concluded that it could not possibly grant citizenship to this elite; but neither could it continue to include them in the great mass of uneducated subjects, where discontent would only fester. The emergence of this new elite thus posed a crisis for French policymakers. Administrators and politicians had to figure out a way to contain this threat to the authority of the Third Republic while appearing to remain loyal to its democratic ideals. The depth of this crisis was revealed in the responses it provoked. Between 1925 and 1933 officials in Paris and Dakar revised the 1912 decree and also defined more precisely who was white and who was not. Older colonial categories were scrutinized and new ones contemplated; skin color increasingly became a decisive marker of Frenchness. The result was a realignment of cultural and racial boundaries which effectively excluded all claims by the colonized to equal status with the colonizer.

Racial and cultural boundaries were nevertheless not the only ones redrawn in France and West Africa in the interwar years. The debate over who was French was also structured in gendered terms. By this, I do not mean, as scholars have demonstrated with regard to Indians under British rule, that West Africans were increasingly equated with the private realm (religion, culture, and the home) and therefore apolitical aspects of society. According to this view, the process of endowing all Indians, regardless of their gender, with feminine—or effeminate— characteristics justified the exclusion of Indians from the public and political world ordered by the state.[4] The new African elite was also feminized, but the terms carried a different meaning than in British India. French-speaking Africans were described as irrational and insufficiently civilized for exercising the full rights of citizenship; these same arguments were used to deny women suffrage in France at the end of World War I. But even more important than the differences in how Indians and Africans were inscribed with effeminacy was the emergence of a specific kind of gendered imperial rhetoric in this period.[5] I show that a crucial aspect of the interwar strategy for safeguarding colonial authority was a growing emphasis on managing relations between the sexes. Ann Laura Stoler, in her study of French Indochina, has concluded that the new politics of exclusion that developed there in the first half of the twentieth century "required regulating the sexual, conjugal and domestic life of both Europeans in the colonies and their colonized subjects."[6] The same could be said of French West Africa, and indeed of France itself.

French discussions in the interwar years about the otherness of Africans thus took a particular form, which raises a number of issues about the exercise of power in an imperial setting. The colonial state was not monolithic; its coercive powers, while extensive, could never be taken for granted, particularly at a moment of intensifying capitalist development. Nor was this state either static or isolated from the metropole. French representations of themselves and of Africans changed in Paris and Dakar as the colonial balance of power evolved, and as metropolitan developments reverberated overseas. The French eventually had to confront potent African nationalist movements—a product of France's presence in the colonies—demanding a voice in policy making. Criticism from those excluded from power led the authorities to attempt to reassert control in a variety of ways, such as redefining citizenship and clarifying racial, cultural, and sexual boundaries. Intensifying concerns in the metropole about declining French birthrates and the rising numbers of immigrants in the 1920s and 1930s also contributed to this change in attitudes, as did the post–World War I emigration of French women to West Africa. By exploring how the French colonial administration reacted to these various developments, I highlight the differential position assigned to all women—African and European, metropolitan and colonial—as part of maintaining French hegemony overseas in the twentieth century.[7] In the murky, shifting sands of interwar French and African politics, the female body and the black body together became the sites of unprecedented concern, as nervous white males did everything to stay on top.

THE HOLLOW YEARS: WORLD WAR I
AND ITS CONSEQUENCES

Before turning to these men and women, however, it is necessary to ask what precipitated this process of cultural, racial, and sexual realignment. Three separate but nonetheless interconnected factors stand out: the outbreak of World War I and the growth of protest movements in West Africa; the arrival of the first white women in the colony; and the further development of eugenicist, pronatalist, and social hygiene movements in France.

The eruption of war in Europe in 1914 led France to recruit soldiers by force in all of its overseas territories. This decision had disastrous consequences in West Africa, both for the local populations and for French authority there. The French eventually recruited 200,000 of the most able-bodied men of the federation over a four-year period, of whom approximately 30,000 were killed in France. The French military and government, and public opinion at large, accepted the idea that the men of certain West African ethnic groups were natural warriors and should be used on the European front lines to terrorize the Germans. Initially heaviest in the Western Sudan, recruitment eventually affected all the colonies of the federation—although urban areas were largely spared. Africans everywhere described military recruitment as a return to the horrors of the slave trade and resisted enrollment in a variety of ways: flight to neighboring British colonies, self-mutilation, and outright revolt. Before the war's end disgruntled chiefs had led rebellions in the Western Sudan, Dahomey, Ivory Coast, Guinea, and the military territory of Niger.[8] French authorities in West Africa were able to contain these revolts, but their confidence was nevertheless considerably shaken.

More serious in the long run, the first generation of French-educated Africans—known as *évolués*—also began to contest the legitimacy of French rule during the course of the war. The election in 1914 of the first black African ever, Blaise Diagne, to the French Parliament from the Four Communes of Senegal considerably emboldened this new elite to press for concessions. Diagne demanded that all évolués throughout West Africa be given the full political rights of citizenship but still be allowed to preserve their Muslim status (which the French maintained was incompatible with their Civil Code).[9] In other cities in the federation, members of the new elite began to agitate for rights; in the early 1920s strikes and tax revolts broke out in coastal Dahomey, which French political reports did not hesitate to blame upon the emerging pan-African movement and international Bolshevism. Most urban Africans protesting in this era, however, were motivated more by local grievances against the French than new international ideologies: excessive taxation, poor working conditions, and forced labor. This contestation, increasingly nationalist in tone, continued throughout the interwar years.[10]

A second factor that contributed to the new postwar politics of exclusion was the arrival of white French women in West Africa. French Equatorial and West Africa were among the last French colonies to attract women. These were not, and were never expected to be, settler colonies, because of their climate and reputation for disease.[11] Nevertheless, by the 1920s sufficient strides had been made in colonial hygiene to lower French mortality rates in Africa. The subcontinent was now deemed a healthy enough place for the one category of women considered most likely to go there: wives of administrators, who had previously remained in France with their children. Like the war, the presence of women introduced another variable into the colonial relationship. Indeed, coinciding with Dakar's sudden sense of insecurity, the arrival of these women practically ensured that any realignment of cultural and racial boundaries within the colony after the war would involve a sexual dimension as well.

Despite the fact that many administrators chose to have their wives accompany them to their posts, no sooner had white women arrived than certain old colonial hands began to accuse them of complicating, if not ruining, harmonious relations between the races. Because white women needed protection, and because, as supposedly narrow-minded bourgeoises, they clung to social conventions unsuited to the colonial setting, they were charged with accentuating French awareness of racial differences. It was this increase in racism, these same critics continued, which was indirectly responsible for the growing native unrest plaguing the colonial world in the 1920s and 1930s.[12] Until recently, historians of imperialism have drawn similar conclusions.

To make a handful of women responsible for increased racial tensions in French West Africa was misguided. Tensions were growing in the colony for reasons that, initially at least, had little to do with the presence or absence of white women. Yet the accusations of racism leveled specifically at women were not wholly wrongheaded. There is no doubt that with the arrival of women new—or at least different—barriers arose between colonizer and colonized. Older forms of racial intermingling, both sexual and social, were discouraged, and administrators did not tour their districts as frequently as before. Entertaining other Europeans became an important priority, while concubinage and prostitution, previously tolerated, were now frowned upon.[13] The relevant question here, however, is who was more responsible for establishing this new code of behavior, men or women?[14] Given the timing of women's arrival in the colonies, there is every reason to believe that the answer is men. This point is important because it places the very real racism of colonial women in its broader political context. In the wake of challenges to French authority, women and men together redrew racial boundaries in French West Africa; but they certainly did not do so as equals.

The third development that helps explain the racial, cultural, and sexual realignment of the interwar years was the growth in France of three related movements: eugenics, social hygiene, and a resurgent pronatalism. None was entirely new in the 1920s; what was new was governmental support for their common objectives. Despite slightly different agendas, all three movements sought to improve both the quantity and quality of the French race. They also shared a renewed concern with upholding traditional morality and collectively displayed a greater willingness than in the past to subordinate the rights of the individual— and of women in particular, who were now ordered *faire naître*—to the interests of the nation-state.[15] The growth of these movements can be attributed to a wide array of recent changes in France. On the one hand, the use of colonial labor in France during World War I and a sizable influx of foreign immigrants after the war exacerbated latent racial tensions. On the other, continuing fears of depopulation and decline due to the devastating loss of life occasioned by war, the perceived need to return female war workers to the home, and advances in preventive medicine made the French government more willing to enact and subsidize policies designed to biologically regenerate the nation.[16]

Both directly and indirectly, the emergence of these linked movements combined to further encourage the new distancing between colonizer and colonized that the growing postwar nationalist movement in West Africa had inaugurated. A new governmental Office of Social Hygiene (1924) stipulated that one of its goals was to disseminate in France and the colonies "the hygiene and prophylactic measures necessary for the maintenance of health, the fight against social diseases and the preservation of the race."[17] The subsequent addition of a Colonial Social Hygiene Service proved how serious the office was about spreading its social hygiene message overseas. The 1920s witnessed the publication of a variety of manuals on colonial hygiene; as in the past, most of these were directed to men, but, for the first time, some were specifically written for women. Implicit in all the hygienist literature of the 1920s and 1930s was the notion that the white and black (or yellow) races should be kept physically separate, to prevent the spread of disease in the short term and the dilution of superior white stock through miscegenation in the long term. Colonial fiction, eugenicist literature, and legal treatises reinforced these views by worrying about what place to assign the mulatto (*métis*) in French society. Was he or she French or native? Even to pose the question was to reveal anxiety over white prestige and confirm that new boundaries of all kinds between blacks and whites were in the process of being drawn.

CITIZENSHIP REVISITED

A report of the Colonial Ministry noted:

> The point is to know to what degree it is possible to satisfy the aspirations of the indigenous populations without jeopardizing our domination. . . . Is it politic, is it in our interest to encourage naturalization? Generally speaking, no. Certainly, we must welcome those . . . of our subjects who can genuinely be assimilated, that is to say who have sincerely moved close to us by abandoning their customs, their mores and adopted ours. . . . But how many will we find who fit this category? Obviously very few. The others, those who solicit the status of citizen . . . only to obtain certain advantages, will always be dangerous.[18]

This comment summarizes the dilemma facing colonial officialdom in West Africa after World War I. The principle of granting citizenship to Africans, which in 1912 had seemed relatively unproblematic, now appeared fraught with peril.[19] The difficulty was that too many Africans who were not yet culturally French aspired to obtain citizenship for the wrong reasons. The 1912 decree stipulating the conditions under which Africans could become citizens had not anticipated this turn of events. Its assumption had been that if adequate hurdles were erected, only truly assimilated Africans would seek naturalization.[20] Was this premise simply wrong? Were there other categories of Africans in the interbellum period who aspired to citizenship out of self-interest and without the requisite degree of Frenchness? French-educated Africans, the principal targets here, would surely have answered no—at least publicly. In a prolonged discussion over this same issue, however, the minister of colonies, the Paris-based Superior Council on Colonies, and the governor-general of French West Africa reached a very different conclusion. Rather than endorse the idea that certain Africans could become French, they began to reconsider the generous principles undergirding the extension of citizenship.[21]

French reassessment of the policy of granting worthy Africans citizenship began in 1924 and lasted until 1933. Colonial Minister Daladier inaugurated this reevaluation when he drew up a legislative proposal designed to transform citizenship from a favor granted to individual subjects at the discretion of the colonial administration into an automatic right if certain criteria were filled. Such a law, if passed, would have represented a significant liberalization of citizenship. It is unclear, however, whether this law ever made it before Parliament; and in putting such a bill forward, Daladier seems to have been oblivious to the actual stakes involved.[22] At any rate, the law was not passed; instead, the legal branch of the Superior Council on Colonies was asked in 1925 to study the "status of the natives in France's colonies and protectorates." The reports issued over the next two years, along with the council's correspondence with Dakar, reveal that all parties interpreted their task as one of defining more clearly who was French and who was not— and who could ever hope to become so. This did not mean eliminating outright the principle that citizenship could be selectively granted to individual Africans judged sufficiently French. In practice, however, the commission made the extension of such citizenship extremely unlikely by recommending the creation of a new legal category intermediate between subject and citizen for the majority of "evolved" Africans.

This recommendation proved to be the major finding of the Superior Council.[23] The colonial minister was sufficiently impressed with the idea to prepare a decree proposal on the subject. If the legislation had passed, eligible Africans would have found themselves now classified as native elites; this status would have enabled them to vote in local elections, exempted them from the penal code for indigenous populations, and allowed them to sit for the entrance exams to France's most prestigious schools.[24] Such concessions, while not entirely meaningless, were a far cry from the rights of citizenship. The new intermediate civil classification, however, was to be all that educated Africans could ever hope for. It had now become clear to most officials that "a Frenchman born in France of French parents and whose ancestors always lived on French soil . . . was not of the same nature as a subject born . . . on recently annexed territory." The latter belonged to collectivities whose ethnic characteristics were "incompatible with our own." When one scratched the Frenchified surface of an educated African, "the old [i.e., primitive] man" always reappeared. It was therefore necessary to abandon the notion of "fusing through naturalization two such ethnically distinct populations."[25] Only "a born European is a citizen"; to offer citizenship to an African would not only be dangerous but "a lie." Yet it would be wrong to ignore completely the aspirations of "deserving subjects." To keep them "in the humiliating and materially disadvantageous conditions" of serfs was only to invite further revolt.[26] The ideal solution was officially to recognize the existence of a new group of Africans, neither subjects nor citizens but a "native elite" who—true to their ethnic destiny—would always remain just that.

In the end the new status never became law, but not because the French disagreed with the sentiments that had motivated discussion of the issue. Governor-General Carde (1924–30) had long opposed extending citizenship to evolved Africans yet was aware of the need to make certain concessions. He too felt that profound differences made it impossible for most Africans to become truly French. Yet when asked to approve the creation of the new category of native elite, he refused, and his refusal convinced the Superior Council and the minister to drop the project. Carde's point was a simple one: West Africa did not need an official status for "deserving Africans," because such a status already existed de facto, if not de jure.[27] Since the war Dakar had granted qualified Africans positions on local councils, the right to participate in council elections, and access to administrative posts previously open only to citizens and had exempted them from the native penal code. The governor-general would continue granting such concessions as Africans evolved and did not want his hands tied by the creation of a new legal category to which specific rights were automatically attached. In addition, in the most politically advanced parts of the federation, the institution of such a category would only be seen as a new means of avoiding the extension of citizenship and would generate more discontent.[28]

Although Carde's arguments helped to bury the native elite proposal, they were not the last word on the subject. On August 8, 1932, the colonial minister issued a new decree regulating access to citizenship in West Africa.[29] The most notable innovation compared to the 1912 decree was that the citizenship granted would no longer be strictly personal but would apply to the applicant's extended family (including illegitimate children). This apparent liberalization, in keeping with the new naturalization law in France, was offset, however, by another proviso. In order to qualify, the individual African and his family now had to satisfy much more rigorously defined criteria proving that they all were culturally French. A circular by Carde explained that naturalization clearly would be misguided if the evolved African was "subjected to influences in his home that were directly opposed to the direction of his evolution." To prove that he and his wife lived as French, he had to be monogamous but also to have availed himself of the French civil status to register his marriage and the birth of children at the time they occurred. Such early and continuous use of French civil status would be a precious indication "of a constant tendency toward our civilization." Another requirement was that he had provided his children with a French education. Finally, the applicant had to prove that "he had elevated himself above his original milieu," that "he had sufficiently detached himself from customary institutions to renounce them," and that "by his mentality, conduct and tendencies, he was worthy of the favor being solicited."[30]

The manner in which the French discussed the extension of citizenship to West Africans in the 1920s is highly revealing. Racial and cultural chauvinism obviously was growing more intense. Republican universalism required that the possibility of naturalization be preserved, but there was nothing generous about the new guarantees of Frenchness that Africans had to satisfy. The declaration that most Africans were ethnically too different ever to become French was a statement of unequivocal exclusion. Yet perhaps even more revealing is the attention paid to gender in the interwar debate over citizenship. Such attention was also new; neither the colonial nor the metropolitan legislator had previously concerned himself with the role women played in the household of educated Africans. In the 1920s not only did authorities assume these women to be the primary bearers of archaic cultures, they also saw them as impediments to genuine male acculturation to metropolitan values. This awakening French interest in the influence that African women exercised was not limited to the question of citizenship. A more conscious awareness of gender in the colonial relationship was typical of the interwar period; it also reflected growing French insecurity and resulted in yet another form of distancing from the colonized: one sexual and social in nature. This gendered distancing, moreover, affected not just African women but all women and all men—white or black—in West Africa.

PRESERVING THE NATION: SEX, RACE, AND THE FRENCH FAMILY

That a sexual and social distancing should occur along with a racial and cultural one is hardly surprising. Studies of British India and Dutch Indonesia have shown that renewed emphasis on racial difference in those colonies involved the erection of new social boundaries between the races and sexes and an explicit taboo against interracial sex.[31] French West Africa is another case in point. At the same time officials determined that Africans were too ethnically different ever to become culturally French, metropolitan publicists and colonial policymakers began to condemn the same sexual contact between the races that they had earlier tolerated; instead they endorsed white endogamy and traditional French family formation. Meanwhile, handbooks on life in the colonies not only reinforced this message but also spelled out more explicitly the degree of acceptable social mixing between French and Africans.

Both historians and colonial apologists have vastly exaggerated the extent to which newly arrived French women were responsible for this retreat from interracial mixing. There is, however, no question that French women figured prominently in enforcing the new barriers that the deteriorating political situation helped to configure. Scientific, medical, and colonial opinion all saw the life of the overseas wife in the same terms. She was to reinforce the colonizer's prestige by formalizing his relations with the colonized, keeping him healthy, and allowing him to produce white French offspring. She was also urged to help the French win their subjects' trust by influencing African mothers to whom she had unique access. French women appear to have embraced these roles, which, after all, did not differ much from the ones that strident demographers were encouraging them to play back home.

In the interwar years a variety of experts popularized the notion that the practice of interracial unions was dangerous for two reasons. First, the illegitimate offspring, the métis, of such unions were considered potentially as rebellious as the évolués with whom they were sometimes compared. It was assumed that the métis, like the évolué, automatically aspired to the rights of French citizenship because of the white blood that coursed through his or her veins.[32] The general feeling, however, was that half-breeds could not and should not become French. Thus, spurned by the country he or she most identified with, the métis was likely to rise up in revolt. Writers of colonial fiction also depicted the métis in this way.[33] The best way to avoid such a problem in the future, everyone agreed, was to ban *métissage* altogether. The second reason for the growing alarm about miscegenation was the fear that interracial sex might contribute to the degeneration of the white race. The very existence of métis children was proof of this degeneration.

Large-scale immigration in the postwar years, principally from central and southern Europe but also from North Africa, fueled growing racism and xenophobia in France in the 1920s and 1930s. Popular sentiment, and even the medical establishment, favored immigration quotas against "inferior, undesirable types," especially in the wake of riots involving North Africans in 1924 in Paris.[34] The onset of the depression, Hitler's rise to power, and new racial theories based on the discovery of human blood groups further exacerbated French fears of miscegenation.[35] These fears inevitably reverberated in the colonies at a moment when local officials were feeling particularly insecure. In West Africa the first decree since 1854 specifically regulating the conditions under which métis could acquire citizenship was passed in 1930; the very fact that particular legislation was now deemed necessary for this group indicated how racialized the issue of French identity had become.[36] Even ostensible liberals were affected, as the work of René Maunier suggests. In 1932 he published the first volume of his *Sociologie coloniale* (Colonial sociology), a compilation of lectures on the subject of contact between the races throughout history. At one point he cited approvingly an ancient author who argued that the only permanent contact between different peoples "occurred through the woman." Such "sexual union" was the superior form of contact between the races.[37] Maunier, however, went on to imply that although such unions might have been encouraged in the past in places like South America, Algeria, and South

Africa with positive results, they should not continue in the present. Métis in French colonies were problems, because they demanded the rights of their white fathers.[38] Concubinage was dangerous in another way as well: it exposed single white males to exotic mores and decivilized them. Finally, France itself now faced "penetration" by "thousands, hundreds of thousands of natives" arriving as immigrants. Such penetration invited the utmost caution.[39] From all these developments Maunier drew one major conclusion: that the swelling exodus of white women to the colonies was a positive step, because it ended the harmful influences of *petites épouses* (native "wives" or concubines) and miscegenation. Henceforth, "peopling [of the colony] would occur—which was really for the better—through white households."[40]

From endorsing racial fusion, Maunier had ended up at the other extreme, advocating strict racial segregation. He had, moreover, assigned to white women a critical role in enforcing segregation. The theme of the white woman's civilizing influence on white men also began to appear in the practical literature on how to prepare for life in the colonies. Like Richet and Maunier, the authors of these books were concerned with the question of how best to preserve the prestige of the white race in the Tropics. Their answer was two-pronged. First, the colonizer should separate himself as much as possible from the colonized, in dress, behavior, and domestic relations. Second, the bush outpost was to become a more attractive and hygienic place to live. Both strategies demanded the presence of white women in order to succeed.

The notion that Europeans required a special health regimen to survive in the Tropics was, of course, a long-standing one. One of the discoveries of the fin de siècle was that with the proper scientific management, white males could adapt easily to even the most inhospitable climates. In West Africa a Public Health Service founded in 1903 drew upon the latest available research to make the colony more salubrious.[41] Back in France a variety of prewar manuals explained how to build houses and which diet to follow, clothes to wear, and exercises to do to stay fit and healthy. Such manuals were already mindful of the need to retain a certain distance from the colonized. Europeans should not adopt even the most suitable native clothing. They should never work as servants because it meant close contact with the natives. Although capable of physical labor, whites should be the head that directs; opium and sexual excesses—two temptations for the new arrival—were to be avoided at all costs. Studying local customs and history was a far better way to get to know the colonized.[42] Most desirable was the presence of one's family, for the stability and companionship it would guarantee.[43]

Even if scores of physicians predicted that the presence of wives overseas would provide numerous advantages, many also agreed that this option existed only for colonies in the temperate zone. In West Africa, where diseases such as malaria, yellow fever, and typhoid were still endemic, women's physical needs placed them at a distinct disadvantage compared to men; a common refrain was that "their sexual functions expose them to hemorrhages and anemia."[44] "We do not believe it will be possible for a long time yet for white children to be born and brought up in the equatorial or tropical climates of Africa."[45] This medical prejudice against female expatriation to Africa conveniently coincided with the conviction of most early administrators that French wives, far from securing their spouses' mental and physical health, hindered their effectiveness as civil servants. Maurice Delafosse wrote in his popular account of bush life that "any married colonial loses a third of his value and a married field administrator loses at least ¾ of his."[46] Although he did marry a French woman later in his career, Delafosse took a Baule wife during his service in the Ivory Coast in the early 1900s.[47] Marriages with local women, according to Louis Sonolet—an administrator with extensive experience in West Africa and author of an ostensibly humoristic tract on "African love"—were the norm for Europeans in the prewar period and had much to recommend them. African wives did not demand constant attention "like their white sisters." Their docile and submissive nature made them more amenable to obey the "prescriptions of our [Civil] Code" than their "European sisters," and they gladly followed their masters everywhere.[48]

By the end of World War I, however, the colonial administration changed its views regarding cohabitation with native women. Along with the medical and scientific community, it began to recognize the virtues of marriage with a white woman. The shift is already apparent in Sonolet's account from 1911. Having praised the virtues of native wives in West Africa, he concluded that most colonials longed for a white wife, because only she can satisfy the need for "love in the superior and ideal sense."[49] Sonolet also briefly criticized métis offspring, "who always cause trouble for the French administration."[50] In the end, his paean to African love subtly reminded white-skinned male and female readers (both of whom were periodically addressed) of obligations to their race. In a similar vein Georges Hardy, who served as director of the Ecole Coloniale from 1926 to 1931 after a long stint in West Africa as inspector of education, did not say his administrators should marry. But as part of an effort to introduce more rigorous standards in the selection and training of the colonial service, he did say they could marry. His only concern was that they choose the right wife: "For women as well as for men, certain specifically colonial virtues exist. . . . Attempt to find out whether she will adapt to being isolated among the natives, far from tea dances and the idle talk of salons. Because it is with the natives above all that you will live, and not everyone can accept such a situation."[51] Despite the negative female stereotype that Hardy invoked here, he acknowledged that fewer administrators than in the past were currently "decivilizing themselves," thanks to the ever greater presence of European women.[52]

What administrators had determined on their own, the medical community now seconded by arguing that West Africa was a safe and suitable place for white women. In the 1920s and 1930s, reservations about white women's ability to adapt to the West African climate disappeared. Doctors increasingly assumed that women were as likely as men—but no more so than them—to succumb to certain tropical diseases, including a kind of nervous exhaustion known as *cafard* or *colonialité*.[53] Instead of seeing the female sexual organs as a source of weakness, medical manuals became enthusiastic about white women's chances of reproducing in the Tropics.[54]

Doctors and administrators not only agreed that woman had a place in the colonies. They also described her role in similar terms that again echoed the racist and sexist arguments of eugenicists like Richet. Preeminent among her tasks were assisting in the maintenance of French authority and preserving her race through aid to her husband and "softening the crude mores" prevalent among white males deprived of French female company; these roles were particularly important since "one Frenchman had to be the equal of thousands of natives."[55] One way "to maintain our prestige" was to separate European living quarters from those of the autochthonous populations.[56] The theme of separation runs through much of this prescriptive literature. Manuals cautioned women to keep a certain distance from their servants, who would invariably be male.[57] Men and women alike should preserve a certain elegance, "for elegance does not exclude strength—rather the opposite."[58] Elegance imbues one with dignity, and "it is necessary to prove [to the natives] that *la Française* . . . is a worthy and elevated women."[59] French women should also decorate their homes in such ways that not only distinguished them from the colonized but also kept the colonizer content and comfortable in his domestic environment. The best way to fight the climate was through "the charming [household] objects" that every French woman carries with her.[60] Too many objects, however, would provide a breeding ground for mosquitoes and other insects. The house should be empty enough to be easily washed. French women in Indochina never bought Chinese furniture "first because we are French and uncomfortable [in it] . . . and finally because these pieces cannot be properly cared for and do not correspond to our family life."[61] In short, it was the job of woman "to create France" wherever she went.[62] And just to make sure that the colonial couple remained thoroughly French, husband and wife should return to the metropole every two to three years.[63]

There was another way in which white women could contribute decisively to the "creation of France" overseas, because "it is not sufficient to possess territory, it is also necessary for the French to establish themselves there . . . in order to secure our prestige."[64] How better to implant themselves than by starting a family? All guides assumed that motherhood was the colonial woman's first vocation and devoted as much attention to instructing women on child rearing as on household management.[65] Women should be especially well versed in the modern science of *puériculture* (infant hygiene). In this new emphasis on reproduction, the focus on separation from the colonized—especially those of the opposite sex—was even more apparent. At the most basic level, the exhortation for whites to reproduce among themselves condemned sexual relations between the races. Commentators repeatedly contrasted the richness of French family life with the emptiness of concubinage; a native mistress "constantly suffered from . . . emotional poverty, intellectual insufficiency."[66] On another level, modern child-rearing techniques clearly excluded the involvement of the colonized. To ensure both the fitness and Frenchness of the children, contact with the servants should be carefully regulated; when the children reached a certain age, the parents ought to send them back to France. Once they were gone, the woman could be useful by introducing African women to basic hygiene, as well as by studying local customs. In this way she would become a true partner of her husband—an intellectual as well as a sexual companion.[67]

The practical literature on colonial hygiene confirms that a sexual realignment, as well as a cultural and racial one, emerged in the interwar years. The underlying concern of doctors and administrators was no longer Europeans' survival in the Tropics. Rather, their focus shifted to the more complicated question of how French men and women could retain their "true" identity in an environment that threatened to overwhelm it, through miscegenation, disease, or cultural contamination. In addition to redefining citizenship, they cast white women in the role of guardians of hearth, health, and racial purity. These women, moreover, were to assume this weighty role not only in their own family circles but also in African homes. The French, far from labeling the home as apolitical in this period and relegating it to the domain of frivolous women and effeminate natives, began a concerted effort to seek to penetrate and control it—with the help of colonial wives. French women would teach their African counterparts how to raise healthy and loyal subjects, thus preventing the nascent nationalist movement from ever taking root.[68] Such was the naive hope of the French administration, now seeking to contain a process of political modernization that it itself had inaugurated a generation earlier.

CONCLUSIONS

That all European nations manipulated the languages of gender and race to justify their domination overseas in the age of the new imperialism is not, of course, in doubt. Yet the racialized and gendered images of themselves and the colonized that Europeans formulated from the late nineteenth century on were often as unstable as the unequal social and political relations that these images encoded in the first place. Changes in the existing balance of power could and did unleash deepseated anxieties about the status of French civilization in the world and its continued ability to preserve imperial hegemory—anxieties that produced major shifts in the rhetorical and real positioning of women and men of all races. In this essay I have argued that the disruptions occasioned in France by World War I, the rise of African nationalism, and the arrival of white women south of the Sahara represented a key moment of change for the French West African Federation. Indeed, we can measure the mounting insecurity of the French in this era through the new discourse on race, gender, and Frenchness that these years spawned. By policing female sexuality and demarcating more clearly the cultural and racial differences between French and Africans, embattled white Frenchmen attempted to recover and reinscribe the power that the colonized were now contesting. Amid the growing tensions of the 1920s and 1930s, restricting French citizenship, strengthening traditional families, and preserving French domination overseas were inextricably related.

What is especially striking about the interwar debate on citizenship and on proper gender and race relations is that it took place on both sides of the colonial divide, within France as well as in West Africa. Mary Louise Roberts has recently shown how dramatically public policy debates privileged gender issues during the 1920s, as the French attempted to come to terms with a postwar world so changed that "it threatened to become unrecognizable to them."[69] I would argue that during these same years—that is to say, well before the Nazi seizure of power in the early 1930s—French politicians and intellectuals also privileged race issues, due in part to a growing unrest in the colonies. In short, at the French Empire's high noon, right relations among the sexes and among the races were together being exalted as the best guarantors of right order in the nation. This was as true for the metropole as for the colonies, particularly once Africans began to lay claim to the same rights as Frenchmen.

5. SECRETS AND DANGER:
Interracial Sexuality in Louis Couperus's *The Hidden Force* and Dutch Colonial Culture around 1900

❦ Pamela Pattynama

In a passage that appears on one of the final pages of Louis Couperus's *De stille kracht*, or *The Hidden Force*, Eva Eldersma, a white female character, whispers:

> I think that I also experienced it once . . . when I was walking with Van Helderen by the sea, and the sky was so huge and the night so deep, or the rains came rustling from so very far away and then came down . . . or when the nights, silent as death and yet brimful of sounds, quivered around you, always with a music that no one could grasp and you could barely hear. . . . Or simply when I looked into the eyes of a Javanese, when I spoke to my *babu* [nanny] and it seemed as though nothing of what I said got through to her and as if what she answered concealed her real, secret answer [226] [1]

The Hidden Force is among the most famous Dutch novels about the colonies in Southeast Asia. Almost always narrated from a European perspective, this genre of colonial novels tends to explore a series of recurrent themes, such as the intangible mysteries of the oriental world and its inhabitants or the unbridgeable difference between East and West. As in the passage just quoted, the differences between the colonized and the colonizers are often rendered metaphorically as the unfathomable secrets and dangers that enveloped the Dutch colonial community of the East Indies.

Written in 1900, *The Hidden Force* is situated in the Indies just before the turn of the century. A smoldering conflict is brewing between the Dutchman Otto van Oudijck, the resident of Labuwangi, an administrative region on the island of Java, and Sunario, a Javanese regent or local administrative official. Behind this all-male battle is the Dutch colonial system of indirect rule. Until the end of the colonial era, the government in the metropole retained the Dutch East India Company's (Vereenigde Oost-Indische Compagnie; hereafter VOC) methods of ruling areas under their full control by employing native regents; often these were aristocrats who had once served as regional rulers or as retainers of indigenous sultanates. Drafted into the business of governance by the VOC's representatives in Batavia, Javanese regents were supervised by a Dutch resident, although they were left to their own devices as much as possible. In the course of the nineteenth century, however, European surveillance had become more intrusive, because the expansion of economic activity and European settlement required a more direct, efficient administration. By 1900 indirect rule concealed the fact that indigenous leaders had been reduced to the role of subordinate colonial administrators. Nevertheless, the local prestige and ceremonial authority they continued to wield over the peasants in their districts facilitated Dutch colonial rule.[2]

The Hidden Force's narrative structure reflects this framework in the antagonism between the Dutch resident, Van Oudijck, and the Javanese regent, Sunario. Van Oudijck represents a high-minded sort of colonial administrator, who relishes governing a major region such as Labuwangi with its extensive coffee plantations and numerous sugar refineries. In fact, the public visibility and independent power associated with his senior stature in the civil service harmonizes perfectly with his authoritarian nature. In the realm of his private life, Van Oudijck has a young wife, Léonie, and four children from a previous marriage. His seventeen-year-old daughter Doddy and his twenty-five-year-old son Theo are pivotal characters in the elaborate narrative structure of *The Hidden Force*. The reader soon learns that Theo is sexually involved with his stepmother Léonie, whereas Doddy is in love with a handsome Indo-European (Eurasian) man, Addy de Luce, an infatuation that has raised her father's ire. As the novel unfolds, Addy is seduced by Léonie, while the conflict between Sunario and Van Oudijck flares up once Van

Oudijck dismisses Sunario's brother from his post as the regent of a neighboring district. Their conflict is never openly battled out, but gradually Van Oudijck's house is afflicted by strange and incomprehensible phenomena: anonymous letters accuse family members of indecent activities, stones are hurled, betel juice is spat at them, and white-clad *hadjis* (Muslims who have made the pilgrimage to Mecca) hover around the house. Members of the Van Oudijck household hear plaintive cries as if a child is being strangled, and the golden glow of whiskey turns a dull yellow.

These eerie events are not perpetrated by anonymous outside sources alone. Claiming to be his son, a hitherto unknown and quite seedy figure invades Van Oudijck's private life, and suspicions and jealousy contaminate his soul. Van Oudijck succumbs to a gradual downfall. In the end he is portrayed through the eyes of Eva Eldersma, who consistently but in vain has tried to introduce European culture to colonial society. Van Oudijck's adulterous wife has departed for the city of sin, Paris, and his children have left him. Eva finds the former resident happier than before but living in the native village with a Javanese woman and her family, far from the colonial European community: Van Oudijck has gone native.

THEORETICAL CONSIDERATIONS: ORIENTALISM AND FEMINISM

Since the appearance of Edward Said's *Orientalism* in 1978, the complicity between historical discourse, literary representation, and European strategies of cultural domination has emerged as a major preoccupation in postcolonial studies.[3] Said shifted the study of colonialism to its discursive operations and has shown that the history of colonialism and imperialism is intimately connected to language. However, Homi Bhabha has criticized Said's idea of colonial discourse as merely an instrumental construction of knowledge. He specifically opposes Said's views on oriental knowledge and practice as intentional inventions on the part of the West. By adding psychoanalysis to Said's argument, Bhabha has emphasized that colonial discourse also operates through the ambivalences that are generated by desire.[4]

At the same time Third and First World feminists have merged the

Louis Couperus, the Dutch colonial writer and author of *The Hidden Force*, at Toba Lake in northern Sumatra, Dutch East Indies, ca. 1900. (Photograph KIT, Amsterdam)

fields of colonial-discourse analysis and feminist theory. Feminist scholars, above all, try to delineate the intersections of race, gender, class, and sexuality in both colonial and feminist postcolonial discourse.[5] Hence, this analysis of *The Hidden Force* is indebted to a feminist refinement of postcolonial studies. Since historical realities shape the conditions for literary representation, my approach combines colonial historiography with a semiotic analysis. In addition to Said's proposed contrapuntal mode of reading, I draw upon the resisting reading methods developed by feminist literary critics in an effort to locate, in the margins of literary discourse, the "unsaid" or the "absent text of history."[6]

Louis Couperus's novel about the East Indies occupies a unique position within the genre of Dutch colonial fiction. As historical fiction, it is implicated in larger colonial structures, cloaked in a mixture of orientalism, covert sexual desire, and Western ambivalence.[7] Although it appeared almost a century ago, the book continues to wield an evocative power. Ambiguous and enigmatic, the novel both mystifies and enchants the reader. Celebrated as one of the highlights of the Dutch literary canon, it is firmly embedded in the cultural heritage and historical memory of the Dutch nation.[8] Moreover, the novel's significance is not limited to high literary culture alone. Since its serialization for television in the 1970s, *The Hidden Force* has entered the popular imagination and become part of a collective unconscious in the contemporary Netherlands.[9]

In fact, the all-pervasive yet elusive "it" that gives Eva Eldersma's whispers such an evocative force has become a commercialized figure of speech that refers to the emotional resonance and cognitive impact of any exotic thing or person. The continued influence of this novel raises questions about its lingering source of fictional power. What does the "hidden force" entail? What exactly is the all-encompassing yet unfathomable "it"? And, to pursue these questions further: how can this "hidden force" still wield such alluring imaginative appeal in contemporary Dutch culture? Here I address these questions and concentrate on the novel's ambivalences and ambiguities. Such an analysis may grant us insights into the novel's literary forces and psychological tensions as well as its hidden ideologies and coded imperialism.

NATURAL FATHERHOOD

The opening portion of the novel situates Van Oudijck at the very heart of the colonial milieu. It foregrounds the *totok* (white, European-born) male administrator as its central figure, while rigid boundaries separate diverse ethnic groups from each other. This setting mirrors the Dutch community's reliance upon its apparent natural right to govern the Indies. Faith in European supremacy as the outcome of God's will or belief in the inherent racial superiority of Europeans was a necessary precondition for colonialism.[10] Firmly implanted in this ideological context, Van Oudijck is introduced as a hardworking, imperious senior official in the civil service. Represented as an archetype of the rational, vigorous, yet compassionate sovereign, his portrayal is primarily articulated in masculine terms. "Soldierly briskness" and "robust virility" coincide with great responsibilities that "delight his authoritative nature." We hear him voice his enthusiasm for his job or, as Léonie puts it, his adoration of the colonial government. Pleased with himself, Van Oudijck articulates both his deeply felt concern for his district as well as his pride in its progress and prosperity during his administration.

In Couperus's characterization of Van Oudijck, one can see the influence of the so-called Ethical Policy that emerged at the turn of the century in the East Indies. This policy resulted from a growing awareness in the Dutch community that during the previous three hundred years of colonial rule, the Netherlands had incurred a debt toward the Indonesian people. Following centuries of outright abuse, the colonial administration now would offer the indigenous population more educational opportunities and better health care. Colonial society in the East Indies was to be reformed, and the spoils of economic exploitation would be distributed more equitably between the Dutch and the indigenous population. Instead of subjugating native people, in the twentieth century the Dutch colonial government would ostensibly teach, nurture, and guide them.[11]

Nevertheless, the attitudes and behaviors associated with indirect rule lingered on. Couperus depicts Van Oudijck as ethical in his efforts to give the local Javanese regents their due by allowing them to maintain their traditional social prerogatives and economic rights. Notwithstanding this liberal stance, the main male character evinces self-indulgent, paternalistic characteristics typical of the late nineteenth century: the Dutchman loves the Javanese like a father. Newly developed parental imagery, which acquired prominence around the turn of the century, derived from rhetorical practices that were deployed to legitimate colonial mastery. Symbols of fatherhood—and by implication motherhood—cemented the relationship of Europeans with native people by emphasizing the benevolent tutelage of fathers and mothers. In turn, these parental figures had the right to insist on deference and obedience from the indigenous population. As a fatherly tutor to both his aristocratic Javanese retainers and, indirectly, the humble peasants in the villages, the protagonist is portrayed as the idealistic, noble master.

A similar self-image is presented to his European secretary, assistants, and comptrollers, because Van Oudijck, in spite of his stern regulations and dictates, knows when to be a jovial paterfamilias. Rapidly moving up the social ladder, he believes himself to be the right man in the right place: his daily existence, his work, his house, and his Indies all bring delight, and nothing in Holland can compete with the good life in Java. Obviously, Van Oudijck's glorification of the Indies is closely linked to his own central position as a powerful father in colonial society.

The Dutchman's presence in the colony, however, turns out to be a liability. With his masterful treatment of an approaching tragic fate, Couperus inscribed a series of disruptions in *The Hidden Force* that undermine Van Oudijck's position from the very first pages. Exposing the unstable foundations of Van Oudijck's self-glorification, these disruptions gradually unsettle the colonial order and the naturalness of the Dutch presence in the colony. The first disruption weakens Van Oudijck's secure and solid position as a father of a family:

> This tall, sturdy man, practical, cool headed, decisive (due to the long habit of authority) was unconscious of the dark mystery that drifted over the native town . . . though he was conscious of a longing for affection . . . it was like a morbid tenderness, like a sentimental discomfort in the otherwise highly practical mind of this superior official . . . the almost independent power of his post harmonized entirely with his authoritative nature. A longing, a desire, a certain nostalgia filled him more than usual. He felt lonely, though he was the father of a family. He thought of his big house, he thought of his wife and children. And he felt lonely and supported only by his interest in his work. [47]

The emphatically mysterious Eastern context in which the male protagonist is situated heightens his loneliness, all the more so because Van Oudijck, rational and down-to-earth, denies the reality of the spiritual forces that permeate the Javanese cultural landscape. This image of solitude culminates in the absence of his wife and children. In contradiction to the resident's forceful, paternalistic nature and inconsistent with his success in administering his district, his family life is portrayed as a source of sadness and vulnerability. His wife and children seem to belong to a realm that is beyond Van Oudijck's control.

A second disruptive feature is Van Oudijck's companion, the Javanese head servant, who is portrayed as having "watching eyes." Not only does the servant's place, squatting behind his master, distinguish the Javanese from the Europeans, but his other perspective also destabilizes the dominant position of the white-skinned, Western father-ruler. Through the servant's gaze the colonial subject questions the naturalness of the Dutch presence in the colony: "Strange people those Hollanders! . . . What is he thinking now? . . . Why is he behaving like this? . . . Just at this time and on this spot. . . . The sea spirits are about now. . . . How strange those Hollanders, how strange!" [47, 48]

A third discordant element emerges in Van Oudijck's portrayal as a natural father. While exalting in his life in the Indies and, implicitly, acclaiming his central position in colonial society, the resident evokes his only regret—his uneasy relationship with the Javanese regent Sunario. Whereas he had always sympathized with Sunario's deceased father, he finds the son nothing more than a "stiff enigmatic shadow puppet." He laughs at Sunario's reputation as a holy man among his Javanese underlings. Instead, the resident calls him "fanatical," "impractical," and "degenerate" or an "unhinged Javanese fop" who shrouds himself "in mystery" (124). In fact, Van Oudijck harbors a lingering suspicion that Prince Sunario keeps his distance out of disdain for the common Dutch burgher, who happens to be his superior in the colonial hierarchy.

Van Oudijck's fond memory of the prince's deceased father and his active dislike of the current regent can be linked to a recurring orientalist image of the colonial "other." As an exotic descendant of the sultans of Madura from the VOC's era, the older native ruler had embodied the romantic European image of the "noble savage." As a result, Sunario's father was burdened with, but at the same time divested of, his otherness. Unlike his father, however, the young regent resists being framed by the colonizer's gaze. His subtle resistance escapes the intellectual grasp of the Dutch resident, and he is dismissed as a negative other: "unreal, not a functionary, not a regent" (68). Moreover, the change in perceptions of otherness, on which the discord between the Dutchman and his Javanese subordinate is founded, alludes to an actual transformation within colonial society.

Toward the end of the nineteenth century, new and conflicting trends had begun to emerge. Since the late 1890s education had slowly become available to natives, albeit exclusively for the Javanese aristocracy. Western education gave members of Java's upper class a chance to fill posts in the colonial administrative structure that had previously been reserved for the European caste; as a result, Javanese nationalist consciousness was awakened. As was true in all European colonies at the time, education played a major role in provoking nationalist unrest. On the other hand, modern Dutch policy led to a more stringent racial apartheid. Thus, disparities between various ethnic and political groups became glaringly evident. Van Oudijck's uneasy feelings about the incomprehensible Sunario in comparison to his gentle, pliable father must be viewed in the light of a budding Indonesian politicization that opposed modernizing colonial rule.

The beginning section of *The Hidden Force* emphasizes a public discourse of politics. Yet the three forces that have begun to undermine the natural position of Van Oudijck as a father are the first implicit signs of a palimpsest narrative in the novel. This latter narrative concentrates on the private sphere and eventually becomes intertwined with the first web of public intrigues.

CREOLE FEMME FATALE

The palimpsest narrative first surfaces in the text with subtle hints about Van Oudijck's sexual biography and the three women he was involved with in the past. His daughter Doddy and son Theo disclose the fact of Van Oudijck's first marriage to a woman of mixed race, a "good-looking nonna" who was Indo-European (50). As mixed-race children, Doddy and Theo expose the domestic arrangement their father had maintained before he married Léonie. Couperus's representation of both Doddy and Theo underscores their half-caste status and hybridized nature. Doddy in particular is shown to be her mother's daughter: the name Doddy indicates the girl's racially mixed origins just as the indication "nonna" registers her mother's Indo-European descent. Doddy's misuse of the Dutch language is another sign of her Indo background.

It should be noted, however, that here *The Hidden Force*'s racial discourse coincides with the conventions of literary naturalism. Within the literary tradition of naturalism, a detailed registration of any character's physical features determines his or her inner psyche. Doddy's dark features, therefore, indicate her precocious sexuality: "She was not tall and already too fully formed, like a hasty rose that has bloomed too soon" (50). Her brother Theo is similarly marked with the languid and lazy sensuality that stereotypically identifies persons of mixed race. Like Doddy, he looks years older than he actually is, and although he is "pale and blond as a Dutchman," he has "full, sensual lips, which he had inherited from his *nonna* mother" (103). With the "discontent of a fat, blond *sinjo*" and angry at his father's refusal to help his own son to get ahead, Theo lazily hangs around the house (196).

The children's mother still lives in Batavia, where she is reputed to maintain a secret gambling house. Their mother's sordid practices associate Van Oudijck's children (and by implication, Van Oudijck himself) with forbidden activities and dirty money. This aura of illegality is subsequently reinforced by the disclosure of Doddy's infatuation with Addy de Luce. Although the latter belongs to a very rich and prominent local family, Van Oudijck censures the liaison because of De Luce's mixed racial background. The atmosphere of pollution culminates in the revelation of Theo's illicit passion for his stepmother, Léonie (51).

While Doddy's affair violates racial boundaries, Theo's affair with Léonie is even more unlawful and in violation of Victorian values. The disclosure of this semi-incestuous and clandestine relationship introduces the Oedipal drama into the story. The exposure of her sexual involvement with Theo establishes Léonie's representation as an adulterous and outrageous female character, even before she actually appears. Evincing scandalous desire, Léonie assumes the guise of the quintessential femme fatale, the paradigmatic femininity that occupied a central role in the Décadence movement, which is so often linked to Louis Couperus.[12] "She was a tall woman, with a fair complexion and fair hair. . . . She had something that attracted attention at once. It was because of her eternal smile, sometimes very sweet and charming and often insufferable and tiresome . . . one could never tell whether she concealed anything behind that glance, whether there was any depth, any soul, or whether it was merely a matter of looking and laughing, both with that slight ambiguity" (54).

Figuring as an object of the male gaze, Léonie is nothing but a fair, beautiful body. Devoid of intellectual interests or responsibility, she symbolizes an unpredictable and immoral femininity. Her narcissism and erotic self-indulgence make her immune to human suffering; hence, this female character functions as a counterpoint to the resident's powerful but tragic male figuration: "There was something strong about this woman, something powerful in her sheer indifference. There was something invulnerable about her. She looked as though life would have no hold on her, neither on her complexion, nor on her soul. She looked as though she were incapable of suffering, and it seemed as though she smiled and was thus contented because no sickness, no suffering, no poverty, no misery existed for her. An irradiation of glittering egoism encompassed her. And yet she was, for the most part, lovable" (55).

Reminiscent of the psychoanalytic views on femininity of Couperus's contemporary Sigmund Freud, the juxtaposition between Léonie's narcissistic sensuality and Van Oudijck's conscientious rationality is underpinned by gender differences.[13] The two characters also display an orientalist opposition between East and West. Consistent with Van Oudijck's image as a forthright and self-righteous Western man is the fact that one never learns how long he has been living in the East Indies. Conversely, Léonie's designation as a Creole (i.e., an individual of European descent but born in the Indies) identifies her with the colony, despite her full-blooded European parents and her creamy white complexion: "[She] possessed the languid dignity of women born in Java, daughters of European parents on both sides. . . . Yet though she looked very European, it may have been her leisurely walk, that languid dignity that was the only thing characteristic of the Indies that distinguished her from a woman newly arrived from Holland" (54–55).

The "very European" Eva Eldersma, the wife of Van Oudijck's secretary, represents the woman newly arrived from Holland. Eva regards the Indies with a curious combination of bitter disappointment and naive delight, due to her "soul of an artist" and "Arabian Nights illusions. . . . The character of the Javanese had been a revelation to her: his elegance, his grace, his salutation, and his dance, his aristocratic distinctions, so often evidently handed down directly from a noble race, from an age-old chivalry, now modernized into a diplomatic suppleness, worshipping authority by nature and inevitably resigned under the yoke of the rulers whose golden braid arouses his innate respect" (74, 77).

Because Léonie gladly delegates to Eva all the social obligations that a resident's wife should have fulfilled, Eva's house becomes the real center of European social life in Labuwangi. Importing "a little European civilization" to the district, Eva breaks with "good old Indies customs" when she organizes charming dinners, giving instructions on how to wear formal clothing such as tails, stiff collars, and white tie for the men. Her elusive "something that reminded everybody of Holland" and her "literary mind" fiercely oppose Léonie's Creole indifference and her erotic nature. Emblematic of this opposition is Eva's rejection of an Indo suitor, whose longing for the "unknown purity" of Europe he projects onto Eva. His desperate outcry—"I love you Eva, Eva"—meets her sarcasm: "I don't think that there's another country where there's so much love going on as in the Indies. It must be the heat." Symbolizing the essence of Europe's culture, Eva Eldersma also personifies its liabilities when relocated to the Tropics. More than Léonie she resembles the resident. Contrary to all the other characters, Eva and Van Oudijck reveal psychological development, while sharing a European ideal of the Indies. Thus drawing closer to the Dutch resident, Eva injects the fear of lassitude and of going native into the text: "She, after only two years in the Indies, understood more and more easily how to let things go—in dress, in body, and in soul—now that every day she lost something more of her fresh, Dutch blood and her Western energy" (77, 79, 96, 156).

Opposed to Eva's freshness and her enthusiastic embrace of European civilization, Léonie is eroticized and rendered obscure and vulgar. Surrounded by "affected little cupids," she indulges in "vicious schemes," "motives of perverted passion," and gossip about "this resident" or "that inspector" who found his way to her bedroom. Her entry into the text turns her liaison with her stepson from a matter of hearsay into a narrative fact: "She stood peering for a moment and then opened the blind further. And she saw that the blind of Theo's room was also opened a bit. . . . Then she smiled, she knotted her sarong more firmly and lay down on the bed again. She listened. . . . He came nearer. He was dressed in pajamas and he sat on the edge of the bed and played with her soft white hands. Suddenly he kissed her fiercely. At that moment a stone whizzed through the bedroom" (62, 63). This ominously interrupted encounter is the first of a startling series of mysterious events that happen to Van Oudijck's family. Significantly, it is Léonie's perverse behavior within the walls of the residential house that is the initial target. Already marked by the links between her promiscuity and her descent from hybridized early Dutch settlers in the colony, Léonie gradually becomes intimately associated with the Orient. Her illicit affair with Addy de Luce articulates a further transgression of the boundary between East and West. It is specifically this interracial adultery that is depicted as an implosion at the heart of the Dutch presence in the colony.

As the embodiment of an aestheticized, exotic East, Addy de Luce is a sultry, bronzed beauty. Highlighted as her counterpoint in their sexual union, he is introduced through Léonie's lustful eyes—a portrayal that reflects Couperus's distinctly homoerotic aesthetics:

> She judged him once more; his comely, slender sensuality and the glow of his tempter's eyes in the shadowy brown of his young Moorish face, the curve of his lips meant only for kissing, with the young down of his mustache; the feline strength and litheness of his Don Juan limbs . . . she suddenly became smitten with the wild young animal vigor which breathed like a fragrance of manhood from his boyish frame. She felt her blood throbbing, almost uncontrollably, despite her great art of remaining cool and correct in the circles around the marble tables. She was no longer bored. [107]

Addy de Luce, with his "strong scent of tiger enchantment," "golden glitter of eyes," and "sinewy litheness of stealthy claw," occupies a position in the text which ironically is often ascribed to Western women (108). This is all the more so because his pampered and hollow, unfaithful and fickle behavior belongs to the Eve side of the equation in the opposition between Eve and Mary the Madonna, or between the Virgin and the whore that structures Western femininity. In this configuration Léonie's new affair is not merely another sign of her outrageous behavior. The union of the adulterous femme fatale and the feminized oriental male occupies a central place in *The Hidden Force*'s narrative web. Narrated as dangerous, if pleasurable, sexuality, their union both blends and reproduces two of the dominant myths that support and reinforce the illusory self-image of the patriarchal West: the myth of the egotistical, ruthless femme fatale and the emblem of the weak and effeminate oriental man. By invoking what in psychoanalytic terms is called revulsion, these fused myths reveal the danger of interracial sexuality that threatens to castrate Van Oudijck's white, European ideal of male authority and rational superiority.[14]

So far, perverse femininity, jeopardized masculinity, and dangerous interracial sexuality form the elements of the palimpsest narrative. Embedded in the novel's primary narrative that explores the public colonial order, it exposes how the oppositional meanings attributed to race, gender, and sexuality intersect with the boundaries set by the family relations that were so crucial in the Dutch East Indies.

INDO CULTURE

Apart from the Van Oudijcks, two other families function prominently in the plot of *The Hidden Force*: the Adiningrats, who comprise Sunario's aristocratic Javanese family, and the De Luces, an Indo-European, racially mixed family, of which Addy is a beloved son. We find Van Oudijck, in his role both as paterfamilias and as father of the region, consumed by hatred for the Adiningrats as well as the De Luce family. His aversion to the Adiningrats focuses on the steady degeneration of noble Javanese aristocrats caused by liquor, gambling, and superstition. But his animosity is also fueled by anxiety. The Javanese regent's mother's fondness of gambling, his brother's alcoholism, and, of course, Sunario's own elusiveness escape Dutch control. Hence, these Javanese signs constantly remind Van Oudijck of his position as an outsider in what he understands to be his region. His contempt for the De Luce clan emerges from a similar displacement of anxieties. Although the Dutch ruler is as yet unaware of his wife's secret affair, the mere existence of the half-caste family seems to threaten his private, that is, his familial space:

> That Addy should ever get Doddy for his wife! True, there was native blood in his daughter too, but he wanted a full-blooded European as his son-in-law. He hated anything half-caste. He hated the De Luces and all the provincial, Indonesian, half-Solo traditions of that Patjaram of theirs. He hated their gambling, their hobnobbing with all sorts of native headmen, people to whom he officially granted what was theirs but otherwise regarded as nec-

essary tools of government policy. He hated their pose as an old Indies family and he hated Addy: an idle youth who was supposed to be employed in the factory but who did nothing at all, except run after every woman, girl, or maid. To the older, industrious man, such a life was intolerable. [197–98]

Descendants of an enterprising, bohemian French adventurer and a princess related to the sultan of Solo, the De Luces typify the Indonesian family clan as described in Jean Taylor's *The Social World of Batavia: European and Eurasian in Dutch Asia*. During the seventeenth and eighteenth centuries, social-sexual relations between Europeans and Asians had produced a mestizo society. In contrast to British imperial rule in India, miscegenation and concubinage in the Indies had not always been condemned. Instead, from the early days of the Dutch East India Company's presence in Java until the late nineteenth century, the mixing of European men and Asian women had been condoned. Because the political authority of the Netherlands remained remote, and full-blooded European women were scarce, locally born women of mixed Asian and European ancestry dominated the female population of settlements in the Indies. Through continual intermarriage with mestizo women, male immigrants from Holland forged alliances that conferred control of positions of power and wealth within the VOC. Thus, a thoroughly hybridized community had evolved in which Indo-European women occupied a central position.[15] Historians, in fact, routinely point to Couperus's fictional description of the extended De Luce family as an example of the wealth and high social position that mixed-race landowners, with their heterogeneous mestizo culture, occupied in nineteenth-century Java.[16]

Significantly, Van Oudijck expresses a hatred of half-castes and their mestizo culture as a pretext for banning his wife and daughter from the social circle that revolves around the seductive, charismatic Addy de Luce. Van Oudijck's outbursts may also result from his envy of a younger man's polymorphous sexual charisma. Yet this violent rejection raises questions: why would he, who in the past married a mixed-race woman himself, now only consider a "full-blooded" European as the appropriate husband for his half-caste daughter? One possible answer in this turn-of-the-century novel is found in the fluctuations of colonial attitudes toward interracial unions and, subsequently, toward the mixed Indo culture that had long existed on Java.

Van Oudijck's disdain for the decadent Adiningrats and the half-caste De Luce family establishes distinct boundaries between European, Indo-European, and aristocratic Javanese families. His contempt, however, excludes the numerous and nameless native servants, whether male or female, who silently watch the Europeans trapped in their self-imposed plot. In 1900, when *The Hidden Force* was first published, an enormous number of European men still lived with colonized women who were their housekeepers and concubines. At the same time, however, racial identities were in the process of acquiring starkly distinctive meanings. The colonial politics of modernity and apartheid in the Indies coincided with an emerging fear of miscegenation in Europe. Invented as a term in the late nineteenth-century vocabulary of sexuality, miscegenation became associated with a set of discourses about degeneracy and eugenics. The object of European fear was less interracial sexuality per se than it was the decline of the white population that would be its inevitable result. Europeans were thought to decline, both physically and psychologically, if they remained in the colonies for too long. In addition to their geographical distance from true civilization, this anxiety was linked to Europeans' long-term exposure to native culture and its vile racial influences by having to live in the sultry equatorial heat. In *The Hidden Force*, Eva Eldersma emblematizes and expresses these common fears of a rapid racial degeneration among Dutch people in the Indies.

Such changes in mentality provoked a radical turn in racial and sexual politics in the Indies. From about 1900 on, miscegenation was increasingly perceived as negative. Concubinage and miscegenation, both fundamental elements of the good old days of the Netherlands Indies, came to be considered the source of the psychological breakdown and ill health of European men. However, miscegenation was increasingly viewed not only as a sign of racial deterioration but also as a cause of political unrest. Until the late nineteenth century, mixed Indo children had been regarded as physically and psychologically better equipped to flourish in the tropical climate. After the turn of the century, in contrast, Indo-European children were depicted more often as the tangible evidence of their white father's sexual weaknesses, as if they were suddenly tainted, both physically and morally, by the supposedly inferior qualities of their Indonesian and Indo-European mothers.

Hence, at the beginning of the twentieth century, the time-honored social rules of mestizo Indo culture, with its constant blurring of racial boundaries, were to be repressed in order to make way for a Eurocentric Indies with clear-cut barriers between rulers and ruled. Just as the tolerance of interracial sexuality and miscegenation had been pivotal in earlier centuries, its condemnation became crucial to twentieth-century colonialism. As a result, Asian-born women lost their central position in colonial society. Concurrently, it became important to identify who was white, and by implication, who was native, or whose children could be recognized as European and which offspring should be regarded as illegitimate.[17] In accordance with this racial pigeonholing, Europeans were white, hence easy to distinguish from the native and mixed-race others. In contrast to such an imaginary, essentialist view of Europeanness, Europeans in the colonies, however, did not form an easily identifiable natural, white community with common attributes, political affinities, and superior culture. Based on the long-standing tradition of interracial unions in the Netherlands East Indies, it was the father's recognition, rather than physical features, that determined who counted as a real (white) European.

The Hidden Force exposes the emotional tensions and ambiguities that were involved in the transformation from an eclectic, mestizo world into one that was molded and shaped primarily by totok sensibilities. At the apex of the social hierarchy of the colonial body politic was theoretically the resident's family—the symbol of high morals, European culture, and above all, pure whiteness. Yet there is nothing clearly defined or pure and unadulterated about any of them. Instead, all family members have something ambiguous, indeed something secretive or downright immoral about them. In their association with illegal activities, such as gambling, or their violation of sexual taboos, they are represented as thoroughly hybrid, if not overtly impure or contaminated. This impure cast of the resident's family reflects the utterly mixed reality of the Indies. The white Van Oudijcks demonstrate how the boundaries between colonizers and the colonized were constructed on the basis of imaginary fictions. Similarly, they present the complexities and ambivalences of Dutch colonial society in 1900—a world in which the mixed

Indo culture of bygone days had come to be regarded as a sign of evil and danger.

Van Oudijck's dislike of, even disgust with, the Adiningrats as well as the De Luces, his refusal to help his son Theo find an easy career, his effort to keep Léonie and Doddy away from the Patjaram family—and, eventually, his refusal to accept Addy de Luce as his son-in-law—are all desperate attempts to segregate the three families from each other and to distinguish the "First Family" from mixed-race others. Despite these attempts, Van Oudijck's own wife and children escape the grasp of the colonial, white Law of the Father, as suggested from the very beginning of the novel.

IMPURE WHITE

In *The Hidden Force*'s brilliant elaboration of the interplay between psyche and culture, Van Oudijck is not only battered by an outside force embodied in a treacherous female figure. The final blow to his authority comes from within, from his offspring—children who are the tangible result of his own sexuality and desire. A seemingly minor figure, who appears long after all the other characters have been introduced and the drama has long since been set in motion, turns out to be a significant actor in the plot. The outcast, half-breed Si-Oudijck appears as Van Oudijck's so-called *voor-kind* (prechild), a possible son from his pre-marital liaison with a native woman. Like scores of other Dutchmen, Van Oudijck had taken a concubine before his marriage to his first wife. Until the end of the nineteenth century, concubinage had been a widespread, customary domestic arrangement but one in which the native woman had no rights whatsoever. A European man was free to acknowledge his offspring and take his children away from their mother. Or he could dismiss his concubine and send her back to her ancestral village with their mixed-race children without assuming financial responsibility for any of them.

Hence, the relatively late introduction of the uncouth Si-Oudijck into the story serves a distinct purpose. Upon finding out about the affair between Addy and his stepmother Léonie, the emasculated Theo confronts Addy as a male rival. But Addy, "with his instant forgetfulness after an hour of love," calms Theo down, counseling him not to get upset about a mere woman (117). In a variant of an Oedipal homosocial arrangement, Addy and Theo agree to possess and exchange Léonie—their father's wife—between the two of them. In addition, they plot the demise of the paternal figure—the paterfamilias of their social world—by visiting Si-Oudijck. On that occasion "the two brothers looked at each other: Theo curious, glad to have made his discovery as a weapon against the old man . . . the other, Si-Oudijck, secretly restraining, behind his brown, crafty, leering face, all his jealousy, bitterness, and hatred" (120). It gives Theo pleasure to listen to Si-Oudijck, who demolishes their father's aura of morality and honor. The scene illustrates the ambivalences within colonial structures, in which intricate male anxieties, racial sentiments, and family relations complicate each other:

> In his innermost self, [Theo] was more the son of his mother, the *nonna*, than of his father . . . he hated his father . . . from a secret antipathy in his blood, because, despite the appearance and behavior of a blond and fair-skinned European, he felt a secret kinship with this illegitimate brother. . . . Were they not both sons of the selfsame motherland, for which their father felt nothing except as a result of his acquired development, the artificially, humanely cultivated love of the ruler for the territory that he governs. [121]

Si-Oudijck's sudden appearance serves a double function. He reminds Van Oudijck of his interracial sexual desires in the past; and, having spent his whole life in the native quarter, Si-Oudijck anticipates Van Oudijck's later abandonment of European civilization for native culture. While it is uncertain whether or not he is really the long-forgotten, unacknowledged child that Van Oudijck had sired with his former native concubine, Si-Oudijck is able to blackmail his alleged father through his mere existence. Already weakened by a string of incomprehensible events which have offended his rational nature, Van Oudijck supplies the money demanded. This defeat again refers to a changing society in which the memory of previously accepted practices—such as sleeping with a native housekeeper—should be suppressed. After the reversal in racial and sexual politics, Van Oudijck's first liaison is considered a dubious one, subject to blackmail and reminiscent of a scandalous lust to be repressed at all costs, even if it requires the payment of hush money.

Another mixed-race member of the family—this time in the form of a sleazy blackmailer, whose claim to be his father's son remains unresolved—is added to Van Oudijck's Indo-European children, Doddy and Theo.

Van Oudijck's defeat results from his daughter's yearning to belong to Addy de Luce's mixed-race world, the hateful betrayal of his legitimate son, and, finally, the anonymous letters of a presumptive illegitimate son. Spawned by the Dutchman's interracial longings—desires he attempts to conceal at any cost—his own children's actions crush his faith in reason and logic, undoing his sense of European masculinity and honor. In the novel this internal crisis is sustained by an emasculation, or rather feminization, of the once self-possessed man. Unable to master his own position, Van Oudijck begins to "hesitate." While passively giving in to long periods of musing in a lazy chair, he enjoys the "weakening of his muscles" and the "aimless drowsiness of his thoughts" (201, 202).

In terms of narrative strategies, the palimpsest narrative has unsettled the father's central position as well as his story. Van Oudijck's own wife and children, instead of the regent Sunario, have endangered his authority from the outset. Moreover, in the stereotypes, such as lack of ambition and flawed morality, which are associated with those of mixed racial background, the hidden narrative exposes the emerging European fear of contamination of the white race. Returning in the form of that which has been repressed, Van Oudijck's acknowledged as well as unacknowledged mixed children signal male desires and anxieties, rather than Indo qualities. Similarly stereotyped, Creole Léonie is presented as the evil genius who has contaminated a superior white family. We see her white, beautiful body soiled and filthy in what has become the novel's most infamous scene.[18]

Naked, she glanced in the mirror at her soft, milky white shape. . . . She lifted her hair, admiring herself, examining herself. . . . At that moment she saw on her thigh a small red spot. . . . The spots came from the corners of the bathroom—how and where she did not see—first small, then larger, as if spat out by a mouth drooling with betel juice. Deathly cold she screamed. The spatters thicken, became full, like purple globs spewed at her. Her body was befouled and filthy with a grimy, dribbling red. . . . She was all red, befouled, as though defiled by a shame of filthy vermilion that invisible, betel-juice stained mouths hawked and spat at her from the corners of the room, aiming at her hair, her eyes, her breasts, her lower belly. [184]

As the sexualized images of her affair with her mixed-race stepson and, worse yet, her masculine desire for Indo Addy de Luce take over in the colonial conflict, the Creole Léonie is forced to assume the burden of guilt.

CONCLUSION

At the beginning of this chapter I raised the question of the hidden forces in the novel. Subsequently, my analysis has disclosed a submerged narrative which exposes illicit sexuality, dangerous liaisons, and racial interbreeding. The novel's haunting ambiguities emerge from this submerged space. However, many a literary critic has deciphered the ominous ambiguity of the novel by interpreting its intangible hidden forces.[19] Such attempts tend to search in Couperus's personal biography for clues to an understanding of the novel. Often these biographical approaches assume a preconfigured East and West by concentrating on the opposition between the colonizers and the colonized or by focusing on Van Oudijck's resounding defeat in a relentless battle between Western rationalism and Eastern spiritualism.[20] Following this line of argument but opposing critics who dismiss *The Hidden Force* as primarily an exotic tale of black magic and witchcraft, Rob Nieuwenhuys has asserted that it would be a mistake to regard the supernatural hidden forces as the novel's central theme. As the preeminent Dutch East Indies literary expert, Nieuwenhuys maintains that the novel is about "the tragedy of the European individual, whose lack of superstitious belief leaves him helpless in the colony."[21]

In his fatal hubris the Dutch resident does indeed fit the classic archetype associated with European individualism and masculinity. Western culture has routinely represented heroes as lonely male figures who emerge when the stability of the social order is in danger. Fueled by "isolation, social confusion, and existential anguish," Van Oudijck's herculean struggle can be traced back to such a foundational fantasy of Western civilization.[22]

However, *The Hidden Force* (and by extension, colonial fiction in general) is not solely implicated in the history of male European heroism; the novel is also imbricated in the contested experiences of gender, class, and sexuality through race. Any attempt to understand its colonial discourse through feminist theories would have to move beyond a Eurocentric tale of tragic male heroism and its implied dichotomies. My reading locates the ambivalence of colonialism in Van Oudijck's representation as a white father. Situated in a colonial context, Couperus's tormented hero carries the white man's burden at a time when the Dutch seem to have lost faith in their natural right to govern. Couperus's story of "decay, fear, and disillusion" not only presents the defeat of the male individual but also portends the demise of the colonial enterprise in the Indies as well as the collapse of the Dutch Empire in Southeast Asia.[23] Therefore, my analysis has focused on the frictions and apprehensions of the colonial community, with its newly embraced politics of racial segregation and taboos on interracial sexuality. It exposes how boundaries blur in the face of a complicated colonial reality in which the histories of public and private spheres are not distinct but always overlapping and intermingling.

In the novel's primary narrative of public politics, Léonie is fixed as the angel of doom who causes Van Oudijck's tragic downfall from his august position as paterfamilias as well as his political role as father of the administrative district. Yet intertwined in the novel's public discourse, the palimpsest narrative tells us a different story. In her betrayal of patriarchal dictates, in wanting both Addy's "wild animal type" and Theo's "white-skinned Dutch type only slightly influenced by the Indies," Léonie transgresses colonial laws, which are expressed in increasingly clear-cut lines of demarcation between white, mixed-race, and native people (108). Watched by her silent Javanese maid, Urip, she challenges and subverts the rigidity of colonial injunctions that mandate the racial boundaries between East and West. Both her Western figuration and the disconcerting presence of an indigenous female gaze function as conflicting spaces that destabilize and denaturalize the myths surrounding masculine European stability. Similarly, as the protagonist of the dark palimpsest narrative, Léonie undercuts the novel's primary plot, in which her ethically upstanding, hardworking husband is to maintain his authority as a ruler and a father.

I would argue that the fictional power of the hidden forces in the novel revolve around the interweaving of narratives in this ambiguous story. Populated by Creole women and Indo "half-breeds," the obscure narrative flares up in the conflict between Van Oudijck and Sunario. Projected onto Leonie, a pervasive, if subliminal, angst about racial contamination is displaced to patriarchal fears about women's unruly and voracious sexuality. Eventually, the intertwined narratives reveal that the denouement of Van Oudijck's grandiose, masculine drama, which takes its eventual shape in his going native, exemplifies the ultimate fears and fantasies of the colonizer in which miscegenation occupies a central position.

POSTSCRIPT

In 1949 the Netherlands finally relinquished its most treasured colony, the Dutch East Indies. Decolonization took place during four bruising years of struggle and war that followed upon Indonesia's unilateral Declaration of Independence on August 17, 1945. The loss of its former colony has since become one of the most traumatic features of Dutch national identity. No longer either embodying a geographical time-space that belonged to the Dutch nation or representing a lucrative career for adventurous Dutch men, the former colony continues to be reinvented through a circulation of histories, narratives, and memories. Among these circulating texts two narratives dominate the collective memory of the East Indies. The first one is the story of a proud, almost heroic, past: *Daar werd wat groots verricht!* which can be translated as: "Those were our glory days, when we accomplished something great over there." In the shift from colonial to postcolonial sensibilities, however, this narrative has been largely overtaken by a second story, which indulges in feelings of shame and guilt and talk of racism and exploitation. While Holland's colonial past used to be a matter of indifference to the majority of Dutch people, an undercurrent of collective guilt has recently surfaced in memories of the Indies.

However contradictory these narratives may seem to be, both stories—the celebratory tale as well as the story of regret and contrition—

have contributed, in fact, to the obscuring and forgetting of mestizo Indo-European histories, in which miscegenation was pivotal. Hence, Holland's dominant narratives not only persist in suppressing Indo people's colonial past, they also tend to muzzle the many voices in contemporary Dutch culture that tell tales about difference, hybridity, and mixed identities. As a hidden element in Europe's history, miscegenation is one of the concealed dramas of intercultural history. With its oblique allusions to a guilty past, it generates fear and undermines fixed identities by effacing Western limits between the civilized Self and, in Gayatri Spivak's terms, its not-yet-human Other.[24]

Stowed away in the attic of Western memory, miscegenation remains either forgotten or repressed. While it may be speculative, I would suggest that *The Hidden Force*'s continuing enchantment touches upon a shrouded space in contemporary Dutch national fantasies: that is, the taboo of miscegenation. Associated with the contested history of race mixing in the Dutch East Indies and the cultural taboo on interracial unions imposed since the early twentieth century, the novel reveals, even exults in, the practice of interracial sexuality. Seductive and ambiguous stories such as Couperus's *The Hidden Force* reinvent miscegenation as a disruptive element that both haunts and captivates the Dutch nation's collective self-image.

6. WOMANIZING INDOCHINA:
Fiction, Nation, and Cohabitation in Colonial Cambodia, 1890–1930

ꝏ Penny Edwards

Imagine a European man in a suit of spotless white, hunched over his writing desk in the French quarter. Dear Mother, he begins. The letter-head places him in Phnom Penh, capital of the French protectorate of Cambodia.[1] The date is harder to decipher: is it 1910, or 1920, or 1930? No matter. Barely audible above the office fan, his pen scratches a hero's trail through warring tribes, wild beasts, and jungle fever. Later, in the post office, he fingers a Cambodian piastre to pay for the letter's stamps. Embossed on the coin is La France, a helmet to protect her values, a lion to defend her virtue. The image unnerves him, for in her matronly demeanor, he sees an echo of his mother. It is as if she had been there in his office, spying over her little boy's shoulder as he spun tall tales of hardship and adventure. But when the postal clerk cashes the coin and hands him a stamp, his mood lifts. Smiling, he licks the stamp, then smooths it down. Beneath his proprietary fingers, immortalized in philatelic brown and cream, a Cambodian nymphet parts her lips in mute invitation to a kiss.

On this trigonometry of gender, colonial constructions of Cambodia were built. First was the mother figure of the metropole, iconized as La France or Marianne, in colonial monuments and currency. National mythology had feminized France since the seventeenth century.[2] Depicted as a "beautiful, strong-willed" young woman in the first years of the Republic, France was refigured after the loss of Alsace-Lorraine in 1870 as "noble, warlike and sheltering."[3] This was the symbol of maternal authority which colonial wives were implicitly urged to imitate. Translated into the imperial context, however, the image was ambivalent. Many colonial writers equated the feminine realm of the metropole with the "sickly over-refinement . . . of an over-subtle civilization, in which the vitality of the race is being drained away." [4] A plethora of colonial novels portrayed French wives as monstrous incarnations of the metropole whose essential femininity was stifled by modernity.

Opposed to this image was the virile colonizer, a man of action whose energy would revitalize the nation by building a new France overseas. "A colonialist must be a man, a real man, the strongest of the strong," wrote Georges Hardy, director of the Colonial Academy from 1926 to 1933. Hardy's dictum encapsulated over fifty years of folklore that eulogized the virility of colonial life, constructing an exotic Wild East in opposition to the flabby degeneracy of the metropole. [5] The colonizer's masculinity was further underscored by imagery depicting the colonies as feminized, sexualized spaces. Unlike France whose matriarchal demeanor implicitly challenged the colonizer's manhood, *la Cambodgienne* (the Cambodian woman) represented a Rousseau-like ideal whose atavistic calling to serve man was still intact. Matronly metropole, virile colonizer, and nymphlike colony were joined in a conceptual triangle which privileged French manhood as the vital link between the raw earth of the colony and the bright hearth of the homeland.

This chapter explores how notions of race and gender were fused to produce such mythology. However, in dismantling these orientalist stereotypes, I do not mean to reinforce the stereotype of the occidental "other" which has emerged in recent scholarship in the form of an essentialized, wicked West. [6] Rather, this essay links colonial representations of Cambodia to the contemporary intellectual climate in France. Anchoring abstract notions in the realities of colonial administration, it charts the private visions and social conventions shaping the ways in which Cambodia was imagined.

My sources are colonial novels, travelogues, guidebooks, journals, bulletins, postcards, monuments, and the archives of the French administration of Cambodia. I give special scrutiny to the works of two scholar-officials. Roland Meyer (b. 1889) experienced colonial Cambodia as a low-ranking clerk whose attempts to straddle French and native worlds ostracized him from his European colleagues. Publication of his semiautobiographical novel *Saramani* allegedly cost him his job. George Groslier (1887–1945), born into the colonial establishment, spent close to thirty years in Cambodia as a high-ranking administrator. His second novel, *Le retour à l'argile* (Return to the clay), received the Grand Prix de Littérature Coloniale in 1929.

Writing from the edges of Greater France, Meyer and Groslier strove to prove both the importance of their colonial domain and their own indispensability as men of superior knowledge and literary prowess. Their novels conjured up an inverted dreamworld, with Cambodia at its center and France on the periphery. In this colonial utopia all the heroes were portrayed as French men, the colonized were Cambodian women hungry for male domination, and the metropole was a brooding matron.

COLONIZING CAMBODIA: DISCOVERERS, DAMES, AND DEGENERATION

In 1860 the French naturalist Henri Mouhot discovered the vast twelfth-century temple complex of Angkor Wat. Mouhot died in Laos the following year, but developments in print technology and the new fashion of travel literature ensured the rapid dissemination of his findings to a rapt audience. Rescued from oblivion by Mouhot's native guides, marketed by his wife and brother, rehashed by a ghostwriter, and enhanced with elaborate engravings, Mouhot's diary was soon serialized in the *Tour du Monde*. A major platform for French explorers, this lavish travel journal showed the French public and politicians "what they were worth, these countries which European governments seek to possess. . . . Who these peoples are . . . what we should take, and what we should leave." Painting Cambodia as a land of cultural and material plenty, Mouhot urged France to add this "magnificent jewel" to its crown.[7]

Mouhot's disclosure sealed Cambodia's political fate. In 1863, swayed by the heady climate of imperial rivalry, the French government established the Protectorate of Cambodia (1863–1953). Until the retrocession of Siem Reap to Cambodia under the Franco-Siamese Treaty of 1907, Angkor Wat stood in Siamese territory. However, the French government used its new foothold in the region and its new ally, the Cambodian monarchy, to win privileged access to the temples. France had soon established a monopoly on the production of knowledge about Angkor in the Western world. Contrasting Cambodia's "degenerate" present with the majesty of Angkor, scholars, explorers, administrators, and novelists mistakenly concluded that the Khmers, who had built Angkor, were now extinct and argued that decadence had led to the decline of an empire and demise of a race. Such analyses were less a lens on Khmer history than a mirror of contemporary French mentality. Reflecting on the ruins of Angkor Thom, Governor-General of Indochina Paul Doumer swore to do everything in his power to prevent France "from slithering down the slope of decadence."[8] Menaced by a burgeoning working class, dogged by the memory of France's losses in the Franco-Prussian war of 1870–71, and threatened by falling birthrates, the French establishment shared Doumer's obsession with national entropy. From the 1880s to World War I, countless voices warned that France was on the verge of vanishing.[9]

These fin de siècle fears were intricately linked to notions of race, class, sex, and gender. A vulgarized Darwinism—or neo-Lamarckianism—emerged which suggested that "like families, societies and social groups were subject to degeneration." In Paris bipolar stereotypes of decadent prostitutes and bourgeois wives were consolidated, while fears of a decline in bourgeois births saw an enhanced emphasis on the role of women as wives and mothers.[10] In marriage the implication was that sexual intercourse was a "racial duty." Against this intellectual backdrop, the invocation of women as both mothers and symbols of nation had particular significance, for "when women and nation are fused, the desire to protect the virtue of one becomes a civic duty to defend the other." Family and race, private and public spheres, were synthesized across nineteenth-century Europe in such female icons of the nation as Germania, Britannia, La France or Marianne, Finlandia, and Polonia. These latter-day secular Virgin Marys often were armed with sword and shield to guard their chastity—and thus the purity of their race—from despoliation by foreign others.[11]

Fears of degeneration informed colonial policy in two key areas— cultural conservation and biological reproduction. From Fiji to Tanganyika, administrators and scholars vowed their noble intent to salvage colonized civilizations from the demons of decline through scholarship, art education, and museums. Indeed, it was the very notion that the Khmer race had disappeared that led to the creation of the Ecole Française d'Extrême Orient (EFEO) in Hanoi in 1898. Fourteen years later

George Groslier claimed that the Cambodian royal ballet was "at the point of death." [12] Similar fears about the "overly rapid decadence" of Cambodian arts, "denatured and mongrolized" by Western influence, led to the formation of the Friends of Angkor, whose vision of a vanishing Cambodia shaped colonial policies vis-à-vis museums and art education. Policies toward the monarchy and the monkhood further entrenched French notions of the Cambodian ethnonational essence. Colonial ritual and architecture magnified the cultural symbolism of the Cambodian crown, while French restrictions on Buddhist monks isolated Cambodian religion from Siamese and Vietnamese influences. [13] European fears of cultural decline were thus projected onto Cambodia. Conversely, the degeneracy of the Cambodian present was used as a warning of how low the French race could sink if it succumbed to decadence.

While colonized cultures were routinely held up as emblems of degeneration, the colonies themselves ironically were seen as sites of regeneration for the French race. Harking back to the loss of Alsace-Lorraine, the writer Hugues le Roux urged his readers in 1898 "to save the race" by creating "an overseas France." French women were vital to healthy eugenics in the colonies, crowed Indochina's leading colonial journal, the *Revue Indochinoise*, because without them a mixed-blood population would emerge, "with all the vices and none of the virtues" of the French and native races. [14] Joseph Chailly-Bert, president of the French Colonial Union, shared these views. With the exception of Catholic nuns and the chorus girls who staffed ocean liners, most fin de siècle female émigrés to Cambodia traveled as the spouses of administrators and investors. Chailly-Bert blamed the shortage of eligible French women in the colonies for pushing decent French men into the beds of native women, thereby jeopardizing the future of both the French race and French rule. In 1897 he founded the Society for Female Emigration to the Colonies to ship virtuous, marriageable women to the colonies in order to "impregnate these distant lands with the genius of our race." [15]

Later that year Minister of Colonies André Lebon wrote to heads of government in Indochina seconding the society's request for jobs for French women. The negative response to this, and to later initiatives, revealed keen tension between metropolitan desires to domesticate the colony and the dreams of colonial officials to preserve their patch as the stamping ground of European males. Protectorate officials replied that the only suitable jobs for women there were teaching posts, and no more female instructors were needed. Stating that the "female element" could not usefully contribute to any department, the governor-general refused to reserve a single place for female émigrés. Undeterred, in 1903 the society's president asked the Indochinese administration to reserve posts for women as postal and telegraph workers, dactylographers, and teachers. "Indochina has no female immigration," replied Governor-General Beau.[16]

Despite such resistance, French women soon were arriving in Indochina, ending "the reign of the native woman, the regime of the concubines." As Phnom Penh's colonial community expanded, so did the demand for female teachers and nurses to staff girls' schools and maternity hospitals. Male critics later blamed white women for erecting "a field of barbed wire" between Europeans and natives.[17] In fact, the policy and mentality of male administrators helped to anchor colonial women in their much-resented role as housekeepers of the empire by closing off other avenues. Civil service positions were consistently categorized as masculine and unsuitable for women. In the late 1920s women were the principal targets of a propaganda campaign to stem a flood of French émigrés arriving in Indochina in search of work. French women in Cambodia as in the metropole were denied the right to vote. Marginalized professionally and politically, they were encouraged to channel their energies into such maternal endeavors as the Society for the Protection of Cambodian Children and Mothers, founded in 1926. An arbiter of hygiene and watchdog of racial purity, the French woman was "destined to civilize and police, to inspire and purify, to ennoble and augment all that confronts her." However, this gender role was class-bound. The spectacle of poor-whitism was feared and condemned across the global colonial map as a serious detriment to imperial prestige. White women who violated bourgeois ideals were considered dangerous threats to the racial and moral hierarchy of colonial rule.[18]

"A Mme Français going to market!" scoffed journalist Jean Ajalbert in an attack on poor white wives who frequented native spaces and assumed native roles. "The Asians cannot understand such a fall!" The image of the debauched white whore, anathema to the cult of the chaste

On the banknote: GIẤY NĂM ĐỒNG VÀNG

SEB. LAURENT FEC.   E. DELOCHE SC

French Cambodia as represented on a five-piastre bank note issued by the Bank of Indochina

white wife, was particularly feared. In 1906 Ajalbert panned the policy of sending Indochinese officials to France, where they could discover that "we are frauds of corrupt morals, our women as easy as dogs." Echoing these sentiments, novelist Pierre Mille condemned the colonial exhibitions for giving natives a window on a world where "white women slaves can be had for twenty francs." In order to maintain the optical illusion of the universally moral and maternal French female, authorities intercepted obscene postcards sent home by Cambodian troops deployed to France during World War I, despite an apparently uninhibited traffic in erotic postcards of Cambodian women to France.[19]

Colonial horrors of degeneration and hybridity led to an obsession with constructing and maintaining bipolar native and European milieus as bridgeheads of national, racial, and cultural purity. Noting with alarm that the French official in Indochina sometimes developed "a new mentality close to that of the colonized people, which threatens to destroy his personality and even his morality," French administrator and future governor-general of Indochina Pierre Pasquier exhorted his peers "to conserve all the qualities of [their] race" so as to prevent their absorption by the native milieu.[20]

Urban planning provided one defense against such absorption. The expansion of Phnom Penh's European population from 150 in 1900 to approximately 530 in 1904 led to the first freestanding villas for whites and the consolidation of a French quarter, cordoned off from the Cambodian quarter by a moat. White wives and mothers had a key role to play in keeping their families French by maintaining such cultural ramparts of the milieu as furnishings, cuisine, their "French manners . . . grace and spirit," and clothing. While oriental costume parties were a fashionable pursuit in fin de siècle Paris, dressing native was considered a dangerous gateway to assimilation in countries where Europeans formed the minority. European women in Indochina were protected from the sun, and the native gaze, by "caps, dark glasses, veils, parasols, gloves." [21] As fashions changed, they were advised that pith helmets were compulsory, as was "dress[ing] appropriately and keep[ing] a distance from the natives." Color as well as style of dress sustained the emphasis on difference. In Cambodian tradition white symbolized the invisible, immaculate, and divine. An insignia of race and rank, the white uniforms of colonial officials contrasted strikingly with the dark attire of Cambodia's majority peasant population. "With the assumption of this uniform," observed novelist Marguerite Duras, "the first step had been taken. From then on, the distance augmented." [22] The white suit became a shield against European assimilation to native culture, a social skin which won instant acceptance and respect no matter what vices of the Frenchman it veiled. But maintaining the European milieu was only half of the battle. Equally important was preserving a quintessential Cambodia as a bulwark against Europeans' cultural slippage.

Just as white women should not fall from their place, so Cambodian women must not be allowed to rise from theirs. Natives who spoke the wrong tongue or dressed the wrong way threatened to unravel a status quo predicated on the entrenchment of social distance and ethnic difference. Cross-cultural exploration and experimentation were the privilege of whites. While the Parisian diva Cléo de Mérode was applauded for posing as a Cambodian dancer at the 1900 Exposition, Cambodian aristocrats and artisans at the international and colonial exhibitions in Paris (1900) and Marseilles (1906) were ridiculed and reprimanded for wearing Western dress. Many provincial chiefs in Indochina reportedly forbade their native subordinates from wearing European clothes. To preserve both French power and a pristine Cambodia, male colonialists fulminated against the pernicious effects that learning the French language had on native women, maintaining that it would corrode their quintessential femininity and create *déclassées* and prostitutes.[23] Such concerns reflected deeper fears of miscegenation. Buttressed through cultural, educational, religious, and political policies, French visions of Cambodia's ethnonational essence were embodied in a racially pure native woman.

The official art of empire cloaked these conceptions in the legitimizing veneer of France's cultural mission. In museums and international expositions, Cambodia featured as an *apsara*, the celestial dancer who embodies "purity of spirit and eternal beauty." In royal court dancing the apsaras were traditionally used to mediate between the king and heaven. Colonial representations divorced the apsara from this cultural context, using the fabled dancer as an intermediary between the French pantheon and the Cambodian people. Emblems of an antiquity that France was sworn to protect, flesh and blood apsaras—the royal dance corps—were repeatedly deployed to represent Cambodia at colonial exhibitions (1906, 1922, 1931). On their knees, bearing gifts, or puzzling over French books, paper and stone apsaras cast Cambodia as the grateful but needy beneficiary of France in numerous monuments and propaganda posters. Sporting a helmet, and sometimes a sword, the powerful protectress France often towered over these supple sylphs.[24] A similar matrix shaped Théodore Rivière's massive monument, *La France*, built in Hanoi in 1908, and his Sisowath Monument, sculpted in Paris and transplanted to Phnom Penh.[25] Designed to reflect an ideal, these depictions bore little resemblance to contemporary Cambodian women, who covered their breasts and whose hair was cropped short at puberty in a style considered androgynous by numerous Western writers. Instead, imperial iconography constructed a mythic Orient imbued with a fantasy femininity that was at once inviting and rewarding.

Outside of public spaces, between the covers of colonial novels and postcard albums, Cambodian women were stripped of the apsara's angelic veneer and cast as sexual playthings. Such depictions emphasized the degenerate status of Cambodia's present, again underscoring France's restorative mission. These images depicted la Cambodgienne as a voluptuous *congaï*, a Vietnamese term coined by the French to refer to Asian concubines in Indochina.[26] Her role in the gender matrix was to transmit the secrets of her culture through amorous encounters with her French protectors. She was a "skin dictionary" (*le dictionnaire en peau*), through whom the French could master the language and culture of the conquered. Like the British and Dutch colonial euphemisms "sleeping-dictionary" and "walking dictionary," the metaphor equated carnal knowledge of the colonized with knowledge about the colony.[27] Male infallibility was maintained by the myth that Europeans had taught Asian women passion. Such stereotypes bolstered notions of the sexual prowess of the white man, emasculated the Orient, and cast the congaï as a purely physical object incapable of the tender emotions and maternal instincts of *la Française* (the French woman). Before 1900 relationships between French men and native women were an accepted feature of life in Cambodia. Gaspard Faraut, a pillar of the French community, moved to a Khmer temple to study the culture and language and married a Laotian who bore him two sons. Faraut's prominence in late nineteenth-century colonial life indicates that no censure surrounded his partial "indigenization."[28] Several other leading colonial figures also settled in Cambodia with native wives. Religious missions in fin de siècle Indochina helped to institutionalize concubinage by hosting the congaïs of French officials during their masters' home leave. Yet by the 1920s few colonial residents enjoyed public relationships with native women. Those who did were considered traitors to the European camp.[29]

These changes in attitude may be traced to Governor-General Doumer's term in office (1897–1902). From the 1860s to the 1890s, Cambodia had been dominated by a loose-knit group of gunslingers, missionaries, adventurers, and carpetbaggers interested in furthering their own military, religious, or commercial gain under a figurehead French government representative. Disgusted by this, Doumer overhauled Cambodia's inert administration, centralized the Indochinese Union, unified bureaucratic procedures, and institutionalized colonial scholarship. Coinciding with the inauguration of the Ecole Coloniale in Paris to train

France's new colonial civil service, Doumer's policies tightened links to the metropole, homogenized French rule throughout Indochina, and ultimately changed the complexion of colonial society in Cambodia.[30]

In a radical departure from earlier laissez-faire policies, Doumer took immediate steps to police the private lives of French administrators; he acted swiftly to end the relationship between Resident Superior of Cambodia Huyn de Vernéville and a high-society Cambodian concubine, Dame Ruong, who was subsequently jailed.[31] Interracial liaisons came under new scrutiny throughout Indochina. In 1898 the prosecutor-general for Cambodia and Cochin China warned subordinates not to take native concubines on pain of dismissal. Soon thereafter, Doumer instructed all French officials to avoid relationships with native concubines, whose influence "is nearly always disastrous." In a 1908 circular the chief prosecutor warned French legal officers throughout Indochina to guard against the corrupting influence of native women or face strict penalties. By contrast, the law was lenient on nonofficial colonial men who maltreated their concubines, even when it ended in murder.[32]

Despite such measures, cross-cultural liaisons continued, leading to the establishment of the Society for the Protection of Children in Cambodia in 1913 to care for the abandoned offspring of native mothers and European fathers. The continued prominence of the congaï in colonial novels and memoirs of the 1910s and 1920s suggests that French-native sexual liaisons did not diminish but were simply pushed from the public to the private sphere. In life as in literature, the presence of the congaï exorcised sexuality from the image of the "irreproachable French-women of Indochina, our wives."[33] At the same time, the banishment of the congaï to back rooms and back streets prevented her racially tainted love from tarnishing the facade of the French administration. The popular literary stereotype of Cambodian women as creatures of the boudoir is testimony to the thinking that informed such constructions. Nevertheless, Cambodian women were far more active in the urban and agricultural economy than their French counterparts. At home they enjoyed financial clout and property rights in a matrilineal society which challenged French colonial and metropole gender ideology. Yet colonial educators and administrators urged la Française to domesticate and elevate native woman.[34] As the century wore on, such role playing became increasingly out of step with socioeconomic changes in France.

World War I had mobilized women to enter the European labor force in unprecedented numbers. Nevertheless, colonial society creaked on as a last frontier of male dominance. In this context, male writers had a vested interest in depicting Cambodian women as weak vessels and helpless children.

Maintenance of the status quo thus hinged on manufacturing and preserving racial, cultural, and sexual identities through the strict application of a trifocal vision of gender. At home the colonial wife and mother upheld the sanctity of the French race and nation. Hidden from public view, the Cambodian concubine yielded intimate knowledge of her body and culture to her French masters. And in the offices of the French administration, men such as Meyer and Groslier articulated and preserved native tradition.

ROLAND MEYER: THE PERILS OF CROSSING CULTURAL BARRIERS

Born in Moscow and educated in Paris, Roland Meyer entered the Indochinese colonial service in 1908. After three months in the cabinet of Governor-General Paul Beau in Saigon, Meyer completed ten years of service in Cambodia, then moved to Laos where he became chief of security and political affairs and permanent secretary of the Franco-Siamese Mekong High Commission. Awarded the Legion of Honor and appointed to the cabinet of the minister of colonies in Paris in 1933, Meyer later became chief administrator of Overseas France. In tandem with his bureaucratic career, Meyer wrote a number of fictional and scholarly works. His *Cours de Cambodgien* (Lessons in the Cambodian language; 1912) was followed by a series of books consisting of a semi-autobiographical novel, *Saramani: Danseuse cambodgienne* (1922); *Cours de Laotien* (Lessons in Lao; 1924); a volume of fiction and essays, *Komlah: Visions d'Asie* (Komlah: Visions of Asia; 1929); and *Indochine française: Le Laos* (French Indochina: Laos; 1931). In 1952 Meyer published his memoirs, *Le propos du vieux colonial* (Proposal of an old colonial), a staunch defense of colonialism, which reinforced the image of a man utterly dedicated to the French colonial project.[35]

A careful reading of Meyer's work, however, reveals a more complex picture. As a boy, he succumbed to the bourgeois fad for armchair travel, reading Daniel Defoe's *Robinson Crusoe* and the works of Jules Verne and James Fenimore Cooper. At age eighteen, with only six hundred francs in his pocket and carrying a trunk and a pith helmet, Meyer embarked on his own adventure. His youthful ambition was to become not minister of the colonies but "the most Asiatic Frenchman in Asia" and to "write the book of Angkor." In Phnom Penh, Meyer found a country, people, languages, history, religion, traditions, literature, and arts waiting to be "conquered" (*Le propos*, 34–35).

During the next decade Meyer defied the prescribed boundaries of colonial life, living a hybrid existence between the offices of the administration where he worked and the Cambodian quarter where he lived. His French peers treated him as "a pariah, a degenerate" for his "wild retreat" into this native space. In turn, Meyer mocked the "rootless whites" who "curse[d] and ignore[d]" Cambodia from the confines of the European quarter, where they "preserve[d] the puerile manias of their civilized life" (*Komlah*, 99). Framing his mission in terms of humanity and knowledge, Meyer saw his self-imposed exile from the material trappings of colonial life as a sacrifice necessary for the completion of his book. By 1918 Meyer had risen several times through the colonial ranks; he had also mastered the Khmer language. His novel was nearing completion, but deteriorating health forced him to leave his "primitive hut" and to descend to the "sterile mediocrity" of his colleagues by opting for the creature comforts of a brick house. It was here that Meyer finished *Saramani*.

Based on Meyer's own life, *Saramani* tells the story of a Frenchman, Komlah (Khmer for "bachelor"), who in many respects epitomizes then prevalent notions of France's mission in Cambodia. Komlah falls in love with what he sees as Cambodia, and he devotes himself to the study of Khmer language and history in order to rescue them for posterity. Like Meyer, the protagonist Komlah, whose name hangs like a question mark over his Frenchness throughout the text, is so charmed by Cambodia that he settles there. He gradually forgets his origins, race, even his language, and becomes the Khmer's adoptive son.

Komlah marries Saramani, a Cambodian dancer who represents "the falling race in all its ancient nobility, the last flicker of a sacred fire whose trembling flame, he, Komlah, would save" (*Saramani*, 23–25). Saramani's white, powdered performer's mask veils the secrets of an ancient race on the verge of extinction. It is this allure which seduces Komlah and compels him to marry her, renouncing his past in the process. Yet his hopes are dashed. Komlah's attempts to adopt Cambodian culture end in failure. Overpowered by the native milieu, he falls sick and returns to France to stop the erosion of his Western personality by "the morbid elements of the Khmer and Buddhist soul" (*Saramani*, 41). Saramani dies alone, shunned by friends and family for having betrayed her race and culture. In this respect Meyer's message is deeply conservative: any attempt to subvert the status quo is an open invitation to disaster.

The story also serves as a parable regarding the dangers of Western decadence. At one point in the book, a Cambodian prince in Paris buys photos of French women in positions that "the prostitutes of Cambodia could never have imagined." Meyer served as Khmer language instructor to French civil servants. Yet when Saramani asks Komlah to teach her French, he refuses because it is a "fatal poison for Khmer girls" and will kindle "thoughts and vices for which your mother tongue has no words" (*Saramani*, 152, 59). Both the French language and modernity serve as metonymies for the destructive effects of women's liberation in the Western world, a prominent theme in Meyer's later work. In 1952 Meyer argued that the emancipated women of the West had invaded the world of men, bringing nothing but disorder and passion: "Love is women's function and vocation. Open the doors of her cage, and what does she do with her liberty? She invents love and its complications. . . . Women are men's physical and intellectual inferiors, and are often irresponsible, a victim of their own weaknesses. The Orientals understood them well, in sheltering this weakness behind walls. For them, and for us also, to let woman free is to lose her" (*Le propos*, 33).

By the same token, *Saramani* implies that to free Cambodians from French rule would be to lose them. Only Komlah stands between the Cambodian race and its erasure from history, personifying France's mission as savior and curator of Cambodia's past. Meyer's Cambodia is indelibly feminine. The land seduces him with "magical charms," luring him deep into its riverine interior, where he is "conquered body and soul" (*Saramani*, 10–11). The native protagonists of his novel are women, guided by instinct and atavistic tendencies. By embodying Cambodia in Saramani, a nubile dancer who dies when abandoned by her French husband, Meyer underscores the vulnerability and dependence of the colonized.

Meyer's novel also offers important testimony to the price of transgressing colonial boundaries. Publication of *Saramani* provoked such outrage among the colonial community that Meyer allegedly was condemned to exile. "Within days, everything was destroyed: his work, his reputation, his modest fortune . . . his career and his future." Meyer accused "a coalition of ignoramuses and jealous people" of conspiring to destroy him and of doctoring *Saramani* to make it more palatable for colonial readers (*Komlah*, 25, 24). Meyer's claims are hard to verify. But it is easy to see why *Saramani* might have offended colonial sensibilities. The novel's detailed coverage of Cambodian customs may well have threatened the prestige of such mainstream scholar-officials as Groslier.[36] Its depictions of colonial society further challenged the legitimacy of French civil servants who claimed to represent the interests of the Cambodian people yet lived isolated in the sanitized cocoon of the European quarter. While writers such as Pierre Loti, Pierre Mille, and Emile Pischari were renowned for attacking the superficiality of colonial lifestyles, Meyer breached convention by attacking those standards from within.[37]

Meyer also broke with colonial tradition by depicting a native woman as a moral and principled individual. Passionate yet forthright, Saramani challenges the hackneyed formula of the cold-blooded Asiatic Eve. Her devotion to her husband is beyond question and resembles any white wife's dedication. Meyer's description of Saramani's lesbian love affair with a younger palace dancer also stresses her capacity for tender sentiment. Sensitively handled and nonjudgmental, this account might have fueled the hostility of his readers by painting a world of female passion beyond the reach of white men.

In a further challenge to his peers, Meyer depicted colonial officials as racists and buffoons. Walking near the French quarter with Saramani one evening, Komlah hears cruel remarks and sees "a group of Europeans . . . still laughing from their hateful jibe . . . hideous and deformed in their white cloth suits, bearded, sweat staining their brows and armpits, enveloped in a fetid smell suited to their insipid flesh. A woman was among them, strapped into her ugly corset, her hair coiffed in an incredible style; under the coarse growth of her faded hair, she fixed her panther's eyes on Komlah and Saramani, innocent victims of her haughty disdain" (*Saramani*, 190). Just as Saramani represents the quintessential beauty and innocence of the golden era of her race, the colonial madam personifies the evils of modernity. By juxtaposing Saramani's natural simplicity with the horrific emblem of a French emancipated woman, Meyer held up a mirror of what Saramani—and thus Cambodia—could become if France failed to respect and preserve native traditions.

Through the reflected gaze of these Europeans, Komlah first becomes conscious of Saramani's outward markers of difference. It suddenly dawns upon him just how petite and dark she is. Realizing that their children would be branded with the color of their origins and condemned to a lifetime of European contempt, Komlah faces up to the failure of his mission. Between his aversion to the whites and the "hopelessness of all conversion" yawns a "chill void," the gaping abyss between French and native milieus (*Saramani*, 195).

GEORGE GROSLIER: THE PERILS OF MODERNITY

The son of a colonial administrator and his French wife, George Groslier was born in Phnom Penh in 1887. In 1891 his parents sent him to France for schooling.[38] He returned to Cambodia in 1909; for the next five years the ministry of public education gave him various assignments. Ever mindful of his cultural heritage, Groslier "kept his extremely civilized habits in the thick of the jungle, and put on his evening dress before sitting down—alone—in front of a collapsible camping table."[39] In 1913 he published the first European study of the Cambodian ballet; his second work was a romantic travelogue entitled *A l'ombre d'Angkor* (In the shadow of Angkor).[40] Upon Groslier's return in 1917 from service in World War I in Europe, the governor-general of Indochina, Albert Sarraut, entrusted him with the portfolio of arts education in Cambodia. Sarraut, a leading advocate of associationist policies, believed that the future of colonial rule lay not in assimilating cultures but in allowing them to evolve "under our tutelage, in the framework of their civilization."[41] These principles guided Groslier's plans for a Phnom Penh School of Fine Arts, opened in 1919, and his expansion of the National Museum into the Albert Sarraut Museum, opened in 1920. Through these institutions the French obtained substantial control over the Cambodian plastic and figurative arts. From 1919 until his death in Phnom Penh in 1945, Groslier continued to direct museum and arts education policy in Cambodia. A prolific writer, he produced scholarly articles on Cambodian dance, arts, traditions, and colonial architecture that regularly appeared in the *Revue Indochinoise*. He restricted his fictional output to novels.

Groslier's artistic vision centered upon replacing the historic patrons of indigenous art—the Cambodian ruling elite who by then invested their wealth in Western imports—with a new clientele: tourists and colonial residents. But to supply the demand Groslier correctly predicted for Angkorean statuary and trinkets, he needed to create a new cohort of artisans whose "pure blood" could save Cambodian art from "decadence" and "bastardization."[42] In addition to recruiting Cambodia's few surviving craftsmen as instructors, Groslier sent students to Angkor to copy and perfect motifs for reproduction.

Praised by some as disinterested and benevolent, condemned by others as a cynical ploy to deprive the colonized of Western progress by shackling them to their own traditions, Sarraut's and Groslier's rescue mission of Cambodian art was guided by a deep-seated horror of modernity.[43] The carnage of World I exacerbated such feelings. Increasingly, Groslier and other French intellectuals looked East for models of civilization that could benefit the metropole. A deeply romantic view of Cambodia emerged, often with highly conservative ramifications. Like Meyer, Groslier saw the emancipation of women as a catalyst of Western decline. A vision of Angkor as the quintessence of Cambodia informed Groslier's lifework; his novels incarnated this ethnonational essence in the female form. Groslier's fiction thus provides important insights into how he conceptualized the Cambodia he helped to authenticate through his cultural policies.

Both of Groslier's novels—*La route du plus fort* (The road of the strongest; 1925) and *Le retour à l'argile* (Return to the clay; 1929)—mirror the trigonometry of gender. *La route du plus fort* begins not in Cambodia but in Paris, where Hélène falls in love with Ternier, a colonial administrator on home leave. Ternier represents the colonizer, a "powerful machine," driven by "the egoism of the strong, the weight of logical thinking" (*La route*, 235). Hélène, personifying France, is eager to transcend the mediocrity of the metropole and journeys to Cambodia for the exoticism and vitality of colonial life. She finds the Cambodian landscape replete with trophies of male colonial endeavors, such as the newly completed road from Sangke to Sisophon, Ternier's pride and joy. In a letter Hélène compares herself to the colony: "I am one of the provinces he has penetrated. . . . Like the province, I am peaceful and happy, limited in my habits . . . and he has advanced upon me. He has thrown me upside down with his world of ideas and new passions, [making me] thirst for riches I'd never seen. Like the villages that his road pushes back and sucks up, all my poor thoughts, my projects, and even my memories are unrecognizable. And in spite of all that suffers in me, the hard and deep groove which tears me, I feel enlarged." Lean, hard, young, and strong, the masculine motif of the road bisects the feminized, fertile terrain of Cambodia, "germinating tirelessly for centuries" (*La route*, 232).

Changeless as the landscape are Cambodian women, represented by Vetônéa, Ternier's concubine. *Vetônéa* is Khmer for "misery," a name apparently chosen to underscore her manipulative characteristics and to evoke sympathy for the hapless French men doomed to sorrow by Cambodian female wiles. Vetônéa is a marginal figure, a literary foil to enhance the exotic atmosphere and to signal Ternier's closeness to the people he rules. The archetypal congaï or *prâpôn* (Khmer for wife), she encompasses both the white man's hope and his burden.

Moreover, Vetônéa is a Siam-Khmer métis abandoned by her father. Embodying France's colonizing mission, Ternier is portrayed as a valiant knight who has rescued Vetônéa and "set her on his throne as well as in his bed." The segregation of space and its role in constructing the colony is stressed as Ternier dictates to his new Cambodian "wife" her code of conduct in his home: she must stick to her three rooms at the rear; she may not appear in any of the windows in the housefront; she may not chew betel indoors or have Cambodian visitors. Penalties for transgression range from economic sanctions to "divorce," a further indication of the colonial obsession with racial and spatial hierarchy (*La route*, 76, 79).

All congaïs, Groslier explains, are governed by the same proclivity to engage in manipulation and deceit. There is thus no scope for emotional depth in Vetônéa. Within months, Vetônéa's transformation to the archetypal congaï is complete. She waits on white men hand and foot; no one is safe from her charms. Seduced by her languid limbs and flattered by her constant attentions, these men soon find themselves irritated beyond belief by the insubordinate rantings and egocentric poise of white women: "With this fluid, supple, passive body constantly before you, la Française seems heavy, thickset, vulgar, raucous. . . . [She] suffers from the climate, she sweats, her body-hair repels you, while this native keeps fresh, dry and gentle as ivory" (*La route*, 137, 83). Only the passing of time reveals the insidious intrigues of the congaï. In due course, Groslier cautions his audience of colonial Frenchmen, she hardens and roles are reversed: now your "shy" native dominates you. What you took to be spontaneous, loving charms proves to be womanly cunning. You learn to live by the clock and never to stay out too late, because "if you do anything to displease your passive servant, she'll refuse to untie her *sampot* tonight!" Before long, she knows all about your finances, has her own set of keys, and controls the other servants. But you know you are not alone in having fallen into this trap, Groslier counsels, for all over Indochina one can see "men of all ages and positions . . . emptied, emasculated by a Cambodian *prâpôn* . . . a subtle and patient female who, like the praying mantis, succeeds in devouring her male" (*La route*, 83, 85). By ruling Vetônéa with a firm hand and keeping her in her proper place, Ternier ensures that this will never happen to him. The weakness of the metropole and the notion that all things feminine should stay in their allotted sphere, while man alone has free rein to change the world, are reinforced by the death of Hélène. Rejecting Ternier's advice that the bush is too hardy for a Parisian woman, Hélène convinces him to take her on a tour of his roads and falls fatally ill. The law-abiding Vetônéa stays in her prescribed space and lives on; Hélène ventures beyond the woman's domain and dies.

Groslier's award-winning second novel adopts the same gender matrix. *Le retour à l'argile* is narrated largely through the eyes of Claude Rollin, a French engineer residing in Phnom Penh with his wife, Raymonde. Representing the metropole, Raymonde is a shallow, weak woman who retreats into memories of Paris and shrinks from all things foreign. By contrast, Claude embraces his new life with true "masculine" vigor (*Le retour*, 16). Cambodia again figures as a congaï, in the forms of Kamlang (Khmer for "strength") and Nakri, his concubines.

The novel relates Claude's violation of the racial barriers of colonial society and his subsequent transition from an aggressive shaper of colonial Cambodia to the passive plaything of his concubines. A major departure from Groslier's previous glorification of France's role in Indochina, *Le retour à l'argile* surprised readers and reviewers.[44] After two years in Cambodia, the once happily married and hardworking Claude abandons his wife, friends, career, colonial costume, and European luxuries for life in the Cambodian quarter. A tale of social decline and descent into decadence, the novel may be interpreted as a warning against the dangers of dabbling with the native milieu. But Claude suffers no moral dilemma at the story's end. On the contrary: "What peace!" Claude sighs in the closing chapter. "What pride to no longer be a civilized man who thinks himself the number one man in the world" (*Le retour*, 269).

Parodying colonial society as shallow nonsense, Groslier applauds Cambodian culture for its simplicity and closeness to nature. Moreover, France has much to learn from Cambodia, Groslier argues in his narrative intrusions, particularly concerning the role of women. An attack on Western civilization and bourgeois convention, *Le retour à l'argile* bitterly condemns the "defeminization" of women in the West. In France progress has turned natural-born mothers into individualistic monsters whose demands for equality have splintered society and the family. Just as progress has erased femininity in France, Groslier contends, it also threatens to destroy the essence of Cambodia. Admiring "the powerful body" of his nearly completed bridge, Claude is suddenly filled with regret that "he will have dealt one more blow to this ancient country ravaged by the West" (*Le retour*, 191).

Claude compensates for his guilt at defacing the Cambodian landscape by protecting his congaï from modernity. He builds her a traditional Cambodian wooden house, furnished with rattan mats and a hard wooden bed, and insists that Kamlang wear authentic Cambodian clothing and jewelry. For Claude she has no existence outside the trappings of his imagined Orient. Yet Kamlang longs for Parisian chic and a Chinese-style brick house on a fashionable street. While Claude indulges his taste for the exotic, Kamlang must suppress her desire for diversity. Claude's aesthetic hegemony mirrors Groslier's sculpting of Khmer artistic identity through the School of Fine Arts. Kamlang's tra-

ditional raiment become the defining features of her persona and to-
tems of Claude's desire. Just as Groslier condemned Western imports as
contaminants of Cambodian culture, so his novel parades la Française
as the ominous fate awaiting Kamlang should she acquire the ways of
the West. Variously sulking, aggressive, tyrannical toward the servants
and disinterested in her husband's work, Raymonde incarnates the nag-
ging metropole. Had she shrugged off her bourgeois soul, shared her
husband's love of the colony, and wallowed in the raw beauty of Cambodia, their marriage might have survived. Instead, her failure to play
the supportive spouse creates "a denuded terrain upon which the congaï advances" (*Le retour*, 126–27, 142, 38, 97).

Once Claude has returned to the clay of a fictive Cambodia where
women are docile creatures living to serve man, he breaks free of the
fetters of Western civilization. Despite his renunciation of colonial ap-
parel for Cambodian costume, Claude remains a voyeur, while Cambodian women and the landscape are leveled and unified into a sen-
suous terrain of warmth and light. Just as his engineer's hands had
tamed nature while building bridges, so Claude now transforms the raw
material of Cambodian women: "She is the flesh, while I am the soul;
she is weakness, and I, strength. . . . I see no room for foggy theories between her and me. I see a man and a woman; a hand and clay"
(*Le retour*, 193, 137). Claude, Groslier implies, by being open-minded
enough to live with Cambodian concubines, who offer themselves to
him four or five times daily, has attained a noble ideal and rejected
Western artifice. For this he is to be admired, not derided. Instead, the
target of Groslier's derision is Raymonde. By failing to anchor her husband in a domestic environment, she has pushed Claude into the arms
of native concubines and thereby Cambodian culture.

CONCLUSIONS

Groslier's and Meyer's novels resonate with the tensions between the
metropole, French colonial society, and the native milieu. Reflecting
obsessions with the demarcation and preservation of Cambodian culture, both authors delineate these separate spheres with notions of race
and gender. But why was Cambodia represented in the feminine? A
possible explanation is that congaïs were the only point of contact be-

tween French administrators and the Cambodian population. While urban planning ensured the segregation of French and native living spaces, employment policies favoring Vietnamese over Cambodian personnel meant that colonial officials rarely encountered Cambodians during office hours. Yet this argument cannot hold true for either Groslier or Meyer. By 1931 Groslier's art school had several hundred male pupils. Meyer's memoirs indicate he met with monks and other Cambodian males. Feminine representation might equally have been a reward for Cambodia's good conduct as a pliable, submissive colony.[45] Reflecting an asymmetry established at the colonial and international exhibitions from 1889 to 1937, Cambodia dominates Louis Botinelly's 1927 monument *Our Possessions in Asia* in Marseilles. Sporting an Angkorean headpiece and a decidedly Parisian hemline, Cambodia reclines as she is waited on by younger, scantily clad Laos and Vietnam. While all three colonies are feminized, Cambodia's beauty, emblematizing its goodness and purity, is exaggerated. David Chandler has analyzed this bias as France's way of rewarding Cambodia for being the easiest and oldest protectorate.[46]

Yet these hypotheses do not mesh with real historical conditions within Cambodia. The gentle, serene, and feminine facade of colonial literature and iconography belied decades of banditry in the vast Cambodian hinterland beyond the narrow frontiers of European enclaves.[47] The decision to represent a colony or nation in the feminine is thus not necessarily a reward for its submissive behavior. Nor can such gender imagery be explained simply in terms of a colonial will to dominate and penetrate. Such an analysis ignores how the colonizer's own nation was framed in feminine terms: Britannia fair or Marianne.

Many factors conspired to produce the stereotype of Cambodian femininity, but chief among them were the anxieties of male administrators about the future of their own sex. Afraid of the emancipation of Western women, colonizers like Meyer and Groslier retreated into a fictive world where woman's place was to serve and obey. Despite their efforts to divorce themselves from the metropole, both writers were deeply influenced by the intellectual climate in Europe. Reflected in a constellation of monuments, exhibitions, and museums, their female typecasting of Cambodia was rooted in generic occidental conceptions of a quintessential feminine East. Such gender imagery was by no means exclusive to the colonial era, as witness the lasting appeal of Puccini's Madame Butterfly and the recent popularity of Andrew Lloyd Weber's Miss Saigon. However, the stereotype of oriental femininity was greatly exaggerated in colonial society, which gave an increasingly anachronistic male hierarchy the power and privilege to plot the place and space of native women's (and men's) lives. The arrival of white wives in Cambodia curbed this freedom and exposed the fallacy of colonial virility, showing that white women could survive in the colonies as well as men. Reluctant to concede this, writers such as Meyer and Groslier sculpted their fictional French women in the image of a decadent metropole and deranged suffragette.

Whether through deliberate ploy or subconscious whim, depicting Cambodia in the feminine fulfilled the fantasies of male scholars, artists, and administrators. The gangland of Cambodia was remade in their hands as a docile, female creature. Meyer's and Groslier's notions of an essentialized femininity fused with a horror of modernity in the image of la Cambodgienne, whom valiant Frenchmen must protect from the onslaught of the modern world. But there was a flip side to these imaginings. Meyer warned of Cambodia's potential to "paralyze" and "suffocate" France, personified by Komlah (*Saramani*, 41). Groslier stressed the destructive appetites of Cambodian women, who "devour their master" (*Le retour*, 85). While emphasizing the femininity of the colony, both writers stressed its potential for insubordination if not properly contained and firmly ruled.

7. SO CLOSE AND YET SO FAR: The Ambivalence of Dutch Colonial Rhetoric on Javanese Servants in Indonesia, 1900–1942

Elsbeth Locher-Scholten

During the past decade historians and anthropologists have become increasingly aware of the lingering importance of colonial discourses in a postcolonial world.[1] As a result, historians in Europe and North America as well as in formerly colonized societies have focused their attention on the subject of colonial mentalities again. In an exploration of this topic, women have also emerged on the scene: even if Dutch colonialism in Indonesia before 1900 had been largely a male affair, the twentieth-century colonial mind-set was no longer a male prerogative. As newly arrived partners of the men who ran the colonial enterprise, white women expressed this colonial mentality in their own right and in their proper female domain, whether within the household or within various women's organizations. Their mind-set was most sharply delineated when it touched upon the Indonesian, or native, population, whom white women met mainly through their Indonesian servants. By examining these white women's voices as they expressed views on their servants, we can refine our analyses of the colonial mentality and provide new insights in the paradoxes and complexities of colonial cultures in the past.

In this essay I explore the attitudes of European women toward Javanese domestic servants by examining their views as articulated in two different genres: first, household manuals for new colonial residents who were not yet familiar with tropical surroundings and, second, novels for children and teenage girls. Both genres offer a rich fund of information since they were highly prescriptive and were meant to be so. I have limited my investigation to the books written in the heyday of colonialism, the period from 1900 to 1942, which started with a new modernization policy (the so-called Ethical Policy) and ended when Japan attacked the Indonesian archipelago and quickly defeated the Royal Netherlands Indies Army.

In the colonial household different combinations of race and gender were forced to coexist. European women, men, and children lived in the same space as indigenous subordinates, who were both male and female. Discrepancies in status and power overlapped with gender differences, illustrating the complicated sociopolitical patterns of colonial society. I address the following questions: What can European representations of domestic servants from this period tell us about race and gender relations at home, in the personal sphere where women wielded control? Were European women more race-conscious or openly racist than European men, a hotly debated issue in current colonial historiography?[2] And finally, to what extent did women's discourses on servants echo a more explicitly male rhetoric on the nature of colonized subjects as articulated in the political arena?

ORIENTALISM OR RHETORIC OF THE FAMILY?

Before I probe these issues, another set of wider questions must be addressed. In most colonial societies Western representations of colonial subjects tended to reflect European ideas about the "East," which comprised a normative set of opinions on the Orient. Such wide-ranging ideas functioned not only as a generalized body of knowledge but also as an incentive for practical political behavior, as Edward Said has argued.[3] Different not only in race but also in class—and frequently, in gender—servants illustrated the otherness of the oriental subject in its most poignant form. Hence, we must wonder to what extent European female writers of household manuals and children's literature orientalized servants and transformed them into inscrutable others, who could be inscribed with a variety of European fantasies or fears—from a safe psychological distance.

However, these servants resided within the same households as Europeans. Intimately connected to the family, they formed an integral part of a paternalistic family system. Views on domestic servants as part of the family had a long tradition in Europe; in early modern Europe the term *family* had meant originally "all who belong to one house(hold)."[4] The Ethical Policy, for instance, was articulated as a rhetoric of the family—Indonesian children under the tutelage of the West—with strongly paternalistic overtones. Indonesians, the elite in particular, were considered as part of the family of man but still a younger generation or as creatures occupying a lower rung on the evolutionary ladder, waiting to be educated by their Dutch tutors.[5] Indeed, both orientalism and the rhetorical celebration of the family or familization molded colonial views on domestic servants.

AUTHORS AND DOMESTICS

Other questions to be addressed focus on the authors of our sources and the social history of servants in the prewar Dutch East Indies. The female writers of household manuals and children's novels belonged to the so-called European population group and were either *totoks* (born in the Netherlands) or *Indisch*; the latter category included both Eurasian and white families who had resided in the Indonesian archipelago for several generations. Both groups belonged to one legal category, that of Europeans, a term I will employ here. Even if Europeans controlled much of the political agenda of Indies colonial society, they formed only a tiny minority within the Indonesian archipelago. In 1930, for instance, only 0.4 percent of the total population of 60 million people in Indonesia were classified as European. Moreover, most of the Europeans lived on the island of Java—80 percent—which explains my focus on Javanese domestics.[6]

Whether these twentieth-century female authors were full-blooded Europeans or mixed-blood Indies women, their opinions about Javanese servants were quite similar. Regardless of their descent, all European women were involved in the process of Westernization of colonial society that took place in the first half of the twentieth century. A distinct sense of a "Netherlands in the Tropics" developed in the interwar years. This process of Westernization was heavily influenced by a steady influx of Dutch men and women from the European metropole.[7] Improvements in both the technical and the social infrastructure of the Indies fostered the immigration of growing numbers of European-born men and women. Positive developments in the field of hygiene and health, education, and recreation made their (temporary) migration not only possible but also attractive. These immigrants in turn supported and nurtured further infrastructural progress. Inevitably, this process of Westernization affected the culture of the colonial community and influenced Indo-European groups. Newcomers from the Netherlands imported contemporary Western ideas and theories about family life and home economics, considered essential for general well-being and family welfare. At the same time, they had to be educated for their future life in the Indies by books or other means. These cultural exchanges, consisting of lessons about the East and imprints from the West, can be found in the domestic manuals of both Indies and totok authors as well as in children's fiction.

While these European women left behind their opinions in writing, we know little about the experiences of the Javanese servant group. Silenced by the subservient nature of their work and their subordinate social class, these servants were neither expected nor allowed to speak for themselves. They did not acquire a voice through the pressures of a tight labor market, as was the case with domestic servants in Europe in the twentieth century.[8] Because of the ample availability of servants on the densely populated island of Java, the principle of demand and supply functioned to their disadvantage. However, we can reconstruct fragments of their social history from the statistical evidence gathered in colonial censuses and by analyzing Western representations of them.

Domestic service was hardly a Western invention in Java. It had a long tradition there as well as in other parts of the archipelago, where domestic service appeared in many different forms. Members of the indigenous elite employed servants in small or large numbers, depending on their status and wealth. These could be common villagers who had become servants because of debt bondage or corvée obligations. In other instances, impoverished relatives could join the households of their more prosperous family members and attend to them. In a socially layered society such as Java, relationships between employers and servants were always grounded in an elaborate hierarchy. They could resemble patron-client bonds and contain all the elements of distance, power, and fear; on the other hand, such attachments could also embrace warm family feelings.[9]

Dutch colonial residents, having constructed a pecking order that placed them in a superior position to the indigenous aristocracy, adjusted to the social patterns of Javanese society. Eurasian women, married to and heading the household of Dutch immigrants, had played a major role in these processes of acculturation since the seventeenth century.[10] This ironic process of "mimicry," to use Homi Bhabha's phrase, was reinforced by the heat and a social climate that defined Europeans' prestige in Java as demanding a leisurely pace of life.

Domestic servants were thus considered indispensable to Dutch colonial society. It was the married woman who was responsible for these servants in the first place. Often the only Indonesians whom Dutch women in the Indies met in their daily lives were servants. At the beginning of the twentieth century, a European household required, at a minimum, a houseboy, a housemaid or nursemaid (*babu*), and a boy for the horses and the garden.[11] The most popular household manual of 1913 reckoned that seven servants were needed: in addition to the houseboy, the cook, the nurse, and the gardener, a seamstress, and someone to do the washing, as well as a coachman and/or a driver. Another manual recommended ten.[12]

The most universally accepted number among Dutch colonial residents in the twentieth century was between four to six servants. Rich people employed more, while poorer Europeans might have less, perhaps just one servant. In fact, in Java's cities where tap water, gas, and electricity were gradually introduced after 1900, the number of servants declined. New city planning and residential construction produced smaller houses with modern sanitation. They provided less room for servants who traditionally used to live in the quarters to the rear of their employers' house, often together with their spouses and children. In the modern city life of the interwar years, servants might come in only during the day, while maintaining their private residence in a nearby *kampung* (native quarter). But whether servants resided on the grounds of the house or in the kampung, domestic service remained an essential feature of colonial culture. Even when economic fortunes plummeted, such as during the depression of the 1930s, Dutch colonial families tended to cling to their employment of servants as an ostentatious privilege or a sign of status.[13]

In terms of actual numbers, however, only a few Indonesians worked as servants. In 1930, for instance, a mere 2 percent of the total Indonesian working population was classified as domestics, i.e., 350,000 persons (300,000 in Java and Madura, 50,000 in the Outer Regions). The actual proportion of Indonesians employed and registered as domestic servants in 1930 seems to be geographically linked to the presence of Europeans, rich Chinese, and indigenous courts. Wherever these were concentrated, the largest numbers of servants could be found.[14] Domestic service formed part of a stratified, elitist society, which was sustained by an abundant supply of labor.

The numbers and composition of this section of the labor force illustrate the preindustrial character of Javanese society in the first half of the twentieth century. Contrary to the situation in Europe, where a feminization of domestic employment had accompanied the Industrial Revolution and where household service had become the main occupation for women, domestic servants in colonial Indonesia were not exclusively female. In Java and Madura in 1930, only 61 percent of the servants were female. Among the female members of the domestic labor force, 72 percent comprised unmarried women.[15] Neither was it as significant a sector of the labor market for Indonesian women as it was in Europe, where domestic service had developed into a major occupation for women. According to the 1930 census, only 4 percent of the total female labor force worked in households, while merely 1 percent of all workingmen were registered as domestic servants. For Indonesian women it remained a less than appealing activity, attracting only those among the landless population who had few or no alternatives. Agriculture, absorbing 40 percent of all workingwomen, or small-scale industry and petty trade—occupying 25 percent and 12 percent of the female labor force—prevailed over domestic labor.[16]

Within the household, family servants were informally ranked in an internal hierarchy. Most often the houseboy stood at the top of the pecking order; in other families it might be a trusted and experienced older nurse. The houseboys had the task of preparing breakfast, dusting and cleaning the galleries of the house, and serving food at family meals or during social gatherings. Although he performed tasks which in European eyes might belong to the domain of women, he resided in the outer world of display and representation. His work space was located in the open front galleries where guests were welcomed: he functioned in the part of the house that Javanese tradition identified as a masculine arena. Second in importance might be the cook, who was always female. A cook who could "prepare a nice rice table and serve a reasonable European dish" was considered "of inestimable value and incalculable dignity." [17] The female nurse's task was to dust and clean the bedrooms and to care for the children, while the gardener, who was always male, worked outside. Sewing and washing were not restricted to one sex; they belonged to the more flexible tasks open to either men or women. The sexual division of labor among servants appeared rather fluid; it echoed hierarchies of age and replicated the permeable gender boundaries that characterized Javanese social structure. Moreover, it conformed to the traditional lines of spatial organization in the Javanese household where the outer world was reserved for men, while the inner world of the house and its back galleries belonged to women.[18]

Recruitment of servants took place mainly by word of mouth, either on the recommendation of other trustworthy servants or through the intercession of European friends. In the 1930s some professional employment agencies for servants in Batavia began to mediate between employers and servants. The Association of Housewives in the Indies, which formed only in 1931 and lagged behind the professionalization of female activities elsewhere in the world, did the same. This association provided its members with labor passports that registered evaluations and kept on file letters of recommendation written by employers after one year of service; the association also published advertisements and organized contact addresses.[19] For others the rumor mill accomplished its work: some families found their personnel waiting for them when they returned from a home leave in Europe. From these patterns, we can deduce that servants absorbed a distinct professional identity. One was a servant—either a nurse or a cook.

Javanese domestics were trained on the spot. They learned the work from their mistress or from other servants. The issue of simple basic education in housekeeping skills for village girls emerged as a point of discussion only in the second half of the 1930s with little tangible results. The Association of Housewives organized some short-term courses in preparing European dishes for Indonesian cooks as well as courses in sewing for nurses.[20] In the 1920s and 1930s some secondary schooling became available to prepare girls of all population groups for household activities. Schools for girls of the privately funded Kartini and Van Deventer Foundation also focused on home economics, but they were open only for girls of the Javanese elite.[21] A specialized school of home economics for girls was founded in 1931, but its requirements of a high school certificate put it beyond the reach of Indonesian personnel.

Regarding the salaries and fringe benefits of servants, we remain in the dark. The Association of Housewives in the Indies made lists of standard wages available when their members requested advice, but these lists were not published. Holidays or regular days of rest were not common for indigenous personnel; just before World War II the association recommended days off, but for European personnel only.[22]

In the 1920s and 1930s, however, the Westernization of colonial culture produced some changes in the positions of servants. The demand for higher standards imposed upon Javanese domestic personnel was translated into practical guidelines and other enticements such as medals for faithful service or courses in domestic work offered by the Association of Housewives. The economic crisis of the 1930s, on the one hand, restricted the number of servants of individual households, since that was a way of trimming expenses. On the other hand, it pushed new groups into the labor market, among them Eurasian girls, better trained in home economics. These changes, however, were barely reflected in Dutch representations of Indonesian servants in domestic advise manuals and children's fiction.

MANUALS AND ADVICE LITERATURE

Dual messages characterized the manuals and instruction booklets for travelers and newcomers. In the first place prescriptions for the spatial arrangements of a European home marked the otherness of domestics. Servants lived on the grounds in specially designated quarters at the back of the house, where the kitchen, the washroom, and the larder were situated: they were expected to live near the places from which they attended to the material and physical needs of their colonial superiors. Servants did not come into the house of their masters except to do work. The mistress was not expected to come to the servant quarters either, except in case of illness or internal conflicts.[23]

The allocation of separate spaces to masters and servants shaped the

Photograph taken in 1922 of a mixed-race Dutch East Indies colonial family. The young Indonesian woman on the far right is probably the family's *babu* or nurse-maid. (Photograph KIT, Amsterdam)

social geography of daily life. In the nineteenth century mistress-servant relations, especially those between the Indies mistress and her maid, may have been warm and familiar, as colonial fiction set in the Indies depicted them. In the twentieth century, however, more distance was prescribed. According to the manuals, a cordon sanitaire should be constructed socially around each home as well as around each individual within the home.[24] European children should not be allowed to eat food that servants gave them. Mothers should feed their offspring themselves. European children should be forbidden to fraternize with the Indonesian servants. Especially as teenagers they should be kept away from the servant quarters to avoid an initiation into the easy sexuality of servants, which according to the puritanical mores of early twentieth-century Europeans was improper and uninhibited. In the 1930s a medical doctor cautioned mothers against surrendering their children to the care of the native nurse, since her unclean hands might infect small girls with venereal disease.[25]

Strict rules reigned in the field of hygiene. The nurse should never wash the clothes of her master and mistress together with her own textiles, which represented "a serious offense against tradition." If she did so, she could be fired on the spot. Neither should she wash Europeans' clothes at the well near the servant quarters; her employers' bathroom was the proper place. The two disparate worlds of masters and servants should not touch each other in such an intimate way, the same author informed her audience. Fear of the other was articulated through the rules of cleanliness. The white body itself ought to be beyond reach of the other race. This message was repeated constantly, both explicitly and implicitly.[25] Clearly, these manuals preached lessons that moved away from the normative race relations that had prevailed within a majority of the nineteenth-century Indo-European households, in which maids massaged their mistresses and could forge close bonds of friendship with them

The twentieth-century dictates of distance and circumspection conveyed a message that was full of contradictions. Servants were physically the nearest of all Indonesians the colonizers encountered. They were the ones to prepare food and serve it; they washed and cleaned and looked after the children. If we take seriously the manuals' messages, we might conclude that most Europeans found their servants' proximity painfully difficult to endure.

Indeed, stories about servants registered a deep-seated ambivalence. On the one hand, Indonesian servants were depicted as dirty, lazy, and unreliable. On the other hand, European women writers praised them for their gentility and inner culture, their skills, compliance, and modesty. In fact, these servants were frequently lauded for being easier to hire and easier to get along with than servants in Europe. Similarly, nursemaids were accused of spoiling European children: by fulfilling all their demands, native nurses presumably created little potentates. The Indonesian custom of not tolerating children's crying clashed directly with European pedagogical notions about the productive role of frustration in building a child's character. Yet babus were applauded for their loyalty as well as devotion. Europeans praised their dedication as far superior to that of a Dutch nursemaid.[27]

Virtually all authors underlined the differences in the culture, language, and emotional natures of colonial employers and indigenous servants. However, they did so in diverse ways. Some authors vilified the latter, while others described their actions in more understanding terms. Some manuals, for instance, denounced servants' lack of respect for the private property of others, while other household guides explained their behavior by claiming that their culture considered theft a sport, i.e., simply taking what was left over or behind.[28] Servants' habit of asking for an advance in wages was either smiled upon or indignantly rejected.

J. Kloppenburg-Versteegh, one of the most important spokeswomen on domestic servants and Indo-European herself, held her Indonesian servants in very low esteem. Of all authors, her racism was most explicit: "In everything you will see that Javanese servants are not like European personnel but only machines."[29] Repeatedly, she depicted them as filthy, lazy, and untrustworthy. But despite all those negative characterizations, she also concluded her book with the common rhetoric of the family: "Our servants are like big children. Let us try to understand their situation and feel compassion for them; this will urge us to improve their lot, to uplift them." European women should educate their servants, teach them hygiene, and elevate their standard of living. The metaphor of the child, one of the most commonly used linguistic devices in the description of Javanese servants, required a motherly attitude on the part of the mistress.[30]

These images of the other, of servants, mirrored images of self. European women should be clean and active themselves. They should control their servants. Order and regularity should reign supreme in the home. "We Europeans are obliged to set an example in everything, even if it gives us trouble and displeasure." One effective means of doing so was to learn Malay, the lingua franca of the Indonesian archipelago, as soon as possible because it would enhance their prestige among the servants. Moreover, women should react in a wise and restrained manner. Only by maintaining their equanimity could European women control and supervise their servants.[31] Behavior toward the servants should be calm and self-possessed, never angry, but always resolute and superior. One should not express complaints in the form of heavy-handed scolding. Or as Kloppenburg-Versteegh formulated it: "Remember not to speak to the servants when in anger: in the first place you will not impress them; in the second place you will upset yourself, while the servant might ridicule your words.[32]

This emotionology—the culturally defined range of permitted emotions—coincided with Javanese distinctions between "refined" and "crude or blunt" behavior. It reflected, too, the cultural ideals of the white colonial upper class of that period, which exacted the same attitude from women toward husband and children.[33] For European women anger was the least appropriate of all emotions, since it would lower white prestige, and to bolster prestige was one of the most important tasks of colonial wives. It was the primary reason to have servants because manual work by Europeans would undermine their dignity; the concern with prestige was also the main motivation behind proper and restrained behavior and acted as an incentive to learn the servants' language and culture. Just like men in the world outside, women should maintain white prestige within the domestic sphere.

Of course there were Dutch and Eurasian women in the Indies who were genuinely interested in the society and the people among whom they lived. But these women were the exception rather than the rule. And their curiosity was met only to a limited extent by the Colonial School for Girls and Women in The Hague, founded in 1920. This school demonstrated a similar ambivalence of orientalism and familization. As an institutionalized alternative to earlier short courses on tropical hygiene for women going abroad, the school formalized a new pragmatism: the growing need for hygiene and medicalization as well as the necessity for a more professional approach to women's domestic obligations. Both forms of pragmatism were exported to the Tropics. Between 1921 and 1938 approximately a thousand women followed the school's three-month curriculum in tropical hygiene and medicine, food preparation, ethnology, and Malay.[34]

Behavior toward servants formed part of the lessons in home economics. On the one hand, the school provided its pupils with the negative images of Kloppenburg-Versteegh, whose 1913 book was the main text on domestic servants. On the other, the school depicted Indonesians, painted so often in "unnecessarily somber" terms, as completely different people but "not less" worthy than the Dutch.[35] Although servants did not figure prominently in the curriculum, the school's success was attributed to its efforts to increase the knowledge of the language and the habits of servants. It achieved its goal of assuaging unnecessary fears of the strange surroundings, "of natives, wild beasts and serpents [sic]" that awaited the students in the Indies. As former pupils reported, servants were "not absolute strangers" to Dutch females newly arrived in the Indies: "The idea of necessary contact with the silent, dark population of their future country no longer seems ominous, since we have learned to understand the language and the religion and know how to respect it." [36]

But the Colonial School wanted to do more. It wanted to prepare Dutch women for the "beautiful and educational" task they faced in Indies society and to make them "pioneers" in medical care, by stepping outside the narrow confines of their Indies home. The image of self engendered in these Dutch women was one of active "mothering." Mothers in the Indies, especially those in the Outer Regions, were held responsible not only for their own family but also for lots of other families, including those of their domestics, especially in cases of illness. The school wanted to teach women "how they could be a helpmate and an adviser to them and for other natives in their surroundings." [37] Embracing the ideas of the Ethical Policy, the school should raise "women's consciousness of her future, her commission, her calling, when she possesses the means to find the way to the soul of the people she is going to live with . . . when she feels that she also has a national task, that is to create bonds of appreciation and devotion between the people of the Netherlands and the people of the Indonesian archipelago." [38]

It was this larger framework of mothering that incorporated white women into the realm of colonial domination; it enlisted them in the "ethical" colonial project and diminished the boundaries between the home and colonial society at large. To married European women, servants embodied this society in the first place. The Colonial School's ideology suggested that the task of white women was broader and nobler than being enclosed in the house. It might even convert the housewife's role into an attractive occupation, endowing her day-to-day existence with an honorable social purpose. In this discourse we find again a familial rhetoric, in close, if problematic, harmony with the otherness of domestic servants. This female discourse was completely in tune with the male-dominated political rhetoric of twentieth-century Dutch colonial society, which represented the colonized Indonesian as a family member to be educated but also as a totally different other.

Race, class, and gender, "the axes along which inequalities of power between men and women [and between colonizer and colonized] are organized and maintained," each played their own role in this discourse.[39] Domestic servants were to a large extent desexualized. Europeans scarcely distinguished between male and female domestics. They tended to treat servants as an amorphous, ungendered group in which only the babu might be granted a special place, since she, due to her devotion to the children, entered the family circle most intimately. While perhaps replicating the fluency of sexual markers that prevailed in Javanese culture, Europeans' undifferentiated attitudes also expressed the authors' Victorian prudery and their lack of interest in the individual personalities of their subordinates. Neither did the women writers of household manuals take into account the class differences between employers and employees; in fact, they rarely commented on this subject.[40] However, the racial otherness of servants figured most prominently in the discourse, which the manuals' authors articulated as a difference of culture and education.

In sum, we find double messages in the European manuals on domestics in the Indies: they expressed both distance and nearness, unreliability and loyalty, and represented servants as orientalized others as well as family intimates. This female discourse reflected male colonial discussions about Indonesians as members of the family of man to be educated or as fundamentally different creatures. The rhetoric on servants betrayed the deeply ambivalent attitude of Dutch women and men toward their Indonesian surroundings in general and their Indonesian servants of different race and culture in particular. Servants, both male and female, were psychologically and ideologically kept at a distance, in glaring contrast to their daily proximity. It was this nearness, undeniable and unchangeable, as well as the experience of being dependent on Indonesian servants that, paradoxically, stimulated the ideology (and practice) of distance. Mistress and servants were tied together in an ambiguous relationship; their lives were interwoven in a most intimate manner.[41] This intimacy constituted one side of the employer-servant relationship. The other side of the coin revealed European power, prestige, and superiority, which produced the subconscious efforts to establish a safe distance from that part of the Indonesian population that touched Europeans' bodies and souls.

It is significant that literature about Indonesian servants published in the Netherlands during World War II tended to accentuate the rhetoric of the family more strongly than before. During this period of national trauma and the outspoken racism of Nazi ideology, former Indies residents apparently idealized the colonial relationship, exalting the nation's colonial record of harmonious coexistence of different races, within the home and beyond.[42]

In practice, being a white or Eurasian housewife in the Indies was to reign over the known (a house) and the unknown (servants). It meant being armed with a firm faith in Western superiority and European conceptions of hygiene and education. It entailed an adaptation to tropical circumstances and Indonesian habits, which often remained incomprehensible and frightening. This created the psychological tensions and contradictory attitudes among most colonial employers that Javanese servants had to endure on a daily basis.

CHILDREN'S LITERATURE

How were these double messages translated into children's literature, if at all? What visions of the other did Dutch children in the Indies absorb? Children's fiction incorporated those values and ideals about colonial society that European middle-class writers of children's novels considered important enough to pass on to the younger generation. This literature emphasized how it should be, rather than how it actually was.[43] Hence, children's fiction can be used as an entry into adolescents' perceptions of the nature of colonial society and its inhabitants. Like domestic manuals, this genre can be excavated as a source which yields information on Dutch colonial attitudes toward servants.

Indies children's fiction—Dutch books that told stories about the life and adventures of European girls in the Indonesian archipelago—was thoroughly colonial. Editors in the Netherlands dominated the Indies market and determined the themes and characters of the genre. Because of the limited demand in the Indies, very few books—only about 4 percent—were actually published in colonial Java. Authors were predominantly of totok origin, born in the Netherlands. With an occasional exception, children's books written by Indonesians were not published during the prewar period. In the 1930s there were virtually no books for Indonesian children in Malay or Javanese, except for the editions of the government's Commission for Popular Reading Material.

This commission published stories from the shadow puppet theater and Indonesian legends as well as translations of European fairy tales and children's classics.[44]

The subject matter and themes of this literary genre were colonial as well. Children's books portrayed Dutch colonial society as a stable and enduring world. Narratives about Dutch colonial history—such as the early modern period of the East Indies Company or the Dutch colonial war against the inhabitants of Aceh in north Sumatra of the late nineteenth century—figured prominently. However, children's books rarely included a discussion of contemporary politics or the urgent reality of an Indonesian nationalist movement. Instead, Indonesian culture was most often conveyed to children in the form of entertaining fairy tales or legends; such publications gave them a sadly limited view of Indonesian society in general. Java's glorious nature was present in lyrical descriptions of rejuvenating holidays in the island's cool mountain air. Indonesian children as central characters figured only in tales about missionaries or those written by a few progressive writers. In books for adolescent girls, the protagonist was almost always a Dutch girl in the Indies. Some novels depicted Indo-European girls, but quantitatively they constituted a minority.[45]

Indies literature for girls conformed to the general pattern of Dutch children's fiction in the early twentieth century. Children's books were hortatory or ethical rather than aesthetic: they communicated a rigid set of moral prescriptions. As an Indies government report stated in 1920, "If a book has an eye-opening, reinforcing, and comforting effect, if it has touched your conscience, if it has reconciled you to your work, your duties, your surroundings, to nature, to people . . . then you have read a good book." The report went on to say that a good book "arouses loving thoughts and noble deeds; a bad book . . . engenders doubt."[46]

Books for adolescent girls were even more specifically morally upright and "good." They described reconciliation and compromise as the proper solution to all conflicts, whether personal problems—such as the hot-tempered girl who evolved, in due course, into a serene wife and devoted mother—or problems within the family. The plot often consisted of a stereotypical narrative: the death of either a mother or father—or a beloved brother—constituted a crucial moment; this tragic event offered a young girl a new vision, albeit a poignant one, of personal growth and reconciliation. Presumably, death endowed a children's story with emotional depth; it allowed the heroine to cope with real grief and show her readers that she could confront misfortune by adjusting herself to a painful emotional loss.

Not surprisingly, children's literature from the interwar period extolled conventional gender roles and a Victorian ideal of marriage. A Dutch mother was routinely depicted as being at home and functioning as the emotional center of the family. Kindness and friendship characterized relations between the parents. Novels for girls conjured up girls who loved and respected their parents as friends and tutors. Although some female protagonists yearned for a career, such stories for teenage girls ended often with the dictum that "the most beautiful role for a woman is that of wife and mother" [47]

Similar to the household manuals, the genre's portrayal of race relations was cloaked in ambivalence. Most books featured totok families as protagonists, who denounced discrimination; however, such renunciations did not involve a racial prejudice toward Indonesians but focused on the painful experiences of Eurasian children who were scorned by whites. Personal interactions between Europeans and Indonesians were restricted to relations with servants or with Javanese mothers. In this literary genre a silent Javanese mother of an Indo-European daughter exhibited nothing but admiration for her light-skinned children. In many novels' final unraveling, however, such Indo children wished to treat their native mothers with respect, even though they felt they should live with their white relatives after their father's death. [48]

SERVANTS IN CHILDREN'S LITERATURE

In youth literature the representation of servants was situated within traditional, Europe-oriented families. Small wonder, then, that the rhetoric of the family prevailed. In one of the most popular books, *De Canneheuveltjes* (The Canneheuvel family)—published in 1912 and reprinted four times in the 1920s and 1930s—Marie Ovink-Soer portrayed servants as the natural friends of children. [49] The babu Tjidem took them for walks to visit her mother in the village, where the youngest dreamed about being a buffalo boy when he was older. Servants took part in all the games at a birthday party. Having to leave them behind when the family returned to Holland was a painful experience, especially for the youngest, because babu Tjidem had saved his life during the same earthquake that killed his mother.

Race relationships were depicted as most harmonious. There was a gentle cooperation between the new stepmother and the seamstress, who together created party costumes for the four children. The evil character was Chinese, not Indonesian. However, the novel clearly delineated the lines of authority. Succeeding several authoritarian European nurses and an indulgent Eurasian aunt, the new Dutch stepmother finally brought order into the household: "She did not rule but guided and advised, did miracles with a soft, appropriately spoken word, both in the contact with family members and with servants." [50]

The same mixture of familiarity and authority was repeated in many other books in this genre. The relationship of the Indo-European Dona Alve with the servants was even more natural and close, for the babu was her aunt.[51] In *Kitty's leed en vreugde* (Kitty's sorrow and joy) the Dutch high school student Kitty deplored the departure of the Ambonese girl-housekeeper Nel who had quickly become an integral member of the family. The children of a Dutch family in *Tussen sawah's en bergen* (Between rice fields and mountains) were close to their servants, whom they found waiting for them after their return from European leave. These servants organized a ritual meal for the new house, at which the father invited the children "to make this house a good one for everybody, also for the servants." [52] The ideal representation of harmonious race relations ended with one of the children, after a holiday on a tea plantation in the mountains, wishing to become a planter himself. The message of these books was clear: the glorious Indies would function as a permanent home country for Europeans.

But the genre communicated other messages as well. In *Een moeilijk jaar voor de Van Heerdentjes* (A difficult year for the Van Heerden family), the widowed father admitted that he continued to yearn for Holland: "In spite of all those Indies years I have always had the strong feeling that we do not belong here." [53] In this novel we find more distance and superiority toward the servants. The latter may "love Nonna Elly, but native servants are just like small children: one has to keep a tight rein on them." [54] As prescribed in the manuals, the oldest girl, who took the deceased mother's place, washed and fed the twin babies herself. Servants were not allowed to do so.

Adults' accusation of babus, who spoiled and overindulged Dutch children, had its resonances in children's literature, but only mildly so in the books under review. A more prominent theme was admiration for servants' loyalty such as in *Ams houdt van Indië* (Ams loves the Indies). This book, published in the Netherlands in 1941, summarized many aspects of the underlying ideology of both the household manuals and fiction for teenagers. The novel was highly informative on totok family life in Semarang; it is also typically Dutch in its focus on the coziness and intimacy of the family.[55] The fifteen-year-old high school student Ams, the oldest of four children, was born in the Indies, where her father was a businessman. Servants functioned as integral figures in the narrative. At first glance, the book seems to convey a natural and relaxed contact between Dutch children and servants. But a variety of ambivalent images of servants resurface. Should the youngest learn Malay from the servants? Did the babu pamper her? In a long dialogue between Ams and her mother—who remained alive in this book—the latter explained that as a totok she had been afraid that this might happen, which made her decide not to hire a nanny when Ams was born. The mother, in fact, confessed her earlier racism: "I still had such an antipathy toward the natives, and the idea that one would touch your dear pink skin with its brown hands made me rebellious. What a nonsense, Ams!"[56] Illness, however, forced her to give up on her refusal to hire a babu.

Relations with servants appeared to be easy and relaxed. However, if we look at the story with Toni Morrison's eyes, we see other "black perspectives."[57] Turning points in the plot evolve around the mistakes made by servants or other Indonesians. Because the driver had forgotten to put on the car's hand brake, the toddler and babu Roes, while playing in it, caused the car to start moving. Had it not been for the resolute behavior of the second son, who jumped on the car's hood and managed to reach the wheel, they certainly would have crashed. When the mother was ill, servants became unruly; the gardener tried to break into the house, but Ams, warned by Roes, prevented the burglary. The novel featured the servants as the ones who made the errors, while courage, as a uniquely European attribute, was inscribed in Ams and her brother.

Orientalism and paternalism are not absent either. Father provided the servants with their salaries; he also taught them how to save money.

At difficult moments—for instance, when the driver, being ashamed of the near-accident, asked permission to leave—the father confessed that "they are difficult people, those natives." [58] Such attitudes of paternalism and orientalism are expressed at moments when Javanese behavior—its withdrawal, its silences—contrasted most strongly with Dutch directness, and when European openness was not understood. At the story's end a more concealed form of paternalism clearly emerges.

When Ams and her brother Wim went for a walk in the mountains during a long holiday, they found a Javanese boy who had fallen in the woods and rescued him. They discovered that he was a classmate of Ams, named Soedarso, who in turn realized that he owed his life to her. After meeting his uncle, a Javanese civil servant, Ams's mother admitted, although she had already lived in the Indies for fifteen years, that "it is for the first time . . . that I have met such a Javanese. Except for our servants we are not in contact with Javanese families." [59] If we read the story as a metaphor, the messages are clear: brown is where the danger lurks, whether in a runaway car or in a dishonest servant; white educates and even saves lives, for which brown should be grateful.

Cultural association and the harmonious coexistence of both races constituted the final imagery of this novel. Together the children, Ams, Wim, and Soedarso, who had recovered from his accident, went for their last holiday walk. The following conversation took place:

"We have a very nice country indeed," Ams said, with satisfaction. "But this is not your country," Soedarso said calmly. "This is not my country?" Ams, replied with indignation. "Holland is your country," said Soedarso while looking at Ams, a little shy about the effect of his words. "Holland," said Ams, "Holland is the country of Mother and Father, they belong there. But not me, I belong here." In her excitement Ams got up and stretched out her arms. "I belong here," she repeated, "I was born here. I love these mountains and the people here!" Soedarso looked at Ams as she stood on the mountaintop and he felt a deep sympathy for this blond girl from a different race, who had accepted him so simply as a comrade and now also made his country her own.

This dialogue appeared at the end of the story. It reflected the strong identification Dutch children felt toward the country of their birth; like many of their parents, they could only distance themselves with great difficulty. The quote itself is utterly colonial. The idea of cultural or political association was expressed by appropriating the Javanese mountains and therefore the Indonesian archipelago, without asking the original inhabitants (Soedarso) for their opinion. Even stronger: the Dutch author inscribed into the Javanese boy a tacit agreement with her gesture. Or as Soedarso "softly" replied to her outburst: "I did not know . . . you considered it that way." The rhetoric of the family implied ownership of country and people without having to solicit the opinions of Indonesians.

If we compare the views on servants in these children's novels with those from the manuals, more similarities than differences appear. More than the manuals, youth literature stressed harmony and family; its messages of difference were more implicit than in domestic literature. Class issues were not touched upon; they were subsumed in the ideology of the family in which everybody has his own natural place in the hierarchy. Differences in gender were not acknowledged either, although women servants might sometimes play a more prominent role, since they were closer to the family. Racism was rarely explicitly stated; at most it was described as an emotion that belonged to the distant past. However, all differences, especially those of class and race, are subtly present when we read these stories at a more abstract level. The relationship between employer and indigenous servant is not only illustrative of the ambivalent coexistence of two races within the household but also becomes symbolic of the colonial relationship itself: Dutch masters supposedly educated and uplifted the Indonesian population to a higher level, while Indonesians were seldom addressed directly.

CONCLUSIONS

Female discourses on servants in the prewar Indies consisted of two ingredients: orientalism and otherness versus nearness and familialization. It reflected the male political discourse of the period, which had incorporated both of these aspects as well. Although colonialism as a practice of institutional dominance may have been primarily a male affair, European women were not separated from it. The ideology of the colonial state as the white paterfamilias of many different races was derived from the home situation and was expressed in metaphors relating to the household. Tacitly, gender was included. Explicitly, European women occupied their place in the colonial structure as colonial parents or guardians in charge of servants, their first pupils.

Domestic service thus became another trope for the colonial relation, being both included in, and excluded from, the colonial family. Since the family at that moment of history was hierarchically structured—as it still is in many parts of our contemporary world—the ideology of the family gave colonial masters, whether male or female, a superior position and the right to rule, both inside and outside the household.

Were European women in the Indies more racist than European men? It seems doubtful. The discourse on servants clearly harbored racist overtones. European women displayed ambivalent attitudes and formulated contradictory messages in the private sphere, which was culturally defined as their space. Men, however, employed the same rhetoric in the political and commercial arena that belonged to them. Was female racism perhaps more painful because it was expressed at home, in the informal setting of the family, where personal feelings were closer to the surface and abstract political structures could not conceal inhumanity? Even there, racism was not a female prerogative. In many novels, such as *Ams houdt van Indië*, it was the father who emphasized the otherness of servants.

Otherness and familialization seem to be paradoxical opposites. Difference and nearness created complicated and contradictory models of relationship. Manuals warned housewives about the first; literature educated girls about the second experience. But orientalism and familialization may have been indissolubly related to each other, woven into a yin and yang entanglement. On the one hand, the nearness of indispensable servants and the average European family's dependence on them caused a psychological reaction of distancing, in terms of spatial design as well as in symbolic categorization. On the other hand, migration to the colonies introduced newcomers to a frightening world. This otherness could only be mastered by making it, both literally and figuratively, familiar. And what is more familiar than the family? However, too much familiarity required simultaneous distancing—once again. Dutch colonial residents were caught, it seemed, in this vicious cycle. Female rhetoric about servants illustrated the paradox of the Dutch colonial mentality, which in the early twentieth century moved between the opposites of domination grounded in social distance and development policies that incorporated Indonesians into a family model. Orientalism and familial ideology belonged to each other as opposite sides of the same colonial coin.

Of both attitudes, the rhetoric of the family might seem the more progressive; it had its shortcomings, however. It reduced servants to the status of children, who had to behave well, to do what they were told, and to be "clean, honest, compliant, and capable."[60] It had its own hierarchy and was used in a progressive as well as in a conservative mode. Moreover, family rhetoric masked many differences, especially those of race, class, and gender, while obscuring inequalities of power.

It is the quality of concealment or obscurity of this rhetoric, which made (and still makes) its use politically worthless, or even dangerous, for subordinate groups trying to delineate their (op)position. This criticism of familial ideology is not new. It has been expressed again in recent years with regard to Asian countries such as the independent Indonesian state or to the modern industrial organization of Japan.[61] In the case of modern Indonesia, we may conclude that while the current Suharto government's rhetoric on the family does not have its roots in colonial discourse, it has been strongly reinforced by the ideology of Western colonialism.

8. ISLAM, GENDER, AND IDENTITIES IN THE MAKING OF FRENCH ALGERIA, 1830–1962

Julia Clancy-Smith

The peculiar settler society that came to maturity in Algeria during the Third Republic was initially the work of General Thomas-Robert Bugeaud, who conquered and then governed the country during the 1840s. Despite his military vocation, Bugeaud's grand vision for Algeria entailed conquest by the plow as well as the sword.[1] The general advocated luring French yeoman farmers across the sea and implanting them on Algerian soil as a sort of nursery for the later flowering of France's civilization. Nevertheless, the general observed that "the Arabs elude us because they conceal their women from our gaze."[2] The remark regarding Arab women was quite uncharacteristic of both Bugeaud and the period in which he lived. Women were not yet explicitly part of the imperial project—that would have to wait until pacification rendered Algeria secure enough for European women to settle permanently and produce offspring.[3]

From Bugeaud's era until the late nineteenth century, colonial observers of North African society employed two principal measurements to gauge native inferiority—political institutions and levels of technology. These measurements, however, served as mere indicators of indigenous cultural underdevelopment relative to Europe. The wellspring of all Algerian social relations was Islam—the Islam of the militant Sufi brotherhoods and charismatic rural rebels. From 1830 on, colonial administrators wrote obsessively about political Islam, regarded as primarily a religion of revolt and resistance.[4] As military dominion gave way to civilian rule and moral subjugation after 1870, the status of Muslim women became increasingly significant for judging the culturally different, subordinate other.

Accordingly, the dominant colonial discourse regarding an active, masculine, seditious Islam came to be accompanied by a parallel discourse about an unchanging, monolithic Islam which undergirded all family structures and sociosexual relations. In the imperial imagination, behind the high walls of the Arab household, women suffered oppression due to Islamic laws and customs. As the colonial gaze fixed progressively upon Muslim women between 1870 and 1900, Islam was moved by many French writers from the battlefield into the bedroom.

In this same period a profound transmutation occurred among the European settlers; from a quarrelsome Mediterranean flotsam and jetsam, they grew into something new. By 1900 Maltese, Italian, French, and Spanish settlers had intermarried, produced numerous progeny, and sunk roots deep into Algeria's unwilling land. Between 1872 and 1927 the number of Europeans residing in French Algeria's departments soared from 245,000 to 833,000. During the Third Republic they assumed a novel collective identity whose political project was proclaimed by the notion of *Nous Algériens*—"We the Algerians." This ideology held that the European Algerians constituted a cultural race distinct from both the inferior Muslims and the racially degenerate, even effeminate French in the metropole.[5] Simultaneously, a second proto-nationalist community was in gestation. Algerian Muslim nationalists, educated in French institutions, began to campaign vigorously for expanded rights under French law, while arguing that these rights could coexist with Islamic legal codes governing personal status, particularly marriage.[6]

This chapter argues that the construction of French Algeria was as much the forging of a gaze—or spectrum of gazes fixed upon Muslim women—as it was the assembling of mechanisms for political and economic control. Moreover, that gaze, its discourses and representations, constituted a critical force in the complex cultural politics of French Algeria as well as in the metropole's relations with its fractious African territory.[7] By 1900 issues of sex and gender, particularly the status of Arab women, came to be privileged in debates over Algerian male suffrage. Manipulated as a political and rhetorical strategy, female status was marshaled to refute the notion that the Arabs' assimilation to France was desirable or even possible. Thus, the flood of literature—official pronouncements, popular fiction, pseudoscientific tracts, etc.—

ostensibly devoted to Muslim women must be read in another way. The
Arab woman, as represented either visually or discursively, functioned
as an inverted image or negative trope for confirming the European
settlers' distinct cultural identity, while denying the political existence
of the other.

In the metropole notions of France's civilizing mission in North Africa also were transformed as French men and women, often influenced
by domestic social reform movements, increasingly directed their attention toward Arab females. It was not accidental that the presumably
degraded state of colonized women became an arena for public debate,
or that colonial representations of the female cultural other, eroticized
and offered for public view, proliferated at the turn of the century. Yet
visions of empire and of the colonized as seen from Paris were not
necessarily in harmony with realities on the ground in French Algeria.
Rather, a triangular set of shifting relations and struggles existed between the metropole, the settler community, and the indigenous population. Finally, a supreme irony emerged by 1900: both societies in
French Algeria, European and native, came to evaluate each other's cultural worth in terms of the female question.

TEXTS AND IMAGES IN THE IMAGINING OF FRENCH
ALGERIA, 1830–1900

Military authorities first raised the issue of women in bureaucratic
or semiofficial writings after roughly 1850, although erratically and
obliquely.[8] Increasingly, however, nonofficial writers began to have a
voice in the unfolding debate, that is, Europeans outside of the colonial
hierarchy, who roamed around North Africa in search of material for
travel accounts, quasi-scientific works, or sensationally sexual fiction
masquerading as authentic travel narratives. Also by 1900 European
women created a voice and literary space for themselves by writing
about indigenous women or describing harem visits.[9] In some cases this
literature was also subverted to argue for various social causes back in
the metropole. One striking example is the Parisian feminist writer
and activist Hubertine Auclert (1848–1914), who published *Les femmes
arabes en Algérie* (Arab women in Algeria) in 1900.[10] By the start of this
century nonofficial participants in French colonialism played an ever

greater part in the representation of the colonized and indirectly in imperial policies.[11]

Throughout the nineteenth century nontextual forms of representation also increased as the supply of, and demand for, paintings and then photography of strange and wondrous peoples swelled in Europe.[12] As a result, an implicit as well as explicit dialogue emerged between texts devoted to indigenous societies, on the one hand, and visual material, on the other. This complicit dialogue, however, shifted as the issue of identity came to the foreground among the settler community in French Algeria. In his disturbing study *The Colonial Harem*, Malek Alloula traces the preoccupation with the veiled or unclothed Arab female body as depicted in salacious photographs and postcards.[13]

These postcards, available to the French public from the 1890s, were the product of profound changes in the way that the colonizer looked at, and ruled over, the colonized. Lurid photographs and oil canvases of Arab prostitutes in seductive poses supplanted the older, folkloric representations of women in their luxuriant native costumes done by French military officers often sympathetic to indigenous society. Before the probing, manipulative camera, Algerian women were transformed into nudes whether robed or disrobed. The ideal spectator was the European male in Algeria or France, who was denied any contact with respectable Muslim women. Photographic images of these woman were contrived to provide visually erotic access to the inaccessible.[14]

The camera's masculine lens, however, had not always portrayed Algeria's inhabitants in this manner. The first uses of photography dated from the late 1850s when the photographer Moulin arrived to celebrate the French army's exploits. These were principally in the genre of "military manhood"; nonetheless, they cannot be divorced from a more general desire to capture local native color. Yet by 1900, photography, for all its proclaimed documentary precision, nurtured the sexual commodification of the Arab woman.[15] In the gradual transformations of visual representations, a prostitutionalization of the Muslim female can be discerned.

The same process can be detected in some fictive travel literature, such as Hector France's *Musk, Hashish, and Blood*, which, judged by the standards of the day, constituted pornography. Composed sometime after 1854, the novel, in guise of a travel account, opens with the imagined rape murder of a young Algerian woman. By framing his story as a true narrative, the author legitimated the illicit sex for a prurient European audience The text then chronicled the author's sexual escapades as he sleeps with the daughters of the Ouled Nail, a Saharan tribe some of whose nubile women marketed their sexual favors to amass a dowry. The fact that this work was translated into English and privately published both in London and by the Panurge Press in New York around 1900 in an American edition limited to 2,000 copies is significant.[16] It suggests that French colonial representations of the Arab Muslim woman as hooker and harlot had begun to feed into the underground pornographic press of the English-speaking world.

The existence of the Ouled Nail tribe, with its unusual sexual practices, was known from the first decades of the conquest era. Only later did abundant studies of these "libertine Saharan beauties" appear in the colonial literature, cloaked in the respectable mantle of semiscientific ethnography.[17] By then the designation "daughter of the Ouled Nail" had become a code word for prostitute—as it continues to be today.[18] Finally, in the Universal Exposition held in Paris in 1900, female dancers supposedly from the Ouled Nail tribe were displayed in the Algerian pavilion as a sort of colonial trophy to titillate the jaded Parisian public, which by then no longer found the older standard erotica from North Africa all that scintillating.[19]

A related question regarding textual or visual representations of women and gender in the colonial setting is that of how European females figured in that literature. Official discussions of colonization schemes for both Algeria and Tunisia, while delving into fertility and peopling, hardly mention the women settlers' role in productive or reproductive processes.[20] The relative absence of female settlers in much of the official colonial literature is intriguing, particularly because gendered constructs permeated the cultural grammar of French imperialism. The mother country or *la mère patrie* was a universally utilized concept employed to translate the relationship between rulers and ruled into a language expressing maternal bonds between mother and child.[21] Algerian Muslims, who enrolled in the French army as soldiers, were assured, "If you serve France as you would cherish your own mother, she will treat you like a son."[22]

French Algeria thus appears as an imperial man's world even as

Mediterranean women arrived in large numbers by 1850.[23] The official silence regarding the presence of European women in the country during the conquest decades can be explained by the social origins of the first female settlers and the professions open to them. Although it was rarely admitted, European females served as prostitutes or consorts for the troops as part of colonial policy. In the 1840s General La Moricière ordered the commanding general in Tlemcen to "proceed with the recruitment and settlement of a female 'personnel' who can cater to the pleasures, if not the health, of the men."[24] Apart from a few furtive references in military correspondence to either organized or freelance trafficking in sexual favors by European women, the only published inquiry into the colonial sex trade is Edouard Duchesne's *De la prostitution dans la ville d'Alger depuis la conquête* (On prostitution in the city of Algiers since the conquest), which appeared in 1853.[25]

SEXUAL LIAISONS AND THE DANGERS OF CULTURAL HYBRIDITY

Duchesne's work reveals the implicit sociosexual attitudes as well as anxieties characteristic of colonial officials in this period. The author, a Parisian health official, espoused the conventional view of medical authorities at the time that female prostitution resulted in "the degradation of the physical and moral force of those who engage in it."[26] However, in a population with a high percentage of single males, it was a necessary evil because without female prostitution "a greater danger may occur." That "greater danger" was, of course, homosexuality.[27] The threat of homosexual activity by European males was higher in Algeria because "homosexuality is rampant" in the native society, according to Duchesne.

In characterizing North African men as prone to homoeroticism, Duchesne echoed universal Western beliefs about the innately perverse nature of oriental sexuality. He explained Arab Muslim deviance by invoking natural conditions in Africa—"in this [hot] climate, passions run higher"—and socioreligious conventions. Because Algerian women were covered and secluded, and "young Algerian men are so handsome and go about in public unveiled, side by side with veiled females, homosexuality is thereby encouraged."[28] While Duchesne and other colonial authorities were truly alarmed by the public health crisis, particularly for the French army with tens of thousands of soldiers, there lurked another, perhaps larger, menace behind the issue of female prostitution: that of sexual relations between European and indigenous men.

The presence of large numbers of Arab female prostitutes in Algiers was striking to Duchesne, who explained this by pointing to the debased moral state of the indigenous population, the product of Islamic legal and sociosexual practices. North African girls were nubile when very young and were married off at an unnaturally early age to protect virginity and family honor. "Sexual activity on the part of young people enervates them and leads to the degradation of the race; this also leads to premature aging." Arab women's habit of frequent bathing, their laziness, and early pregnancies rendered them elderly before their time.[29] Their spouses, lusting after younger flesh, divorced or repudiated them after a few years of marriage. Left with little means of support, these women had no other recourse than the brothels of the cities where large numbers of colonial men were stationed. Thus, Islamic law and traditions increased the pool of public women.

However, the author widened his critique beyond Arab Muslim society when he noted the "extreme repugnance of women of the Midi [i.e., Mediterranean world] for manual work," a northern European stereotype frequently invoked in portrayals of not only North African females but also Sicilian and other Mediterranean women.[30] In addition, education was entirely lacking among the native women, and "education is the best weapon against vice and sin."[31] Duchesne did invoke "misery," the loss of native wealth due to the French conquest, and the destruction of native handicrafts and industries as additional causes for prostitution. No suitable work existed in the public sector for honest but poor Muslim women, whereas in France impoverished women earned money by being seamstresses or laundresses.[32] Ironically, Duchesne's awareness of the role of poverty and ignorance in forcing native women into prostitution contradicted his representation of Arab Muslim society as distinctly perverse in the domain of sexuality and morals.

What really worried colonial officials was not only uncontrolled

French postcard made from a photograph of veiled Algerian Arab Muslim women in the narrow streets of the Casbah in the city of Algiers ca. 1900

prostitution but also the increasingly promiscuous promiscuity—cultural as well as sexual—in the capital and other cities with large European populations. As Duchesne pointed out, "In looking at the question of nationality and prostitution, it is probably certain that the French soldiers seek out Arab women due to their strangeness and newness."[33] Not only did these cross-cultural sexual encounters threaten political barriers between ruler and ruled, but also moral boundaries were at risk: "the exchange of vice and methods of sexual debauchery between indigenous and European prostitutes" was the consequence of the mixing of the populations.[34] As Stoler and others have persuasively argued, women in the colonies were fundamental to erecting and maintaining social ramparts based upon race and gender; sexual relations with the indigenous population sabotaged the colonial pecking order.[35]

THE ARAB MUSLIM WOMAN IN THE EYES
OF OFFICIAL FRENCH COLONIALISM

Duchesne's study of one dimension of sexuality stands out as an exception. In most official writing on Muslim women during this earlier period, indigenous female sexuality seems to have been considered beyond the pale of polite discussion. Besides, until late in the century, the military establishment monopolized the colonial discourse on indigenous society; pacification rather than sexual morality was the most important consideration. Nevertheless, from the 1840s on, some French officers, particularly those attached to the Arab Bureau, described, frequently in textual asides, the native women they discerned against the larger backdrop of North African culture. Largeau's *Le Sahara algérien* (The Algerian Sahara) is representative. In this quasi-ethnographic study, he offered a careful description of female costume worn in the desert, accompanied by detailed sketches. Women's desert garb was, however, but one of many other topics Largeau examined; the real purpose of his study was tribal political economy rather than the semiclosed universe of women.[36] Colonized women in the countless works from this particular colonial milieu and this era are an ethnographic curiosity among so many others. Visually and textually they functioned as appealing decorative objects; they had not yet been invested with an offensive or subversive aura.

When colonial male writers broached the topic of Muslim sexuality, they tended toward disquisitions about Arab men, believed to be "oversexed." The social consequences of exaggerated Arab male sexuality, symbolized by polygamy and the harem, were momentous for North African Muslim civilization. As Michel Chevalier, the Saint-Simonian writer, sermonized in 1865, "Polygamy in Algeria prevents the development of social institutions, social movement, refinement of usages, culture of the spirit, and the progress of arts, literature, and science."[37] His views on polygamy were later taken up by Auclert who declared that the practice of multiple wives led to "intellectual degeneracy."[38]

One of the first military officers to speak about—if not for—Algerian women, and to offer them up to European view, was Eugène Daumas (1802–1871). General Daumas went to Algeria in 1835 with the African army and soon acquired a profound knowledge of Arabic. Instrumental in organizing the Arab Bureau, Daumas's vocation as an interpreter of North African culture overshadowed his military career. From the 1840s until his death, he produced a large corpus of works on native society; in his writings, one can detect the outlines of what later became the French colonial ethnographer's craft.[39]

Daumas left behind a curious study entitled "La femme arabe" (The Arab woman), comprising fourteen chapters and 154 pages of ostensibly documentary material devoted solely to native women. To justify studying women, Daumas employed the language of Frédéric Le Play to argue that "it seems to me that in all the countries of the world the condition of woman allows us to evaluate the social state of a people, their mores and level of civilization. [Thus], it is extremely important, particularly for our domination of Algeria, to know where we stand on such a controversial subject, given the fact that women are viewed so differently [in native society]."[40]

Daumas was by no means the first European to decry the existence of polygamy, divorce, and repudiation in Islam—that tradition had its origins in medieval Christian polemics; nor was he the first to denounce what was seen as the universally abject moral, sexual, and social condition of Arab women.[41] Yet he appears to have been the earliest official to establish women as a distinct object of inquiry, worthy of systematic, scientific scrutiny. Moreover, Daumas was the first colonial writer to state explicitly the triangular relationship between knowledge, colonial domination, and the need to penetrate the hidden world of indigenous women.

Daumas's treatise raises two main issues: What rhetorical use does he make of Algerian women in discussing colonial rule? And, second, Why was his manuscript only published posthumously when issues of political identity had come to the foreground in French Algeria?

Significant was the fact that the author entitled his treatise "La femme arabe," which tends to reduce the cultural complexities of North African females to a single, textual monologue; moreover, Arab becomes, wrongly, synonymous with Muslim. Daumas's expository strategy for laying bare the condition of the Muslim woman, and thus of Algerian society as a whole, was fundamental to the emerging colonial ethnographic gaze. He traces her life cycle from birth and childhood through adolescence and marriage, ending with the rituals surrounding death.

This life-cycle strategy, which might be characterized as "womb to tomb," was subsequently taken up by numerous other French writers. (A second strategy, which became scholarly practice toward the end of the century, was to commence discussions of Muslim women with analyses of Islamic injunctions regulating female condition and status and then to demonstrate how practice diverged from Islamic legal prescriptions, particularly from any laws beneficial to women, such as those governing inheritance.)[42]

Daumas's proclaimed purpose in writing was "to tear off the veil that still covers the morals, customs, and beliefs" of Arab society.[43] Is there not a suggestion of rape here? Only by exposing what has previously been concealed can remedies be found for the "moral sickness" that the colonizer has diagnosed in North African Muslim society; naturally, the antidote was superior French civilization. Daumas warned his readers, if rather coyly, that he will be obliged to speak about sex, although the word itself is not used. This in turn raises the question of intended audiences. According to the general, his scientifically impartial work would be of practical use for statesmen and administrators as well as writers, artists, and scholars.[44]

Daumas noted that there were two schools of thought regarding the state of Muslim women. According to the first, woman is nothing but an "object of luxury": a sensual, indolent, and bored creature, caged like a bird in the harem. The second viewed woman as a servant or slave condemned by her husband to forced labor and, implicitly, coerced sex. Daumas then addressed the debate raging both in France and Algeria on assimilation versus association, which also had produced two irreconcilable stances. The first saw fusion between Christians and Muslims in Algeria as an idle dream; the second held that marriage between the "daughters of the vanquished" and the sons of the conqueror would result in an inevitable assimilation; eventually the entire Arab people would be uplifted.[45] Daumas, however, dismissed the second position as implausible, if not outright impossible.

In his role as ethnographer and voyeur, Daumas traced the informal education of the young Arab girl who, from early on, is taught "voluptuous behavior" and "flirtatious habits." These emphasized seductiveness yet contradicted the extreme social value placed upon female purity and virginity in Muslim culture. Assuming the mantle of ethnographic objectivity, Daumas's prurient gaze followed in narrative fashion the social and sexual biography of the Arab female. While remaining undetected, he invited his readers to peer through the keyhole of an urban Arab home or to lift up the tent flap of a Bedouin dwelling to behold the uneasy intimacy of the Muslim family.[46]

Because the Arabs' conception of love differed so fundamentally from European attitudes, marriage institutions offered the most insuperable barriers between French and Muslim. In detailing marriage ceremonies Daumas felt compelled to warn his readers about salacious material: "As the reader prepares to penetrate into the most intimate domain of Muslim society, may he show indulgence for customs which might be repugnant to European sensibilities."[47] Yet he disarmed potential critics by maintaining that the scientific aim of narrative keyhole viewing rendered the Arab family suitable for contemplation. After all, his study was based upon irrefutable textual and ethnographic evidence: his long, personal acquaintance with native society; passages from the Koran; and anecdotal material, popular proverbs, and folklore gathered on-site. It is important to note that most of his material was from pastoral-nomadic communities, largely in the Sahara, the only place where a French man could have had some contact, however limited, with indigenous females. Suggesting that class, region, and ethnicity made significant differences in female status and condition, Daumas in depicting the Arab woman nevertheless converted her into a totemic or formulaic construct: "There is nothing in Arab life—be it religion, honor, pleasure, danger, or fatigue—from which the idea of woman is absent."[48]

Daumas's work on women was completed toward the end of his life. He may have also had a bourgeois French audience in mind when writing the manuscript; otherwise warnings about indelicate material and justifications for discussions of sexuality would not have been necessary. Only in 1912 did the *Revue Africaine*, the paramount colonial journal devoted to things Algerian, publish his work—forty-one years after his death. Significantly, this volume contained no other articles devoted to women, although in his short introduction to "La femme arabe," Augustin Bernard justified the work's posthumous publication because "the indigenous [Algerian] family is still for us a closed sanctuary, forbidden to the gaze and investigations of the nonbeliever."[49] Its tardy appearance suggests that the motivations for publication were mainly polemical; Daumas's treatise offered additional evidence that the Algerians could never be politically assimilated to France due to the degraded status of Muslim females.

Although its early composition made Daumas's treatise atypical, it anticipated later official writing as well as the academic discipline of ethnography as practiced in North Africa. A number of colonial scholars, including Adrien Leclerc and Louis Milliot, who published legal studies of Muslim women in 1901 and 1910, respectively, drew upon Daumas's numerous writings, even though they did not always explicitly acknowledge their intellectual debt to the general.[50]

For Milliot, Leclerc, Depont, and other French administrators in the post-1871 era, the Arab woman functioned as a trope for indigenous Algerian culture. Increasingly that trope was deployed to demonstrate that the natives could neither absorb French civilization nor merit political or civil rights comparable to those enjoyed by the European settlers.[51] As French rule in the Maghrib entered its second century, *la femme arabe* became another way of talking about Islam—about the procreation of the Muslim family and, therefore, of a social order so utterly different as to make assimilation inconceivable.

Moreover, obsessions with Muslim women intersected with the colonial fixation on Islamic saint cults and Sufi orders. Both the Sufi order and Arab woman were partially or fully hidden from European view; their very concealment rendered them mysterious, alluring yet threatening. When discussing Sufism (Islamic mysticism) and native women, colonial writers employed metaphors of penetration, disrobing, and unveiling.[52] Nevertheless, the linkages between the Algerian Sufi brotherhoods and colonized women rested upon more than similar figures of speech or rhetorical devices. By 1900 an unspoken alliance had been concluded between the conservative leadership of the Algerian Sufi orders, representing popular Islam in the countryside, and the colonial regime. That alliance meant that efforts to improve the status of Muslim women encountered overt hostility on the part of colonial officials who argued that tampering with Islamic laws and customs shaping gender relations would incite co-opted religious leaders to rebellion.

Returning to the question of why Daumas's study was published when it was, a further hypothesis can be advanced. The appearance in

Paris of Auclert's provocative *Les femmes arabes*, and her spirited campaign from 1888 on to improve the condition, legal and otherwise, of Algerian women, may have been a factor. Auclert's work partially supported what Daumas asserted, while conversely arguing for assimilation in an era when colonial policymakers, for the most part, had renounced that objective for French Algeria.[53] Inadvertently, Auclert may have provided yet more ammunition for those influential turn-of-the-century colonial authorities on Muslim culture such as Octave Depont, who wrote in 1901 that "assimilation would necessitate the exclusive application of our laws and the adoption of our customs, which are diametrically opposed to the [natives'] social state, and this would undoubtedly breed revolution [among the Muslims]."[54]

By the turn of the century, female sexuality and gender, as well as the closely related question of race, become the favored rhetorical haunts of male writers, both in official and nonofficial discourse. In addition, European women writers seized upon the sexual oppression of Muslim women as a political cause. Hence, European men and women contributed to the gradual fusion of the emerging discipline of ethnography with the imperatives of colonial rule and to the mingling of the official world of French imperialism with the nonofficial realm. Representations of Muslim women shaped, in turn, the contours of a distinct French Algerian community acclaimed by the settlers as the nineteenth century drew to a close.

HUBERTINE AUCLERT, METROPOLE FEMINISM, AND ARAB WOMEN

Hubertine Auclert's entry into the emerging debate offers an intriguing site for exploring gender, colonial discourses, and the politics of identity in French Algeria. Auclert was the founder of the radical wing of the French feminist movement. She was born in 1848 into a family of provincial bourgeoisie from the Allier. At the age of sixteen, she entered a convent, the Sisters of Charity of Saint Vincent de Paul, but was asked to leave the order since the nuns characterized her as a bit demented. Auclert was not crazy but merely rebellious. Her father had been a dedicated republican who adhered to unpopular political principles and openly disagreed with established power. Auclert was truly her father's offspring; throughout her life she too espoused unpopular causes, the most unpopular of all being the enfranchisement of women in France and improvements in Muslim women's condition in Algeria. Indeed, these two projects were intimately connected in several ways: Auclert's proposals for Algerian women were the logical extensions of the "familial" or "maternalist feminism" that she had articulated for women in France.[55]

Auclert's militant public career to win the vote for French women began in 1873 when she left home for Paris. She mobilized the women's rights campaign through her organizations Droit des Femmes and Suffrage des Femmes. She founded and edited the first suffragist newspaper in France, *La Citoyenne*, providing most of the paper's financing and writing many of the articles herself. Auclert was also one of the "first feminists to practice civil disobedience."[56]

Auclert's decision to leave Paris and reside in Algeria permanently was somewhat fortuitous. Antonin Lévrier, Auclert's longtime lover, received a post as *juge de paix* in Frenda (Oran), while learning that his health was in jeopardy. Algeria's dry climate was to restore Lévrier's vitality. In July 1888 Auclert married Lévrier in Algiers, apparently under pressure from conservative elements in the European settler society. She spent four years in the country, living first in western Algeria, then in the oasis of Laghouat, and finally in the capital where her husband took an editorial position on the staff of *Le Radical Algérien*. During her Algerian interlude Auclert closely studied the daily lives of Arab women, keeping extensive written notes of her observations.[57] In 1892 she returned to Paris a widow; North Africa's climate had not saved her husband.

What sort of Algeria did the leader of French suffragists encounter? While still in Paris, Auclert had anticipated finding an "earthly paradise"; she found quite the opposite. Racism, anti-Semitism, and bigotry were rife and undisguised; the politics of exclusion and constructions of identity among the Mediterranean settler population increasingly made Muslim women (and Jews) the objects of scorn and contempt. In the first pages of her study, she stated that "in Algeria there are very few Frenchmen who would classify the Arabs as part of the human race."[58]

Racial politics and discourse in French North Africa differed somewhat from those in European colonies in sub-Saharan Africa.[59] Clear-cut racial boundaries between colonizer and colonized did not always exist in Algeria; the vast majority of Arab-Berber peoples was of similar racial stock to the conquering Europeans, many of whom were from nearby Mediterranean countries or islands. Moreover, throughout the nineteenth century northern Europeans frequently characterized the Catholic Maltese and Sicilians as being of the "African race." [60] Thus, race had been a highly unstable category of difference in early French North Africa, and a multiplicity of meanings and behaviors could be associated with it. In the hands of colonial apologists in Algeria, the classifications of "Arab" and "Muslim" became a cultural-religious racial grouping deployed to deny even the most basic rights to the indigenous population. As Prochaska observed: "The formation of a colonial society recognizably Algerian occurred between 1890 and 1914. It included all the Europeans—French, Italian, Spanish, Maltese—and excluded Jews as well as Muslim Algerians. Contemporary observers perceived a melting pot effect, a fusion of the European ethnic groups which resulted in a new 'race.'" [61] F. Dessoliers, one of numerous colonial publicists writing on race as constructed at that time, declared that in Algeria had been born "a new people, a race which is superior in intelligence and energy [to the French of the metropole]." [62]

Auclert noted the way in which this new race of Europeans calling Africa their homeland represented and thus treated the indigenous peoples: "In the eyes of foreigners, officials, Jews, settlers, and traders, the Arab, accorded less respect than his sheep, exists solely to be crushed. The dream [of the Europeans] is to push the Arab back into the desert in order to take from him what has not yet been taken. The French Algerians, who declare that fanaticism renders the Arabs uncivilizable, do everything possible to keep the Arabs in a state of ignorance so conducive to exploitation and domination." [63] And Auclert found a parallel between male prejudice against women as social and political beings and racial prejudice directed against the colonized. [64]

For Auclert the Arab woman symbolized all that was politically amiss in France's domination of North Africa. Her condition had been degraded, not ameliorated, by seventy years of French rule. Moreover, Auclert accused colonial officials of collusion with Arab males in respecting Islamic laws and customary practices, such as child marriage, the sale of brides, and polygamy, practices which rendered native females "little victims of Muslim debauchery."[65] Further evidence of complicity between conservative Muslim male elites and French administrators was provided by the lamentable state of education for Muslim girls. After 1861, colonial officials argued against state-supported instruction for indigenous females, claiming that schools were too costly and, worse, created a group of educated Arab Muslim women accepted by neither society.[66] Auclert's remarkably astute analysis attacked not only the European settler lobby and antiassimilationists but also the Arabophiles. Those few Europeans in Algeria who professed sympathy for Arab and Islamic culture paradoxically opposed modernization of indigenous society since modernity threatened to erode *le pittoresque Algérien* or "authentic, traditional" native life. If the Arabs appeared barbarous, France—French men—were to blame.

Many of the positions and causes advocated by Auclert in the metropole were introduced into her arguments on the moral duty to uplift the Arab women—to turn harem inmates into voters. If Arab men sought access to the ballot box, so did Arab females who also aspired to be assimilated—to become Frenchwomen, freed from their cages, walled homes, and cloisters. If Arab males were backward, it was partially due to racism on the part of both the settlers and administrators. But the least advanced socially, morally, and culturally were indeed colonized women, subject to masculine whim and tyranny, oppressed by a system of dual patriarchy, one French, the other Arab. The "mother country" was in reality a "cruel stepmother."[67]

Auclert also employed the discourse of universal sisterhood—"our Muslim sisters"—in her writing. Nevertheless, as was also true of British feminists, who often used an identical discourse to express concern about the Indian woman, sisterhood for Auclert was imperial and hierarchical.[68] Unlike many other writers, however, she clearly perceived the nefarious influence that French colonialism had wrought upon indigenous society and culture.

It is hardly surprising that in Auclert's passionate polemic, French suffragist agendas found their way into the Algerian context. Yet the reverse was also true; the colonial encounter in North Africa furnished additional evidence for the need for women's rights in France.[69] The disenfranchisement of French women exerted a deleterious influence not only upon colonial policies generally in Algeria but specifically upon native women. True assimilation could only be realized when French women were drafted by the colonial state to serve as cultural mediators and house-to-house activists; only women could bring France into the domestic spaces of secluded Arab women. The ideology of European women as moral beacons and guardians, as agents of civilization in the colonies, was a view widely shared and promoted by many British female activists. Yet this notion was not as fully articulated in French feminism—or at least not with regard to Algeria. To Auclert, the Arab woman represented more than a simple foil to measure progress in feminist causes back in France: "If women in France were accorded their share of power, they would not permit in a French territory the existence of a law allowing the rape of children." [70]

The most provocative section of Auclert's 250-page work deals with what she called child rape: "Arab marriage is child rape." [71] Here Auclert cited unsettling examples of young girls given through marriage contracts to men, often much older, in exchange for the bride price. Yet she suggested that the impoverishment of the indigenous population had much to do with these practices, which deviated in some respects from Islamic law. [72] While the consummation of the marriage was legally postponed until puberty, in actual fact this was not always respected, with tragic consequences for the young girl. [73] Unnatural sex—in the decades when the naturalization (i.e., the conferring of French citizenship) of Europeans in Algeria and the granting of even limited political rights to some Arab Muslims were hotly debated issues—provided additional ammunition to antiassimilationist forces.

Auclert's work expanded upon, in much more candid fashion, what General Daumas had merely hinted at—the morally perverse sexual customs of the natives. Yet at strategic points she asked different questions of the ethnographic material presented so fervently to her audiences, mainly found in the metropole. French law as applied (or not applied) in colonial courts was as much to blame for these lamentable sexual crimes: "French justice allows the application [to Arab girls] of Muslim customary law which is in total violation of French law." [74] Auclert also posed a fundamental challenge to the bourgeois liberalism of the Third Republic, one which she frequently raised in lobbying for women's suffrage in France—the Republic could not claim to be a true republic until women's rights and concerns were legally redressed. And until Algerian Muslim women had been culturally elevated through education to the level of French women, should not the Third Republic assume a legal and moral guardianship over them?

A sincere, if self-appointed, advocate for Algerian women, Auclert returned to Paris in 1892 without having achieved any concrete results. While still in Algeria, she had submitted petitions on behalf of indigenous females to Paris; all of them met with indifference. (We have absolutely no information regarding how Auclert's advocacy was viewed by Algerian Muslim women, if indeed they were even aware of her efforts on their behalf.) Back in France, she continued to submit petitions demanding education, the abolition of polygamy, and legal changes in the status of Algerian women until the end of her life. Auclert left Algeria a "lonely pioneer," but she did have her imitators, although not until several decades later.[75] Auclert's arguments were taken up by the Algerian novelist and writer Marie Bugéja in her work entitled *Nos soeurs musulmanes* (Our Muslim sisters; 1921) and in Bugéja's other works published during the interwar period.[76]

COLONIAL POSTSCRIPTS: NATIONALIST DISCOURSE AND THE ARAB WOMAN

Auclert appears to have succeeded in the one domain where she would have wished to fail. By bringing to bear her considerable "skills as a publicist to the education of [metropole] French opinion about Algeria, much as she had done for the woman question in the previous decade," Auclert ironically may have convinced many in both Algeria and France of the unsuitability of the colonized for political or civil rights.[77] Not only did she publicize the condition of Arab girls and women under Islam and customary law in the Algerian press, such as *Le Radical Algérien*, but she also used the Parisian feminist paper *La Citoyenne* as a vehicle for her campaign.[78] In the hands of antiassimilationists, *Les femmes arabes* may have offered yet more evidence for demonstrating the immutable difference of the indigenous population, especially when it came to matters of sexuality by then thoroughly imbricated in questions of citizenship.[79]

Thus, colonized women were becoming the measure of all things by the eve of the Great War—hidden and concealed yet on display. More

than this, the Arab woman in Algeria was being transformed into a political pawn. For Arab nationalists and Muslim liberals at the time, the
woman question became, and still is today, an ideological terrain for
debating issues of identity, cultural authenticity, and moral integrity. By
1900 indigenous Muslim reformers in Egypt and North Africa advanced
the novel premise that Islamic law was not immutable; the Tunisian
Tahar al-Haddad proposed a new reading of Arab female nature and
rights, waging campaigns to educate women to be national mothers.[80]
In 1899 the Egyptian intellectual Qasim Amin published *Tahrir al-mar'a*
(The emancipation of women), followed the next year by *Al-mar'a al-
jadida* (The new woman), arguing for unveiling and legal reforms in
marriage and divorce. The prominent Algerian jurist Kamal Muhammad ibn Mustafa composed in 1903 *Les droits de la femme* (The rights
of women), which reconsidered female status under Islamic law.[81] That
this treatise was written in the language of the conqueror is of fundamental significance; its audiences were French-educated Muslims, then
pressing for admission to French Algeria's political city, as well as officials and policymakers in both the country and the metropole.

In contrast, the new race of French Algerians vigorously promoted
another vision of Islam and the Arab woman. They proclaimed the existence of an invincible Islamic legal system and unchanging indigenous
mentalité toward women and sexuality; together these produced the
harem which embodied the threat of "a state within a state."[82] At the
same time the influential colonial novelist Louis Bertrand, who published a number of literary and polemic works dealing with *pied-noir*
identity from 1899 on, portrayed the Algerian Muslims as aliens or exiles
in their own land, while exalting the sensual, virile "Africanness" of the
European settlers, "born of the blood of Latin races."[83]

By the time of the lavish 1930 Centenary, the colonial gaze, with its
peculiar discourse on gender, race, and religion, was fully articulated.
Its quintessential academic spokesman was Emile-Félix Gautier, a professor at the University of Algiers. Gautier was commissioned to com-
pose a study devoted to the Muslim family specifically for the 1930
commemoration. His argument in *Moeurs et coutumes des musulmans*
(Mores and customs of the Muslims) is constructed from strategic code
words for gender and sexuality. Family functioned as a code for harem,
and harem for (deviant) Arab Muslim sex. There was no home or

hearth in the Arab North African household due to the debased status allotted its women by Islamic law and custom. In Gautier's learned view France and the French culture could never truly be "at home" in Algeria, because the requisite domestic foyer did not and could not exist among the Arabs. Implicit was the notion that French citizenship and Muslim sexuality could never be reconciled. Nevertheless, France would continue eternally to rule the country.[84]

In the metropole at the same time but at the other end of the political spectrum, the French Left also focused upon native Algerian women. A modest effort was launched to improve conditions for colonized women as part of a larger modernization program to offset militant nationalism.[85] In 1936 the socialist-inspired Blum-Viollette bill sought unsuccessfully to extend limited suffrage to Algerian Muslim males to counter growing political unrest. As Maurice Viollette, a former governor-general of Algeria and minister in the Popular Front of 1936, intoned: "Many people think that the indigenous woman counts for nothing. This notion is utterly false. The indigenous woman is extremely influential in Arab society."[86] The next period when Algerian Muslim women came, or were pushed, to the foreground as an ideological cause was during the bitter fighting of 1954–62. By then, however, the presumed deviant sexuality and moral degradation of the Arab woman and Muslim family were no longer evoked. Instead, the newly configured colonial project advocated female education and the enfranchisement of Muslim women to save L'Algérie Française, more or less the same program that Hubertine Auclert had championed over a half century earlier.

9. CIVILIZING GENDER RELATIONS IN ALGERIA:
The Paradoxical Case of Marie Bugéja, 1919–39

᛭ *Jeanne Bowlan*

On February 2, 1921, a middle-aged French-Algerian woman wrote to the governor-general of Algeria, requesting his support for the imminent publication of her first book, *Nos soeurs musulmanes* (Our Muslim sisters). Identifying herself as the daughter, wife, and sister-in-law of colonial civil service administrators, Marie Bugéja (1875?-1957) hoped that the governor-general would approve of her book's goal: "the moral recovery of the Muslim woman for the greater good of the Muslim home and for France above all." Upon receipt of the letter the next day, someone in the governor-general's office wrote, "Who is this?" on the letter and passed it on to the director of the Bureau of Native Affairs, J. Mirante.[1]

Two weeks later the director sent a note back to the governor-general identifying Bugéja as the wife of Manuel Bugéja, a retired chief administrator of a *commune mixte*, a territory with a mixed population of Europeans and Algerians. Mirante acknowledged that, on the whole, Manuel Bugéja's career had been satisfactory. The director briefly referred, however, to several incidents when Bugéja had misused his authority or had not gotten along with his colleagues. One such incident had resulted in Bugéja's being suspended for a month. In 1893 a disciplinary council had found him guilty of forcing Algerians, including a sixty-five-year-old man, to do manual labor for the European population. "Even though in the course of his career he did not prove to be exactly the ardent native lover (*indigénophile*) he boasts of being today," Mirante continued sardonically, "since his retirement, M. Bugéja has

᛭ *175*

believed it necessary to constitute himself the advocate for the most exorbitant native demands. Therefore, he maintains close relations with the Khaled party, works very regularly on the newspaper *Ikdam*, and publishes articles in it—sometimes very violent ones—against the Algerian administration."[2] These activities branded Bugéja as at least suspect, if not downright traitorous, to an official like the director of native affairs. Mirante called the governor-general's attention to Bugéja's active support of both the political organ of the Young Algerians movement and the movement's more radical faction headed by Emir Khaled (Khaled ibn Hashimi).

Disappointed by the limited civil and political reforms of the law of February 4, 1919, Emir Khaled's wing had split from the majority of the Young Algerians nationalist movement which accepted, at least for the moment, the law's limited reforms. Commonly referred to as the Jonnart law, after the then governor-general of Algeria, Charles Jonnart, the legislation had created a separate electorate of about 425,000 Algerian men, or about 43 percent of Algerian males aged twenty-five or more.[3] The electoral power of these so-called half-naturalized Frenchmen was restricted to choosing between one-fourth and one-third of the members of various local governing councils. Emir Khaled continued to push for reforms, such as full French citizenship for Algerians who retained their personal civil and legal status under Islamic law and bilingual education. Although the settlers had managed to resist the more radical changes that Emir Khaled promoted, the Jonnart law's moderate reforms stirred settlers' discontent with what they perceived as the antisettler policy of the national government in Paris. It is not surprising, therefore, given the political context and Manuel Bugéja's activities after his retirement, that the director of native affairs reacted negatively to Mme Bugéja's letter.[4]

As to Marie Bugéja's own endeavors, the director observed that she had mounted a campaign to achieve "the so-called reclamation of Muslim women who, she maintains, are oppressed by the ancestral prejudices of the native masses and intentionally barred from our schools by our administration." Mirante surmised that Bugéja hoped for a subsidy to help publish her book, although she had not requested one explicitly. He recommended that a subsidy be refused because of "the manifest intemperance of her ideas and style."[5]

The life and work of Marie Bugéja, one of the most prolific authors living in colonial Algeria between the world wars, provide a case study of the gendered social taxonomy of womanhood in colonial Algeria that placed modern French Christian womanhood on one extreme and traditional Arab Muslim womanhood on the other. Bugéja's work demonstrated a complex negotiation between the dominant imperialist view that indigenous Algerians needed civilizing and her iconoclastic program for taking that proposition seriously and directing it at her Muslim sisters. Although she was not the first French reformer to advocate improving the status of Muslim women, Bugéja carried previous arguments a step further. She proposed that Muslim women be the fulcrum by which the Algerian Muslim population could be elevated to the level of French civilization.[6] Relying on the notion that women were the center of the family, Bugéja called for the education of Algerian girls. By instilling French notions of domesticity in the heart of the Algerian family, assimilation could be achieved, and Algerians would remain loyal to France.[7]

Between 1918 and 1939 Bugéja published eleven books, both fiction and nonfiction, and more than sixty articles, ranging from descriptions of the people and geography of Algeria to appeals for improvement of Algerian women's status.[8] Although all of her books, except the first, were published in North Africa, she won literary prizes from metropolitan, not settler, organizations. For example, in 1927 she won first prize for prose from the Colonial Literary Section of the Académie pro Arte of Marseille. In 1930 she was awarded the Grand Prix in Paris's Grand Literary Contest for the Algerian Centennial. The Institut de France named her a laureate, and in 1936 she won the French Language Prize from the Académie Française. In contrast to this success in France, Bugéja was never even nominated for the Algerian literary prize offered by the colonial government. Whether by choice or by exclusion, she did not belong to the principal contemporary writers' organization, the Association des Ecrivains Algériens.[9]

Her insistence upon the central role of Muslim women distinguished her from most other contemporary authors, who drew upon the same repertoire of stereotyped characters and stories as their literary predecessors. For example, the weekly magazine *Afrique du Nord Illustrée* printed short fiction by such leading contemporary settler authors as

Charles Hagel, Charles Courtin, Magali Boisnard, and Maximilienne Heller. Many of their stories depicted Algerian men as lascivious brutes and Algerian women as wanton and indolent. In contrast to Bugéja, most colonial novelists did not see any potential for Algerian women to be redeemers of their "race." Instead, prurient fiction and erotic postcards that evoked exotic images of Arabs and Muslims, especially Muslim women, continued to sell throughout the 1920s and 1930s.[10]

Marie Bugéja and several other authors, however, challenged the orientalist fashion in literature established by literary luminaries like Gustave Flaubert as well as lesser lights like Pierre Loti. Although Bugéja's work bore the imprint of a Eurocentric, colonial perspective—as did the fiction and anthropological studies produced by other authors in the interwar period—it did articulate a broader view of Algerians than the fantasies spun by novelists about harems and veiled women.[11] The subtext of Bugéja's melodramatic novels and travel descriptions of her native Algeria and its indigenous peoples was her desire to undermine the prevailing notion that Arabs and Muslims were an unchanging people without history.[12] She wrote with intensity and conviction that "the Arabs are 'a civilized people asleep'; in order to wake them from their long slumber, it will suffice to let the ideas that we have sown in this ground take effect." But as an advocate for Muslim women she added, "In order to see these ideas fully germinate, let us extend the benefits of our teaching to native girls as well."[13] Bugéja believed that education would awaken the Algerians to modern French civilization, thus assimilating them into Greater France, which encompassed all French colonial possessions.

In most of her work, she contended that unless both Algerian boys and girls were educated in French colonial schools, France would fail to win the hearts and minds of Algerians. Bugéja insisted that the colonial administration, in neglecting Algerian women, failed to seize the key to success. "By acting directly on femininity," the administration would find a powerful tool for directing Algerians' "evolution and consolidating it into a durable stability."[14] The administration never managed to meet Bugéja's challenge. Very few Algerians of either sex received French education. In 1928, when 86.4 percent of the population in Algeria was Muslim, only 34.7 percent of the students in public primary schools were Muslims.[15] Of the approximately eight million Algerians in 1954, 94 percent of the men and 98 percent of the women were illiterate in French.[16] Algerians did not evolve into French citizens, as Bugéja had hoped they would.

Most settlers strongly opposed the assimilation of Algerians into the French nation. Having made Algeria French, settlers were intent on keeping the boundaries between rulers and ruled rigid and clearly defined. Boundary definition was essential in Algeria because both the ruling and ruled populations were comprised of so many different ethnicities and cultures.[17] This definition relied, in part, on the settlers' sociolinguistic and political segregation of the population into "Algerians," meaning themselves, the European settlers, and "Muslims" or "Arabs," meaning the indigenous peoples. These terms glossed over the complexity of the two communities. French, Spanish, Maltese, and Italians constituted the dominant European population, while the indigenous peoples included, among several others, Arabs, Berbers, and Jews. Recognizing that naming the various groups of inhabitants in colonial Algeria is no less political today than it was during French rule, in this essay I use the terms *French*, *European*, and *settlers* to distinguish inhabitants of European descent from *Algerians*, those whose ancestors were indigenous to Algeria. The settlers employed physical, economic, and educational segregation in addition to linguistic exclusion to enforce the boundaries between rulers and ruled during the course of their occupation of Algeria.[18]

Maintaining the boundaries of rule in the wake of the First World War presented novel challenges as news of the success of the Young Turks' nationalist movement, the continued attempts of Egyptian nationalists to end the British protectorate in Egypt, and Woodrow Wilson's ideas about self-determination percolated among Algerians as well as settlers. On the Algerian side these external factors mixed with disappointment about the limited reforms enacted under the Jonnart law of 1919. Many of the roughly 180,000 Algerian men who returned from fighting in the trenches for France during the First World War expected French citizenship as a reward for their sacrifices; a virtual promise, after all, had sustained their military valor on the murderous battlefields of the Great War.[19]

The political leaders of the settler community, who had been opposed to the conscription of Algerians, argued that Algerian Muslims were not evolved enough to become full French citizens. How could Muslim men be considered French, settlers argued, if Koranic law governed their lives in matters such as marriage, divorce, and inheritance? To be a French citizen meant that one willingly submitted to the civil laws of the French state. Algerian Muslim men, therefore, could only be granted full citizenship if they renounced Islamic law in the areas where it conflicted with French law. But at the same time the colonial administration claimed that they were obliged to uphold the promise made by the French government in 1830 to honor Islamic customs and religion in Algeria. French "respect" for Islamic tradition became, paradoxically, a justification for excluding Algerians from political and economic power during the period from the French conquest of Algeria until the early 1920s.[20]

Unlike many of her fellow settlers and the colonial administration, Bugéja took the idea of the civilizing mission to heart. She believed that the French were in Algeria to enlighten the indigenous population and to assimilate them into the superior refinement of French civilization. Bugéja's beliefs were undoubtedly influenced by her long and close association with the colonial civil service. As a daughter and a wife of administrators, Bugéja lived much of her life in rural areas, where Algerians outnumbered Europeans about six to one. As a child, she sometimes accompanied her father when he went on his administrative rounds to villages under his authority in the northern mountainous region of Kabylia. While he took care of business with indigenous men, she stayed with local women and girls. As a young woman in 1895, she began her career as an administrator's wife when she married Manuel Bugéja. Among other duties, she gave dinners for visiting dignitaries and civil service officials and accompanied her husband when he had to attend similar occasions organized by either Europeans or Algerians. When Algerians served as the hosts of such ceremonial events, Bugéja visited with the wives of Algerian political and religious leaders in their separate chambers.[21]

Bugéja's experiences, of course, were hardly typical of the existence of most settler women, because the vast majority of Europeans lived in the urban areas of northern Algeria where they outnumbered Algerians. Both demographic factors and her role as an unofficial adjunct in the colonial civil service gave Bugéja the possibility of meeting many more Algerians than the average European. But the civil service also functioned as a cultural filter. Bugéja most likely talked with Algerian men employed as subordinates in the colonial administration and their wives and families. Her most substantial contacts thus fell within a narrow range of the indigenous social strata. Moreover, Bugéja spoke only a few words of Berber, the native language of Kabylia, and had no apparent facility with Arabic. Therefore, her conversations with Algerians, particularly with Algerian women, would have been extremely limited since girls received less French language instruction than boys or none at all. Although this limitation undoubtedly led Bugéja to generalize and simplify her portrayals of Algerians' lives, she was no worse in this regard than most other writers. Yet her more varied experience of the people infused her work with somewhat more authenticity than those who wrote novels based on restricted contact with Algerians. Finally, Bugéja used her partial understanding of indigenous society in original ways—namely, to challenge prevailing interpretations that other writers had made from similarly limited viewpoints.

By converting her memories of her own life in rural Algeria into entertaining stories, Marie Bugéja responded to the burgeoning popular demand in Europe for travelogues and ethnographic descriptions. In these presentations she drew on her conversations with partially assimilated indigenous women and supplemented those insights with more general observations about Algerians' lives gleaned over the course of her career as a colonial civil service wife. That occupation had ended when her husband retired in 1916 and the couple moved to Algiers. It was then that her serious campaign on behalf of Algerian women began. In 1917 she wrote *Nos soeurs musulmanes*. Unable to find a publisher until 1921, Bugéja turned to giving public talks, which were sponsored initially by the Société de Géographie d'Alger et de l'Afrique du Nord and published in its journal. In her first effort in 1918, she described a trip that she and her family had made in the Djurdjura mountain range in the Kabylia region. In the midst of relating her adventures, Bugéja wove in an appeal to her European audience to educate even the poorest Algerians because they "possess in the depths of their hearts qualities that we want to believe the entitlement of our civilization." Although she did not focus specifically on women, Bugéja challenged the notion of "eternal Islam" and the idea that Algerians were culturally so different from the French that there could be no rapprochement.[22]

Bugéja addressed the issue of the Muslim woman in her second lecture held under the auspices of the geographic society on March 26, 1919, at the city hall of Algiers. She relied on the basic argument of her book, *Nos soeurs musulmanes*: "In a society, woman represents tradition; now, if one wants to modify tradition, that is, manners, customs, habits of feeling and thinking, it is advisable to begin with her."[23] For Bugéja, the French civilizing mission in Algeria could succeed only if Algerian females as well as males received a French education. Bugéja insisted especially on the role that Algerian women could play in furthering the cause of Algérie Française: "If their intelligence was cultivated through a well-balanced instruction—there would be no need to prepare them to confront exams—we are certain that, brought out of their ignorance, they would be precious auxiliaries for us."[24] She argued for educating women to help equip them to fulfill their "natural" role in the family. Education would both ensure that the civilizing mission took root in Algerian families and make Algerian women more compatible with their educated husbands, thus stabilizing the Algerian family as an agent in the French civilizing mission.

Response to Bugéja's proposals depended on whether the reviewer was in Paris or Algiers. Parisians like Maria Vérone, the president of the French League for the Rights of Women, lauded Bugéja's role as an agent in the civilizing mission in her 1921 review of *Nos soeurs musulmanes*. "If all the wives of our civil servants resembled Marie Bugéja, peaceful penetration [*sic*] would give the best results."[25] Vérone may have been appropriating Bugéja and her work for the feminist cause, although Bugéja never identified herself as a feminist. Part of Vérone's review appeared in the editor's preface to the second edition of *Nos soeurs musulmanes*, which would indicate that Bugéja did not oppose linking her work obliquely to the feminist cause back in the metropole. Nevertheless, I argue below that Bugéja's focus was not the feminist goals of French women but the amelioration of the status of Algerian women. The metropolitan literary prizes she won for *Nos soeurs musulmanes* and some of her succeeding books confirm that her work appealed to a broader audience than Parisian feminists.

A reviewer in Algiers, however, voiced some reservations about Bugéja's first book. Captain Peyronnet, a secretary of the geographic society and an army officer in the 19th Corps, began his review in the *Bulletin de la Société de Géographie d'Alger et de l'Afrique du Nord*: "Here is a very good book. We already know Madame Bugéja as an orator. Her lectures are well attended." But he quickly raised her point about educating Algerian women and observed that "one may dispute several of her ideas," and a few of her chapters "certainly will give rise to controversy." [26] The accuracy of this prediction was reflected in the colonial government's continued refusal to help subsidize the book's publication and dissemination.

Bugéja had forwarded her manuscript to the director of native affairs after being turned down in February 1921 for a prepublication subsidy. Mirante had suggested to the governor-general that he would review Bugéja's manuscript if she continued to press her request for government help. After meeting with Bugéja's husband on May 10, 1921, the secretary-general of the Algerian government requested an evaluation of *Nos soeurs musulmanes* from the director. In the report of his findings to the secretary-general, Mirante drew a connection between the ominous events in Turkey and Egypt and the possible results of Bugéja's campaign. His analysis of her book derided Bugéja's insistence that the French colonial administration's role was to encourage Muslim women to relinquish obsolete customs. "This program, as bold as it may seem, is not new. It already has been the object of ardent campaigns in Turkish and Egyptian newspapers, between 1900 and 1914, and it is easy to recall the fright that seized the well-read of Constantinople and Cairo when certain pamphlets in Arabic attempted, in 1912, to create a 'Muslim feminism.' The evolution, the instruction of the Muslim woman, the question of wearing the veil, of the gynaceum, etc., are infinitely delicate subjects which it is advisable to address with extreme circumspection." [27] His concluding recommendation was that a few copies of the book might be bought for the government's library. Marie Bugéja did not give up. On May 11, 1922, she wrote to the new governor-general, Théodore Steeg, requesting a subsidy for the diffusion of her by then published book. On May 27, 1922, Mirante sent a note to Steeg informing him of the long history of Bugéja's request and the negative response of Steeg's predecessor, Eugène Abel. [28]

Director Mirante represented the majority opinion among settlers about Muslim gender prescriptions. Most Europeans regarded Algerians as unsuitable for full French citizenship precisely because of what they understood to be typical Muslim gender roles. The oppression of

women, for example, became a central argument in the 1935 French
Senate debate over the Blum-Viollette bill, which proposed granting
citizenship to Algerian Muslims without requiring them to renounce
Islamic law. Had the bill passed, it would have meant that Algerians
naturalized under this law would have been exempted from submitting
to French civil law in matters such as marriage, divorce, or inheritance.
Paul Cuttoli, mayor of Constantine, led the coalition against the bill. In
a long address to his fellow senators, Cuttoli claimed that "the indigenous woman must see the end of this shocking inequality that exists
between the man, the male, the lord, and his companion." [29] If assimilation was to work, it would require years of patient work, not the en-
actment of laws. "To modify legislation before customs have changed,"
Cuttoli advised, "is to throw oneself into the maddest of adventures." [30]

The next day Pierre Roux-Freissineng took Cuttoli's place on the
Senate floor and reminded Minister Viollette of the scenario that one
Algerian mayor had imagined would result from enacting the Blum-
Viollette bill. The mayor, commenting on the hypothetical case of a
French bigamist on trial before an Algerian Muslim judge, had won-
dered if this judge "who would have four wives in his palace and as
many concubines as he can nourish" would be capable of condemning
a French man for having more than one wife. [31]

The status of French women, however, revealed the hypocrisy of
these men who registered their alarm at the "shocking inequality" between the sexes that they found in Algeria. Whereas women in several
Western European countries, such as England, Germany, and the Netherlands, had won the right to vote by the end of the First World War,
French women in 1935 still lacked this right. Moreover, French women
did not have the right to control their reproductive capacities since having an abortion was a criminal offense. These two examples of French
women's civil rights—or rather the lack of them—were but the most
basic indexes of inequality between the so-called civilized sexes in metropolitan France. [32] Nevertheless, most French people believed that their
Christian culture's gender norms were superior to those of Algerian
Muslims.

Bugéja at times expressed a surprising ambivalence about both cultures. The French interpreted "Muslims'" belief in superstitions as
proof that Algerians did not have a civilization worthy of the name.

Bugéja noted that this evaluation was applied to women especially, and that they were most often dismissed as completely ignorant. Arguing against such stereotypes, she juxtaposed Algerian superstitions with French ones. While Algerians might believe that "Fatma's" hand protected people from the evil eye, the French had worn fetishes or talismans during the war. Bugéja compared the Algerian belief that one could get good luck from drinking milk offered by a stranger to Breton women collecting dust from the church altar to throw into the wind while saying a prayer. She concluded that "to whichever religion humans belong, they have faith in a supernatural force that protects them in dangerous times. . . . the Algerian natives . . . have conserved ancient traditions and changed them according to their whims. Some of them are childish, others vulgar; still others resemble our own. They are not an index of either regression or barbarianism." Education, in both the French and Algerian cases, would combat such ignorance.[33]

Bugéja's cultural comparisons tackled more politically volatile questions when she made analogies between two of the most often cited signs of Algerian Muslim women's oppression—polygamy and the veil—and similar conditions in her own culture. In her first book she noted that although Muslim men could be married to four wives simultaneously, most did not actually do so. Whether for financial or other reasons, between 1911 and 1948 the percentage of polygamists in the total male population declined by slightly more than half (from 64 per 1,000 to 30 per 1,000).[34] Rather than simply correcting a common misperception about Muslims, however, Bugéja remarked on the contrast in legal rights between Algerian wives and French mistresses. "These women . . . are recognized publicly as wives, while according to European morality, only one wife is recognized but an indeterminable number of others are hidden. If bastards are born, who cares? Morality is saved. Which is the healthier—our morality or the Muslims'?"[35] Bugéja's analysis of women's legal rights under French law and the relative states of French and Algerian sexual morality contrasted sharply with the views expressed in the 1935 Senate debate of the Blum-Viollette bill. Bugéja's comparisons between the two cultures questioned the superiority of the French; the senators had no doubt as to which culture was better.

Challenging the organization of sexuality and marriage, Bugéja rocked one of the key pillars in the French ideology of cultural superiority. Europeans used their organization of sexuality as a crucial means to distinguish themselves from Algerians and to maintain dominance and cohesion as a colonial community. How could the French be a fit model of civilization if their sexual morality was no better than that of the polygamous Algerians? Subverting French authority in these areas undermined the settler community's cohesion and supremacy. Bugéja compared the lives of French and Algerian women in order to show that the latter were not beyond comprehension. But her correlations muddled the rhetorical and political boundaries between the civilized and uncivilized, thereby complicating the civilizing mission.[36]

On the subject of veiling, for instance, Bugéja made another transgressive parallel. In a book of published letters, she sought to make veiling less of a fixation among her readers. "I have never approved of the veil nor fought against it because I believe that my campaign proves sufficiently that what I want to take away from Muslim women is the veil of ignorance and I have ignored a 'style' that has become an 'obligation . . . A style that can fade like any style.'"[37] In another letter earlier in the book, Bugéja compared veiling to that "horror of civilization," the corset. Since women no longer wore corsets in France, Bugéja was hopeful that one day the veil would disappear as well.[38] Given Europeans' long-term obsession with veiled Arab women, Bugéja's belief that veiling was little more than a "style" that might eventually be abandoned was a striking observation. For early twentieth-century Europeans, the veiled Arab woman embodied the exotic Orient. The veil became a screen onto which Europeans projected their sexual fantasies and fears. All the more stunning, then, that Bugéja indifferently shrugged this off. She shook the veiled woman loose from her static position in the West as the symbol of an eternally unchanging Islam.[39]

By equating veiling to corseting and by claiming that the French had no right to be more sanctimonious about their sexual morality than Algerians, Bugéja called into question the French rationale for the civilizing mission. She also put herself in a paradoxical position. Her conundrum stemmed from the dual role she created for herself. By appointing herself, on the one hand, as a French spokesperson on behalf of the Muslim woman and, on the other hand, by leading a campaign to instill French civilization in the hearts of Algerians, Bugéja had to grapple with continual contradictions. She attempted to raise questions about the supposedly unchanging status of Algerian women in the minds of the French public by exposing the similarities between French and Algerian women. But at the same time she had to stress Algerian women's difference in order to justify the need to make them conform to French gender prescriptions.

This contradiction was most evident in Bugéja's attitude toward mixed marriages between French-educated Algerian men and metropolitan French women. She argued that Western-educated Algerian men wanted to marry French women because they found Algerian women's lack of education unattractive. Educating Algerian girls, then, would produce more compatible mates for the so-called evolved Arab men who had been educated in French schools in Algeria and/or in France.

> As for mixed marriage, the natives themselves have recognized that they are not developed enough, not liberated enough from ancient prejudices to break the bonds that hold them prisoners and slaves to public opinion. But, despite these prejudices, from which they suffer, despite the insults that no one spares them, the young natives, educated and Frenchified, feel pushed, almost in spite of themselves, toward the daughters of Europe, closer to them through common culture and through this certain something—attraction of the mind—that brings together beings with the same intellectual formation. The young women of their own race, unconscious heirs and innocent victims of old traditions without serious foundation and of nefarious idiocies that have become venerable through force of use, seem much more foreign to them. . . . Isn't there danger in that? [40]

Bugéja simultaneously upheld the French ideal of companionate marriage as a model for Algerians and eliminated Algerian men as suitable spouses for French women. The danger allegedly lay not in the intermingling of the cultures but in the division between Algerian men and women. Algerians could help each other to overcome their "backwardness" whereas intermarriage with the French would only make the Algerians more aware of their flaws. Bugéja's discussion of mixed marriages was self-serving in that it provided another justification for edu-

cating Algerian girls. While the number of marriages between Algerians and metropolitan French was minimal, marriages between French
settlers and Algerians were even more rare. With regard to intermarriage and/or concubinage, Algeria is a unique case. Although the First
World War brought many Algerian men to France, relatively few married French women. Sexual relations between colonizer and colonized
simply did not happen to the same extent that they did in other colonial
contexts.[41]

Bugéja's argument in favor of educating Algerian women so that
they would be more suitable marriage partners for Algerian men suggests a more complex motivation than simple maintenance of colonial
boundaries. In accord with contemporary French notions of marriage,
which emphasized the intellectual and emotional partnership of marriage, Bugéja argued that educated Algerian women would be better able
to assist their husbands in maintaining French civilization in their
homes. In learning to be French and to instill "Frenchness" in their
families, Algerian women could win the respect of both Algerian and
French men. Algerian men would see the valuable role women played
in French-style family life. French men would have to give up their
bleak view of the Algerian woman as a "beast of pleasure or beast of
burden."[42] In both cases, Algerian women's condition would improve.
For Bugéja, maintaining Algérie Française did not entail preserving a
traditional Algerian gender role for her Muslim sisters. Rather, she
fought to make Algerian femininity French.

Her struggles with the colonial administration over this issue demonstrate that most French colonials resisted any change in Algerian
women's status, as did many Algerians—although for very different
reasons. The French used the quintessential imperialist political gam-
bit of preserving native "traditions" that would enhance their rule.
The Muslim woman marked Algerians as uncivilized; it was best, therefore, to maintain the gender prescriptions that produced her. Such an
oppressed female justified continued French domination. For their
part, Algerians also equated maintenance of tradition with the Muslim
woman. But Algerians came to see her as the embodiment of cultural
resistance to colonization, as has been discussed by several scholars, beginning with Frantz Fanon.

Moreover, in many colonial contexts the preservation of reinvented traditions was perceived as being grounded in cultural prescriptions regarding the role of women. In the Dutch East Indies, for example, "a Western and essentially middle-class vision of women's maternal destiny and housewifely duties merged with respect for *adat* [tradition], thus revealing a complex pattern of complicity between the indigenous patriarchal norms and Western notions about women's proper place." Bugéja attempted to disrupt this complicity, which operated in Algeria as well. She relied, nonetheless, on the Western vision of "women's maternal destiny."[43]

Bugéja claimed that her vision of different gender prescriptions for the new Algerian woman was humanist rather than feminist: "What a magnificent movement, a movement that is the bearer of this civilization, when the schools will be open, everywhere, to the young native girl. Let us say it again that it isn't a question here of feminism but of humanity!"[44] Despite her rejection of feminism as constitutive of the new Algerian woman, Bugéja willingly used feminism to promote her own cause. In 1932 she participated in the Congress of Mediterranean Women, submitting a report on the status of Muslim women which was read to the conference.[45]

If Bugéja's new Algerian woman was not a feminist, neither was she modeled on the modern woman of the Jazz Age. Bugéja rejected the sort of individual liberation that young French women embraced in the postwar world.[46] "I don't want to see our North African Muslim sisters, without preparation, discarding the veil and plunging into the turbulence of life; they must first be initiated. Only the invigorating atmosphere of a well-established school will allow them to gain liberty wisely." The 1920s women's fashion of short hair, short skirts, and plunging necklines front and back appalled Bugéja. She chastised both her European sisters for following this fashion and European men for tolerating "nudism." "Is there anything more shocking for a Muslim woman, enveloped in her veils, than to find herself in a tram, back-to-back with a 'nudist' who complacently rests her back, bare-skinned down to her belt, on the shared wooden backrest, or even better, on a male companion's encircling arm?"[47] For Bugéja, the liberation of Algerian women was to be closely contained in the bourgeois institutions of education and the family.

Bugéja based her claim to speak for her Muslim sisters on her allegedly common experience with them: being a woman and a mother. Her first book, *Nos soeurs musulmanes*, includes an address to Muslim mothers in which Bugéja invokes their experience as mothers of sons who fought in the First World War. Whether we are "Moorish women in splendid veils, poor women in torn rags, highly civilized French women, or those with work roughened hands, we are all mothers."[48] Through this rhetorical device Bugéja positioned herself as the intimate of the women she wanted to help. Her position as a middle-class woman of European descent nurtured her presumption that sex-gender was the most salient identification for Algerian women. By claiming sex-gender solidarity, Bugéja granted herself moral authority to be a spokesperson. From this position she imagined a sort of civic wifehood and motherhood for these women, not unlike the role she herself had played.[49] I have used "sex-gender" here in an attempt to represent Bugéja's thinking on the subject. She did not, of course, have the benefit of gender theory to distinguish the two, which prompted her to conflate her experience as a mother with Algerian women's experiences. For Bugéja, woman equaled mother and wife.

In many ways Bugéja was a maternal imperialist, a woman who set herself up as both role model and advocate for Algerian women. Her attitude toward her Muslims sisters, as revealed in her copious writing, established her warm regard for Algerian Muslim women and her genuine interest in their condition. This attitude, however, is more aptly characterized as maternalist, rather than sisterly, both because the power dynamics resembled the more extensive power of a mother, and because Bugéja relied on an essential notion of womanhood as motherhood to bind the diverse women of the Algerian colony to one another. For all her sympathetic analogies between the lives of French and Algerian women, however, she continued to assert French gender construction as the model. She offered no space for Algerian women's own voices in her work.[50]

Her project of giving Algerian women a French education was shaped by an imperialist vision, yet the fight that she waged on behalf of Algerian women in her books, articles, and lectures rendered her campaign more complex than a simple assertion of cultural superiority. Bugéja's gendered role as a European woman in a colonial settler society inscribed her with feminine qualities, such as empathy and nurturance, that enabled her "to build relations based on genuine understanding of indigenous peoples, especially women, or at least to act as [advocate] for [her] sisters at a time of rapid social change." [51] In her advocacy role she criticized the colonial administration for its neglect of Algerian women. She went so far as to question the hierarchical construction of French gender norms, especially in regard to sexual relations. For example, rather than castigate Algerians for polygamy, she contrasted women's legal protection as wives to French women's precarious position as mistresses. Bugéja used these incendiary analogies, however, more to keep her French readers' feet to the fire regarding the need to improve Muslim women's condition; her aim was not to change the prevailing gender hierarchy within French culture.

Bugéja stood out from her contemporaries with regard to the goal of her work. She was not part of the cohort of colonial women authors who raised the specter of the oppressed Muslim woman in order to speak to European men about European women's oppression. The literary critic Denise Brahimi noted the scarcity of European men in many of the women's books and concluded with the speculation that "this European man, so little evoked, could not but be implicitly present in the minds of the European women who wrote. It is in part for him, receiver and future reader, that the books were written. The Algerian woman could thus be used as a sort of foil but also as representative of a temptation that it was necessary to exorcise. One thus better understands the virulence of the discourses against polygamy: Muslim men openly realized an old masculine tendency that was more hidden elsewhere, but which it was necessary to show in every way possible how pernicious it was for women." [52] It is significant that Bugéja did not engage in fierce polemics about polygamy. Bugéja's cultural relativism stands in sharp contrast to the work of the other authors (Hubertine Auclert, Magali Boisnard, Henriette Célarié, etc.) whom Brahimi analyzed.

In this regard Bugéja represents a different paradigm than the British women Antoinette Burton examined in her recent book on the connections between British feminism and Indian women. Burton argued that British women such as Josephine Butler and Mary Carpenter saw "Indian women's plight as an incentive for British women to work in the empire and as proof of British women's contributions to the imperial civilizing mission." Butler and Carpenter urged British women to make careers out of social reform in India. Marie Bugéja's main concern was with her Muslim sisters, not her French ones. Perhaps because she did not identify as a feminist, she did not see Algerian women's plight as a polemical tool to be exploited in the struggle to attack gender inequality in French society—metropolitan or colonial. Although Bugéja regarded her own advocacy as a career of sorts, she did not attempt to use it to demonstrate her "social-imperial usefulness" as British feminists in India were doing, according to Burton.[53]

In contrast to her British counterparts, Bugéja revealed more of her contradictory loyalties. In her writing she repeatedly faced the thorny contradictions that arose out of her conflicted position as both a colonial civil service wife and a lobbyist for Algerian women. In every instance Bugéja retreated into her role as colonizer. Thus, she was unable to push her analysis of the similarities and differences between women any further because to do so threatened her identity as an agent of the civilizing mission in Algeria. Nevertheless, by narrowing the seemingly vast chasm between aspects of Algerian and French women's lives, Bugéja attempted to shake her readers out of their complacent belief that Muslim prescriptions about female gender norms were so alien and backward that trying to civilize the women and ameliorate their status would be hopeless.

Bugéja's devotion to a colonial policy of assimilation simultaneously upheld her belief in French superiority while allowing for the possibility that Algerians might attain true Frenchness.[54] Ironically, her belief that Algerians could become French, together with her assurance that as a woman she could transcend racial frontiers or ethnic barriers to become the spokeswoman for Algerian women, threatened the civilizing mission in Algeria, one of the main justifications for French settler society. If a French woman could speak for change on behalf of Algerian women, and the latter could rise to the level of educated French womanhood, then what natural distinctions would remain between these two gendered beings? If the veiled Muslim woman was not eternal, could the civilizing mission be?

10. "IRRESISTIBLE SEDUCTIONS": Gendered Representations of Colonial Algeria around 1930

🍂 *Yaël Simpson Fletcher*

In French travel writing on Algeria in the 1920s and 1930s, the first sight of Algiers from an arriving ship in the harbor inspired visions of pleasure and relaxation, a break from the cold and dark winters of northern France. Gendered in French as feminine (*la ville*), "she" was portrayed as beautiful, white, and sun-drenched: voluptuous in her charm. "The tourist who arrives in Algiers on one of those pleasant winter days . . . immediately falls prey to [her] irresistible seductions."[1] Once seen, the city "bestowed . . . the divine privilege of loving [her] passionately."[2] The very word *Algeria* conjured up images of the Orient, "inspiring in all who encountered it the ardent desire to know the country."[3] The eroticism that suffused French colonial literature expressed a "fantasy of colonial mastery," in the words of literary scholar Emily Apter.[4] Many images were multivalent, however, with an undercurrent of danger or disgust. In fact, disembarkment in Algiers marked a transitional moment in which the French visitor encountered the Arab population for the first time. One writer perceived the dark-skinned porters crowding the docks as a "sudden brutal invasion of a barbarian band." For another recent arrival the glance of a veiled woman prompted a vision of "all the sensuality, all the passion of the Orient." Reality, however, was not quite so romantic. The luggage arrived safely at the hotel, and the face revealed by a momentary drop of the veil was "flaccid and yellow, fleshy, disappointing."[5]

The widespread use of gendered rhetoric and images was crucial for the process of constructing difference between "us" and "them" and for naturalizing the colonial relationship. Not only were French men sexualized and Algerian women eroticized, but also the land, labor, and the "exotic" were seen in male or female terms. France was often portrayed as a powerful masculine figure, despite its traditionally female representations.[6] As in other European colonial discourses, the "demarcation of identity and difference" functioned to establish the authority of the colonizer.[7]

The French conquest of Algiers in 1830 marked only the first of many battles for the region. Spreading out across the new colony in the wake of the military invasion, immigrants from Italy, Spain, and Malta as well as France had settled on land most of which had been confiscated or appropriated by the state from the autochthonous peoples of the region, the Algerians.[8] The difficult victory of the First World War, won with the crucial assistance of colonial native conscripts, served to focus attention on the importance of maintaining French control of the empire. As the largest settler colony in the French Empire and the closest to France, Algeria was particularly significant. The 1930 centenary of the conquest was observed with conferences, exhibits, special publications, literary prizes, and ceremonies. The celebrations included a series of officially sponsored events in Algeria attended by the president of France, Gaston Doumergue, as well as an automobile rally across the Sahara.[9] Some eighty thousand metropolitan French visitors came to Algeria for the special occasion, and the centenary organizers distributed over one million copies of a twelve-volume set of booklets commemorating the colony's economic, social, and political development. In the name itself, Centenaire de l'Algérie, and in the ceremonies and publications, the issue of violent conquest was glossed over; instead, French colonialism was glorified as the progenitor and benefactor of Algeria.[10] This publicity campaign constituted a discourse which can be characterized, without a doubt, as colonialist.

This chapter explores the gendered nature of the rhetoric and representations found in the colonial writings of the centenary period. I begin by delineating the links made between French virility and the cultivated landscape. In the second section I explore images of the desert, technology, and masculinity. In the third and fourth sections I examine the eroticization and exoticization of Algerian women as well as the construction of their primary role as bearers of tradition. Finally, I conclude with a general inquiry into questions of loyalty and difference in Algeria.

THE LAND

In 1929 the French government formed a publicity committee for the centenary. At its first meeting André Tardieu, the interior minister and the president of the committee, gave the welcoming lecture. France, he said, needed to learn that what took place in 1830 was not so much the conquest of Algiers as the creation of the first page of the "French magnum opus in Algeria."[11] This grandiose phrase signified the Algeria created by the settlers over the past century: a new land of modern agriculture and industry, roads, railways, and docks, of well-built cities, good schools, and other beneficial institutions. Integral to the idea of Algeria as a French construction was the belief that before 1830 there had been nothing but decay and chaos. General Bonneval's statement that upon arrival in Algiers the French found "a barbaric, unhealthy region, without culture, without commerce, without industry, where brigandage and piracy raged permanently" was typical.[12] Indeed, the governor-general of Algeria in 1930, Pierre Bordes, congratulated the French soldiers and settlers for transforming Algeria, which in 1830 had consisted of "anarchy, ignorance, and misery in regions abandoned to wasteland, bereft of roads, . . . [and] 1.5 million Muslims of different races in constant struggle with each other, without industry, without commerce, eking out an existence from the dry soil," into a modern country.[13]

These different races included Arabs, Berbers, Jews, and the various nomadic desert tribes of the Sahara. Like other European colonizers, the French had developed racialized hierarchies to categorize and classify people. For Muslims, in particular, insidious tribal customs and alien religious values embodied racial difference and marked their inferiority. Some French observers differentiated the Berbers from the Arabs as less "fanatical" in their Islamic religiosity, more industrious in their work habits, and lighter-skinned; these three characteristics brought them somewhat closer to civilization. But most of the French considered the entire collectivity of Algerian "races" to be barbaric, uncivilized, and incapable of any kind of productive activity.

Jean-François Guilhaume has noted the pervasiveness of the myth of Arab "desertification" of Algeria.[14] It seemed obvious to the French colonialists that the semiarid condition of a region once called the "breadbasket of Rome" was due to Algerian ignorance and sloth. This myth not only provided a justification for the seizure of lands but also functioned as a counterimage that underscored the colonial vision of Algeria's subsequent agricultural productivity. While recognizing the importance of crops like cereals and dates in Algeria before 1830, most writers attributed the very existence of a cultivated landscape to the "scientific approach" and hard work of the settlers.[15] For example, the official journal of the centenary, the *Cahiers du Centenaire de l'Algérie*, claimed that it was "evident that all the agricultural wealth was a pure [European] creation, a creation ex nihilo" brought about by "the personal action of the colonial settler."[16] The invisibility, and the consequent denigration, of Algerian labor reinforced French claims of superiority.

European writers often feminized the African landscape. The "imperialist gaze of desire" saw only a continent languishing in idleness and passivity.[17] Representations of the desertification and subsequent transformation of Algerian land were gendered. Imagery of renewal and rebirth depicted France as the virile partner who inseminated and gave life to a receptive Algeria. In this colonial vision fertilization took place in many different ways. A professor at the University of Algiers, E. F. Gautier, compared the European settlers to germinating seed, and Pierre Deloncle's title, *La caravan aux éperons verts* (The caravan with green spurs), referred to the rain-stained jackets of the French team of surveyors, officials, and writers that identified them with life-giving rain in a drought-ridden region.[18] According to the geographer Julien Franc, the settlers sacrificed "blood and gold" to bring the land to productivity.[19] General Bonneval was particularly proud of the new date palm groves in the Sahara: "One must not forget that these Saharan regions were disdainfully abandoned to the *Coq Gaulois*, so that it could scratch the sand at its ease. In scratching the sand, the Gallic Cock made a large number of artesian wells burst forth, which has allowed the creation of superb palm groves."[20] Both the development of water resources and new methods of cultivating date palms were presented by a government agronomist, Jean Blottière, as examples of the benefits brought by French colonization to the Algerians.[21] The depiction of an orphaned land, abandoned to the French, demonstrated the "backwardness" of the nomadic tribes and justified French occupation. Bonneval claimed that the indifference of these peoples to the land's potential productivity galvanized the French into becoming strutting roosters, who in turn disdained the ignorant Algerians. The Gallic cock, of course, was a traditional symbol of both France and masculine prowess.

Once fertilized by the settlers, the previously barren country itself displayed a youthful and impetuous fecundity.[22] Before reaching that happy state, however, the land, like a growing child, had to go through its own rites of passage. For example, Julien Franc wrote that the plains of the Mitidja "had the most unhappy, tormented, and deadly infancy: the first settlers, transformed into soldiers, pursued an unremitting struggle against native looters and assassins, against terrible malarial fevers, against brushwood covering the fallow soil. 'Her' more peaceful adolescence was nevertheless still a continual struggle for 'her' riches against the stingy soil and deadly climate. Out of this obscure struggle, without glory, the settler of the Mitidja finally emerged as victor thanks to his tenacity."[23] The male soldiers and settlers were viewed as protective parents, defending their families not from Algerians fighting for their land but from Arab thieves; these men, according to Franc, had deserted the plain in 1830.[24] Domination was for the child's own good, bringing "her" to fertile maturity. Although feminized, Algeria was not yet a mother. Rather, the colony as a whole was considered the offspring of the "colonizing genius" of France.[25] Virile and omnipotent, France "had made a living country out of the dead earth," working "miracles" in the desert.[26]

Once brought to life, Algeria had a special significance for the French as a "new country," a land of growth and opportunity.[27] The seminal metaphor was extended to the French-built infrastructure. One newspaper article compared the way in which "railroads, docks, piers, dams, hydraulic works, the clearing or creation of new neighborhoods sprouted up with a rapidity, a vigor, and an astonishing cheerfulness" to the explosion of vegetation in the Algerian spring.[28] Algiers, "more robust and more active" than any French town, had "the happy air which accompanies youth, prosperity, and self-confidence," filled with the "lusty children of Greater France."[29] Indeed, the settlers displayed the "most vigorous qualities of the French race."[30] In a typical statement Director of Indigenous Affairs Jean Mirante suggested that the youthfulness of Algeria would rejuvenate France as a whole, just as "the fecund peace" brought from France to Algeria had led to an increase in the Algerian population.[31] The conservative fear that French power and resources, both human and material, were dwindling spurred the desire for France to be seen (and to see itself) as an active and expanding nation. Colonial writers addressed a France which seemed to need the idea of Algeria as a fresh start, a new land, a frontier where its virility and vigor could be recovered after the losses in the First World War.

In his analysis of the relation between literature and anthropology in Africa, Christopher Miller has suggested that "the processes of projection . . . by which the identity and desires of the colonizer reproduce and satisfy themselves, are directly related to colonial policy. Projection translated into political terms becomes what I would call colonial inscription, the imposition onto Africa of French systems . . . making Africa 'French.'"[32] One of the main goals of the centenary organizers was to promote a vision of Algeria as a province, rather than a colony, of France. The northern part of Algeria ("French Algeria") was divided into three departments which sent representatives to Paris, like all French departments in the metropole. There were numerous administrative distinctions, however: the colonial civil government had a great deal of autonomy; native Algerians had very little representation; there was a separate, harsher legal code for Muslims; and Algeria still had a governor-general, like other colonies. The military ruled the more recently conquered southern regions of Algeria.[33]

Colonial writing expressed the French incorporation of Algeria through images of geographical links and biological metaphors. Because it was just across the Mediterranean Sea, Algeria was considered "simply the extension of French soil."[34] One writer even declared grandiloquently, "Algeria . . . is one of the nerve centers of the French organism, one of the vital points of an extended unit, where the destinies of the *patrie* are, in part, elaborated."[35] Once defined as part of France, French Algeria by a process of metonymy could stand in for all of France. As such, even to imagine a separate Algeria was impossible. "The hypothesis of Algerian independence is inconceivable," declared one of the writers for the *Cahiers du Centenaire*.[36] The very need to make such a statement, however, undermined the presumed merger of identities between France and Algeria.

Algeria might have been an extension of French soil, but the soil itself was very different. Paradoxically, every comparison to France acknowledged the alterity of Algeria. For example, Georges Rozet, the author of two guides to Algeria, described 750 settler villages "as morsels of France, grafted in some way upon the deep red Algerian soil."[37] Traveling across Algeria, Deloncle had a near-hallucinatory experience smelling and seeing "a French field of wheat" outside In-Salah, "this lost corner of the African land."[38] These ambiguous and contradictory images gave a sense not only that Algeria was different, but also that the French were aliens on African soil. They exemplified a particular type of colonial representation, "mimicry." In this discourse the colony and the metropole were presented as "almost the same but not quite," one a slightly distorted reflection (rather than an imitation) of the other. Since colonial domination required the clearly demarcated difference between "them" and "us," any merger of identities threatened the status quo. Mimicry expressed this unsettling and unacknowledged indeterminacy in the colonial vision.[39] Indeed, Algeria was often described as the "Second France," an unremarkable phrase which nevertheless raised significant questions.[40] It marked Algeria as not quite the same as France. Or, was Algeria the livelier and younger inheritor of the first metropolitan France?

The desires of Bonneval, Franc, and other colonial writers were evident in their discussions of Algeria's cultivated landscape. As a natural complement to the feminized land, the French settler was defined as a very powerful, if androgynous, male, capable even of usurping female procreative powers. Indeed, the male writers rarely acknowledged the presence and contribution of European women among the settlers. The masculinization of the whole race was a necessary sign of its superiority. But even within the discourse of empire, various forms of resistance to the "colonial inscription" were recognized, whether from the Algerian people or from the natural environment. The prickly bushes and drought of the Mitidja presented literal and physical obstacles for the settlers, and the image of the alien red earth undermined rhetorical assumptions of the Frenchness of Algeria. However strong the desire, even the rhetorical extension of France to Algeria was ultimately impossible.

THE DESERT

The Algerian desert furnished a testing-ground for demonstrations of French superiority. Descriptions of the Sahara focused on its emptiness, its lack: "nothing to rest the eye on, not one tree, not one house." This infinite immensity, however, was called "voluptuous," the dunes compared to paintings of seductive women.[41] Despite this alluring portrait, the desert held many dangers and was accessible to tourists in 1930 only because of quite recent military victories. French superiority was celebrated in a popular and commercial centenary event, the Rallye Saharien, an auto race across the Sahara in February and March 1930. For the rally ten teams of four cars each left at intervals from Oran, Algiers, Bone, and Tunis. Their goal was to cross the Sahara from the Mediterranean Sea to the Niger River and then return from Gao to Algiers. Most of the teams were sponsored by automobile manufacturers, and some featured specially designed touring cars with sleeping quarters and balloon tires. The passengers included correspondents, a few women, and even one child. At the opening of the rally, the governor-general reminded his listeners that this event was the latest in the great French effort to "attach to the civilized world a huge expanse of desert," a forum to "show to the world the greatness of France."[42]

The automobile epitomized European civilization and technological progress. Nevertheless the auto rally across the Sahara not only faced technical problems but also had to confront the "indecipherable, terrifying" desert itself.[43] The participants often had to dig their automobiles out of the sand. The language of struggle and conquest pervaded the descriptions of crossing the desert. But the successful completion of the rally meant that the Sahara no longer could be equated with "a country of thirst and of fear . . . a wild, gloomy gate of death."[44] Its dangers had been transformed into exotic and picturesque scenes. This conquest of the Sahara took place on two levels, the imaginary and the material. Redefining the desert as a safe but fantastic thoroughfare was as important as actually crossing it without major mishap.

It is interesting to consider one of the bronze plaques designed to commemorate the centenary rally. In a rectangular abstracted style the image on the plaque contrasted heavily robed men on camels, obviously Arab, with the French automobiles. No drivers or passengers were visible in the cars. The two seated figures, in high relief, dominated the foreground, while the two automobiles receded into the background, in a low relief similar to that of the craggy cliffs in the distance. As a celebration of the crossing, one would expect the automobiles to dominate the scene. The visual centrality of the camel riders, however, seemed to indicate their permanency in this barren land. Nevertheless, the automobiles' movement away from the figures gave a sense of progress and the future. This tension between Arab men and French automobiles qualified the "Frenchness" of the Sahara. It also had a broader resonance. In a telling passage the amateur ethnographer and prolific novelist Ferdinand Duchêne compared himself to his automobile, "a vibrating machine. . . . Our brains vibrate also. They are the creators of speed like the motor." This febrility cast doubt on the health and virility of modern Frenchmen, whom Duchêne contrasted with the Arab leaders of a camel caravan: "These are men who have no other worry than to remain men. And are we certain that they might not be the ones who are right?"[45]

THE CASBAH

Edward Said has shown the importance of the fictional construct of the "Orient," as other, exotic, and inferior for the nineteenth-century European colonial project.[46] In poetry and novels the Orient figured as an "imaginary harem."[47] The famous colonial novelist Louis Lecoq described the Casbah, the Arab quarter in Algiers, as a veritable fragment of the Orient, an exotic place existing for the pleasure of the male tourist.[48] Travel guides described it as "impenetrable," nightmarish, with a "fantastic network of tortuous streets," in sharp contrast to the straight and open boulevards of the modern European city.[49] E. F. Gautier compared the Casbah to something that was already dead, "a poor old small cadaver, fossilized and encysted in a large living organism," i.e., the European quarter of Algiers.[50] The exploration of the Casbah was just as much an adventure as crossing the Sahara, but one in which visitors braved dirt and darkness instead of sand and sunlight. It provided an opportunity for the travel writer to display his daring and European superiority over the inhabitants. Already conquered once militarily, both the desert and the Casbah had to be conquered yet again for tourism.

Photographs accompanying articles and books on Algeria usually portrayed the Casbah with a view of a heavily veiled woman in a narrow passage of steep stone steps.[51] Like the image in which a veiled woman's glance initially evoked a sexual fantasy of the Orient only to give rise to dismay as her face was revealed, the Casbah in Algiers inspired dreams of penetration that yielded to a disturbing reality for visitors. In a telling incident in his travel guide *Alger et sa region* (Algiers and its environs), the novelist Antoine Chollier felt compelled to enter a dark, narrow passage which led into the center of the Casbah. It had a "humid and nauseating atmosphere," but "the obscure mystery drew [him] on."[52] The sexual connotations of the dirt, smell, and disease of the Casbah help to explain Chollier's prurient fascination, which inextricably linked debasement and desire.[53] He continued in the dim light on a path slimy with fish entrails, encountering a silent veiled woman and a mewing cat. Chollier described the whole experience as a "phantasmagoria," comparing it to being transported back to a fifteenth-century European town.[54] The French constructed a timeless vision of the Arab quarter as a residual fragment of Algerian urban life and family and gender relations before 1830. James Buzard has noted how the "aestheticizing" gaze creates the picturesque, a view to be seen rather than a place to be experienced. The transformation of a living neighborhood into a historical anachronism also transformed the nightmarish experience into a walk full of voyeuristic thrills and morbid pleasures.[55]

Representations of women played a crucial role in orientalizing Algeria. Over thirty years ago Frantz Fanon noted the peculiar symbolism of the veiled Algerian woman for the French colonizer.[56] Recent scholars have developed his insights, delineating the process by which "clothing becomes emblematic of a cultural or racial group," and more particularly how the veil came to represent Islam, thus manifesting "a colonial relationship which is both gendered and sexualized."[57] The veiled woman was thought to be ignorant, illiterate, and oppressed, and her image functioned as a marker of Muslim cultural inferiority. In the most common depictions in press reports and travel writing, Algerian women were glimpsed only from afar, swathed in veils, on their way to a mosque or saint's tomb.[58] But another version of the trope expressed the writer's desire to get closer, to see underneath the veil. In the male European imagination, the woman veiled in public registered at the same time her sexual availability in private, in the harem.

Of course the prostitutes' quarter of the Casbah provided ample opportunity to view unveiled women from all parts of Algeria. This was not very satisfying, at least for Chollier. He vividly conveyed his dismay at the prostitutes' "woefully dejected faces under the makeup, flowers, and ribbons" and his nostalgia for a supposed female purity. The sight of nude dancers in a dimly lit bar recalled the memory of dancers in the south: "Where are you, modest little Oulaid-Nail dancers, whom I saw on a beautiful night at Bou-Saada, in the hieratic poses of your nude bodies of young ephebes?"[59] These dancers, the Nailiyat, belonged to a southern tribe in which women had an unusual amount of sexual freedom before marriage. Indeed, selling sexual favors was an accepted means for amassing a dowry for the women of the Oulaid-Nail.[60] French representations of the Nailiyat were ambiguous. In the towns and cities of northern Algeria, they were considered a type of prostitute. In both photographs and written descriptions, the Nailiyat were presented arranging their hair, lounging in doorways, and smoking. In the south, however, the Nailiyat were portrayed as dancers rather than prostitutes. In fact, French writers seemed puzzled by the contrasts between their modest dress and ornate headdresses and between their somber expressions and enticing hand movements.[61]

At a performance in the oasis of Laghouat, Pierre Deloncle compared the blue and white outer robes of the Nailiyat to those worn by French peasant women in religious processions. But then, as if realizing how shocking his comparison actually was, he emphasized that this was the only element in common between the Muslim dancers and the Catholic Enfants de Marie. Just the fact that he thought to draw a parallel between devout French women and the Nailiyat was significant. Despite his denials, it suggested not only the religiosity of a dance performance but, more generally, the eroticization of women in public. Nonetheless, he felt compelled to defend the Nailiyat: "Yet, at rest, their comportment is perfectly correct and, while dancing, even when they mime the most precise gestures of love their faces rest absolutely impassive." The "yet" indicated his confusion about the Nailiyat and the sexuality expressed in their dances. Indeed, the dancers served as a screen for Deloncle's fantasies. In his sleep he imagined that he had "realized a childhood dream" of rescuing a storybook heroine, Chryséis, who had been abducted by nomad fighters from a French fort in the desert.[62]

Orientalist stereotypes triumphed over determined images of actual women, evoking desire even in the most unlikely settings. For example, Chollier encountered in a clinic on the edge of the Casbah a "little Moorish girl," heavily veiled, with red slippers, whom he imagined among the "princesses of yesteryear" at the palace of the Dey. He described her in unabashedly erotic language: "her eyes, limpid as a gazelle's, smiling languishingly." Despite the fact that her eyes were the only things he could see of her, Chollier seemed to envision the girl as an unveiled odalisque. As though in response to his unstated desire, the nurse teasingly lifted the girl's veil to give Chollier a glimpse of her face. He just had time to see "the exquisite features of this little offended Venus. . . . She was not yet fifteen years old, and in her body, which was already that of a woman, she had the soul of a child." As he left the Casbah already treasuring in his "sachet of memories the pungent perfume of the red carnation of her lips," Chollier purchased as a souvenir a pair of "darling" coral slippers.[63] And so he turned a trip to an otherwise drab clinic into an erotic fantasy of the Dey's harem.

This was not all. To his delight Chollier was able from his privileged position as a European man to "contemplate at leisure the entire female race who hide behind the barred windows in the Casbah: Berber, Arab, and Saharan women." It seemed as if the women were part of an anthropological collection, a veritable counterharem. Chollier was not the only French writer to classify the women of Algeria according to stereotypes of race and tribe.[64] The Algerian anthropologist Malek Chebel has suggested that this practice of inventorying reflected "the wish to find some paradigms in an ocean of uncertainties." The "scenes and types" of colonial books, postcards, and exhibitions provided a reassuringly simple and understandable typology for the heterogeneous peoples and cultures of the French Empire.[65]

THE WORKSHOP

The recognition that a woman was a worker seemed to dissipate the erotic charge aroused in orientalist visions of the harem. Chollier, for example, commented that in the European part of Algiers, "veiled women . . . are far removed indeed from the odalisques of the *Tales of the Arabian Nights*: they are simply decent Moorish girls, maids-of-all-work." [66] The gendered discourse of French domination and superiority over Algeria took a particular turn in the representations of women weavers in the carpet industry. Descriptions of precolonial carpet making in North Africa focused on the *reggam*, the master craftsman, who went from tribe to tribe instructing the women in new designs. The French, however, disdained his skills. The official Jean Mirante wrote that "the reggam was far from being an artist; he has contented himself with maintaining the tradition received from his fathers, sometimes deforming it in the process." [67] He was blamed for incorporating alien designs and diluting "pure" regional styles. The degradation of tradition brought about by the reggam's visits to weaving households had sexual connotations: "Sometimes, in order to demonstrate his genius to the women, he innovates, that is to say, he blends the styles." His reputed success as a seducer of women who were thought by the French to be otherwise secluded from men evoked moral disapproval mixed with a touch of envy.[68]

By the nineteenth century Algerian carpets had lost many of their distinctive qualities. The problem, according to French authors, stemmed from the "contamination" of "traditional" designs by external influences, the use of unstable chemical dyes, and the poor technique of unskilled female and child labor. With the production of rugs "left to the fumbling inspiration of ignorant women with no taste, the fabrication [of carpets] was from the artistic point of view completely decadent at the beginning of the last century." Even the guiding hand of the reggam had apparently disappeared. The decline was blamed squarely on the cultural backwardness of Algerians, with no recognition of the vagaries of world market forces. Despite the disarray, the French thought it "easy to resuscitate the Algerian carpet industry, to infuse it with fresh blood." [69] This biological metaphor suggested the female maladies of fainting and wasting away. Like doctors, the French took charge of the industry's recovery. In contrast to the descriptions of agricultural development, however, women were included in this effort. The administrator A. Berque, for example, praised a number of European women for setting up workshops and "infus[ing] new life" into disused patterns.[70]

The task of technical training and support was taken up by the Algerian government. The director of indigenous affairs established schools and sponsored research into "authentic" designs, techniques, and colors for both embroidery and rug making. The researchers turned for inspiration to precious carpets from the fifteenth and sixteenth centuries, labeling their patterns the "traditional" ones which had been either lost or diluted. The French specialists then provided both the state- and church-run schools and workshops with renovated designs, appropriate for each region, and advice on materials and dyes.[71] "Authentic" and "tradition" are loaded terms, particularly when used in reference to ' Oriental" carpets, which as the very name suggests gain value from their recognition as a product of the "East." Brian Spooner suggests that "authenticity lies in cultural distance," which incorporates "the survival of traditional relations of production."[72] In the *Cahiers du Centenaire* the "renaissance" of carpet design involved a "return to classical tradition." But this tradition was invented, or at least redefined and re-created, by the Europeans. While the French built large, modern workshops, some for as many as one hundred workers, the techniques of production did not change. Indeed, both Berque and Blottière emphasized the impetus given by the revival to isolated household production of carpets. The French wanted to keep carpet weaving as a family industry, but with their own experts, rather than the reggam, determining the designs.[73]

By insisting that the survival of precolonial handicrafts required official management and expertise, Algerian industry was translated into French achievement. By labeling these largely female professions as "traditional" pursuits and then reviving them as such, the French obscured the history of such industries and, more generally, the impact of colonialism on "native" society and economy. By denigrating the skill and creativity of female labor, the authors of the *Cahiers du Centenaire* limited the role of women to passive bearers of tradition. While accepting the need for technical education, the French imposed limits that only consolidated the archaic and backward position of Algerian women. Young girls learned weaving, embroidery, and French in the small training workshops. These were skills they could bring into marriage and continue to practice even if secluded at home. While this was certainly a change from fantasies of odalisques either waiting on or waiting for their master, the vision of a de-eroticized and moralized harem maintained an aura of profound difference.

GREATER FRANCE

French representations of Algerian men varied a great deal. In general, colonialist literature stereotyped them as weak, lazy, and insincere. During the centenary celebrations, however, an image of the loyal, if exotic, subject briefly predominated. President Doumergue's official tour of the colony provided newspaper readers in the metropole with an introduction to the colonialist vision of Algeria. In cities bedecked with red, white, and blue, he received an enthusiastic welcome during parades, banquets, and meetings arranged by the Algerian government. Reporters focused on the men in white robes, brilliant jewels, and colorful headdresses among the crowds greeting the president. Descriptions of the hot African sun and the brilliant blue sky framed the narratives of outdoor festivities, from Doumergue's entry into Algiers on May 4 to his departure from Oran on May 12. These images not only formed an unfamiliar and picturesque backdrop to ceremonies of French dominance but also produced the meaning of the ceremonies themselves. Evocations of difference and inferiority gave value to the French attack on Algiers in 1830 and the subsequent battles of "pacification" which continued into the twentieth century. The once-threatening Muslim "other" was transformed into the safely subordinate "exotic."

The literary scholar David Spurr posits a "paradox of colonial discourse: the desire to emphasize racial and cultural difference as a means of establishing superiority takes place alongside the desire to efface difference and gather the colonized into the fold of an all-embracing civilization."[74] This paradox can be clearly observed in the depiction of local Algerian leaders' ritual declaration of loyalty to France, an important feature of Doumergue's tour. For example, the May 3, 1930, cover of a popular illustrated biweekly, *L'Illustration*, featured an impressive drawing of a banquet in Oran of the Union Fédérale des Anciens Combattants held in honor of the centenary. The central standing figure was an Arab in elaborate white robes, making a toast. He was identified as Boussif-Caïd, speaking on behalf of his father standing behind him, the chief Ben Chika, a veteran of the First World War. His words, quoted in the caption beneath the picture, contained a striking contradiction: "There is no longer present, on this African earth, an Algeria and a France; there is nothing but France." [75] The French, of course, welcomed just this sort of rhetoric, but it was undermined by the very presence of the dignified Arab veteran, distinguishable by his robes and by his silence. He was clearly neither French nor assimilated but the inhabitant of a place and society, Algeria, that had been extinguished by his son's words. Loyalty to the state, the image seemed to suggest, put French and Algerian men on the same footing. Notwithstanding the chief's irreducible difference, it is tempting to interpret his son's declaration as a subtle bid to claim the rights as well as the duties of Frenchmen. [76]

For the French the extremely high ratio of Algerian men who fought the First World War signified their enduring solidarity with France. Press coverage of the centenary included the suggestion that the Algerian contribution to the war effort justified its inclusion in "Greater France." [77] Furthermore, colonialist writers claimed that the Algerians' demonstration of loyalty proved that Algeria was not just part of Greater France but was, indeed, French, a significant identity shift. [78] The many images of bemedaled Arab veterans indicated this bond with France. Their white robes, however, imprisoned them in their difference. [79] Too much similarity was problematic. The French anxiously distinguished the indigenous Algerian from the European Algerian. The "not quite" part of almost being the same, an essential element of mimicry, was illustrated by Chollier's description of university students in Algiers. In a curiously contradictory passage, he made it very clear that he could tell the Arab and the European students apart. But then he emphasized that there was nothing in the dress or bearing of the Arab students "that on first glance recalled their origins." They are betrayed only by speech: the "hoarse" sounds of Arabic and their "singsong and unctuous" tone in French. The men he admired were the rural Algerians who looked out of place on the streets of Algiers and reminded him of biblical patriarchs, "glorious relics of picturesque old days." [80] As long as Algerian men maintained their identifiable difference, French self-confidence could be maintained.

CONCLUSION

Colonialist discourse aimed at a rhetorical incorporation of Algeria into France's national self-image, despite the obvious difference between colony and metropole. Gendered representations were crucial in resolving this apparent contradiction. The simultaneous feminization of Algeria and masculinization of France naturalized the colonial relationship. Kristin Ross demonstrates the continuing power of gendered rhetoric in her discussion of representations of France and Algeria in the decades following 1930, up through the 1954–62 war of independence. She shows the pervasiveness across the political spectrum of images of a common household, cohabitation, and marriage, with Algeria, of course, as the female companion or wife.[81]

In 1930, however, Algeria had yet to have a unified female identity in political discourse. Rather, separate elements of the colony were eroticized. Portrayed as seductive, passive, and available, the landscape seemed to exist for the sole purpose of French penetration and fertilization. The idea that potentially productive land was foolishly abandoned by the Algerians facilitated the elision of conquest to creation. In a complete usurpation of all procreative powers, every aspect of agricultural, industrial, and demographic growth was attributed to French men. But, almost as if this power of creation was too much, concerns emerged regarding the degeneration of the French race. The losses of the First World War had eroded French self-confidence. Technology and the fast pace of modern life seemed to be changing human nature. The "natural" Algerian nomad in the desert appeared as the signifier for a primordial masculinity no longer attainable by French men. The nostalgia that suffused this hagiographical portrayal of earthy "natural" masculinity, however, indicated the Algerian's exclusion from modern life. He was allowed back into the landscape only after he had been definitively conquered, transformed into a picturesque presence in the desert and a wistful emblem of archetypal manhood.

By contrast, Algerian women were pictured as already restricted to the interior of the home and subordinate to men. The issue for French writers was one of contact and control. They portrayed themselves in situations which excluded Algerian men: women lifted their veils, danced, or worked for Europeans. In the public sphere, however, French men allied with Algerian men as fellow veterans. But the exoticization of Algerian war veterans, even while portrayed as loyally French, indicated their subordination. The "fantasy of colonial mastery" provided the filter through which the French perceived the reality of colonial power. Its gendered imagery and erotic scenes filled French colonial vistas while it blocked the glare of harsh inequalities and oppressive laws. The force of these gendered metaphors and highly charged rhetoric obscured for the French the development of the other Algeria, a subaltern Algeria transforming itself into a nation in revolt.

11. EMANCIPATING EACH OTHER: Dutch Colonial Missionaries' Encounter with Karo Women in Sumatra, 1900–1942

ℑ Rita Smith Kipp

This essay examines a colonial encounter, extending over a period of fifty years, between Dutch missionaries and the women of a particular Indonesian society—the Karo. The Karo are one of several Batak peoples whose homelands lie along the Sumatran mountain range called the Bukit Barisan. The missionaries worked for the Dutch Missionary Society (Nederlands Zendelinggenootschap, abbreviated as NZG), an organization that represented the more liberal branch of Dutch Reformed churches, although it was officially nondenominational. The misunderstandings that marked this encounter were no doubt mutual, but this chapter's focus is primarily on the missionary perspective.

The missionaries hoped to lead Karo women to emancipation through a grounding in Christian morality and education. The primary outcome of this emancipation, so the missionaries reasoned, would be that women might claim greater autonomy within their families, and especially greater parity with their husbands. Emancipation also meant that women might be educated for professional careers. These intended outcomes were compromised both by the missionaries' misunderstanding of women's status in Karo society and by their limited sense of what emancipation might mean. While Karo women did not enjoy status and autonomy equal to that of men, they were in a far better situation than the missionaries initially reckoned. The missionaries also assumed that professional careers necessarily entailed women's commitment to a single life. Karo girls and their parents, however, did not see women's work as incompatible with marriage and family life. They continually challenged the missionaries' assumptions, utilizing education and opportunities provided through the mission to reach their own goals, thereby forcing change or gaining concessions from the missionaries, and partly emancipating them, as it were, from their preconceptions.

The Karo heartland is a high plateau that was relatively inaccessible until the early twentieth century, but Karo also occupy the foothills and lowlands between the plateau and the city of Medan on the northeastern coast of Sumatra. They cultivate both wet and dry varieties of rice and a wide range of other subsistence and cash crops. The Karo are distinguished from lowland Malays by speaking a Batak language, by a patrilineal social order, and a preference for asymmetrical cross-cousin marriage. Ideally, men should marry someone from their mother's patrilineage, the closest example of which would be a mother's brother's daughter. (The daughters of a father's sister are like sisters, expressly off-limits for romance or marriage.)[1] A man's mother's and/or wife's family are his *kalimbubu*, wife-givers, and his ritual superiors. The families into which his sisters or daughters marry are termed *anakberu*; they are his ritual inferiors. Relations of siblingship and equality mark those who share patrilineal descent, while social hierarchy prevails in the affinal kalimbubu-anakberu relationships. These kinship statuses are for the most part ritualistic and social, not economic.

The Karo became the target of missionary work in 1889, in a classic divide-and-rule scenario, when plantation owners on Sumatra's east coast desired to make them a "Christian bulwark."[2] The planters wished to shield their investments from an Islamic war of resistance that was simmering to the north by making the Karo their Christian allies. Inviting the Dutch Missionary Society to establish itself among the Karo, the planters offered to meet all the expenses of the new installation in its first years. The planters' and missionaries' plans were somewhat stymied when the colonial government denied the missionaries permission to work on the Karo Plateau, not yet under Dutch control, where villages continually skirmished with each other. For the first fifteen years of the mission's existence, the missionaries worked only in the Karo-speaking villages located in the piedmont or foothills regions of the east coast. When the government annexed the highlands into the colonial realm in 1904 through a military expedition, the mission's center of operations shifted to the Karo Plateau.

The missionaries employed a wide-ranging approach to evangelization, opening primary schools and treating the sick as well as teaching and preaching about the new religion. As the decades passed, the mission managed an increasing number of stations, churches, schools, clinics, hospitals, and a leprosarium. It published a newspaper in the Karo language, as well as the Bible and other literature, primarily to teach about Christianity. Despite its expansion, the mission was singularly unsuccessful at gaining converts, a failure some attributed to its close relationship with the land-voracious plantations and its general association with the Dutch regime, of which the Karo grew increasingly resentful throughout the colonial period.[3]

ASSESSING WOMEN'S STATUS

In 1920 missionary E. J. van den Berg, addressing a meeting of missionaries and indigenous evangelist-teachers, expressed the need to reach Karo women.[4] He explained that in other mission fields, missionary wives were able to teach and influence young girls through hiring them as household servants. Missionaries had hoped to use this "student system" not only to win girls to Christianity but also to teach them Dutch standards of housekeeping and hygiene and to make them fitting partners for a cohort of mission-educated men who, as teachers and church leaders, would exemplify new standards of dress, cleanliness, and comportment in their communities. The method had borne little fruit up to that time (although it would show some success later) because Karo girls seldom agreed to work as servants. In the mission's early years, it had been difficult to find any Karo willing to work as house servants, although boys were generally more willing than girls, because parents were more comfortable with allowing a son to live with a missionary family than allowing a daughter to do so. Dina Wijngaarden-Guittard, the first missionary wife to live among the Karo, was frustrated not only by girls' reluctance to become servants but also by the way her neighbors perceived her housekeeping role. Hoping to impress her neighbors with new standards of cleanliness and domesticity, she appeared to them to be "just sitting" at home while they worked in the fields, carried water and firewood, or pounded rice.[5] In 1901 J. H. Neumann had two girls working in his house; one had been a debt slave whom he had redeemed and the other had been placed with him by her brother. The community was quite suspicious of his intentions.[6]

Girls' reluctance to be servants exemplified what the missionaries felt to be a general characteristic of their gender. Missionaries perceived Karo women as the "conservative element" in society and thus an impediment to religious change. Writing in 1929 from Sibolangit, Jan van Muylwijk reported that 184 persons were studying for baptism and that many others showed interest. Often, he reported, it was the wife who would not agree to the idea, citing the case of one headman whose wife threatened to kill herself if he converted. As the headman continued with his study to become a Christian, the wife ran away into the forest, where she was found two days later. In Van Muylwijk's next annual report, he remarked on an overall increase in interest, but he still noticed a strong resistance from women, "precisely those most difficult to win." While these reports of resistance by Karo women were no doubt accurate, it was also true that the missionaries expected to see this pattern. The board agreed with Van Muylwijk's report that it was a pity women resisted Christianity "because they have only to gain by changing. . . . But as is the case so often elsewhere, women are the conservative element." The idea that women were conservative in accepting conversion was an old saw in mission circles.[7]

The board did point out that in Van Muylwijk's statistics for the same year, women comprised a slight majority in his congregation. Almost a decade later, writing from the plateau, Hendrik Vuurmans listed 776 men and 694 women as church members in the Karo Highlands but also noted: "Concerning church attendance at Kabanjahe, it must still be remarked that the women's side is always much more crowded than is the men's side." At the same time he reported that he had baptized 47 men and 52 women in 1938.[8] It is difficult to know how early the attendance pattern favoring women started, because statistics on attendance and membership from the various posts were not usually broken down by gender. It is probably safe to generalize, however, that while some Karo women may have shown the most vehement resistance to Christianity at first, women increasingly formed the majority of the faithful.[9]

The seeming paradox that women both resisted and were drawn to the missionaries' message can be partly resolved by clues suggesting that in the beginning they might have systematically overlooked or discounted women's interest. Writing from the new post on the plateau in 1906, Van den Berg found that people were quite reserved about the new religion. He observed that men, especially, were reluctant when they learned that it entailed giving up gambling and smoking opium, but he added, "The woman I leave out of consideration because she forms an element in Batak society that does not count, and thus her attendance has but little value." Evangelistic strategy, in this NZG field as in others, always placed great value on winning and influencing headmen and other male leaders, on the presumption that once the high-status men of influence were won over, they would pull their followers into the fold.[10] Given the tenuous quality of leadership in Karo society, the strategy was miscalculated in this case.[11]

The missionaries' overestimating the influence of male leaders paralleled their underestimating the importance and influence of Karo women in their families and communities. Van den Berg's argument at the teachers' conference of 1920 about the problems of reaching women had included the point that Batak women occupied a low status, presenting a barrier to their becoming Christian. Missionary views of Indonesian women in general and the Karo in particular were not always consistent. On the one hand, they portrayed women as powerless and passive.[12] On the other, they hinted that women exercised enough influence to thwart the missionaries' best-laid plans. Van Muylwijk, who bemoaned Karo women's conservatism, also felt that "from the beginning it was clear that nothing could be achieved here without reaching the women with the Gospel and winning them to it," a judgment that contradicted his colleague's earlier opinion that women in Batak society did not "count."[13]

Missionaries supposed that making Christians of indigenous women in the Indies should, as a matter of course, improve their position in society. The missionaries assessed the low position of Karo women from a number of social criteria. First, the practice of polygyny indicated to them that women's status was particularly low. Also, in this patrilineal society women had no legal rights to inherit land. Moreover, the missionaries thought that the practice of bride payments showed that women were traded like chattel.[14] A bride payment attached future children to the groom's clan; in case of divorce, then, the children belonged to the father. Women did the bulk of the agricultural labor as well, and although missionaries repeatedly commented on women's strength and industriousness relative to Karo males, they tended to see Karo women as bonded servants if not slaves to their husbands.[15] In reality, women's position in Karo society was not as disadvantaged as it seemed at first glance. Women were probably not particularly happy if their husbands took another wife. But women in polygynous marriages maintained separate households, and men with multiple wives were generally headmen or other men of influence. The material and social benefits of marrying such a man frequently balanced the disadvantages of being in a polygynous union. Although women had no rights to land, women sometimes received land as "gifts" or had lifetime right of usufruct in their parents' land.[16] In many cases couples chose to live in the wife's village if her family granted them property or the use of property, and this usage sometimes passed on to their children. Thus, women in effect controlled property and transmitted it to heirs in some cases.

Karo attitudes about bride payments in the past were no doubt similar to those held by contemporary Karo, who continue this practice. In Karo thinking a bride price symbolizes a woman's value, especially her economic and reproductive value. Western women appear, from the Karo's perspective, to throw themselves into marriage without the dignity of a payment marking their worth. Regardless of how high a woman's bride price is, however, it remains only a symbol of her worth, not a monetary measure of it as if she were a commodity for sale in the market. Ritual expressions, especially funeral payments, suggest that even a man who has paid his bride price in full remains perpetually "indebted" to his wife's family. After death, a person's funeral payments acknowledge the continuing "debt" he or she owes the kalimbubu.[17]

The missionaries felt that Karo men spoke disparagingly of their wives when they referred obliquely to them as "the one who cooks my rice," "the one who feeds my livestock," or "the one I bought with gold." These circumlocutions, however, had an opposite purpose. They enabled a man to refer to his wife without uttering her name or saying bluntly "my wife," for to use her name would have signaled great disrespect. Furthermore, saying "my wife" (likewise, "my husband") also violated etiquette, sounding obscenely crude to Karo ears, as if one had alluded to the sexual act.[18] The missionaries and other European observers misinterpreted this polite hedging as disrespect, when it was, in fact, just the reverse.

The missionaries, who had quickly gauged women's status from a checklist of customs, came only later to a more nuanced consideration of the options and maneuverability available to women. Vuurmans, one of the later missionaries to the Karo, realized that the social-juridical position of women in this patrilineal society appeared to be lower than it actually was in the practices of everyday life. Women controlled the finances in most families and were "outgoing in behavior," exhibiting the outward signs of "emancipation." [19] Because the missionaries worked from a faulty analysis of what the limitations and powers of Karo women were, and because they wrongly assumed that Christianity, almost in itself, would correct the restrictions imposed on women, the strategy of raising women's status through conversion was not particularly effective in the long run.

EDUCATING KARO WOMEN

Missionary education proved to be an important agent of change in Karo women's lives, although the outcomes of this change did not match what the missionaries had intended. Formal education was virtually unknown in traditional Karo life, and the schools the mission introduced had a profound and lasting effect on Karo society. Through formal education and informal modeling, missionaries attempted primarily to mold Karo men and women into Christians but also into gender roles that matched more closely their own European experiences.

An article in an NZG journal in 1909 reveals the general tenor of missionary thinking on the question of women's careers in this era. "De plaats die de Jaavansche vrouw inneemt in de samenleving en in de Christengemeente" (The place which the Javanese woman occupies in society and in the Christian community) was originally presented as a lecture in the Netherlands before the annual meeting of the Dutch Missionary Society. The speech began, ironically, with the caution that we should not identify the Gospel with Western civilization, and that in the process of bringing the Gospel, missionaries should not expect the peoples of the Indies to adopt other cultural aspects of the West. The author, Arie Kruyt, had been struck by the pervasive dominance of women in Javanese markets, buying and selling with expertise and carrying goods and produce through the streets. Javanese women managed tea shops or other small businesses until late at night, made batik, or labored in the rice fields, in addition to working in their households. These economic roles gave them a measure of independence from men, especially as women usually managed their own income apart from their husbands. Wherever Islam had exerted its influence on Java, it had restricted women's freedom and their inheritance rights, Kruyt observed. He worried that the importation of Western law might also diminish women's legal rights, "for example, as with us, in giving the management of a woman's property to her husband."

Yet in other ways Kruyt could not see beyond the possibilities of women's emancipation, as defined in the Netherlands of his time. Speaking of what became of Javanese women who converted to Christianity, Kruyt remarked, "for the Christian girl, marriage remains the goal of her life." The missionaries counseled young girls not to marry too early, however, and were glad when they insisted on marrying someone whose education and "development" matched their own. Yet Kruyt wondered with despair whether these Christian women could ever manage their own evangelistic work among women, for none among them was willing to renounce the idea of marriage. "But then it is not possible to have among the Javanese people, for example, deaconess [nursing] work as we know it, nor shall a class of female teachers emerge." Javanese women who worked as nurses in the mission hospitals committed themselves for only two years, and all eventually married.[20] Kruyt did not consider their education wasted, however. "For our work they are indispensable as housewives and mothers."

Kruyt never questioned why educated Javanese women should have to choose between their work or having a family, although Javanese men did not have to do so. For him, it went without saying that female deaconesses, nurses, and teachers in the Netherlands expected to remain single, while most male careers were predicated on the expectation of marriage. Javanese women, who worked in fields and markets and usually controlled the money in their families, including their husband's earnings, must have assumed that both work and family would be part of their lives.[21] They would not conform to the missionaries' notion that

Postcard made from a photograph of a Karo Batak woman
in traditional dress ca. 1920

with "emancipation" would come, as in Holland, a class of unmarried
professional women who had felt compelled to trade marriage and
family for careers.

Although girls attended mission schools, they generally were in the
minority in the early years. When Jan Wijngaarden opened the first
primitive school with about a dozen students, parents would not let
their daughters attend, claiming that they were "too dumb" and, anyway, did not need an education. Wijngaarden also speculated that avoidance rules between brother and sister and other kinds of kin would
make coeducation impossible.[22] He supposed that girls would have to
be educated separately by women missionaries. By 1900, however, girls
had begun to attend the mission's schools in the east coast foothills, and

one small school had fifteen girls attending—despite the fact that the seating on benches rather than desks made the avoidance practices difficult to follow.[23]

Just after the turn of the century, the Karo's interest in education suddenly ignited. On every side villagers begged the missionaries to open schools. In 1907 an enthusiastic civil servant in charge of the region made education compulsory for all Karo boys and girls who lived within a one-hour walk from a school. He levied fees from parents to support the plan and opened some new government schools, which eventually came under missionary leadership. The missionaries and the local government were both stretched beyond their resources to manage and staff these new schools. In 1911, when more students showed up than could be accommodated, a directive from the government stipulated that boys should have priority in government schools, and in some locales girls also dropped out of mission schools in deference to this ruling.[24] The schools employed Minahassa and Toba Batak teachers, but Neumann began as early as 1901 to train Karo as teachers.[25] It would be decades, however, before any of the aspirant teachers were girls.

The Karo's sudden enthusiasm for education began to abate around 1915, and school attendance started to fall. Villagers might have had unrealistic expectations of what an education would do or did not understood that it required a steady commitment over a number of years. They also resented the school tax and the compulsory attendance. In addition, new economic conditions may have affected people's calculations of the benefits of schooling.[26] Now under colonial rule, highland Karo were required to pay taxes, and with a new road connecting the Karo Plateau to the lowlands, a new market for their agricultural products emerged. Markets were also filled with novel things to buy. Families marshaled all their members, boys and girls alike, to meet these new economic burdens and opportunities, so the cost of sending children to school interfered with families' short-term economic interests.[27]

In addition, however, two complaints about the mission schools surfaced repeatedly: they spent too much time on religion, and they did not teach Malay, the lingua franca of the Indies. The charge of too much religious education had plagued even the earliest mission schools, but the regrets about the lack of Malay instruction only developed later.[28] The linguistic policy of the mission—to teach and preach in Karo and to produce a literature in that language—was aimed specifically at keeping the Karo insulated from the influences of the surrounding Muslim world. Facility in Malay would have allowed Karo to migrate to urban areas or elsewhere, but Malay speech might also have been the first step in "becoming Malay," which in this region was synonymous with Muslim conversion.[29] Meint Joustra, writing in 1896, remarked that the Karo had little practical use for literacy—few jobs required it—and he did not want to educate them for jobs outside the region, where Karo would surely encounter the influence of Islam.[30] More ominously, by the 1920s Malay was also becoming the language of an emergent Indonesian nationalism.

Whatever the causes of the Karo's disenchantment with education in general and missionary schools in particular, the missionaries retaliated against their withdrawal by closing all elementary schools in October 1920. The move was intended as a dramatic threat, gambling that when people realized the loss, they would contritely beg the missionaries to reopen the schools. Instead, communities seized the opportunity to found their own schools, and the missionaries later regretted having lost control of elementary education.[31] In the wake of this miscalculation, the missionaries tried all the harder to monopolize advanced levels of education in Karoland, including teacher-training programs. Even with the primary school system collapsing, ten girls were among those who applied in 1920 to study at a "continuing" school the mission hoped to preserve in Kabanjahe.[32]

Missionaries aimed to use the schools as a vehicle to spread Christianity and to equip Christian Karo to read the Gospel in their own language. The missionaries expected the Karo to remain as cultivators in their home region—a literate peasantry. They never intended the schools to become a means of transforming the Karo into mobile, urban wage earners who followed job opportunities wherever they might lead. This was especially true for girls' education. The missionaries did not at first imagine educating Karo girls for jobs outside the home, and when Karo girls applied for advanced levels of education, the missionaries sometimes reacted with surprise. In 1936, when the mission had begun to train evangelists and teachers once more, Van Muylwijk wrote the board that sixty people had applied for the program, "including ten girls!"[33]

TRAINING NURSES OR TRAINING MOTHERS

The misapprehension between the missionaries and the Karo is most clearly seen in a nurses training program centered at the mission hospital in Sibolangit, a market town in the foothills. The program did not originate as a nurses training course, but it was forced into that mold by the demands of young Karo women and their parents. It began, in fact, not for educational purposes at all but to take care of infants whose mothers had died in childbirth.

Throughout the nineteenth century Karo newborns whose mothers had died were usually killed and sometimes cremated with their mother's corpses. The reluctance to let motherless newborns live was expressed through various whispered fears. Such children began life in unlucky circumstances, and as their fate, they would bring bad luck to all with whom they had contact. The ghosts of women who had died in childbirth would attempt to take with them into the grave some close family member, especially, in the case of a woman who died in childbed, her own child.

The early missionaries perceived the Karo as crassly materialistic, cold-blooded, and self-interested.[34] And they painted infanticide with this brush: people killed infants to save themselves inconvenience or expense. Pagan selfishness contrasted with Christian love was also a theme in the mission's care of lepers. Starting in 1906, the missionaries, heavily subsidized by the government, undertook the care of lepers in an asylum. Exemplifying Christian love for hopeless outcasts, this community was the most successful locale for making converts in the entire Karo field. It also garnered a tremendous amount of publicity and goodwill for the mission among Europeans in the Indies and in Holland, not to mention spectacular donations, becoming a favorite photo stop for visiting dignitaries and common tourists.[35]

Jan Wijngaarden took a motherless newborn into his home as early as 1894, and his wife Dina Wijngaarden-Guittard raised this baby, named Sangap, with her own infant son for about a year, until her husband's untimely death ended her sojourn in Sumatra.[36] The story of Sangap, from the Wijngaardens' letters, was published in the NZG's scholarly journal. Although the NZG director privately advised Mrs. Wijngaarden not to bring Sangap with her when she returned to Holland, the boy remained attached to the missionary families that followed her. News of his rescue must have spread by word of mouth throughout the Karo area, because families began bringing motherless infants to missionary homes shortly thereafter. In one instance Hendrik Pesik, a Minahassa teacher who was working for the mission in a small village, reported in 1896 that a man had visited him to ask what Batak day it had been three days earlier, that is, what day it would have been on the Batak lunar calendar. The man's wife had died on that day, and someone had said it was a "bad" day and that she would return to take him or one of their children with her in death. Pesik consulted the notes he had written about this calendar. The day was Budaha, truly an unpropitious day. He used the opportunity to talk with the man about good and bad days and about spirits, saying Christians feared none of these things. Some days later the same man returned with a sick baby, and although Pesik fed it canned milk and rice porridge, the child eventually died. The mother had come back for it, people said.[37]

In the same year Benjamin Wenas, another Minahassa teacher who was working for the mission in a village, took in two motherless infants, both girls.[38] One of these was reclaimed by her family and died within a matter of days. Only a few weeks later, two women from another village arrived at Wenas's door with another baby, desperate to have Wenas take it. One of the women, the baby's aunt, insisted when Wenas demurred, saying that if he did not take it the child would die. Again, Wenas and his wife conceded to try, naming the baby Si Ruli, the Lucky One. She lived five months, succumbing to a mysterious stomach pain. "We were very sad at her death," Wenas wrote, describing her burial which the child's relatives also attended.[39]

Wijngaarden's account of rescuing Sangap from infanticide two years before had suggested that behind the Batak's superstitions, selfishness was the real root of mothers' refusal to become wet nurses to other women's children. (His wife, nursing her own child at the time, did not nurse the infant Sangap but rather used a bottle.) In his assessment infanticide was the grisly evidence of the pagan's hard-heartedness and lack of love. Wijngaarden's successor, Joustra, did not agree with this judgment. The survival of Sangap had become an example that must have spread from ear to ear among Karo in the foothills. The same year that Wenas and Pesik recorded their experiences with orphaned babies,

Joustra wrote that two fathers of motherless newborns had come to ask him for bottles and milk. "Certainly this is a sign that the earlier custom of letting a baby die was not just out of cruelty," Joustra decided, "but more because of the impossibility of raising it." [40]

E. J. van den Berg, the first missionary to live in the Karo Highlands, found that the story of Sangap had preceded him there. Soon after settling into Kabanjahe in 1905, Van den Berg received a baby from a man whose wife had died some weeks before. The child had been kept alive but was in poor condition, and it died after several weeks. Two years later, with Dutch law newly imposed on the plateau, infanticide had become a crime, but surely one that still went unreported and unpunished in most instances. In that year Van den Berg took in six infants, three of whom died. Thus, people still came asking the missionary to harbor motherless infants. Mrs. van den Berg, with two small children of her own and pregnant with a third, did most of the supervising of the infants' care. But Van den Berg had stipulated that each family leaving a baby with him must also provide a family member to help with the work. [41]

These ad hoc arrangements in missionary homes were seldom mentioned in letters or publications after 1908 and probably declined as missionaries found themselves with more than enough to do with the expanding schools and other work. Such arrangements may well have occurred sporadically and without comment, however, until the time a hospital provided an institutional setting for the same practice.

The hospital at Sibolangit had already been open for ten years before it took up the care of motherless babies. In February 1925 the wife of one of the Karo teachers died of complications after childbirth. She had intended to have the baby in the hospital at Sibolangit but had not been able to get there. The baby, a boy, was kept in the women's ward from February to September. Two young Karo women who had begun to work in the hospital in 1923 and 1924 nurtured the baby while attending to the other patients. Between September 1925 and the beginning of the new year, there were four other orphaned newborns in Sibolangit's hospital. The staff realized that keeping them with sick female patients was not in the best interests of either those patients or the babies, and a linen storage room was then converted into a nursery. Van Muylwijk, the missionary at Sibolangit, advertised in the mission newspaper that the hospital needed girls as helpers for this work, and to his surprise five girls applied. By the next year there was a total of twelve girls. Before this time there had been at most four Karo girls or women working at Sibolangit. Pieternella Wynekes, a nurse who managed the hospital, had to struggle in the beginning to recruit any.[42]

Van Muylwijk saw in the baby care a way to expand the work of the hospital and perhaps to attract girls to work there. He envisioned an opportunity to teach and influence young women, while at the same time providing a health service that he was sure would win the hospital much good publicity. He wrote asking the board to support the expansion of this project financially. The board reacted cautiously, explaining its thoughts in a letter to Van Muylwijk. While the board saw some good "perspective" in this work (at a time when church growth, schools, and other mission activities at Sibolangit were virtually dead), the project seemed a "circular argument" and somewhat contrived. Certainly the training of young women was worthwhile, but was it necessary to promote the care of motherless babies to achieve that end? "Is there much mission potential in this work," the board asked, meaning does it have much evangelistic promise, "or is it purely a work of charity?" While the board did not suggest that Van Muylwijk abandon the plan, it urged him to be careful. "Perhaps it is better if the people themselves take on this infant care."[43]

Despite his superiors' lack of encouragement, Van Muylwijk continued to make his vision a reality. The goal of the girls' training, as he saw it, was not to produce professional nurses but to produce wives and mothers, each "more suited for her task later in her own family." Eventually he hoped to reach other women with the Gospel through the example of these nurse apprentices. Most of the girls who came to Sibolangit to work had had no previous education. They took sewing lessons from Mrs. van Muylwijk and learned to make their own uniforms, of which they were very proud. They also received instruction in religion, and they attended church on Sunday, making up a majority in attendance during the first years of the program. They received no salary but only food, clothing, and a little spending money.[44] Van Muylwijk was correct in anticipating that this work would strike a responsive chord. Karo parents liked it and wanted their daughters to participate in the training. Benefactors liked the concept, too. In 1928 a Medan doctor contributed seven hundred guilders to the program, and an article in the *Deli Courant* brought in additional gifts. Van Muylwijk proceeded with his plans, building a dormitory large enough to house twenty girls.[45]

It was clear, too, that the Sibolangit baby ward offered a service that people had long needed. "The more it is known, the more people bring them to us," wrote Wynekes.[46] By 1928 there was a daily average of twenty-three babies in the hospital, babies brought "from the edges of Karoland." Fathers from as far away as the Simelungun Batak region, Lau Baleng, and Kuta Cane brought their infants to Sibolangit. Van Muylwijk determined to take only babies whose mothers were dead (rather than sick or simply negligent), and the babies' fathers were required to pay five guilders a month for the service, "to ensure the father's care and interest" in the child. When they were between eighteen months and two years of age, the babies were returned to their fathers, that is, if they lived that long. Of the fifty-two babies who were brought to the hospital in 1928, twenty-five died, but Van Muylwijk reasoned: "That's not bad. Even in Europe, the survival rate of such babies is only about 50 percent."[47]

With motherless infants gathered in one place, the very cause of their being there became the more flagrantly obvious: the high mortality of childbearing women. Van Muylwijk used this evidence to argue for the need for a government-paid midwife. Without keeping careful statistics on this, Van Muylwijk had noted twenty-five deaths from childbirth in twenty months spanning 1925 and 1926. As a result of Van Muylwijk's efforts, a Karo woman named Pertumpuen br. Purba was placed at Sibolangit in 1929. She traveled to surrounding villages for deliveries and also supervised births within the hospital, although hospital deliveries were still very rare. Unused to the idea of a professional midwife, Karo women did not call on Purba much at first, so she busied herself with helping in the baby ward. In her first year at Sibolangit, there were thirteen hospital births compared to three the year before, and the demand for her services gradually became commonplace.

The girls who came as baby caretakers often had different ideas about their future than Van Muylwijk had for them. In 1929 four of the girls who had finished their three or four years at Sibolangit found work in other hospitals, and Van Muylwijk could have placed even more, if only there had been suitable candidates. Another left to attend a government high school. Five returned to their villages. While Van Muylwijk admitted that it would be acceptable in some cases for the girls' experience at Sibolangit to lead to a nursing career, he regretted to think that the girls who applied might be motivated by "the desire for diplomas and making a lot of money." Van Muylwijk found that there were always more applicants than places, and that even Simelungun and Toba Batak girls wanted access to the program. Through time, the applicants themselves changed, increasingly becoming girls who had already received some previous education, many of them beyond the primary grades. In 1936 Van Muylwijk wrote: "In twelve years the times have also changed in this respect. And so, because the girls themselves and their parents increasingly asked for it, we must accommodate, although it is unfortunate, the demand that this training should earn one a diploma and suit one for a well-paying job elsewhere. In this way the emphasis of this work was laid ever more on the material value and the profit rather than on ideals, and increasingly the real value of this work for our mission was lost." [48]

SEWING EMANCIPATION

Missionary wives and missionary nurses undertook the first evangelistic work directed specifically at women. The vehicle for this was sewing lessons. Dina Wijngaarden was chagrined in 1894 that only two boys were eager to learn sewing from her, probably in order to make trousers. At this point Karo dress for both men and women consisted of cloths or sarongs wrapped at the waist or above the breasts, shawls, and head wraps. Fitted clothing was rare and was generally the prerogative of headmen or other men of influence. In general, males were more likely than women to take up Malay or European dress, so the women Dina Wijngaarden hoped to teach probably could not see much use in learning how to sew. Fashions changed, however, and by the early 1930s Karo women began to adopt what Sandra Niessen has called the Sumatran *vestimentun communis*, a combination of Malay and European clothing that elides ethnic distinctions.[49] Now they wanted to learn to make Malay blouses, dresses, or nurses' uniforms for themselves, and perhaps appropriate (i.e., Western) school clothing for their children.

A progressive leader on the plateau, Pa Sendi, established a home economics school for girls in Kabanjahe in the 1920s, a move the missionaries regarded as competitive with their own control of education. Mrs. van den Berg thus began to offer sewing lessons, also in Kabanjahe, and was quickly inundated with work. The Van den Bergs successfully lobbied the board to hire a woman leader for the student hostels that the mission ran at that time in Kabanjahe, envisioning that such a person could relieve Mrs. van den Berg of the sewing clubs. This leader, Linda Wilkens, assumed leadership of the sewing clubs in Kabanjahe in 1931. In Sibolangit, J. M. J. Meyer, a nurse who began managing the hospital there in 1929, performed similar duties but cited this as one of the things she most enjoyed about her assignment. In the 1930s Mrs. W. A. Smit continued the Sibolangit work and at one time was leading five different groups in weekly meetings.[50]

The sewing clubs grew to movement proportions in the 1930s, involving all the missionary wives. Mrs. Neumann, now in her fifties and with her children grown, was an especially active leader in this movement. In 1933 Mrs. Neumann and others made the informal sewing groups into a club with the polyglot title Christelijke Meisjes Club Maju—a Dutch-English-Malay composite meaning Christian Girls Club Forward (or, perhaps, Progressive Christian Girls Club). Everyone simply called it by its initials, CMCM. The first one was formed at Kabanjahe and, in the next two years, divided into five chapters. By 1939 another eighteen clubs had formed elsewhere on the plateau and some twenty in the foothills. The missionary women intended the clubs for unmarried girls above the age of sixteen, but then married women wanted to join, and even younger girls, so the club was split into three age grades.

Mrs. Neumann wrote later that in the first two years of the organization's life some people had expressed suspicion and distrust. "And then people said, 'Why go to so much trouble for women and girls. That is just the female sex.'"[51] The suspicion did not quickly abate in all areas. In 1937 W. A. Smit reported that when a girl who had joined the CMCM asked to study for baptism, people attributed this to the magical powers of the evangelist, and as the rumor spread, that evangelist saw people slipping out their back doors as he entered the villages. Smit wondered whether the CMCM girls should not be made to wait at least two years before being baptized to prevent the impression of being bewitched.[52] CMCM members served as good "propagandists for Christendom" in their families and sometimes refused to marry any young man who would not become a Christian.

Through this activity women also learned about the phenomenon of a club as a modern bureaucratic form, and these clubs were the forerunner of today's women's groups, called Moria, in the Karo Batak Protestant Church.[53] Each chapter elected officers and had a treasury to meet the costs of its activities. In fact, the wives of Karo evangelists, following the model of the missionary wives, took on the leadership of many of these clubs, and all chapter leaders gathered monthly to coordinate activities and to receive Bible instruction to pass on to their groups. The missionary wives began to train Karo women to carry out the work of leadership, sending them on tours of widely scattered villages where women had asked to have a CMCM group set up. "We are thus striving to make this work independent," Mrs. Neumann wrote, "but control (i.e., leadership) will still be necessary for a long time."[54] The reference to control here is to European control and leadership. Just as the male missionaries to the Karo were slow to train an indigenous clergy and to imagine that Karo Christians were ready to manage their own church, so Mrs. Neumann could not imagine Karo women carrying on the sewing clubs entirely without European supervision.

The missionaries saw this CMCM growth as evidence of a great "emancipation struggle" on the part of Karo women. While they admitted the need for emancipation and encouraged their wives' involvement in the clubs, they also showed some apprehension as the movement mushroomed. How far would it go? Was it possible that the women were simply using Christianity as a convenient path to emancipation? Once they had acquired some useful and perhaps marketable skills, would they abandon the faith? "Indeed, people now see a way through Christianity," Neumann felt. "The great advantage is that, from this, spiritual interest can be kindled." Smit worried that the feminist ferment would overshadow the spiritual: "This work manifests itself in an emancipation struggle, and the evangelizing character is driven ever more into the background, as far as I can judge. Naturally this is not the plan and intention, but perhaps just the consequence of some methods. Don't the women and girls place too much emphasis on the idea of 'going forward'? Isn't it excessive to say: 'Oh those lazy men and boys; forward girls, show your strength'? This is very surely a good stimulus, but one that can eventually become a danger." [55]

Yet Vuurmans, who seemed more comfortable with emancipation than some of his older colleagues, noted that the emancipation of Karo woman was proceeding with or without the mission and its CMCM work. Some well-to-do families sent their daughters to Padang Panjang, in West Sumatra, to the normal school there and were pleased if their daughters began to wear Western dress. "People are much concerned at the present time with the education of their children, and not just for the boys, but also for the girls," Vuurmans wrote. "There are now six girls in the new course for teachers . . . and mothers have come to me with their daughters, pleading with me to take their daughters into the program. One father wrote me a letter asking if I could not see to it that his daughter was accepted." [56]

Girls were enrolling in increasing numbers in the public schools, and some took the finishing school course at Kabanjahe where they learned home economics. Yet Smit noted that most of them continued or returned to work as agricultural laborers, and although they often dressed and looked differently than other village girls, he found they had not become "unbalanced" for the most part or disdainful of physical labor. Furthermore, Karo men seemed not at all threatened by this "emancipation" of women but, on the contrary, encouraged it, especially by seeking educated girls as spouses for themselves or their sons. [57]

In imitation of the CMCM work, Smit, assigned to Sibolangit in 1936, tried to establish a similar club for boys—the Karo Christian Boys League or BKDK. In its first year BKDK counted 358 members in 23 chapters, but from the beginning it encountered more problems than the CMCM, perhaps because it missed having a set of skills to sell and a form of busywork around which to structure its meetings as its sister organization had with needlework. Significantly, adult males were not attracted to this organization as adult women were to CMCM. Neumann and then Vuurmans had helped supervise the boys club at Kabanjahe, but Vuurmans felt it was not doing well in 1938. It attracted only a small number, "what you might call the pick of the congregation at Kabanjahe," and consisted largely of young men who worked as hospital staff. Smit obtained movies to show at one "youth evening" at

Sibolangit, and some fifteen hundred people came to view them. As a result, some non-Christian boys in the town formed their own organization, whose purpose was to sponsor monthly film showings in the marketplace. This organization attracted virtually all the non-Christian boys in the area and thrived much longer than Smit had expected. Although he tried to effect some sort of cooperation between this group and the BKDK, he did not succeed.[58]

In 1937 Smit organized what he hoped would be an annual convention of CMCM and BKDK chapters. Expecting about 500 people, Smit watched astounded as 20 buses arrived, some from as far as 100 kilometers away, and 1,500 young people gathered for the event. In 1939 some 2,000 gathered for a similar youth rally, but Smit felt that the boys' enthusiasm had already begun to wane. In the same year Smit's wife reported that some CMCM members had begun to drop out as well, especially after they had learned what they wanted about the art of sewing.[59]

CONCLUSIONS

The housewife role was invented in Europe in the nineteenth century, "a function of the sexual division of labor under which men were allocated paid, women unpaid, work."[60] The diffusion of the concept of the housewife followed the path of capitalist penetration. Ingrid Rudie, returning to a rural Malay village in the 1980s, found that the term *housewife*, which was part of no one's vocabulary in the 1960s when she had carried out dissertation research there, had become a commonplace identity, nourished by classes in cooking and other domestic arts. A new emphasis on Muslim family values gave men responsibility for supporting their families and suggested a corresponding dependency appropriate for women paradoxically when more and more Malay women were working outside the home for wages.[61]

The missionaries to the Karo did not think they were abetting the penetration of capitalism, but their mission field, with its unique history of support from the region's plantations, illustrates the contorted relationship between colonial capitalism and colonial missions. The missionaries' financial dependence on the "money men" of Deli was a continuing source of uneasiness and ambivalence. They did not approve of the planters' lifestyle when it included, as it often did, hard drinking, native mistresses and the economic and physical abuse of workers. The missionaries regarded their own lives of relative poverty and humanitarian service as morally superior to those who lived in the pursuit of earthly treasures. But their antipathy to the capitalist system—even if it paid their bills—did not prompt them to question the gendered division of labor that underpinned that system, just as they did not question the imperialism that had paved their way to the Indies. On the contrary, they more often explained the conquest of the colony as God's hand in history, creating opportunities for the spread of the Gospel.[62]

One of the intellectual lights of Dutch missions, Hendrik Kraemer (who visited the Karo field on a trip through the Indies in 1939), argued that in order to erect a truly universal church, Christianity would have to be adapted in various ways to become relevant in a multitude of other cultural settings.[63] Even the earliest missionaries in the Karo field, however, were sensitive to the idea that peoples of the Indies did not have to adopt European culture in the process of becoming Christian.[64] In fact, if the missionaries could have transplanted Christianity without the materialism, secularism, and other ills that coexisted with it in Europe, they would have been quite happy. Nor did they wish for a total transformation of the Karo's social order and way of life, especially since they hoped that linguistic and social distinctiveness would prove to be a barrier against assimilation into the surrounding Islamic majority. Missing from the missionaries' consideration of Christianity and culture, however, was any significant critique of gender in Western societies. They were oblivious to the possibility that the gender relations of European societies were part of the cultural baggage best left behind as unessential to the Gospel. They were confident that European Christian women were already emancipated compared to women in Asia, so the missionary wife—especially her role as housekeeper—was held up as a model for emulation.[65]

Missionaries attempted to mold the Karo into gender roles and occupations that fit their taken-for-granted sense of naturalness or propriety. The first missionary to the Karo scoffed at men dandling babies on their hips and cooking rice in little huts while their wives, working in fields nearby, wielded hoes.[66] Mrs. Wijngaarden, not giving up on those neighbors in Buluh Hawar who rejected her offer of sewing lessons, wrote, "Later I hope to shape them into housewives as far as I am able to do so."[67] In the 1930s, with girls attending school in increasing numbers and beginning to work in hospitals, the missionaries still envisioned women's primary work as domestic work and hoped to educate them for that future. This goal reflects, perhaps, the class standing of Dutch missionaries, whose origins (or in some cases, their aspirations) were in the middle class.[68] At least the education they offered Karo girls was not class-differentiated. Unlike Javanese society, Karo society had no aristocratic layer until policies of indirect rule attempted to create one. In Java education for girls was largely restricted to the daughters of the elite, who were supposed to become exemplars for common women to emulate. Even so, the goal of "uplifting" the aristocratic women of Bali and Java remained essentially to prepare them for their housewifely duties and maternal destiny.

Dutch missions were comparatively slow to respond to feminist currents in missionary thinking. A women's missionary movement of great proportions captured the imagination of women in Britain and the United States in the late nineteenth and early twentieth centuries. This movement, conceived as "woman's work for woman," was predicated on the assumption that the gender segregation of Asian societies prevented women from having access to the missionary message. Professional women missionaries were thus thought to be essential in order to reach women in these gender-segregated settings.[69] By the 1920s and 1930s, however, the movement in America was beginning to wane, partly because of secularist and isolationist trends within American society after World War I but also because the societies where missionaries worked were changing. "It was simply no longer true in the non-Western cultures, where the efforts of modern missions were focused, that only women could reach women."[70] Educational and occupational settings were becoming increasingly gender integrated, and missionary schools were part of this process, as the history of mission schools among the Karo also demonstrates.

In this comparative view the Karo mission's requests for a professional woman missionary during the 1930s appear to come rather late. Dutch missions started to take up the charge of missions by and for women when the movement was already on the wane elsewhere. Missionary wives among the Karo, facing the burgeoning CMCM demands on their time, made the request again and again throughout the 1930s for the board to send a woman missionary to the Karo field.[71] Mrs. Smit felt that the foothills region could even use two women missionaries. The board refused these requests, having no one available. The first professional woman missionary under NZG sponsorship was commissioned only in 1934, after years of fierce lobbying in the Netherlands from women's missionary support groups.[72] She was stationed in Java. The requests on behalf of the Karo field for a woman missionary were, therefore, not fulfilled before the war interrupted or, more precisely, ended the mission to the Karo.

The missionaries saw their work as emancipatory on a number of levels. Above all, they wanted to free all Karo from what they regarded as superstitious paganism, selfishness, and morose fatalism, dissolving these through the experience of Christian love and faith. No doubt they also viewed the literacy and numeracy taught in mission schools as empowering for both males and females. Judging women's position as degraded and restrictive, they felt women had the most to gain from accepting Christian teachings and were chagrined to find that women were initially less attracted to their message than men. Because women did not "count" for much in Karo society, the missionaries tended to discount women's interest and church attendance, thinking that evangelization would succeed only if male leaders converted. Their assessment of women as powerless and passive contradicted a growing realization that unless they succeeded in winning Karo women to Christ, they would not succeed at all. Near the end of the colonial period, the missionaries came to reassess women's status and to understand better the sources of women's autonomy and influence, and by then Karo women were becoming increasingly numerous among that small minority of Karo who defined themselves as Christian.

The persistent demands by Karo women and their parents—for access to places in programs of advanced education and for shaping infant care service into a diploma-granting program for professional nurses—resisted the missionaries' attempts to define and limit emancipation. The missionaries had to concede to some of these demands or risk forfeiting an opportunity for contact, as they did in 1920 when they lost control of the primary schools. The sewing clubs of the 1930s made some of the missionaries a little nervous, as if emancipation, once ignited, might burn out of control. In time, the missionaries, especially those who joined the field toward the end of the colonial era, Hendrik Vuurmans in particular, became more comfortable with the premise of women's emancipation. Vuurmans perceived, rightly, that women's emancipation was not going to come as a paternalistic bequest by the missionaries but was being impelled by forces quite outside the missionaries' control.

In the 1930s Karo were just beginning to join the migration to the cities. Members of other ethnic groups—Toba Batak, Minangkabau, and Chinese—were beginning to migrate into the two major towns of Karoland. People were learning to apprehend a new economic environment where education would be necessary for success. They were also coming to imagine themselves part of a new "community" where peoples of different ethnic groups would forge a common identity as Indonesians against a common enemy, the Dutch. In this process women's emancipation would be enveloped by the emancipatory movement for nationhood. In this process, too, the missionaries would lose control of the church whose foundation they had laid. The Karo Batak Protestant Church was born in 1941, under the threatening advance of the Japanese. While the missionaries were imprisoned in war camps and later during the stressful years of the revolution, this new church was sustained by men and women whom the missionaries believed to be incapable of carrying on without them.

12. GOOD MOTHERS, MEDEAS, OR JEZEBELS: Feminine Imagery in Colonial and Anticolonial Rhetoric in the Dutch East Indies, 1900 –1942

ᕯ Frances Gouda

In this chapter I explore the parental metaphors—of both a motherly and fatherly variety—that infused the rhetoric of Dutch colonial officials intent on validating their position of authority over colonized subjects in the Indonesian archipelago. I also probe the ways in which Indonesian nationalists in the twentieth century invoked the same gendered vocabulary in order to ridicule or subvert the legitimacy of European mastery. In the Dutch East Indies, as elsewhere, justifications of colonial governance were often saturated with both paternal and maternal imagery. Colonialism, it seemed, supplied its practitioners with a flexible parental style, enabling them to define themselves as representatives of either the mother country or the fatherland who were commissioned to educate native children.

In the Netherlands itself the author of the ideological platform of the Anti-Revolutionaire Partij (Antirevolutionary party), Dr. Abraham Kuyper—who served as the paterfamilias of the orthodox Dutch Reformed political forces in the Netherlands—inaugurated a self-consciously parental discourse in 1874. Colonial practice, Kuyper proposed, should inspire the Dutch in the East Indies to perform the role of faithful tutors to indigenous pupils. They ought to think of themselves as guardians who are dedicated to the instruction and edification of their native children. God in his infinite wisdom had forged the bonds between the Netherlands and the Indies, Kuyper held forth, and the policy of the Antirevolutionary party should be "to maintain all things ordained by God."[1] Since 1830, however, the Dutch government's exploitation of Javanese peasants through the lucrative system of the forced cultivation of cash crops had committed a cardinal sin by violating his commandment that "Thou shalt not steal." From now on the role of Dutch colonial rule in Southeast Asia, Kuyper sermonized in 1874, would be to replace these "greedy tendencies" with a moral obligation to "uplift" Indonesians. In the Antirevolutionary party's political lexicon, ethical colonial governance inspired by Christian faith implied both selfless dedication and stern instruction on the part of those who wished to execute God's will on earth. In short, beginning with Abraham Kuyper's formulation of *Ons Program* (Our program) until the Japanese conquest of the Dutch East Indies in 1942, the terms *ethical trusteeship*, *moral tutelage*, and *parental guidance* were inextricably linked to any and all discussions about Dutch colonial practice in Indonesia.[2]

Almost forty years later, on November 14, 1918, during the second session of the newly created protoparliament of the Indies, the Volksraad (People's Council), one of its Indonesian members, a prominent nationalist from Java named Tjipto Mangoenkoesoemo, boldly criticized the Dutch colonial government; in doing so, he exhibited his wizardry with the Dutch language by displaying a mischievous sense of humor. Tjipto also parodied the wide range of complementary, if paradoxical, tropes about strict paternal instruction, on the one hand, and the maternal nurturance of indigenous children, on the other, which had permeated the "ethical" rhetoric of Dutch colonial legitimacy since the turn of the century.

Dutch civil servants in Indonesia were hardly unique in this regard. The idiom of parental obligation or the vocabulary of family ties, in fact, often served as a constitutive metaphor of many colonial discourses.[3] Whenever Europeans asserted the validity of colonial rule, they frequently alluded to their parental duties toward their native progeny. Discourses fashioned to justify colonial regimes contained a mixture of maternal prototypes of empathetic caring for the welfare of indigenous peoples, which both competed and overlapped with paternalistic models emphasizing the rigorous training of groups of native children. Europeans in a colonial setting tended to conjure up this language of motherhood and fatherhood to represent colonial societies as a great happy family composed of benevolent but strict white-skinned parents who guided their brown-skinned offspring to basic literacy and psychological maturity. Europeans' appeal to family imagery was often designed to bolster the myth of colonial societies as a natural, organic whole.

Tjipto Mangoenkoesoemo, for his part, employed similar figures of speech, but he intentionally turned them upside down or inside out in order to mock the colonial rhetoric of legitimacy. Despite the government's solemn vow to labor with all its might on behalf of the welfare of the Indonesian people—a pledge the reigning governor-general had repeated at the ceremonial opening of the People's Council earlier in the year—Tjipto informed his parliamentary audience in 1918 that he could not fail to notice a major weakness of character. In his anthropomorphized vision of the Indies colonial state, the government resembled a capricious schoolmaster who was incapable of keeping a promise. Having established the Volksraad, Tjipto intoned, "the government received so many feathers in 'her' cap that in my imagination 'she' acquired the appearance of an [American] Indian with a feather head-dress." Tjipto then switched genders to describe the impact of this plumed headgear, as if it were a tangible implement of power and the colonial state could only be masculine when it adopted an aggressive posture. The Dutch East Indies government donned these feathers, Tjipto continued, "to give 'him' such a bellicose look that the enemy might flee in confusion." [4]

In his criticism of the colonial state, Tjipto's transition from feminine to masculine imagery must have been a deliberate strategy, since the Dutch word for government (*regering*) is a female noun. After all, parental metaphors invoked either a motherly image or a fatherly model in order to accentuate discrepancies of power; these linguistic practices endowed the agency of Europeans with supple meanings that were grounded in the different emotions commonly associated with either motherhood or fatherhood. Gendered figures of speech signified all sorts of unequal social relationships that were not intrinsically connected to actual sexual differences between men and women. Such tropes, instead, tended to summon symbols that expressed differences in power, status, moral style, or social sensibilities.

As Helen Haste has recently argued in *The Sexual Metaphor: Men, Women, and the Thinking That Makes the Difference*, femininity, in the course of history, has come to epitomize "expressive, rather than instrumental roles." Women seem to embody feelings, while the pursuit of instrumental goals is often associated with men, not only within the family but also in social groups in general.[5] Through the use of metaphor, the idea of gender has been dislodged from the tangible realm of physiological distinctions between men and women. As such, gendered language tends to provide an array of narrative tools designed to illuminate social hierarchies or to illustrate differential positions of command and subordination, of strength and weakness, or of intellectual logic and irrational emotions. Gendered tropes, in other words, have emerged as descriptive elements of many aspects of social organization or political structure.

Hence, Tjipto's abrupt shift from a feminine to a masculine government—facilitated, of course, by certain peculiarities of the Dutch language—was a rhetorical trick he pulled out of his orator's hat to expose the contradictory character of colonial policies in Indonesia. Tjipto applied his rhetorical tactics more transparently when he continued his address to the People's Council in Batavia, a parliamentary institution that was in reality a debating club with both Dutch and Indonesian members. Whether the governor-general appointed its members or whether they were elected by means of a limited franchise, since 1918 the People's Council constituted a ceremonial forum where delegates discussed legislation or budgets and advised the Indies government on policy issues.

In his speech Tjipto joked irreverently about the government's so-called Ethical Policy which he portrayed as "Miss Ethics," a woman who reputedly "is gentle and warm-hearted: she has beautiful eyes, a classic nose, and such a delectable mouth that the lonely voices which register their indifference to her beauty are dismissed as people with vulgar taste, who thereby forfeit their right to participate in the discussion." When these dissonant voices, he quipped, wondered publicly whether the pretty and elaborately made-up "Miss Ethics, whose real face is hidden beneath a thick layer of powder," was not, in fact, an "old hag," they were silenced by the Dutch-language press in Java or Sumatra.[6]

Tjipto's sarcasm knew few bounds. In the same Volksraad oration he raised several other questions that both exposed and exemplified the government's bad faith. About recent events near the town of Kediri in

East Java, where hungry Javanese men had stolen cassava from a European plantation, he ridiculed the government's saber rattling as a shameful display of macho military power in its suppression of desperate, starving peasants.[7] Tjipto also called Dutch civil servants in western Java (Sunda) to task for terrorizing people in Madjalaja, who had shown the courage to join a populist Muslim organization (Sarekat Islam or Islamic Union) that espoused a form of nationalism perceived as dangerous by the Dutch colonial regime. Because the Dutch government had fabricated the story that the Sundanese had elevated Tjokroaminoto, the chairman of the central board of Islamic Union, to the position of a king with supernatural powers, Tjipto accused Dutch administrators of telling a tale that was sinister so "it might send a young lady to bed, shivering with fright, even if it is a fairy tale no thoughtful man can take seriously."[8]

In his conclusion Tjipto returned to the wily tricks of Miss Ethics. All these developments, he said, are internally related and seem to indicate that the government is afraid that Miss Ethics has "overstimulated us natives by casting too many amorous glances in our direction." It appeared, Tjipto continued, that government officials had decided that the time was ripe "to reintroduce to center stage her mean-spirited older sister—the virago, the witch—whose actual name is Ancien Régime: this old young lady with her wrinkled face, who in the past has catered so well to the needs of the Dutch East India Company, now must tuck us into bed and temper our ardent declarations of love for greater human rights and delay our march toward a happier future."[9]

With sardonic humor Tjipto Mangoenkoesoemo employed masculine and feminine images to exhibit the hypocrisy of Dutch colonial policies in the Indies and to register his opposition. When he emphasized the government's abuse of its superior military power, he invoked the emblems of a fierce Native American with a feather headdress engaged in truculent, masculine behavior. By portraying the Indies government's ethical welfare policies on behalf of the native population as either an old shrew or a Jezebel intent on seducing Indonesians in order to render them more pliable, Tjipto mocked the ways in which the Dutch colonial regime justified its rule as charitable.

The Indies government's so-called Ethical Policy, after all, was based on a "moral obligation." Because of the prodigious profits garnered through the system of forced cultivation of cash crops such as coffee, tea, sugar, and indigo imposed on the inhabitants of the island of Java between 1830 and 1880, the Dutch nation had incurred a "debt of honor." This liability was publicly acknowledged by Wilhelmina, the very young queen of the Netherlands, at the turn of the century. In her annual Royal Address to Parliament in The Hague in 1901, she announced that henceforth the Dutch colonial state in the East Indies would pay back its debt of honor to Indonesians by nurturing their educational and material well-being.[10] Tjipto's depiction of the Ethical Policy as Miss Ethics, however, conjured up a voluptuous lady not in the least concerned with preserving her dignity by fostering with motherly zeal the prosperity of her children. Instead, he painted a picture of a shameless hussy, whose ruddy cheeks concealed all sorts of insidious symptoms beneath. Her superficial charm, Tjipto suggested, camouflaged the fact that she was really a harridan no different from her older sister, whom he described as a "virago" or a "witch" because she had only been concerned with satisfying the commercial appetites of the Dutch East India Company.

Tjipto's deliberate use of feminine emblems was striking, since refined Javanese aristocrats who served as indigenous retainers of the Dutch East Indies state were bound by a straightforward patrilineal vocabulary. They were expected to address local Dutch civil servants as "Father" and to refer to the governor-general as "Grandfather." As late as December 13, 1939, when R. K. A. Bertsch, a senior administrator of Central Java, retired, the oldest Javanese member of the Provincial Council, Soerioadikoesoemo, said farewell to the departing Dutch civil servant by noting that he had been "a father, a good father, who had always seriously minded the well-being of his brood (*kroost*)."[11] However, most Indonesians with a formal role in the colonial administration were fully aware that a female queen in a distant land on the other side of the globe required the greatest deference of all. The recognition that in the overall hierarchy of authority a female monarch rather than a male governor-general embodied the most august position of power may have added an ambiguous twist to Indonesians' understanding of European constructions of power, gender, and parenthood. But this ambiguity captured the ways in which colonial rule conflated masculine and feminine emblems of parental authority in order to envelop colonial governance in a comforting aura of family rhetoric.

Accordingly, "as colonial fathers, we must acknowledge that our children are utterly dependent on our guidance," the Dutchman J. J. B. Ostmeier wrote in 1911 in *Insulinde,* the biweekly magazine of a nationalist organization of permanent Indies residents who were officially classified as "Europeans." Even though many of *Insulinde's* subscribers had Indonesian mothers, a law of 1898 had stipulated that the children of Dutch fathers and native mothers would receive European status if their father officially recognized them. "If we were to ease the gentle pressures imposed upon our big children, they will inevitably stumble over the many obstacles all human beings encounter in the course of life. No one can blame us for treating the little Javanese as an overgrown infant, and the education of every child," he pontificated, "requires both clemency and indulgence, although on occasion it is necessary to be stern and exacting. No positive development will occur if we, as fathers, are only gentle and tolerant merely because it is too difficult to determine the appropriate boundary between severity and leniency." However, Ostmeier conceded, as colonial fathers we sometimes do not heed "the golden lessons of maternal experience," and this failure to learn from motherly intuition is the reason why the Indies government sometimes "implements well-intentioned but awkward measures which produce nothing but inimical results." [12]

Nationalist intellectuals, in turn, whether in the Dutch East Indies or French North Africa, concocted similar gendered images in their assaults on colonial exploitation, and they did so by deliberately destabilizing commonly held assumptions. Many a nationalist argued that colonial civil servants did not want the natives to perceive European rule as a tender mother engaged in protecting her child from a hostile environment but rather as an eagle-eyed matriarch who shielded her perverse offspring from their innate, self-destructive instincts. "The colonial mother protects her child from itself, from its ego, its physiology, its biology, and its own unhappiness," Frantz Fanon wrote in *The Wretched of the Earth,* in order to rescue colonized peoples from their own involution. [13]

Native intellectuals, it seemed, intentionally conjured up an oxymoron: by representing European rule as a cruel mother, they invoked a wide range of disturbing and contradictory images. The depiction of colonial regimes as Medea, for example—or as a female incarnation of a Minotaur who swallows up her own children with the gluttonous appetite of mother countries in the European metropole, always hungry for raw materials—corrupted notions of natural and loving motherhood. In addition to paradox, pathos surrounded this symbolism, too, since an array of nationalists glorified revolution as a harbinger of the bountiful world that would fulfill their utopian dreams. However, these socialist reveries often degenerated into a nightmare because many revolutionary leaders ended up committing suicide by consuming their own progeny. During the early 1920s an Indonesian Communist, Tan Malaka, used a well-worn cliché when he observed that the revolution in Russia, as had previously occurred during the French Revolution, "was devouring its own children."[14]

Accordingly, when addressing the Volksraad in 1918, Tjipto Mangoenkoesoemo incorporated complex layers of meaning when he caricatured prevailing notions of proper motherhood; simultaneously, he elicited the primordial duality of women as Madonna, on the one hand, and whore, on the other. The colonial state was both a mercenary harlot and a wicked mother who sold her sexual favors to the highest bidder, thereby serving the interests of rapacious European capitalists while muzzling or sowing discord among her native offspring. Tjipto's contemporary, the Javanese nationalist Soetatmo Soeriokoesoemo—despite their disagreements about the essence of Javanese culture and its proper relationship to European values—also represented Dutch rule in gendered terms. The capitalist state, wrote Soetatmo, resembled a family consisting of a father "henpecked" by a mother who does nothing but "primp" herself while neglecting her obligations to her children.[15]

Quite predictably, the ubiquitous trope of the evil stepmother also entered Dutch colonial discourses. When the political journal of Dr. Abraham Kuyper's Antirevolutionary party accused the European residents of the Indies who regarded the archipelago as their "fatherland" of harboring a "love for the mother country [in Europe] barely above the freezing point," the magazine of the Indies settlers' association *Insulinde* responded with cynicism. Love for the mother country is a beautiful word but a vague notion, *Insulinde*'s author scoffed; instead, a simple deference to our fatherland should suffice. It is shameful to ask permanent Indies residents to love a mother country, he proclaimed, that has never shown her children on the other side of the globe any affection. How could they adore a mother country that has treated permanent Indies residents in nothing but the most blatant "stepmotherly fashion"?[16] The nationalist magazine *De Beweging* (The movement), for its part, switched genders and struck a stepfatherly theme in 1921. If the Dutch colonial government wants to be a genuine father to his children who were born and raised in "Our Indies," *De Beweging* declared with indignation, then he will have to make amends and treat his children with "love and devotion, with compassion and patience" as is proper for a good father. If he conducts himself like "a heartless stepfather or foster parent," his children will fear him and tremble at his sight rather than bear him affection.[17]

Some American diplomats stationed in the Dutch East Indies during the late 1930s used the exact same figure of speech. In a confidential memorandum to the State Department in Washington, D.C., in early 1939, for instance, U.S. Consul General Erle Dickover in Batavia commented on the feelings of antagonism between the "Dutch (and Indo-Europeans) in the Indies" and those in the European homeland. "Netherlanders here are toiling and sweating under the tropical sun, trying to build a vast empire and to hold it for posterity," he noted. But most Dutch people in the European metropole, even if they hoard with glee the enormous profits generated by the Indies, "believe that they can treat the Indies like a stepchild—a stepchild who might be the main source of income for the family, but who nevertheless may be starved and neglected with impunity."[18]

The children who presumably were the victims of all this bad mothering, fathering, or stepparenting, meanwhile, wished to assert their autonomy from Dutch tutelage altogether. Another Indonesian nationalist, Semaoen, conceded in 1924, for instance, that the Communist movement in the Indies might still be callow and inexperienced, but he insisted that it had already achieved the status of an independent adult, who does not wish to be "a child of the Dutch but only a child of Leninism."[19] Semaoen asserted that Indonesians were not malleable infants but grown-ups, who relished their autonomy and were capable of selecting their own mentors.

In juxtaposition to the manipulative imperialist parents who provoked bitterness among their flock of children—a direct reference to the Dutch divide-and-rule policies in the Indies—the flamboyant nationalist Sukarno, in his theatrical courtroom defense during his political trial in 1930, concocted yet another female model. He summoned the imagery of an attentive mother figure who fostered brotherhood and sisterhood among her children: the allegory of the goddess Merdeka (freedom, independence), who instructed all Indonesians in the sacred knowledge that "united we stand, divided we fall."[20] In other contexts, though, Sukarno's vision of femininity was a bit more ambivalent; educated as an engineer at the Bandung Institute of Technology and well-versed in Western political ideology, he proudly wore European trousers and reputedly ridiculed any Indonesian man who still dressed in a traditional batik sarong for "resembling a woman."[21]

Similarly contested emblems of womanhood and maternity resurfaced in the postwar independence struggle. A postcard disseminated in Java in 1945 or 1946, for example, celebrated the international solidarity of Indonesians with their nationalist siblings in India with the caption "We Fight for Mother India and Mother Indonesia."[22] After Sukarno and Mohammad Hatta unilaterally proclaimed the nation's independence from Dutch colonial rule on August 17, 1945, it was no surprise that India was one of the very first nations to recognize the sovereignty of the Indonesian Republic. In a certain way nationalists in both Indonesia and India had committed rhetorical matricide. Without equivocation they rejected the predatory mother country in the European metropole, whether Great Britain or the Netherlands, which represented, in the immediate post–World War II period, a fear of renewed exploitation. Instead, Indian and Indonesian nationalists transferred their allegiance to a symbolic mother figure who sheltered her native sons and daughters; inevitably only the latter was worthy of filial obedience. Postwar anticolonial slogans in Indonesia, as a result, called upon all young men "to defend the Indonesian mother country with body and soul" (*Pemoeda2 pertahankan tanah air dengan djiwa ragamoe*) or "to stand shoulder to shoulder" and to "beware of the traitors of the people" (*Bersoesoenan bahoe oentoek kesempoernaan kemerdekaan Indonesia* and *Awas!! pengchianat bangsa*).[23]

The Japanese during World War II, though, reinforced the imagery of the destructive female again. They circulated propaganda portraying the Dutch colonial state as a diabolical "temptress," whose seductive appearance disguised that she was a monster at heart, while a Japanese

Postcards circulated by nationalists during the post–World War II struggle for Indonesian independence. (Courtesy of P. van Meel from his work *Getekend als koloniaal: Een relaas over de belevenissen van een KNIL-soldaat en de mensen die zijn leven deelden in de jaren 1930–1950* [Dordrecht: Stabelan, (1982)], p. 98)

navy official in Java at the close of World War II described himself as the "foster-father of Indonesian independence." [24] Following the defeat of Japan and the return of Dutch civil servants in 1945–46, Indonesian nationalists picked up this negative female symbolism again and made it quite explicit in their representation of the Netherlands Indies Civil Administration as a tawdry prostitute. A postcard with a cartoon of a scantily dressed white woman contained the following caption:

スパイは会議や物を餌にして釣るのである。

De verleidster.
(Japansche propaganda).

Japanese propaganda circulated during Japan's occupation of the Dutch East Indies. The Dutch colonial administration was portrayed to Indonesian nationalists as a seductive temptress whose feminine appearance disguised the fact that she was at heart a monster. (From the *Het Indisch Nieuws*, December 7, 1946)

"Beware! Do not be tricked by the whore N.I.C.A [Netherlands Indies Civil Administration]: Later you Indonesians will be oppressed by her [again]" (*Awas! djangan terpedaja dengan pelatjoer N.I.C.A.: Nanti Indonesia kami aniaja*).[25] Meanwhile, the young Indonesian nationalists trying to evict the streetwalking NICA "temptress" from their country resembled "military infant[s], fresh from the womb of Revolution," who could not imagine that such a jaded woman could have ever possessed any kind of sex appeal.[26]

Such gendered and parental metaphors, of course, were not unique to the colonized world of Southeast Asia. In the European metropole peasants and working-class citizens were depicted, too, as unruly children in need of civic education before they could be regarded as adult citizens. In a similar vein, the dangerous maelstrom of Communism

was sometimes represented as an influx of bewitching females—or seductive "red" nurses—who might engulf honest laboring men and lead
them astray.[27] However, political elites in most European countries presumed that workers and peasants were speakers of the same national
language, who would become more proficient in the nation's cultural
grammar once they recognized the benefits of capitalist democracy and
electoral politics.

In contrast, civil servants dispatched to the colonies often saw their
native wards as preliterate, as not yet capable of intelligible speech, and
most of them embraced one of two contending perspectives on their
indigenous pupils. Professor Johan Christiaan van Eerde, the director
of the Ethnology Section of the Colonial Institute in Amsterdam, for
instance, articulated the dilemma succinctly in the context of the Indonesian archipelago: European impressions of less developed people, Van
Eerde wrote in 1914, tend to oscillate between two extremes. On the one
hand, Westerners harbor a vision of primitive people caught in a web of
"cruelty, magic, cannibalism, and slavery." On the other hand, they in-
vent the idyllic image of a people untainted by civilization and living in
"dreamy tranquillity and harmony in the mild climate of their natural
environment."[28] As an "ethical" Dutch reformer insisted in a letter to a
newspaper in colonial Indonesia (*Bataviaans Handelsblad*) in 1911, "The
fundamental honesty of the genuine ur-Javanese is truly touching."[29]

But the other extreme view resonated just as loudly, and many Dutch
men and women perceived the Javanese as natives whose illiteracy issued from their immaturity or congenital stupidity. Many Dutch colonial residents thought that the primal instincts of the Javanese would
forever lead them astray unless they were kept in check indefinitely.
Thus, some civil servants' empathetic devotion to pristine indigenous
peoples, who, in their eyes, possessed a natural dignity and sweet disposition, clashed with other Dutchmen's contempt for superstitious and
devious natives, whether from Java or more remote outer islands. The
consequence of these competing visions was a contested discourse in
which the "hyperethical" language of motherly affection for native
peoples, grounded in respect for local customs and traditions, collided
with the stentorian masculine discourses of other colonial administrators who called for Western moral discipline and scientific rigor.

The average Dutch colonial resident, an Indonesian member of the

Volksraad noted in 1918, viewed the millions of peasants in Java as "dishonest, stupid, careless, childish, despotic, and servile."[30] Given these impressions of their native charges, firm fatherly guidance, schoolmasterish instruction, and only an occasional motherly embrace were the operative figures of speech of the Dutch Civil Service in the East Indies. Through its high-minded paternalism this European administration had "brought the Pax Neerlandica and with it peace and justice, the possibility of a rise in the standard of living, and the sense that millions of ethnically diverse people are all children of one mother country, the Dutch East Indies." Twentieth-century Dutch colonial residents, meanwhile, chided Indonesian nationalists for thinking "in a childlike and childish fashion that they were called upon to replace the foreign colonial masters."[31] When Sukarno said jokingly that daybreak does not come because the rooster crows but, instead, that "the cock crows because the sun is rising," a Dutchman dismissed him and his nationalist comrades as immature roosters who think that by crying loudly "they can accelerate daybreak."[32]

Nationalist ideas of independence and autonomy, the conservative Dutch civil servant M. B. van der Jagt asserted in the People's Council in 1918, were nothing but symptoms of innocent childhood diseases, which the Dutch had to tolerate as "the measles and chicken pox of a primitive people yearning for progress."[33] Resembling a pediatric nurse, the Dutch administration cared for her young patients during the maladies of childhood: she would hover over their sickbed until an omniscient doctor, steeped in Western medical science, might declare them fully recovered and ready to commence an independent life. A few years before the outbreak of World War II, the British historian John Sydenham Furnivall still mocked the didactic style of Dutch colonialism; its pedantry was personified by self-proclaimed guardians, he noted, who could not refrain from telling their orphans what to do, even when the latter were quite capable of taking care of themselves.[34] And at the end of World War II, after the proclamation of the Indonesian Republic on August 17, 1945, the very last governor-general of the Dutch East Indies used the same language by conceding that the prestige of the Dutch nation in Indonesia could be compared to that of "a schoolmaster in his classroom two days before the beginning of summer vacation."[35]

Obviously, gendered metaphors highlighted notions of superiority and inferiority, only to mask the blatant discrepancies of power between Dutch colonial residents and their Indonesian subalterns by using the euphemistic language of caregiver and patient, of parent and child, or of schoolteacher and student. While mainly paternalistic in tone and designed primarily to justify the harsh measures necessary to teach common sense to indigenous peoples, colonial discourses also appealed to feminine images at strategic moments—if and when they wished to emphasize the altruistic attempts of the West to improve the material standard of living and to protect native peoples from presumably self-destructive, archaic practices. The government's concern with the welfare of the native population was so deeply felt, said a former civil servant, that it displayed an "exaggerated nannyism": the colonial government's "excessively nurturing qualities rather than its shortcomings" spawned the Indonesian independence movement.[36] The Dutch nation, after all, was a "greenhouse" or "nursery" dedicated to the cultivation of the familial bonds of the average native household, because the weak economic conditions of the Indonesian population emanated primarily from "a loose family life." As an "ethical" Dutch-language women's magazine intoned in 1935:

> The mother in the village slogs and slaves away. She carries loads on her back as heavy as lead; in the middle of a pitch-black night she pounds bran or corn so she can trudge the enormous distance to a market far away, where she sells her pathetic products in order to earn a few extra cents . . . if only she would stay at home and learn to care better for her children by fulfilling her housewifely obligations, then enough time would remain to earn additional income by doing some light agricultural work or, even more desirable, by spinning, weaving, or making *batik*, *tritik*, *djoemplat*, or *plangi* [various ornate forms of cloth] and pottery or baskets.[37]

Implicit in these observations was a sense that women, although crucial to Indonesians' economic well-being, should nonetheless be encouraged to embrace their motherly roles. Uniquely Western definitions of domestic propriety and prosperity prompted Dutch colonial inhabitants of the Indies to blame Indonesian women as much as men for failing to construct stable households. Women, they argued, devoted too much time and energy to selling trivial products in the marketplace, which prevented them from fulfilling their domestic duties and maternal destiny. Dutch inhabitants of colonial Indonesia employed tortured logic, though, in their efforts to understand the sexual division of labor among indigenous peoples and its causal relationship to poverty and the lack of economic progress. Javanese men, a Dutch stereotype proposed, were "carefree, artistic, impulsive, rarely and irregularly active."[38] Besides, men in Java or on other islands of the archipelago failed to muster the same kind of "inner impulse," "serious determination," or "sense of duty" as men in the West to provide for their families; as a result, women and children had to survive, by hook or by crook, on their own.[39] However, when a woman worked like an ox, day and night, to generate food and sustenance for her family, she was held liable for the "loose family life" of the indigenous population, which, in Dutch eyes, was the root cause of what they euphemistically called Indonesians' *mindere welvaart* (lesser economic development). This kind of tautological reasoning revealed, above all, that the Dutch habit of viewing the role of Indonesian women through a Western looking glass blurred their vision. Tjipto Mangoenkoesoemo, for his part, confirmed the centrality of women in Indonesian society when he said in the Volksraad in 1918 that "women in our country, as we all know, are much more instrumental in the functioning of our social life than are women in Europe," but he drew the opposite conclusion. Because they played such a pivotal role in the perennial struggle for family survival, Indonesian women should receive an actual voice in the running of the body politic, rather than remain disenfranchised.[40]

In contrast, when Dutchmen employed a feminine vocabulary in their allusions to colonial rule as a "birthplace," a "cradle," or a "public nursery" devoted to the promotion of the maturity and eventual independence of Indonesian people, they nonetheless implied that this was an arena in which men wielded control. To elaborate upon the medical metaphor that the Dutch civil servant Van der Jagt introduced in the People's Council in 1918: the Dutch colonial government functioned as a sympathetic nurse during her patients' childhood infirmities, but it was a male pediatrician who finally declared them healthy enough to sanction their release from the hospital. While the caring qualities of colonial rule could be rendered in terms of traditional women's profes-

sions such as social work and nursing, the ultimate decisions about
the patients' future remained a male prerogative. "Private family life
rather than the public sphere constitutes the proper domain for women
to develop their gifts and talents," a Dutch member of the People's
Council, W. H. van Helsdingen, warned his audience in 1935, "because
women's desire to be men's equal degenerates, only too soon, into doing
what men do—that is, being their equal in smoking and drinking." [41]

However, if the vision of women, whether their own wives and
daughters or indigenous women, as creatures in need of protection prevailed, such visions often merged with a more ambivalent perception of
their other colonial charges, that is, native men. It was true that some
Dutch East Indies residents endowed men belonging to ethnic groups
outside Java, such as the daredevil Buginese sailors of southern Sulawesi
or the defiant Acehnese of northern Sumatra, with a courage or ferocity
that confirmed their quintessential masculinity. But colonial officials often depicted indigenous men as overgrown children who wallowed in
the spectacle of puppet theaters or indulged in games of chance and
were haunted by superstitions and fears of ghosts. At the same time
European men tended to portray both white matrons and girls and the
colonized women they knew most intimately—their concubines or
their children's nannies, who supposedly "mediated" between the cultures of East and West—as caring only about ephemeral things or not
being educated enough to have an interest in any aspect of life beyond
the domestic realm.[42] While the fragility of Dutch-born women in the
colonies rendered them frivolous in the eyes of their fathers or husbands, a Babylonian confusion of tongues typified the communication
between European men and indigenous women, whether they were native housekeepers with whom they also shared a bed or anonymous
women in village communities. Colonial rhetoric thus associated femininity with capriciousness and identified most indigenous men with
childish incompetence, rendering both naturally dependent on "patriarchal tutelage."[43]

In sum, Europeans in the gothic theater of colonialism resembled
dramatists staging an elaborate morality play with a multitude of actors
and actresses, who portrayed both masters and servants of different skin
color, varying levels of eloquence, and distinct styles of elocution. They
forced upon the colonized territories of Asia the shape of their own

culture as well as European meanings of gender difference—embodied in what Stephen Greenblatt has called their "kidnapping language"—in order to make the bewildering world in which they had to function more intelligible, habitable, and, above all, "natural" as defined by a Western lexicon.[44] The legitimation of colonial rule hinged on the description of the "natives" as being unable to speak for themselves or as not yet having a proper language—either for the time being or indefinitely.

A Dutch journalist, for example, argued derisively about Indonesians in 1924 that "a native Indonesian knows nothing and can't do anything on his own. . . . If a native were to be a student at a university and ventured to speak, he would have no voice of his own and would only parrot what [Dutch mentors] have inspired him to say."[45] Accordingly, Europeans claimed that they were colonialists in order to teach basic literacy in the cultural grammar of the civilized world. In the process they imposed a variety of gendered tropes, representing either command or subordination, upon indigenous vocabulary. Some native intellectuals, in turn, reacted like "adopted children" and absorbed European culture with a vengeance in order to become evolved and well-bred, not being content with merely acquiring a cursory knowledge of "Rabelais and Diderot, Shakespeare and Edgar Allan Poe."[46] As a result, a complete mastery of the language of the colonial "other" enabled indigenous intellectuals, such as Tjipto Mangoenkoesoemo in the Dutch East Indies, to invert or ridicule the gendered depiction of authority and subservience and articulate a colorful anticolonial critique.[47]

POSTSCRIPT

The colloquial speech of the young Indonesian Republic after 1945 tried to downplay European masculine and feminine metaphors which signified either power or weakness. Bahasa Indonesia (the lingua franca of the Indonesian archipelago), after all, is a gender-neutral language, making it cumbersome to formulate elusive figures of speech that associate authority with masculinity or conflate feebleness with femininity. But alas, the modern Indonesian Republic has not granted women positions of formal power in the political hierarchy. Neither is it true that in contemporary Indonesia inequalities in status and prestige are less often expressed in the invidious imagery of sexual difference than before independence, if only because the millions of Javanese speakers in Indonesia's heartland still refer to boys and girls, on occasion, as "penis" and "vagina."[48] In fact, one could argue that in its twilight years Suharto's New Order government since 1965 has done all it could to reinforce patriarchal stereotypes by circumscribing women's social and political position more rigidly along gender-specific lines. For example, the panoply of women's organizations and women's self-help cooperatives that are sanctioned by the New Order state tend to reinforce the roles of women as subservient to their husbands' interests.[49] However, during the anticolonial struggle after 1945, when the "infant state began to kick and baw lustily, claiming spontaneous maturity in an atmosphere of chaotic enthusiasm," the invented cultural grammar of the fledgling Republic, albeit unsuccessfully, tried to construct a novel political language that would not reproduce the gendered stereotypes of colonial mastery.[50]

13. TREKKING TO NEW GUINEA: Dutch Colonial Fantasies of a Virgin Land, 1900–1942

꙳ *Danilyn Fox Rutherford*

"The Netherlands Indies will only really be the Netherlands Indies when New Guinea is populated by men and women of Dutch stock," so went a rallying cry heard during the 1930s.[1] But in 1963, when the world had become a very different—and tentatively postcolonial— place, the Netherlands was forced to end a nasty dispute with the Indonesian Republic. Although Indonesia had gained independence from the Netherlands on December 29, 1949, it would take an additional fourteen years before the Dutch nation was willing to let go of western New Guinea.

Three years later the Dutch-born political scientist Arend Lijphart wrote *The Trauma of Decolonization* to explain why it had taken Holland so long to give up this enormous remnant of the Dutch East Indies. For over a decade after relinquishing the rest of the colony, Holland clung to New Guinea, claiming it was guiding its primitive population to self-rule. In the wake of Indonesia's independence, the Dutch invested New Guinea with a significance that far outweighed its material worth.[2] As a replacement for the Indies, New Guinea became a fetish, a symptom of the injury to Holland's national and global self-esteem.

Lijphart's diagnosis revealed the extent to which the possession of a large colonial empire defined Holland's domestic and international identity. But it failed to expose the deeper roots of the Netherlands' pathological attachment to New Guinea. If the postwar mission to develop New Guinea was a symptom of imperial desires and anxieties, so was the category in whose name it took place. Well before decolonization, politicians and journalists shaped a particular image of New Guinea that would justify continued Dutch rule.

In the psychoanalytic theories to which Lijphart vaguely alludes, the fetish is depicted as appearing in the face of uncertainties in knowledge and identity.[3] Fixing on the last thing seen before witnessing the mother's troubling "lack," the fetishist displaces the nervous questions evoked by the fantasy of castration: Does she have it? Do I have it? Could I lose it, too? In light of such formulations, Lijphart's depiction of the Netherlands' postwar fixation on New Guinea presents us with an odd sort of fetish: a figure with no apparent relation to gender. But the underlying fantasies that produced the obsession brought the question of sexual difference to the fore.

In this essay I examine these prewar fantasies, which transformed New Guinea into a maternal fatherland for orphaned Europeans. Profound changes in Indies society gave rise to a movement to settle New Guinea in the early 1920s. Persisting through the 1930s, it yielded three roughly chronological visions of the fatherland. In this late colonial context, I track the shifting place of gender in portrayals of New Guinea as a zone of national, racial, and bureaucratic purity. Moving through the series, I explore how an explicit concern with sexual control yielded to a general fantasy of prowess. By tracing a rhetoric of exclusion through these depression-era texts, I show how this virgin land came to shelter a manly figure of colonial power.

As should be obvious, the subject of New Guinea's mastery invariably appeared in these visions as singular and male. The feminine entered the picture as a pluralized figure of impurity or as the seductive object of a masculine gaze. If the dream of New Guinea was a fantasy, it followed the logic of a complicated symbolic economy. The elite imagination responded to a wide range of threats by projecting sexual difference onto space. As is often the case, the images of women presented in these visions evoked a range of alterities. The feminine both affirmed and disrupted a colonial hierarchy cursed by contradictions in status, place, and race.

Those who promoted the new fatherland in the 1920s and especially the 1930s were not the first to associate New Guinea's (lack of) development with Holland's threatened prestige. But they were the first to insist upon the territory's detachment from the Indies. Nothing happened in New Guinea to account for its changing place in the colonial imagination. When the dream began, advances in transportation were bringing this neglected periphery closer to the imperial core.[4] Although the fantasy changed the future for New Guinea's inhabitants, the Papuans had little to do with its emergence. It started in the heartland of Dutch colonial society, in Java, far to the west.

THE THREATENED EUROPEANS

Sometime in the 1930s a Dutch supporter looked back on the birth of the dream of trekking to New Guinea. "The Indo-European desires to remain European, despite the color of his skin, inherited from his mother, no matter how poor his economic conditions may be. And this desire was the father of the New Guinea ideal."[5] In the 1920s reformers examined the position of "the Indo-European" and decided his future was grim. This perception was a product of significant changes that the twentieth century brought to the Indies. Between the 1870s and the 1930s, political, economic, and technological developments transformed the colony, securing its boundaries and redrafting its social contours. With the liberalization of migration policies and the opening of railways and shipping routes, new opportunities and improved conditions attracted Europeans to the Indies. As their numbers grew, the colony's sex ratios shifted. The full-blooded European housewife replaced the native concubine, and a wealthy, Western-oriented community of newcomers who had been born and raised in Europe (*totoks*) swept away a mestizo cultural world.[6]

These concubines' descendants faced an uncertain future. In the 1930 census 190,000 of the 240,000 persons counted as "European" were labeled as Indies-born settlers (*blijvers*), persons of either mixed or pure European blood who were born and raised in the Indies.[7] The colonial state and private industry had initially promoted mixed-race liaisons by discouraging the migration of married Dutchmen to the Indies.[8] Thus, for several centuries a large portion of the colony's officially defined elite had consisted of Eurasians. Unlike the Philippines' Spanish rulers, Dutch authorities in the Indies never created a distinct legal category for the progeny of unions between whites and natives or whites and persons of mixed race. If many Indo-Europeans (or Indos) were classified as "natives," those recognized by their legal European fathers enjoyed the same status under the law as pure-blooded Dutch men and women. Ranging from the impoverished children of soldiers to the wealthy descendants of Batavia's ruling elite, in the late nineteenth century these Europeans had found employment in private enterprise and an expanding colonial bureaucracy.[9] But around the turn of the century, persons of mixed race began to lose their standing with the growth of a *totok* ("trueborn' or "full-blooded") Dutch community increasingly attuned to distinctions in language, lifestyle, and skin color. Residents born in the Indies gradually adopted totok norms, some shared totok tastes, but few enjoyed the totoks' status or wealth.

The newcomers did more than monopolize the bureaucracy's highest posts. Their arrival set in motion changes that threatened the older community from below. Drawing on Louis Couperus's novel *The Hidden Force*, Pamela Pattynama has argued that the transformation which allowed for the creation of a "white" community also gave rise to a certain unease. Confronted with a native world shrouded in mystery, a new generation of Dutch officials attempted to pull Java's villages into the light of modernity.[10] By expanding the colonial school system, the reforms first helped, then hindered many of the racially hybrid Indies-born residents, who found themselves competing with educated natives who hailed from the archipelago's feudal elite. The Dutch modernization program—called euphemistically the "Ethical Policy"—contributed to the birth of the Indonesian nationalist movement and the replacement of locally hired Europeans by lower-paid native clerks.[11] Many Indo-Europeans lost their steady, if mediocre, income from positions in either the colonial bureaucracy or the private sector; what remained to distinguish such redundant clerks from the competition of educated natives was their superior legal status as Europeans.[12]

The Agrarian Act of 1870, which prohibited the alienation of native land to nonnatives, played a key role in the New Guinea dream.[13] To save Eurasians from vanishing into the native community, attempts were made in the 1920s and 1930s to expand the provisions of the law which offered access to land to European paupers who wished to become small-holders. At a time when nationalist rhetoric appealed to the natives' primordial connection to place, "the Indo-European farmer," living off his own land, was imagined in an attempt to preserve a place in the Indies for this embattled group. Ironically, by attempting to give him roots in the soil, the reformers who spoke for the Indo-European challenged a boundary which defined his privileged status.[14] To beat a system which only recognized peasants or planters, Indo-Europeans needed a space where they could remain European but, at the same time, claim a native's right to own land.

In a dream that reflected desires other than simply the Indo-European's, New Guinea became that space. Ann Stoler has shown how late colonial elites consolidated their position in a variety of settings by reforming or repatriating their "unseemly" compatriots.[15] The plight of displaced Indo-Europeans posed a special challenge to the Dutch East Indies' white masters, who were not pleased by the prospect of mixed-blood colonial residents returning to the mother country in Europe. Obviously, the New Guinea dream's father had a father, too—its grandfather, if you will: the desire of the powerful to remain in control.

The late colonial period saw the birth of a determined, if eclectic, nationalist movement among educated Indonesians. At first, Indonesians' political awakening pleased a Dutch colonial bureaucracy imbued with "ethical" fervor, because their native pupils appeared to be learning to play Western politics. But it frightened them soon thereafter, as they sensed their prerogatives coming under attack. The Great Depression, unleashed in September 1929, played a significant role. Provoking a wave of unemployment in both Holland and the Indies, the depression brought some totoks to their knees. For Couperus's generation of European-born Netherlanders around the turn of the century, danger had resided in the archaic native mysteries that Europeans' enlightened rationality could not penetrate. Twenty years later they faced the threat that enlightened natives might replace them at the top of the colonial world. With the Great Depression looming and radicals lurking in every corner, the image of a haven in the Indies for a threatened elite captured the attention of both Indies-born settlers and Dutch-born newcomers. It was not the first time that the Indies' masters tried to avert disaster by turning potential troublemakers into pioneers on the periphery of Dutch East Indies society. A euphemism for the coolie and the exile's harsh "new existences," a new panacea of colonizing New Guinea became the solution for Europeans who were losing their place.[16]

THE TREK BEGINS

In 1923, four years after the founding of the Indo-European Union, one of the organization's district chairmen had an exciting idea.[17] Speaking at the union's annual convention, A. Th. Schalk proposed the founding of a European agricultural colony in New Guinea. Evoking both the Mormons in the United States and the Boers in South Africa, the head of the Indo-European Union's chapter in Banyuwangi depicted a community grounded in the principles of "self-reliance." While Schalk's speech met with the approval of many members "inside and outside the Indo-European Union," the colonywide leadership of the union remained cool to the idea.[18] Schalk's proposal was dropped until 1926, when A. R. Landsman founded the New Guinea Colonization Society (VKNG).

The New Guinea Colonization Society grew rapidly, opening branches throughout Java. In 1929, after a dispute with other leaders, Landsman and his group from the city of Malang in east Java broke off to found what would be the VKNG's staunch rival, the New Guinea Immigration and Colonization Foundation (SIKNG). The VKNG and the SIKNG, racing to be first, established settlements on the northern coast of New Guinea in November and May 1930. The VKNG chose a site near Hollandia, the town which later became the capital of Netherlands New Guinea. The SIKNG colonists settled close to Manokwari, then the territory's main administrative post.

By 1933 over four hundred Europeans had settled in New Guinea, and their trek was a topic of debate on both sides of the globe. In the Indies those who joined the colonization societies in the discussion included members of the protoparliament of the Netherlands East Indies, the People's Council (Volksraad). Founded in late 1918 as a "school of politics" for native leaders, by the 1930s the racially mixed protoparliament had become a platform for two European political organizations in particular.[19] One was the already familiar Indo-European Union, which has been characterized as "more Dutch than the Dutch" in its loyalties. Claiming to represent tens of thousands of indigent Indo-Europeans, the union had 13,200 members at its height, most of whom were middle-level officials.[20] The other was the ultraconservative Patriots Club, founded in 1929 to disclose the truth about the Indies to a public misled by the propaganda of the Ethical Policy. Said to include among its members one-third of the colony's Dutch-born residents—all men, since women did not receive the active franchise until 1941—the Patriots Club attracted top business and government leaders.[21] Meanwhile, in the political arena of Holland itself, the Hitler-inspired National Socialist movement also took an interest in New Guinea.[22] Playing to fears of the potentially radicalized urban masses, the National Socialists encouraged the handful of New Guinea colonization societies while they lobbied the national parliament for financial support.

Supporters prescribed New Guinea's colonization as the cure for a wide range of social ills. The trek would alleviate European unemployment on crowded Java and open an escape valve for Holland's urban poor. It would offer land and a decent livelihood to the settlers of this "unpopulated" place. New Guinea's development would confirm Holland's control of the colony's border and keep foreign interlopers at bay. Rehashed and recycled among the different factions who pushed the colonization of New Guinea, these arguments cannot account for the fervor shown a cause that was regarded in some circles as "criminally insane."[23] When enthusiasts pictured the new fatherland in New Guinea, what did they see?

One could regard the New Guinea fantasy as the product of the late colonial politics of race and sexual morality. In a variety of settings, the presence of white women both occasioned and justified a new policing of the European self. The enforcement of middle-class mores homogenized the elite, limited its membership, and deepened the divide between the rulers and the ruled. In a futuristic work of late colonial science fiction, New Guinea became a setting for the deployment of new technologies of containment. This empty land became a laboratory for the cultivation of a monitored class identity—the cloning of moral purity in a pristine environment. Through measures protecting the character, hygiene, and health of the colonists, sexual control was perfected as an instrument of colonial power.

However, a wider set of concerns coalesced in this dream. When viewed from another angle, science fiction was transformed into a nationalist romance that was enhanced by unambiguously gendered images. The imagined New Guinea fatherland became a robust surrogate for the colonist's frail native mother, anchoring his claims in purer soil. Turning the pauper into a hero, the trek appealed to the "sublimated eroticism" of Holland's earlier "cults of masculinity."[24] In the 1880s Dutchmen had felt a kinship with the brave South African Boers; in the 1930s they identified with New Guinea's brave pioneers. Like the colonial soldiers who served the virtuous young Queen Wilhelmina at the turn of the century, loyal youth would defend this virgin land.[25]

If nationalism infused the enthusiasts' dreams, fascism gave form to their nightmares. The Indo-European Union and the Patriots Club, as well as both colonization societies, made no secret of the affinity that existed between National Socialism and their version of the colonial mentality.[26] The alternative to settling pure New Guinea was sinking into a swamp of indeterminacy. In Klaus Theweleit's analysis of the male fantasies that arose in the early phases of German fascism, the "communist flood" that threatened to engulf the "soldier male" was invariably feminine.[27] The New Guinea fantasies drew their urgency from a range of colonial discourses that made the indigenous woman the focus of dangerous desires. Descriptions of "the Indo" referred to the "voice" of the "native mother in his blood," who was responsible for his taste for idle pleasures.[28] In the "trueborn" Dutch household, the intimate other took the form of native servants, carriers of alien customs and communicable diseases. Various fears found expression in literature that presented the native mistress as a disruptive force.[29] When propagandists referred to "the woman question" as the most important factor in "successful colonization," they evoked a whole range of threatening images. Far from the masses of native mothers, servants, and lovers, New Guinea became a refuge from the woman within.

Playing to different audiences, different elements of the movement presented New Guinea as a real and symbolic refuge from contagion. As the drama of colonization progressed, three visions of New Guinea came into view: first as the cradle of a nation, then as a crucible of racial purity, and finally as a refuge for a reinvigorated state. As we move from one vision to the next, note the nature of the native Papuan, who must accommodate each scene. The third solution brings us closest to postwar New Guinea. In this virgin land a changing cast of imaginary Europeans seemed to flee the paradoxes of colonial rule.

VISION ONE: THE LAND FOR INDO-SETTLERS

Our first New Guinea, promoted by the New Guinea Immigration and Colonization Foundation (SIKNG), was a space of purified hybridity. Its colonization was a deed which would unify the "Indo-Settler race."[30]

New Guinea would solve the dilemma of European land rights quite simply: just as the Sumatran could claim Sumatra, the Indo settler would claim New Guinea by embracing a newly forged identity that tapped both his maternal and paternal roots. A circular logic made the act of claiming New Guinea the justification for its possession.[31] In epic poetry and strident prose, on Dutch pages scattered with Malay, German, and English words, the SIKNG's newsletters celebrated the future birth of "the New Guineaer." To the Zionist's "Say Yes to Jewishness," the SIKNG echoed, "Say Yes to Indo-ness!" Borrowing from Zionist appeal to Jews to embrace their ethnicity, the SIKNG urged its Indo supporters to recognize who they were.[32]

The New Guinea Immigration and Colonization Foundation charted a way for the Indo settler to go native without vanishing into the masses. The New Guineaer would be indigenous but with a difference: unlike the "stiffened" Europeans or the "ancient" Asians, he would be of vigorous mestizo stock. "Evolution needs new forms, new sorts of plants, animals, men, races. . . . Alas!! Neither the Dutch, as the active agent, nor the Native, as the passive element, appear destined to form a great new race in this region."[33] With the glories of nature bringing out his best, the Indo settler would become the future leader of an Indies federation. The process of settling New Guinea would fill him with masculine vitality. Scarcity would teach him the true value of things. Strengthened by hard work in the clear "glacial air," the young colonist would commune with the "powerful creation process" and come nearer to the "reality of Being: the fields and hills in which the free wind blows are what furnish our bread and our MEN."[34]

The colonists left behind a diseased existence when they set out for New Guinea. In Java's cities, where Indo settlers lived as parasites on the system, insatiable desires and meaningless distractions were sapping the national will. The unemployed joined the "human waste" of poverty that fertilized Communism's evil weed.[35] The idle pleasures of the rich fed the resentment of the poor, which would explode in "bloody excess" when "the crisis" finally came. In place of fratricide, New Guinea offered nourishment, stability, and peace. There would be no hunger or conflict in this "land of unbounded possibilities," where apples and coconuts could thrive side by side.[36]

Far from urban sites of excess and distraction, the SIKNG's New

Guinea could safely employ either local or imported native labor.[37] For the society's supporters contagion was not an effect of exposure to natives: it was the result of performing native tasks. If a colonist did not have coolies, he would become a coolie himself and "lose the Indo's meager capacity to remain lord and master." If his Indo wife did not have servants, she would become her husband's "slave," just like the local Papuan women. And when she rejected this treatment and retreated to Java, the colonist would be forced to replace her with a local girl. Those who refused to associate with Papuan helpers—albeit as their masters—would, according to this convoluted logic, end up with Papuan wives. This reasoning suddenly raised the specter of a New Guinea teeming with natives. By intermarrying, inevitably, the colonists would "assimilate . . . and disappear into the Papuan population."[38]

Marked by the contradictions of this fetishized space—Is it empty? Or is it full?—such a command to associate presented the Indo settler with a paradox. His standing as New Guinea's "first possessor" rested on the Papuans being "scarce." But as the SIKNG newsletters' photographs from the colony showed clearly, he needed Papuan servants to remain who he was.[39] On the horns of this dilemma, SIKNG writers transformed these other "New Guineaers" into the colonist's evil shadow. Papuan women urinated in public and allowed their husbands to lend them to their friends. Naked and dirty, they did all the work, leaving the men to adorn themselves with shells, scraps of Western clothing, and other worthless "finery."[40] These Papuan dandies lacked the "vitality" to last for long. But that was no reason not to employ them before they died out.

In the SIKNG's fantasy about New Guinea as the home for Indo settlers, sexual difference figured as differences in potency. Just as performing native labor would degrade the Indo settler, "manly" Papuan women feminized their men. The same dynamic that produced decadence among the Papuans accounted for the flaws of the SIKNG's other racial others, the Dutch-born newcomers. One contributor portrayed Holland's founding fathers, the Batavians, as loafers who lived off their shrewish, bullying wives until an invasion by the Huns forced them to get tough. "Oh Holland, our land of origin," another lamented, "if only there were a Mussolini among your sons!"[41] Making identity an effect of recognition and will, the SIKNG offered New Guinea as the only place in the Indies where the hybrid Indo-settler could "honor his father and mother [races]."[42]

VISION TWO: WHITE NEW GUINEA

Our next vision of New Guinea was very different. With its fascist supporters in the National Socialist movement in the Netherlands, the New Guinea Colonization Society (VKNG) presented a fatherland whose sons would always be Dutch. A "blank page," just like Australia at the dawn of its history, the VKNG's vision of New Guinea offered marginal Europeans a fresh start. According to the society's leaders, the VKNG's goal in New Guinea was not a political but a socioeconomic one: to rescue "Indies Netherlanders" from Java, where they lived among strangers, and place them in their own European milieu. Far from the servants of the "feudal Indies," the colonists would roll up their sleeves and take up farming, "the natural basis of all things."[43]

Unlike their rivals in the New Guinea Immigration and Colonization Foundation, who would let nature run its course, the VKNG attempted to restore what was natural through a program of moral reform. Training camps on Java instilled prospective colonists with discipline and self-reliance. The trainers faced a challenge in the Indies girl, who had acquired an unnatural disdain for manual labor. Addicted to high heels, dance halls, and other urban pleasures, she "wavered on the threshold" of an agrarian future. But with time, she would shed her "affectations" and take her place at the pioneer's side. The Indies girl would become the happy spouse of an honest farmer or *boer*. A diligent housewife like the matrons of yore, she would savor her toils "in the midst of—and in harmony with—God's beautiful tropical nature . . . without becoming a peasant as some people might assume."[44]

This vision of domestic redemption depended on New Guinea remaining a "totally different setting" than Java. The trek to New Guinea was an escape from the "mixed land," where the competition from cheaper Javanese labor was destroying Indies Dutchmen.[45] For the New Guinea Colonization Society's rescue mission to be effective, New Guinea had to remain pure. The VKNG strictly limited the use of Javanese or Papuan labor in its colony. This prohibition was meant to promote "self-reliance," but the measure also spoke of other fears. "Natural repugnance" was not enough to prevent miscegenation, a writer noted.[46] "The Papuans must stay off the colonists' farms!" The National Socialist movement's propaganda went even further in its tract on "White New Guinea." Exposure to the natives could have "fatal effects." The writer proposed placing the Papuans in special reserves where the government could suppress "customs in conflict with good morals and hygiene, such as head-hunting, cannibalism, and certain sexual practices."[47] Hygiene was an obsession in White New Guinea: the authorities would even sanitize the terrain.

The New Guinea Colonization Society and its supporters fixed the scale linking gender to potency and race. On top was a "man at the peak of his powers." Manning the helm of the Dutch ship of state, the Indies-born Dutchman would ensure that colonization was a success.[48] Next came the "hearty young Hollander," then the "current stock of colonists," and below them the "wavering Indies girl." The "mixed land" lay morally beneath them all, far to the west in the colony's crowded center: a heterogeneous, decaying swamp. White New Guinea was a "barrier to an awakening Asia" and a "bulwark" against a tide of feminine impurity.[49]

VISION THREE: THE BUREAUCRAT'S CROWN TERRITORY

The third vision carried this logic to a different plane. The Patriots Club fantasy about New Guinea did more than transform lax boys into strapping men.[50] It was the stage for a manly apparatus: an unencumbered colonial state. Presented in the People's Council in the capital of Batavia, our third vision of New Guinea reflected the interests of ambitious businessmen and frustrated bureaucrats.[51] While Indo-Europeans' colonization remained the impetus for New Guinea's development, the project now called for massive investments. To prepare for a large influx of Netherlanders from both Holland and the colony's heartland on the island of Java—that is, "the Greater Netherlands"—the government needed to commission soil studies, build roads and harbors, open office buildings, hospitals, and schools.[52] This frontier was animated by the functions of government, not the feats of brave pioneers. It called for a new Ethical Policy of technological development, but this time not focused on improving the lives of the natives. Instead, it would be performed for the glory of the Dutch nation and to reclaim the integrity of the state.

Like the SIKNG and the VKNG, the Patriots Club defined the New Guinea of the future in contrast to the colonial present. But different features vanished from its terrain. For the territory's development to succeed, New Guinea would have to be "set free" from the "purely fictive" system of indirect rule, free from the People's Council's meddling and the bureaucracy's red tape; if possible it should be free from the Indies' corrupted government all together.[53] This backwater should be made a new crown territory, administered and funded directly by the government in The Hague. A "strong young governor" took the place of the intrepid young colonists celebrated in the first two visions. Unchecked by the Indies' moves toward self-rule, he would lead this gigantic land that "lay awaiting a heroic national act" on behalf of the Dutch crown.[54]

Patriots Club writers turned their gaze from Australia to Australian New Guinea to find a model for the new fatherland. Instead of emphasizing the "sinking" European, they depicted the woeful decline of the Netherlands' international prestige. Its shameful performance in New Guinea was striking to anyone who glanced at the island's eastern half, which was run by Australia and featured scores of productive mines and thriving plantations.[55] Holland could only blame itself for its shortcomings, because the two sides of the island were identical. Defined by contiguity, not analogy, Dutch New Guinea was "Australian." Its Papuans (Melanesians) were not of an Asian race.[56]

The Patriots Club vision of New Guinea's cultural essence justified a reinstatement of the penal sanction in the territory.[57] As had once been the case for Javanese migrant workers, Papuan coolies who fled their employers in the New Guinea of the future should be jailed. As the Australian rulers of eastern New Guinea had learned, legally enforced labor contracts had an edifying effect on these primitive workers. But this portrait did more than deny New Guinea's natives the protection of ethical reforms. It mobilized a new discourse to keep its European colonists safe. Harking back to the writings of Friedrich Engels, the Patriots Club's experts placed the "nomadic" Papuans before the dawn of "private property and the state" and declared them *res nulla*, thus without rights to land.[58] In the Patriots Club's vision, New Guinea was distant and empty—far below Europe on the ladder of evolution and entirely empty of law.

The VKNG and the SIKNG cleared New Guinea of native rights and native seductresses—by making the Papuans a race without a future. For the SIKNG, the local population's inevitable demise would make room for the New Guineaer nation. For the VKNG as well, this doomed population fell outside the purview of plans for native autonomy. As the VKNG's leaders almost cheerfully put it, nothing could emancipate natives who were dead.[59] This view left the imaginary colonists from the competing societies with a shared dilemma: how should they deal with the ghosts? The Patriots Club's solution, if apparently milder, more effectively neutralized the Papuan. The Papuan and the colonist could never share the same language, desires, or media of exchange. They certainly could not share the same women or jobs. Placing the colonists among natives who lived in their own cultural infancy, Patriots Club propagandists forgot their fears of contagion.[60] A marginalized community found its salvation in the powerful tools of an unencumbered state that would master a sublimely feminine Nature. In this Stone Age land of slow evolution, racial hierarchies were impervious to change.

CONCLUSION

Of these three visions of New Guinea, the last left the deepest impression. It is not difficult to imagine why. The Patriots Club's study commission in Holland was but one in a series of institutions dedicated solely to the scholarly examination of New Guinea.[61] Academic separation prefigured political divorce. A former governor of Netherlands New Guinea wrote in his memoirs that by the end of World War II, any officer "well-oriented in the literature" who observed the Papuans could see that they had nothing in common with the Indonesians.[62] Colonial scholarship had defined the Papuan as "Melanesian," cutting him off from the ethnic groups to his west.

The question is not whether real differences divided the natives of New Guinea from the native of other parts of the colony. Like the peoples known as "the Batak" or "the Dayak," the Papuan was born in a process of naming in which those designated as such had little part. What is significant is not the truth of the category but the conditions and effects of its development. As the three visions have demonstrated, the Papuan's detachment from the Indies suited a clear set of rhetorical demands.

The 1930s visions infused New Guinea with a significance that was easily rekindled. Arising at the twilight of empire, this maternal father-land was, in accordance with the logic of the fetish, the last object seen before the trauma of its demise. In the 1940s, in Japanese concentration camps in Asia, in Nazi-occupied Holland, and in a colony in revolt, old nightmares of dissolution seemed to come true. New Guinea was more than simply a refuge for loyal colonials; its development was an act of national will. Conveniently, the primitives Papuans seemed to cry out for guidance and protection. In the wake of the Indonesian struggle for independence, Dutch nationals in Southeast Asia did not have to look far for an appendage to replace what they had lost.

The discourse that produced this fetish was anything but neuter. En-gaging the "sublimated eroticism" of nationalist sentiment, virgin New Guinea became a crucible for the making of men. The Indo-Blijverland (land for Indo-European settlers) offered relief from the colonist's struggle for acceptance by creating a newfangled "race" that was neither native nor Dutch.[63] White New Guinea completed the colonist's assimi-lation by erasing his native descent. The crown territory reserved a space for a reinvigorated bureaucracy unimpeded by having to share political power with nomadic Papuans who resembled ghosts. Kindred subjects emerged in this untainted land, far from Java's distracting pastimes, competing natives, and meddling reformers: the white governor, the Dutch colonist, and the New Guineaer, all powerful, young, and male.

In the first two visions, the colonists' regeneration demanded the purging of a negative femininity. The SIKNG's fantasy traded Java's con-fusing seductions for the bounty of mother earth. Offering beauty and sustenance, New Guinea gave the Indo settler the determinate origin that the rest of the Indies could not offer. The VKNG's fantasy sought purity through *apartheid* (segregation). To ward off the horrors of the "mixed land" of "mongrel" Java, the colonists needed pure women as well as pure air. Haunting the sites of contagion at moments of doubt, Papuan women represented the return of the repressed. As the Indo's maternal ancestry, as the full-blooded European's native servants, or simply as the source of Indo-European settler indolence, women signified the ambivalence expelled in pure New Guinea. In the phallocentric logic of late colonialism, they raised the possibility that the other could, in fact, be the self.

These visions of New Guinea illustrate what has been called the "analytic slippage (in colonial discourse) between the sexual symbols of power and the politics of sex."[64] But they also reflect concerns not captured under the rubric of "sexual control." As the distinctions produced by the colonial system began to blur, shaken Europeans looked to a gendered New Guinea for a "slice of eternity."[65] But if land and women stood for origins in this fantasy, they could only present the slippery guise of solid ground. This becomes obvious in the final vision in the series. New Guinea's master was a colonial bureaucratic machine: in fetishized form, the very system that the Indo settler had tried to flee.

And so it was for the Indo-European pioneer, who enjoyed a short revival in the early 1950s when the Netherlands had transferred sovereignty of the archipelago to Indonesians, only to be erased again in Holland's postwar plans.[66] The specter of White New Guinea briefly rose from the ashes in a proposal to purify Holland of the disease of National Socialism after World War II. A postwar plan to deport convicted Nazi collaborators to New Guinea read like a reprint of fascist schemes conjured up in the 1930s.[67] But the Indo-Europeans, having followed the old dream by escaping to New Guinea after Indonesia's independence from the Netherlands was a political reality, soon gave up farming to join an expanding bureaucracy. Within a few years they found themselves caught between high-ranking civil servants born in Holland and Papuans being groomed for self-rule.[68] Postwar New Guinea was a scene for imparting Europeanness to someone other than the Indo. Portraying the Dutch nation as the Papuans' privileged protector, the new rhetoric was grounded in an imagined affinity between the natives and the Dutch.[69] When the New Guinea dream expired for once and for all in the early 1950s, most Indo-Europeans and scores of Papuans fled Indonesian rule and together made the Netherlands their home.

These gendered fantasies of a pure New Guinea mark a moment in the entangled history through which Dutch colonialism created both the rulers and those they ruled. The people of what is now the Indonesian province of Irian Jaya have had to live with the legacy of these delusions. Holland's postwar promotion of Papuan nationalism planted the seeds of the separatist movement that has waxed and waned in Irian Jaya. The authorities in Jakarta have attempted to promote integration through programs that echo colonial policies and plans. Instead of European colonists, Indonesian transmigrants now trek from crowded Java to a promised land far to the east.[70] In the mid-1930s a pioneer wife told a little joke after her home was shaken by an earthquake: "Feel that? My husband finally put his shovel in the soil!"[71] Dutch dreams have given way to Indonesian realities, but in "empty New Guinea," some things have not changed. In the words of Nietzsche, it is distance— "*Distance!*"—that gives woman her allure.[72] The maternal fatherland, the paternal fetish: up close, it never seems the same.

NOTES

1. INTRODUCTION

1. Two examples of this type of scholarship are: A. P. Thornton's *Imperialism in the Twentieth Century* (London, 1978), and Christopher M. Andrew and A. S. Kanya-Forstner, *The Climax of French Imperial Expansion, 1914–1924* (Stanford, Calif., 1981). See Dane Kennedy's critique, "Imperial History and Post-Colonial Theory," *Journal of Imperial and Commonwealth History* 24, 3 (Sept. 1996): 345–63.

2. Lewis Pyenson, *Empire of Reason: Exact Sciences in Indonesia, 1840–1940* (Leiden, 1989), 182. A comprehensive overview of the scholarly literature devoted to empire is Michael Adas, "High Imperialism and the 'New' History," in *Islamic and European Expansion: The Forging of a Global Order*, ed. Michael Adas (Philadelphia, 1993), 311–44.

3. For example, Jacques Marseille, *Empire colonial et capitalisme français* (Paris, 1984).

4. Ronald Robinson and John Gallagher, *Africa and the Victorians* (London, 1961), is the classic work on British financial and economic imperialism.

5. See the discussion of the various uses of the terms *colonialism* and *decolonialism* in current scholarship, particularly in literary studies, where the word *colonial* is employed as a metaphor for any form of elite or cultural domination, in Sidonie Smith and Julia Watson, eds., *De/Colonizing the Subject: The Politics of Gender in Women's Autobiography* (Minneapolis, 1992), xiii-xxxi; see also David Prochaska's "History as Literature, Literature as History: Cagayous of Algiers," *American Historical Review* 101, 3 (June 1996): 671–711.

6. For a discussion of colonialism as a cultural formation, see the introduction to Nicholas B. Dirks, ed., *Colonialism and Culture* (Ann Arbor, Mich., 1992), 1–25.

7. One of the best discussions of the recent scholarly production on gender and empire is Margaret Strobel's "Gender, Sex, and Empire," in Adas, *Islamic and European Expansion: The Forging of a Global Order*, 345–75.

8. Julia Clancy-Smith, *Rebel and Saint: Muslim Notables, Populist Pro-*

test, Colonial Encounters (Algeria and Tunisia, 1800–1904) (Berkeley, Calif., 1994).

9. Nupur Chaudhuri and Margaret Strobel, eds., *Western Women and Imperialism: Complicity and Resistance* (Bloomington, Ind., 1992); the quote is from page 3.

10. On this, see Frances Gouda, *Dutch Culture Overseas: Colonial Practice in the Netherlands Indies, 1900–1942* (Amsterdam, 1995), esp. 45–50; Theodore Friend, *The Blue-Eyed Enemy: Japan against the West in Java and Luzon, 1942–1945* (Princeton, N.J., 1988), 18.

11. See Ranajit Guha and Gayatri Chakravorty Spivak, eds., *Selected Subaltern Studies* (New York, 1988).

12. The number of recent studies devoted to the British Empire by scholars in widely different disciplines is staggering; one only has to consider the twenty or more new titles in the series Studies in Imperialism by Manchester University Press to conclude that Great Britain still corners the academic market in things imperial.

13. Peter van der Veer describes the colonial state as "a nexus of projects and arrangements" in "The Moral State: Religion, Nation, and Empire in Victorian Britain and British India," paper presented to the Ethnohistory Workshop, University of Pennsylvania, Feb. 1996, 29.

14. Nicholas Thomas, *Colonialism's Culture: Anthropology, Travel, and Government* (Princeton, N.J., 1994), 3.

15. David Spurr, *The Rhetoric of Empire: Colonial Discourse in Journalism, Travel Writing, and Imperial Administration* (Durham, N.C., 1992), 184. Spurr's ahistorical approach is, however, a major flaw.

16. As in Clifford Geertz, *Islam Observed: Religious Developments in Morocco and Indonesia* (Chicago, 1968).

17. For example, the renowned Dutch Islamic scholar Christiaan Snouck Hurgronje was invited to give a series of lectures in Paris in 1911 on "Dutch Policy toward Islam" to French colonial administrators; the lectures were published later that year in the *Revue du Monde Musulman* 14, 6 (June 1911): 451–509. Significant for the purposes of this volume were Snouck Hurgronje's assertions that Islam and modernity were irreconcilable because "polygamy, the ease of divorce, the situation of [Muslim] women, who are inferior to their husbands . . . prevents the normal evolution of the household or family" (461). The Dutch scholar's views and the rhetoric he employed were identical to those of many French specialists on Islam. For a discussion of bilateral inheritance arrangements for sons and daughters and women's right to control their own property in Java, see Gouda, *Dutch Culture Overseas*, 95–96, 178–79.

18. Prasenjit Duara, *Rescuing History from the Nation: Questioning Narratives of Modern China* (Chicago, 1995).

19. Ann L. Stoler, "Rethinking Colonial Categories: European Communities in Sumatra and the Boundaries of Rule," *Comparative Studies in History and Society* 31, 1 (1989): 132–49; Robert J. C. Young, *White Mythologies: Writing, History, and the West* (London, 1990).

20. Nancy K. Florida, *Writing the Past, Inscribing the Future: History as Prophesy in Colonial Java* (Durham, N.C., 1995), 393–94. See also Laurie J. Sears, *Shadows of Empire: Colonial Discourse and Javanese Tales* (Durham, N.C., 1996).

21. For an overview, see Ann Thomson, *Barbary and Enlightenment: European Attitudes towards the Maghreb in the Eighteenth Century* (Leiden, 1987).

22. Charles Boissevain, *Tropisch Nederland* (Haarlem, 1909), quoted by J. Van Goor, "Indische reizen in de negentiende en twintigste eeuw: Van verkenning tot journalistiek toerisme," *Tijdschrift voor Geschiedenis* 105, 3 (1992): 457–58. See also the discussion in Henk te Velde, *Gemeenschapszin en plichtsbesef: Liberalisme en nationalisme in Nederland, 1870–1918* (The Hâgue, 1992), 153–61.

23. On constructions of masculinity in the British Raj, see Mrinalini Sinha, *Colonial Masculinity: The "Manly Englishman" and the "Effeminate Bengali" in the Late Nineteenth Century* (Manchester, Eng., 1995).

24. George Lakoff, *Women, Fire, and Dangerous Things: What Categories Reveal about the Mind* (Chicago, 1987).

25. Naomi Quinn, "The Cultural Basis of Metaphor," in *Beyond Metaphor: The Theory of Tropes in Anthropology*, ed. James W. Fernandez (Stanford, Calif., 1991), 60.

26. Edmund Burke III, ed., *Struggle and Survival in the Modern Middle East* (Berkeley, Calif., 1993), 6.

27. The works of the French Algerian writer Louis Bertrand, for example his *Devant l'Islam* (Paris, 1926), 41, employ the language of the enemy—and not that of the bourgeois family—to describe Islam's relation to the West.

28. For a critique of Foucault's inadequate attention to race and colonialism, see Ann L. Stoler, *Race and the Education of Desire: Foucault's History of Sexuality and the Colonial Order of Things* (Durham, N.C., 1995), 75.

29. Terence Hawkes, *Shakespeare's Talking Animals: Language and Drama in Society* (London, 1973), 212.

30. Edward Said, *Orientalism* (New York, 1979), and numerous works by Homi Bhabha and Gyan Prakash, including the latter's edited volume, *After*

Colonialism: Imperial Histories and Postcolonial Displacements (Princeton, N.J., 1995); see the forum devoted to, as well as the critique of, the Subaltern Studies movement in the *American Historical Review* 99, 5 (Dec. 1994): 1475–1545.

31. Robert J. C. Young, *Colonial Desire: Hybridity in Theory, Culture, and Race* (London, 1995), 163.

32. Mackenzie, introduction to Sinha, *Colonial Masculinity* , vii.

33. Edward Said, *Culture and Imperialism* (New York, 1993), 10.

34. Antoinette Burton, *The Burdens of History: British Feminists, Indian Women, and Imperial Culture* (Chapel Hill, N.C., 1994), 36.

35. Young, *Colonial Desire*, 164.

36. Pierre Leroy-Beaulieu, *De la colonization chez les peuples modernes* (Paris, 1872), 293. A recent analysis of the Netherlands as a colonial model is H. L. Wesseling, "Nederland als koloniaal model," in Wesseling, *Indie verloren, rampspoed geboren* (Amsterdam, 1988), 156–58.

37. Ann Laura Stoler and Frederick Cooper, "Tensions of Empire: Colonial Control and Visions of Rule," *American Ethnologist* 16, 4 (1989): 609–21. The most comprehensive historical study of family discourses, images, and narratives as deployed in revolutionary politics is Lynn Hunt's *The Family Romance of the French Revolution* (Berkeley, Calif., 1992).

38. For a discussion of these issues in the context of nineteenth-century France and the Netherlands, see Frances Gouda, *Poverty and Political Culture: The Rhetoric of Social Welfare in the Netherlands and France, 1815–1854* (Lanham, Md., and Amsterdam, 1995), especially chaps. 2 and 4.

39. On this, see David A. Bell, "Lingua Populi, Lingua Dei: Language, Religion, and the Origins of French Revolutionary Nationalism," *American Historical Review* 100, 5 (Dec. 1995): 1403–37.

40. Sears, *Shadows of Empire*, 76–78, 86, 130–35, 168, 202.

41. Paul Rabinow used the phrase "social dust" in *French Modern: Norms and Forms of the Social Environment* (Cambridge, Mass., 1989), 163. Joost van Vollenhoven, despite his Dutch name, was a naturalized French citizen; he was governor-general of French West Africa when he made this statement in 1917. See Alice Conklin, *A Mission to Civilize: The Republican Idea of Empire in France and West Africa, 1895–1930* (Stanford, Calif., 1998).

42. Sinha, *Colonial Masculinity*.

43. Homi Bhabha, *The Location of Culture* (New York, 1994). See the discussion in Young, *Colonial Desire*, 161, and Laurie J. Sears, ed., *Fantasizing the Feminine in Indonesia* (Durham, N.C., 1996).

44. See Stoler, *Race and the Education of Desire*; Anna Lowenhaupt

Tsing, *In the Realm of the Diamond Queen: Marginality in an Out-of-the-Way Place* (Princeton, N.J., 1993).

45. Michael Taussig, *Mimesis and Alterity: A Particular History of the Senses* (New York, 1993), 78–79; Bhabha, *Location of Culture*, 26.

46. The Algerian Arab Muslim leader Ferhat Abbas (1899–1985) is a perfect example of politico-cultural hybridity; see Charles-Robert Ageron, *"L'Algérie algérienne" de Napoleon III à de Gaulle* (Paris, 1980).

47. Ronald Hyam, *Empire and Sexuality: The British Experience* (Manchester, Eng., 1990), 203.

48. Toni Morrison, *Playing in the Dark: Whiteness and the Literary Imagination* (Cambridge, Mass., 1992), 38. See also Gail Ching-Liang Low, "His Stories? Narratives and Images of Imperialism," in *Space and Place: Theories of Identity and Location*, ed. Erica Carter, James Donald, and Judith Squires (London, 1993); Low approaches imperialism as "a culture of masculinity" (188).

49. Louis Couperus, *The Hidden Force*, trans. Alexander Teixeira de Matos (London, 1922; New York, 1924; rept., Amherst, Mass., 1990).

50. Quoted in Henri Tincq, "Les chrétiens d'Algérie, otages et martyrs," *Le Monde*, Tuesday, Aug. 6, 1996, 11.

2. IN PURSUIT OF GREATER FRANCE: Visions of Empire
among Musée Social Reformers, 1894–1931

1. Quote cited by Raoul Girardet, *L'idée coloniale en France de 1871 à 1962* (Paris, 1972), 188; see also Dominique Lejeune, *La France de la Belle Epoque, 1896–1914* (Paris, 1991), 77.

2. See my forthcoming book, *A Social Laboratory for Modern France: The Musée Social and the Rise of the Welfare State, 1890–1914* (Durham, N.C., 1998), and the French edition, *La république sociale: Aux origines de l'Etat-providence* (Paris), and my article "Le Musée social à l'origine: les métamorphoses d'une idée," *Le Mouvement Social* 171 (April–June 1995): 46–69; Sanford Elwitt, "Social Reform and Social Order in Late 19th Century France: The Musée Social and Its Friends," *French Historical Studies* 11, 3 (1980): 431–51.

3. Elinor A. Accampo, Rachel G. Fuchs, and Mary Lynn Stewart, eds., *Gender and the Politics of Social Reform in France, 1870–1914* (Baltimore, 1995).

4. I thank Christopher Thompson for insightful discussions on this subject.

5. See David Spurr, *The Rhetoric of Empire: Colonial Discourse in Jour-*

nalism, Travel Writing, and Imperial Administration (Durham, N.C., 1993); Gwendolyn Wright, *The Politics of Design in French Colonial Urbanism* (Chicago, 1991); Paul Rabinow, *French Modern: Norms and Forms of the Social Environment* (Cambridge, Mass., 1989); Susan Pedersen, *Family, Dependence, and the Origins of the Welfare State, 1914–1945* (New York, 1993); Philip Nord, "Social Defence and Conservative Regeneration: The National Revival, 1900–1914," in *Nation-hood and Nationalism in France: From Boulangism to the Great War, 1889–1918*, ed. Robert Tombs (London, 1991), 210–28; Ann L. Stoler, "Sexual Affronts and Racial Frontiers: European Identities and the Cultural Politics of Exclusion in Colonial Southeast Asia," *Comparative Studies in Society and History* 13 (July 1992): 518.

6. See my forthcoming article, "Le Musée social et ses réseaux réformateurs, 1894–1914," in *Laboratoires du nouveau siècle: La "nébuleuse réformatrice" et ses réseaux en France, 1880–1914*, ed. Christian Topalov (Paris, in press); Françoise Blum and Janet Horne, "Féminisme et Musée social, 1916–1939," *La Vie Sociale* 8–9 (1988): 313–402.

7. "Exposé des motifs à l'appui de l'institution d'une exposition d'économie sociale," *Exposition d'économie sociale: Enquête, instructions, et questionnaires* (Paris, 1887), 18.

8. Emile Cheysson, "L'économie sociale à l'Exposition universelle de 1889," *La Réforme Sociale* 2, 8 (July 1, 1889): 3; Tony Bennett, "The Exhibitionary Complex," in *Culture/Power/History: A Reader in Contemporary Social Theory*, ed. Nicholas B. Dirks, Geoff Eley, and Sherry B. Ortner (Princeton, N.J., 1994), 148; see also Tony Bennett, *The Birth of the Museum: History, Theory, Politics* (London, 1995).

9. Zeynep Çelik, *Displaying the Orient: Architecture of Islam at Nineteenth-Century World's Fairs* (Berkeley, Calif., 1992).

10. Cheysson, "L'économie sociale à l'Exposition," 4.

11. Wright, *Politics of Design*, 94–95; see also Robert de Souza, "L'urbanisme en dix commandements," *Le Musée Social*, April 1929, 130, 135; Alain Cottereau, "Les débuts de plannifcation urbaine dans l'agglomération parisienne," *Revue de Sociologie du Travail* 12 (Oct.–Dec., 1970): 362–92; Jean-Pierre Gaudin, *L'avenir en plan: Technique et politique dans la prévision urbaine, 1900–1930* (Paris, 1985).

12. Stuart Michael Persell, *The French Colonial Lobby, 1889–1938* (Stanford, Calif., 1983), 85; Emile Boutmy, *Le recrutement des administrateurs coloniaux* (Paris, 1895), 11, 37, 40, 46.

13. Georges Picot, "L'usage de la liberté et le devoir social," *La Réforme Sociale* 3, 9 (Feb. 1895): 28, 41–42; Raymond Betts, *Assimilation and Association in French Colonial Theory, 1890–1914* (New York, 1961), 41; Robert

Nye, *Masculinity and Male Codes of Honor in Modern France* (New York, 1993); for the British context, see Graham Dawson, *Social Heroes: British Adventure, Empire, and the Imagining of Masculinities* (London, 1994), 1–166.

14. "Section d'hygiène urbaine et rurale," Musée Social, *Annales*, Nov. 24, 1910, 411.

15. "Section d'hygiène urbaine et rurale," ibid., 1912, 87–88; André Lichtenberger, "La lutte pour la race: Espaces libres et terrains de jeux," *L'Opinion*, Dec. 24, 1910, 801–3; Lucien March, "Pour la race: Infertilité et puériculture," *Revue du Mois* 10 (1910): 551–82.

16. Le comte d'Haussonville and Joseph Chailley-Bert, *L'emigration des femmes aux colonies*, Union Coloniale Française, Jan. 12, 1897 (Paris, 1897), 8.

17. On the influence of Frédéric Le Play and his followers upon social reformers, see Bernard Kalaora and Antoine Savoye, *Les inventeurs oubliés: Le Play et ses continuateurs aux origines des sciences sociales* (Paris, 1989); Antoine Savoye, "Une réponse originale aux problèmes sociaux: L'ingénerie sociale," *La Vie Sociale* 8–9 (1987): 487.

18. In his book *L'organisation du travail*, Le Play expounded his social catechism, or the six essential criteria for achieving peace in the workplace; see Savoye, "Le Play et la méthode sociale," 118.

19. Frédéric Le Play, *La réforme sociale en France déduite de l'observation comparée des peuples européens* (Paris, 1864; rept. New York, 1975), 1:181–98; Emile Cheysson, "L'enseignement ménager et la question sociale," *Oeuvres Choisies* (Paris, 1911), 2:315–30, 345.

20. Betts, *Assimilation and Association*, 106–32.

21. Emile Cheysson, "L'action sociale de la femme et de la mutualité," *La Réforme Sociale*, April 1902, 606.

22. Congresses were held in Oran in 1909 and Constantine in 1911. Bernard Gibaud, "La mutualité française et les premiers congrès internationaux mutualistes," in *Mutualité de tous les pays*, ed. Michel Dreyfus and Bernard Gibaud (Paris, 1995), 193–205.

23. Octave Depont, *La mutualité musulmane: Le Congrès d'Alger-Tunis* (Alger, 1905), 202; *Actes du Congrès de la mutualité coloniale et des pays de protectorat*, Alger-Tunis (Alger, 1905), 251.

24. "Section agricole," Musée Social, *Annales*, 1905, 48; "Section des missions," ibid., 97; Rocquigny, "La coopération dans l'agriculture algérienne," Musée Social, *Mémoires et Documents*, 1906, 281; Rocquigny, "Les associations agricoles de l'Algérie," ibid., 1907, 1–37.

25. Charles-Robert Ageron, *Les Algériens musulmans et la France (1871–*

1919) (Paris, 1968) 2:861–71; Raymond Aynard, *L'oeuvre français en Algérie* (Paris, 1912), 310; Louis Tardy, "Les associations agricoles dans l'Afrique du Nord," Musée Social, *Revue Mensuelle*, 1927, 372; Tardy, "Les institutions de mutualité et de coopération agricole en Algérie," ibid., 1930, 337–44.

26. Emile Cheysson, "Le role de la femme dans la mutualité," Musée Social, *Mémoires et Documents*, 1905, 336.

27. Augusta Moll-Weiss, "L'enseignement ménager en Allemagne," ibid., 361.

28. Cheysson, "Enseignement ménager," 323; Cheysson, "La crèche et la famille," "Le role de la femme dans la mutualité," "L'action sociale de la femme," in *Oeuvres Choisies* 2:307–9, 340, 605.

29. Seth Koven and Sonya Michel, eds., *Mothers of a New World: Maternalist Politics and the Origins of the Welfare State* (New York, 1993).

30. Blum and Horne, *Féminisme*, 319–21; Cheysson, "Enseignement ménager," 322.

31. Kaëte Schirmacher, "Le travail des femmes en France," Musée Social, *Mémoires et Documents*, 1902, 321–72; Augusta Moll-Weiss, "La femme dans le système d'Elberfeld," ibid., 1906, 377–99; Claire Gérard, "La condition de l'ouvrière parisienne dans l'industrie de la fleur artificielle," ibid., 1909, 1–24.

32. Joan Scott, *Only Paradoxes to Offer: French Feminists and the Rights of Man* (Cambridge, Mass., 1996); Christine Bard, *Les filles de Marianne: Histoire des féminismes, 1914–1940* (Paris, 1995); Karen M. Offen, "Depopulation, Nationalism, and Feminism in Fin-de-Siècle France," *American Historical Review* 89, 3 (June 1984): 654.

33. Offen, "Depopulation, Nationalism," 657.

34. Ibid., 673–74.

35. Julie Siegfried, *La guerre et le rôle de la femme* (Cahors, 1915), 8, 15.

36. Yvonne Knibiehler and Régine Goutalier, *La femme au temps des colonies* (Paris, 1985), 88–89, 91; d'Haussonville and Chailley-Bert, *Emigration des femmes*, 6–7, 9, 33; d'Haussonville, *Les non classées et l'émigration des femmes aux colonies* (Paris, 1898): 779–810.

37. D'Haussonville and Chailley-Bert, *Emigration des femmes*, 59.

38. Le Play, *La réforme sociale en France*; G. Vabran, "La femme française et la femme musulmane en Tunisie," Musée Social, *Mémoires et Documents*, 1913, 44; A. Chassevant, "La médecine sociale en Algérie," Musée Social, *Revue Mensuelle*, 1927, 225–27.

39. Vabran, "La femme française," 42–43, 45.

40. Ibid., 31–59.

41. Philip Nord citing Eugène Pelletan, "Republican Politics and the

Bourgeois Interior in Mid-Nineteenth-Century France," in *Home and Its Dislocations in Nineteenth-Century France*, ed. Suzanne Nash (Albany, 1993), 195.

42. Cited by Hodeir and Pierre, *Exposition coloniale*, 33.

43. Girardet, *L'idée coloniale*, 175–99.

44. Albert Sarraut, *Grandeur et servitude coloniales* (Paris, 1931), 12, 18; Hodeir and Pierre, *Exposition coloniale*, 26, 139.

45. "Le Musée social: Son but, Son organisation, Son oeuvre," Musée Social, *Revue Mensuelle*, Oct. 1933, 347.

46. In 1936 Vérone joined the staff of Jean Guéhenno's left-wing newspaper *Vendredi*, where she wrote on women's role in Islam.

47. "Les Etats-Généraux du féminisme," *Le Quotidien*, May 31, 1931; Cécile Brunschvicg, "Les Etats-Généraux du féminisme," *La Française*, June 13, 1931; see, for instance, Paul Gradvohl, "Les premières années de l'Association des surintendantes (1917–1939)," *La Vie Sociale* 8–9 (1986): 379–453.

48. E. Duvivier de Streel, *L'urbanisme aux colonies et dans les pays tropicaux* (Paris: 1931), 10; Girardet, *L'idée coloniale*, 188.

3. "SPECIAL CUSTOMS": Paternity Suits and Citizenship in France and the Colonies, 1870–1912

I would like to thank the French government for a Bourse Chateaubriand, the University of Chicago for a Humanities Overseas Research Grant, and the University of Rochester's Susan B. Anthony Institute for Women's Studies for a Faculty Grant, all of which supported the research for this paper. A Monticello College Foundation Fellowship at the Newberry Library in 1997 provided invaluable time to write.

1. Evelyn Brooks Higginbotham, "The Problem of Race in Women's History," in *Coming to Terms: Feminism, Theory, Politics*, ed. Elizabeth Weed (New York, 1989); Marianne Hirsch and Evelyn Fox Keller, eds., *Conflicts in Feminism* (New York, 1990); Nupur Chaudhuri and Margaret Strobel, eds., *Western Women and Imperialism: Complicity and Resistance* (Bloomington, Ind., 1992); Ann-Louise Shapiro, ed., *Feminists ReVision History* (New Brunswick, N.J., 1995).

2. James F. Traer, *Marriage and the Family in Eighteenth Century France* (Ithaca, N.Y., 1980), 154–65; Crane Brinton, *French Revolutionary Legislation on Illegitimacy, 1789–1804* (Cambridge, Mass., 1936).

3. *Code civil des français* (Paris, 1804; facs., Honfleur, 1977), article 341, 84.

4. For surveys of the literature, see Alexandre Dumas *fils*, *La recherche de la paternité: Lettre à M. Rivet, député* (Paris, 1883); Abel Pouzol, *La recherche de la paternité: Etude critique de sociologie et législation comparée* (Paris, 1902); for analysis, see Jean Elisabeth Pederson, "The Meaning of Motherhood: The Politics of Paternity Suits," paper presented at New York State Association of European Historians, Oct. 1993; Rachel G. Fuchs, *Poor and Pregnant in Paris: Strategies for Survival in the Nineteenth Century* (New Brunswick, N.J., 1992), 68–69, 90–93.

5. Claire Goldberg Moses, *French Feminism in the Nineteenth Century* (Albany, 1984); Laurence Klejman and Florence Rochefort, *L'égalité en marche: Le féminisme sous la Troisième République* (Paris, 1989).

6. Karen M. Offen, "Depopulation, Nationalism, and Feminism in Fin-de-Siècle France," *American Historical Review* 89, 3 (June 1984): 648–76; Karen M. Offen, "Exploring the Sexual Politics of Republican Nationalism," in *Nation-hood and Nationalism in France: From Boulangism to the Great War, 1889–1918*, ed. Robert Tombs (New York, 1991), 195–209.

7. Robert A. Nye, *Crime, Madness, and Politics in Modern France: The Medical Concept of National Decline* (Princeton, N.J., 1984).

8. Gustave Lagneau, quoted in Pouzol, *La recherche*, 169.

9. Jules Simon, quoted in Dumas *fils*, *La recherche*, 22.

10. M. Bry, cited in Pouzol, *La recherche*, 78.

11. Congrès International du Droit des Femmes, "Voeux: Section de législation," *L'Avenir des Femmes*, Sept. , 1878, quoted in Susan Groag Bell and Karen M. Offen, eds., *Women, the Family, and Freedom: The Debate in Documents*, 2 vols. (Stanford, Calif., 1983), 1:455.

12. Maria Deraismes, *Discours prononcé au Pecq, le 14 juillet 1882, à l'occasion de l'inauguration du buste de la République des communes de Jacques France* (Bois-Colombes, Seine, [1882]), 2.

13. Dumas *fils*, *La recherche*, 16–18.

14. Offen, "Depopulation"; Tombs, *Nation-hood*, pt. 3, "Policy in the Era of Nationalism," 231–78; Offen, "Exploring Sexual Politics"; Michelle Perrot, "The New Eve and the Old Adam," in *Behind the Lines*, ed. Margaret Higonnet et al. (New Haven, 1987), 51–60.

15. Pouzol, *La recherche*, 4.

16. Jean Elisabeth Pedersen, "Legislating the Family: Gender, Population, and Republican Politics in France, 1870–1920" (Ph.D. diss., Univ. of Chicago, 1993), especially chap. 4.

17. Unless otherwise noted, all biographical information on politicians is from Jean Jolly et al., *Dictionnaire des parlementaires français*, 8 vols. (Paris, 1960–73).

18. Gustave Rivet, *Journal officiel de la Republique française, Débats du Sénat*, June 7, 1910, 1466–67.

19. Ibid., 1467.

20. Martin's denial of political rights to women in this passage is perplexing given his support of women's suffrage after 1919. One wonders whether his belief in suffrage came after his support for paternity suits, or whether his denial of rights to women in this passage was simply politically expedient. See Steven Hause with Anne R. Kenney, *Women's Suffrage and Social Politics in the French Third Republic* (Princeton, N.J., 1981), 231, 236, 239–40.

21. Louis Martin, *Journal officiel, Débats du Sénat*, June 9, 1910, 1482.

22. Maurice Violette, *Journal officiel de la République française, Documents de la Chambre des Députés*, Feb. 27, 1911, Annexe 796, 1439.

23. Rivet, *Journal officiel, Débats du Sénat*, June 7, 1910, 1466–69.

24. Pierre-Ernest Guillier, ibid., June 14, 1910, 1510.

25. Félix Martin, ibid.

26. Louis Martin, ibid., Nov. 11, 1910, 1731.

27. Jean Richard, ibid., June 16, 1910, 1514.

28. See Raymond F. Betts, *Assimilation and Association in French Colonial Theory, 1890–1914* (New York, 1961); Henri Brunschwig, *L'Afrique noire au temps de l'empire français* (Paris, 1988), 22; Jacques Thobie, Gilbert Meynier, Catherine Coquery-Vidrovitch, and Charles-Robert Ageron, eds., *Histoire de la France coloniale, 1914–1990* (Paris, 1990), 34–37; Denise Bouche, *Histoire de la colonisation française* (Paris, 1991), 1:108.

29. Charles-Robert Ageron, *L'anticolonialisme en France de 1871 à 1914* (Paris, 1973), 19–32; Ageron, "Socialistes et communistes français devant la question Algérienne," *Politiques coloniales au Maghreb* (Paris, 1972), 151–215. On Hubertine Auclert, the most famous feminist anticolonialist, see Stephen Hause, *Hubertine Auclert: The French Suffragette* (New Haven, 1987); Marnia Lazreg, "Feminism and Difference: The Perils of Writing as Women on Women in Algeria," in Hirsch and Keller, *Conflicts in Feminism*, esp. 333.

30. Quoted in Viollette, *Journal officiel, Documents de la Chambre des Députés*, Annexe 796, 1443.

31. Ibid.

32. Ibid. See also Guillier, *Journal officiel, Débats du Sénat*, Nov. 8, 1912, 1345.

33. Later French administrators reported over 200 different peoples along the Somalian coast (Hubert Deschamps, *Côte des Somalis* [Paris, 1948], 21–29). See also Lee V. Cassanelli, *The Shaping of Somali Society: Re-*

constructing the History of a Pastoral People, 1600–1900 (Philadelphia, 1982); and for French West and Equatorial Africa, Commission de Codification des Coutumes Juridiques, *Coutumes juridiques de l'Afrique occidentale française*, vols. 1–3 (Paris, 1939); Georges Bruel, *La France équatoriale africaine* (Paris, 1935); Maurice Delafosse, *Enquête coloniale dans l'Afrique française occidentale et équatoriale* (Paris, 1930).

34. Commission de Codification des Coutumes Juridiques, *Coutumes juridiques*; Bruel, *France équatoriale*; Delafosse, *Enquête coloniale*.

35. John L. Esposito, *Women in Muslim Family Law* (Syracuse, N.Y., 1982); Louis Milliot, *Introduction à l'étude de droit Musulman* (Paris, 1953), esp. 387–411.

36. Quoted in Viollette, *Journal officiel, Documents de la Chambre des Députés*, Annexe 706, 1443.

37. Nigel Heseltine, *Madagascar* (New York, 1971), 93.

38. Hubert Deschamps, "La première codification africaine: Madagascar, 1828–1881," in *Ideas and Procedures in African Customary Law*, ed. Max Gluckman (London, 1969), 169–78.

39. Henri Lavondès, *Bekoropoka: Quelques aspects de la vie familiale et sociale d'un village malgache* (Paris, 1967), 15; Richard Huntington, *Gender and Social Structure in Madagascar* (Bloomington, Ind., 1988), 1–3.

40. C. Keller, *Madagascar, Mauritius, and the Other East African Islands* (London, 1901), 81; Belle McPherson Campbell, *Madagascar* (Chicago, 1889), 28–29; Chase Salmon Osborne, *Madagascar: Land of the Man-Eating Tree* (New York, 1924), 219–21; and, more recently, Raymond Decary, *Moeurs et coutumes des Malgaches* (Paris, 1951), 30; Heseltine, *Madagascar*, 93–94.

41. For example, Yvonne Knibiehler and Régine Goutalier, *La femme au temps des colonies* (Paris, 1985).

42. Allan Christelow, *Muslim Law Courts and the French Colonial State in Algeria* (Princeton, N.J., 1985), 223–74.

43. Bruel, *France équatoriale*, 268.

44. Christelow, *Muslim Law Courts*, 262–65; A. N. Elliott, A. L. Epstein, and M. Gluckman introduction to Gluckman, *Ideas and Procedures in African Customary Law*, especially 9–15, 31–33; Kristin Mann and Richard Roberts, "Law in Colonial Africa," in *Law in Colonial Africa*, ed. Mann and Roberts (Portsmouth, N.H., 1991), 3–58. For the British case, see Margaret Jean Hay and Marcia Wright, eds., *African Women and the Law: Historical Perspectives* (Boston, 1982).

45. Pierre-Ernest Guillier, *Journal officiel, Documents du Sénat*, March 5, 1912, Annexe 88, 699–700.

46. Ibid.

47. Rachel G. Fuchs, "The Right to Life: Paul Strauss and the Politics of Motherhood," in *Gender and the Politics of Social Reform in France, 1870–1914*, ed. Elinor A. Accampo, Rachel G. Fuchs, and Mary Lynn Stewart (Baltimore, 1995).

48. Paul Strauss, *Journal officiel, Débats du sénat*, Nov. 8, 1912, 1344.

49. Guillier, ibid., 1344–45.

50. Maurice Colin, ibid., 1345.

51. Christelow, *Muslim Law Courts*; Charles-Robert Ageron, *Modern Algeria: A History from 1830 to the Present*, trans. Michael Brett (Trenton, N.J., 1991), 47–81; Vincent Confer, *France and Algeria: The Problem of Civil and Political Reform, 1870–1920* (Syracuse, N.Y., 1966).

52. Amédée Knight, *Journal officiel, Débats du Sénat*, Nov. 8, 1912, 1345. For Knight's politics in Martinique, see Fred Constant, *La retraîte aux flambeaux: Société et politique en Martinique* (Paris, 1988), 45–54. On colonial law, see Alain Philippe Blérald, *La question nationale en Guadeloupe et en Martinique: Essai de l'histoire politique* (Paris, 1988), 71.

53. Gerard Cornu, *Droit civil: La famille* (Paris, 1984), 2:385.

54. Alain Bénabent, *Droit civil: La famille* (Paris, 1995), 400–403, 424–25; André Rouast, *La famille: Mariage, divorce, filiation* (Paris, 1952), 590–602, 7211–31, 796–97.

55. Adrien Gaudin de Villaine, *Journal officiel, Débats du Sénat*, Nov. 10, 1910, 1737.

56. Charles Rieu, ibid., Nov. 8, 1912, 1334.

57. See Pedersen, "Legislating the Family," esp. the introduction and chap. 3.

58. Jeanne Deflou, "Le bilan du féminisme en France en 1914," *La Femme de Demain*, no. 7 (Jan. 1914): 2.

59. Maria Vérone, "La recherche de la paternité," *Jus Suffragi*, Jan. 15, 1913, in dossier 347 PAT, "Recherche de la paternité," Bibliothèque Marguerite Durand, Paris.

60. Louis Martin, quoted in "La recherche de la paternité devant l'opinion," *Le Droit des Femmes* (Jan. 1913), in dossier 347 PAT, "Recherche de la paternité," Bibliothèque Marguerite Durand, Paris.

61. M. Bosquet, quoted in "La recherche de la paternité devant l'opinion."

62. "La recherche de la paternité devant l'opinion."

63. Juliette Akar, "La recherche de la paternité," *La Française*, March 7, 1931, 3.

64. Jean Veil, *Le code civil: Textes antérieures et version actuelle* (Paris,

1981), 136–37; Bénabent, *Droit civil*, 425; Michelle Perrott, "Naissance du féminisme," in *Le féminisme et ses enjeux: Vingt sept femmes parlent* (Paris, 1988).

65. Carol Pateman, *The Sexual Contract* (Palo Alto, Calif., 1988); Joan Landes, *Women and the Public Sphere in the Age of the French Revolution* (Ithaca, N.Y., 1988); Joan W. Scott, "French Feminists and the Rights of 'Man': Olympe de Gouges' Declarations'," *History Workshop Journal*, no. 28 (Autumn 1989): 1–21.

66. Bell and Offen, "Women's Fate in the French Revolution of 1848," in Bell and Offen, *Women, the Family, and Freedom* 1:248–49; Laura S. Struminger, "Looking Back: Women of 1848 and the Revolutionary Heritage of 1789," in *Women and Politics in the Age of Democratic Revolutions*, ed. Harriet Applewhite and Darlene G. Levy (Ann Arbor, Mich., 1990), 259–85; Bouche, *Histoire* 2:105.

67. Bouche, *Histoire* 2:146–47; Christian Bruschi, "Droit de la nationalité et égalité des droits de 1789 à la fin du XXe siècle," in *Questions de nationalité: Histoire et enjeux d'un code*, ed. Smain Lacher (Paris, 1987), 42–46.

68. Rogers Brubaker, *Citizenship and Nationhood in France and Germany* (Cambridge, Mass., 1992), xi.

69. Bouche, *Histoire* 2:142–43; Christelow, *Muslim Law Courts*, 267–68; Dominique Sair and Richard Roberts, "The Jurisdiction of Muslim Tribunals in Colonial Sénégal, 1857–1932," in Mann and Roberts, *Law in Colonial Africa*, 131–46.

70. Rachel Fuchs is currently analyzing the trial records of actual paternity suits to determine who used the law and how it worked for women in continental France.

71. Sally Engle Merry, "The Articulation of Legal Spheres," in Hay and Wright, *African Women and the Law*, 86–87.

72. Martin Charrock, "Making Customary Law: Men, Women, and Courts in Colonial Northern Rhodesia," ibid., 53–67.

4. REDEFINING "FRENCHNESS": Citizenship, Race Regeneration, and Imperial Motherhood in France and West Africa, 1914–40

1. Dominique Simonnet, "Devenir Français: Chiffres 1993," *Libération*, Feb. 3, 1995.

2. The federation of French West Africa (Afrique occidentale française) was created in 1895 and placed under the control of a government-general headquartered in Dakar. Five colonies belonged to the federation: Senegal,

Guinea, Ivory Coast, Dahomey, and Upper Senegal–Niger. It also included the military territories of Niger and Mauritania.

3. Ann L. Stoler, "Making Empire Respectable: The Politics of Race and Sexual Morality in 20th-Century Colonial Cultures," *American Ethnologist* 4, 3 (1989): 635.

4. See the articles by Dipesh Chakrabarty, Sandria B. Freitag, and David Gilmartin entitled "Aspects of 'the Public' in Colonial South Asia," *South Asia* 14, 1 (1991).

5. Gender as a category of analysis has been largely neglected in the existing literature on French West Africa. For an introduction to French policies in West Africa in this era, see Alice L. Conklin, *A Mission to Civilize: The Republican Idea of Empire in France and West Africa, 1895–1930* (Stanford, Calif., 1997).

6. Stoler, "Making Empire Respectable," 635. Stoler's conclusions regarding French Indochina and the Dutch East Indies apply to nonsettler colonies such as French West Africa, with one important difference. Concern with miscegenation surfaced later in the sub-Saharan colonies than in French Indochina, probably because they were acquired last, and women did not settle there before the 1920s and 1930s.

7. Nupur Chaudhuri and Margaret Strobel, eds., *Western Women and Imperialism: Complicity and Resistance* (Bloomington, Ind., 1992); Yvonne Knibiehler and R. Goutalier, *La femme au temps des colonies* (Paris, 1985); Helen Callaway, *Gender, Culture, and Empire: European Women in Colonial Nigeria* (London, 1987).

8. Marc Michel, *L'appel à l'Afrique: Contributions et réactions à l'effort de guerre en A.O.F., 1914–1919* (Paris, 1982).

9. G. Wesley Johnson, "The Impact of the Senegalese Elite upon the French, 1900–1940," in *Double Impact: France and Africa in the Age of Imperialism*, ed. Johnson (Westport, Conn., 1985), 155–79; Michael Lambert, "From Citizenship to Négritude: 'Making a Difference' in Elite Ideologies of Colonized Francophone Africa," *Comparative Studies in Society and History* 35, 1 (1993): 239–62.

10. Conklin, *A Mission to Civilize*, chap. 6.

11. The first modern attempt to organize female emigration to the colonies occurred under the auspices of the Union Coloniale in 1897. A committee was formed to recruit 50 to 60 young women who would work and, hopefully, marry overseas. The only colonies healthy enough to be targeted for emigration, however, were Algeria, Tunisia, parts of Tonkin, and the upper plateaus of Madagascar (J. Chailley-Bert, *L'émigration des femmes aux colonies: Union coloniale française-conférence*, Jan. 12, 1897 [Paris, 1897]).

Six years later almost 100 women had been sent to the various colonies, but only 20 had found husbands (M. Pégard, "L'émigration des femmes aux colonies," *La Réforme Sociale*, Dec. 16, 1903, 872–82). By the interwar years French women were actively promoting colonial careers for themselves, usually as female doctors, medical assistants, and teachers. See, for example, A. Querillac, "Le rôle de la femme médecin aux Colonies," *Dépêche Coloniale*, April 10, 1932, and Hélène Gosset, "Les Toubibas, ou l'oeuvre des femmes françaises au Maroc," *L'Intransigeant*, March 7, 1932.

12. For example, Robert Randau's *Le chef de porte-plume* (Paris, 1922), which satirizes the role played by the wife of Governor-General Ponty (1908–14).

13. Before World War I the administration had actually encouraged concubinage. As one manual put it: "How should the European conduct himself in West Africa? For those who lack the moral strength necessary to endure two years of absolute continence, only one line of conduct is possible: a temporary union with a well-chosen native woman" (Dr. Barot, *Guide pratique de l'Européen dans l'Afrique occidentale à l'usage des militaires, fonctionnaires, commerçants, colons, et touristes* [Paris, 1902], 329).

14. Stoler, "Making Empire Respectable," 640.

15. The expression "Il faut faire naître" (we must give birth) is pronatalist Fernand Boverat's, from his article by that name in *Revue de l'Alliance Nationale pour l'Accroissement de la Population Française* 143 (1924): 163–71.

16. William H. Schneider, *Quality and Quantity: The Quest for Biological Regeneration in Twentieth Century France* (Cambridge, Eng., 1990); Lion Murard and Patrick Zylberman, "De l'hygiène comme introduction à la politique expérimentale (1875–1925)," *Revue de Synthèse*, 3d ser., 115 (1984): 313–34; Susan Pedersen, *Family, Dependence, and the Origins of the Welfare State: Britain and France, 1914–1945* (Cambridge, Eng., 1993); Yvonne Knibiehler, *Cornettes et blouses blanches: Les infirmières dans la société française, 1880–1980* (Paris, 1984); Mary Louise Roberts, *Civilization without Sexes: Reconstructing Gender in Postwar France, 1917–1927* (Chicago, 1994); Tyler Stovall, "Color-blind France? Colonial Workers during the First World War," *Race and Class* 35, 1 (1993): 35–55; Gary Cross, *Immigrant Workers in Industrial France* (Philadelphia, 1983).

17. Schneider, *Quality and Quantity*, 141–42.

18. M. Tesseron, directeur honoraire au ministère des colonies, "Rapport sur la condition légale des sujets dans les colonies françaises et sur les prérogatives qui en resultent," 1925, Archives Nationales du Sénégal (ANS), 17 G 59, Fonds moderne (FM).

19. It is interesting to consider the history of French naturalization policy in West Africa. In 1889 the Third Republic passed its first major law

on citizenship. This law was extended to the colonies "other than Martinique, Réunion, and Guadeloupe" in 1897, but its provisions applied only to nonnationals and their descendants residing or born on French territory. The 1897 law expressly stipulated that "it changed nothing in the condition of natives in the colonies" (Décret, Feb. 7, 1897, *Journal officiel de la République française*, 895–97). In 1907 the governor-general of West Africa challenged this exclusion by petitioning the minister of colonies to approve a decree that would permit the naturalization of meritorious Africans (Gouverneur-général au ministre des colonies, Politique indigène: naturalisation des indigènes, législation et projets, no. 1015, May 30, 1907, Archives nationales, section d'outre-mer [Aix-en-Provence] [ANSOM], Affaires politiques [AP] 2759/2). This decree was finally passed in 1912.

20. The May 25, 1912, naturalization decree required the following conditions: a West African place of birth and residence; proof of devotion to France or occupation of a salaried position in the colonial administration; knowledge of French; a certificate of primary studies; proof of good financial standing and tax compliance; no criminal record or history of bankruptcy (arrêté no. 907, May 25, 1912, *Journal officiel de l'Afrique occidentale française [JOAOF]*, 395). An important assumption of the decree was that the extension of citizenship was to be strictly personal, although it could be extended to an applicant's wife married under French law and any children from that union who had been registered with the French authorities.

A second assumption was that any Muslim applicant would agree henceforth to be bound by French rather than Koranic law. The 1912 conditions were slightly modified in 1918 to facilitate naturalization of returning African veterans (arrêté of Feb. 2, 1918, ibid., 51–52).

21. In fact, a 1916 decision by the French Parliament to extend citizenship automatically to all Africans born in the Four Communes of Senegal considerably complicated the naturalization issue in West Africa. Blaise Diagne astutely manipulated Parliament's ignorance of colonial affairs to gain this concession. The government-general was opposed to the new law, because it failed to require that Muslims accept the provisions of the French Civil Code as part of naturalization. As Dakar saw it, there was now a group of French citizens in the colony who were not worthy of the status of citizen, since they continued to follow Koranic law. The new citizens of the Four Communes, in contrast, felt that they had finally received the political rights that they deserved. The presence of these anomalous Muslim citizens, who quickly began to demand further concessions, also helps explain why Dakar became so opposed to any further extension of citizenship in the 1920s.

22. "Projet de loi; accession des indigènes à la naturalisation," 1924,

ANSOM, AP 1638; "Proposition de loi par M. Valude," 1922, ANSOM, AP 145–6. For the laws provisions, see Mario Roustans, "L'accession à la qualité de citoyen français," *Annales Coloniales*, Sept. 17, 1925. Daladier's project had not been voted upon when he left office in the spring of 1925. It appears to have been motivated in part by a desire to unify the existing legislation throughout the empire (each colony had its own set of criteria for extending citizenship); in part by agitation by the French League for the Defense of the Rights of Man and Citizen, which was in favor of the project (Ligue à Président de la République, Dec. 20, 1920, ANSOM, AP 2759–3); and in part by the residual sense of debt that France felt it owed its subjects for their contribution to the war effort. Instead of being debated in Parliament, the proposed legislation gave rise to a prolonged investigation by the legal branch of the Superior Council into the conditions regulating naturalization in the empire.

23. Procès-Verbaux for March 30 and June 15, 1927, ANS, 17 G 59, FM. The idea of an intermediary status between citizen and subject was first debated in these meetings. Discussion continued the following year (Procès-Verbaux for June 13, 1928, ANSOM, AP 1638).

24. Ministre des colonies à vice président du Conseil d'Etat, "a.s. de l'institution dans certaines de nos possessions d'une catégorie de sujets ou protégés dites d'indigènes d'élite," ANSOM AP 1638. His report and *projet de loi* are attached to this correspondence.

25. Tesseron, directeur honoraire au ministère des colonies, "Rapport sur la condition légale des sujets dans les colonies françaises et sur les prérogatives qui en résultent," 1925, ANS, 17 G 59, FM.

26. Conseil Supérieur des Colonies, Session of March 30 and June 15, 1927, "Rapport de M. Bernard Lavergne, professeur à la Faculté de Droit à Lille," ANS, 17 G 59, FM.

27. Gouverneur-général au ministre des colonies, no. 1072, Oct. 8, 1930, ANSOM, AP 1638. Only the governors-general of Madagascar, Equatorial Africa, and French Somaliland favored the proposal to create the new category.

28. Ibid. For earlier drafts of this same letter, which are even more revealing, see ANS, 7G 47, FM. In one such draft, Carde insists that "although the new citizen . . . may have personally and momentarily elevated himself above his [original condition of "native"] he often falls back down before the end of his career . . . from which it is necessary to conclude that [citizenship] is not made for our natives."

29. Arrêté no. 117 a.p. "promulguant en AOF le décret du 21 août 1932, relatif aux conditions d'accession des indigènes de l'AOF à la qualité de

citoyens français," Jan. 19, 1933, *JOAOF*, 155–57; for the local application of the decree, see arrêté no. 118 a.p., Jan. 19, 1933, ibid., 157–60. The 1918 decree on naturalization for West Africans who had served in the French army was also revised by a decree of April 19, 1933, which unified conditions for veterans throughout the empire; see arrêté no. 1410 a.p., June 17, 1933, ibid., 605–7; arrêté no. 1411 a.p., June 17, 1933, ibid., 611–12.

30. Circulaire no. 11 "a.s. de l'accession des indigènes à la qualité de citoyen français," Jan. 19, 1933, ANS.

31. See Kenneth Ballhatchet, *Race, Sex, and Class under the Raj: Imperial Attitudes and Policies and Their Critics* (London, 1980); Ronald Hyam, *Empire and Sexuality: The British Experience* (Manchester, Eng., 1991).

32. Jacques Mazet, *La condition juridique des métis dans les possessions françaises, Indochine, Afrique occidentale française, Madagascar* (Paris, 1932).

33. A whole series of novels from the interwar years explored the plight of the métis: Clothilde Chivas-Baron, *Confidences de métisse* (Paris, 1926); Jehan Cendrieux, *François Phuoc, métis* (Paris, 1929); Herbert Wild, *L'autre race* (Paris, 1930); and Lucienne Favre, *L'orientale 1930* (Paris, 1930). These novels stressed such themes as the métis' hatred for their French fathers, the inability of the métis to fit into French society, and the incompatibility of the two races.

34. Schneider, *Quality and Quantity*, 235–36.

35. Pat Shipman, *The Evolution of Racism, Human Differences, and the Use and Abuse of Science* (New York, 1995).

36. According to this decree, if a métis of unknown but visibly mixed parentage could provide proof of his French culture, this along with his white features was sufficient for citizenship (arrêté no. 2568 a.p. "promulguant en AOF le décret du 5 septembre 1930, fixant la condition juridique des métis nés de parents inconnus en AOF," Nov. 14, 1930, *JOAOF*, 944–46).

37. René Maunier, *Sociologie coloniale*, vol. 1, *Introduction à l'étude du contact des races* (Paris, 1932), 112–13.

38. Ibid., 115.

39. Ibid., 117.

40. Ibid., 171. In his condemnation of miscegenation, Maunier openly acknowledged his debt to eugenicist thinking; he cited the "well-known Mendelian law . . . the law of hybridization, that a return to the primitive takes place, that the native type always carries the day" (ibid., 114). Another clear example of eugenicist thinking penetrating colonial circles is provided by two articles which appeared in *La Revue Indigène*—a colonial journal devoted to "native affairs"—on the eve of World War I. The first article

reported on the latest findings of the Eugenics Society: that "children of mixed parentage resemble most the parent in whose original habitat they are born and raised." This meant that French-Indochinese children were "destined to return rapidly to the Indochinese type." And the article concluded "Is it because they have known this law for a long time that the English have avoided in general mixed-unions in the colonies?" ("La science et les métis," *La Revue Indigène* no. 94 [March 19, 1914]: 143–51). Another article by French colonial employees argued that no Indochinese could acquire the requisite degree of civilization to be admitted to the colonial service at the same level of pay as Europeans. As proof, the signatories cited "the regression which takes place when descendants of métis intermarry"; they "return slowly but surely to the inferior origin" ("Lettre des Amicales de fonctionnaires à M. le Gouverneur Général de l'Indochine," ibid., no. 97 [June 30, 1914]: 354–59). Similar sentiments would develop in West Africa a little later.

41. Emile Roux, *Manuel à l'usage des administrateurs et du personnel des affaires indigènes de la colonie du Sénégal et des colonies relevant du Gouvernement Général de l'AOF* (Paris, 1911), 467–504.

42. Gustave Reynaud, *Hygiène coloniale*, vol. 2, *Hygiène des colons* (Paris, 1903), 373, 386–87, 389. Concern with preserving French prestige is also discussed in Alexandre Kermorgorant and Gustave Reynaud, "Précautions hygiéniques à prendre pour les expéditions et explorations au pays chauds," *Annales d'Hygiène et de Médecine Coloniales* 3 (1900): 384.

43. Reynaud, *Hygiène coloniale* 2:11.

44. Ibid.

45. Dr. Barot, *Guide pratique*, 331.

46. Maurice Delafosse, *Broussard, ou les états d'âme d'un colonial suivis de ses propos et opinions* (Paris, 1923), 79; William Cohen, *Rulers of Empire: The French Colonial Service in Africa* (Stanford, Calif., 1971), 122.

47. Louise Delafosse, *Maurice Delafosse: Le Berrichon conquis par l'Afrique* (Paris, 1976).

48. Louis Sonolet, *Le Parfum de la dame noire: Physiologie humoristique de l'amour african* (Paris, 1911), 202, 204.

49. Ibid., 210.

50. Ibid., 215.

51. Georges Hardy, *Ergaste ou la vocation coloniale* (Paris, 1929), 31–32.

52. Ibid., 78.

53. J. L. Faure, ed., *La vie aux colonies: Préparation de la femme à la vie coloniale* (Paris, 1938), 46–47.

54. Ibid., 7–8, 160.

55. "La femme et la vie coloniale," *La Dépêche Coloniale*, April 29, 1932.

56. Faure, *La vie aux colonies*, 68.

57. Ibid., 101.

58. Hardy, *Ergaste*, 30.

59. Clothilde Chivas-Baron, *La femme française aux colonies* (Paris, 1929), 121.

60. Faure, *La vie aux colonies*, 59.

61. Chivas-Baron, *La femme française aux colonies*, 124.

62. Ibid., 187.

63. Faure, *La vie aux colonies*, 56.

64. Ibid., 11.

65. Chivas-Baron, *La femme française aux colonies*, 176.

66. Ibid., 146.

67. Ibid., 186–87.

68. A. Querillac, "Le rôle de la femme médecin aux colonies," *Dépêche Coloniale*, April 10, 1932.

69. Roberts, *Civilization without Sexes*, 6.

5. SECRETS AND DANGER: Interracial Sexuality in Louis Couperus's *The Hidden Force* and Dutch Colonial Culture around 1900

1. The page numbers cited in this chapter are from E. M. Beekman's edition of *The Hidden Force* (Amherst, Mass., 1990). Beekman thoroughly revised the first English translation by Alexander Teixeira de Mattos done in 1922. He decided to keep Teixeira's translation because of its "congruence of tone" with the original and a "similar somewhat archaic diction" (p. 40).

2. D. K. Fieldhouse, *The Colonial Empires: A Comparative Survey from the Eighteenth Century*, 2d ed. (1966; rept., London, 1991), 328.

3. See Aparna Dharwadker's reading of *Tughlaq*, "Historical Fictions and Postcolonial Representation; Reading Girish Karnad's *Tughlaq*," *PMLA* 110, 1 (1995): 43.

4. Homi K. Bhabha, "Difference, Discrimination, and the Discourse of Colonialism," in *The Politics of Theory*, ed. Francis Barker et al. (Colchester, Eng., 1983), 194–211.

5. See, for examples, Gayatri Chakravorty Spivak, "Three Women's Texts and a Critique of Imperialism," in *Race, Writing, and Difference*, ed. Henry Louis Gates Jr. (Chicago, 1986), 262–80; Jean Gelman Taylor, *The Social World of Batavia: European and Eurasian in Dutch Asia* (Madison, Wis., 1983).

6. For an elaboration of feminist reading methods, see Judith Fetterley,

The Resisting Reader: A Feminist Approach to American Fiction (Bloomington, Ind., 1978). See also Shoshana Felman, "Rereading Femininity," *Yale
French Studies* 62 (1981): 19–45; Naomi Schor, *Reading in Detail: Aesthetics
and the Feminine* (New York, 1987). I borrow the terms "absent text of
history" and "unsaid" from Pierre Macherey, *The Theory of Literary Production* (London, 1978).

7. Edward W. Said, *Orientalism* (Harmondsworth, Eng., 1978), 2.

8. The impact of Couperus's imagination is greatly due to his brilliant,
unorthodox use of the Dutch language. For an analysis of his fin de siècle
style, see P. H. Ritter Jr., "Over de stijl van Louis Couperus," in Ritter Jr.,
Louis Couperus (Amsterdam, 1952), 54–73; also E. M. Beekman, introduction to *The Hidden Force* (Amherst, Mass., 1990), 17–19.

9. For a discussion of the TV series, see Leo Ross, "*De Stille Kracht* als
kijkvoer," *Maatstaf* 22, 8/9 (1974): 11–24.

10. In *The Hidden Force* Louis Couperus demonstrates a remarkable
awareness of Dutch imperialism and colonial culture. Yet, written in 1900,
the novel incorporates an essentialist distinction between East and West. It
therefore inevitably privileges Europe as the center, emphasizing the homeland over the native and the metropole over the colonial periphery.

11. C. Th. van Deventer, "Een Eereschuld," *De Gids* 3 (1899), rept. in *De
Locomotief*, Aug. 30, 1899.

12. E. M. Beekman, introduction to *The Hidden Force*, 6.

13. Sigmund Freud, "Some Psychical Consequences of the Anatomical
Distinction between the Sexes (1925)," in *Women and Analysis*, ed. Jean
Strouse (Boston, 1985), 25.

14. Revulsion is a psychic mixture of fear of losing one's identity and a
fascination with this loss. This ambiguous response was first invoked when,
in its early development, the child detached itself from the mother in a
necessary move. At that moment, which establishes sexual difference, the
child experienced its first loss, a traumatic and fundamental one. Prior to
this, the child was fused with its mother and inhabited a void, an emptiness
in which neither subject nor object, neither masculinity nor femininity existed. Lurking in the unconscious, the memory of this lost bliss will always
ambiguously disrupt the oppositional, rational, gendered, and racialized
order, in which the subject finds herself or himself. The literary image of
an interracial union as constructed in *The Hidden Force* transgresses the
boundaries between masculinity and femininity and fuses different "races."
It thus works by inciting in the reader an archaic mixture of pleasure and
danger which is called revulsion. See Julia Kristeva, *Powers of Horror: An
Essay on Abjection*, trans. Leon S. Roudiez (New York, 1982).

15. Taylor, *The Social World of Batavia;* see also Heather Sutherland, "Van mesties tot Indo: de sociale geschiedenis van families in het koloniale Makassar," in *Bronnen van kennis over Indische Nederlanders,* ed. Wim Willems (Leiden, 1991), 183–99; and for a discussion of mestizo culture, see Edy Seriese, "Indische letteren als Mestiezenliteratuur," *Indische Letteren* 7, 4 (1992): 145–51.

16. See also V. J. H. Houben, "De Indo-aristocratie van Midden Java: De familie Dezentjé," in *Sporen van een Indisch verleden,* ed. Wim Willems (Leiden, 1992), 39.

17. A. van Marle, "De groep der Europeanen in Nederlands-Indië, iets over ontstaan en groei," *Indonesië* 5 (1951–52): 485.

18. F. L. Bastet, *Een zuil in de mist: Van en over Louis Couperus* (Amsterdam, 1980), 86. See also Jacqueline Bel, "Losbandigheid, geldzucht en goena-goena: De receptie van Indische romans in Nederland aan het eind van de vorige eeuw," in *Indisch-Nederlandse literatuur,* ed. Reggie Baay and Peter van Zonneveld (Utrecht, 1988), 144.

19. For an interesting example, see Marion Valent, "Over *De stille kracht* van Louis Couperus," *Literatuur* 1, 4 (1984): 203–9.

20. See, for example, Henry van Booven, *Leven en werken van Louis Couperus* (1933; rept., The Hague, 1981); H. W. van Tricht, *Louis Couperus: Een verkenning* (The Hague, 1965).

21. Rob Nieuwenhuys, *Oost-Indische spiegel: Wat Nederlandse schrijvers en dichters over Indonesië hebben geschreven, vanaf de eerste jaren der Compagnie tot op heden* (1972; rept., Amsterdam, 1978), 257. Similarly, Beekman in his introduction recognizes in Van Oudijck's paternal arrogance and inflexibility a "flaw reminiscent of King Lear" (p. 28).

22. See Lee R. Edwards, *Psyche as Hero: Female Heroism and Fictional Form* (Middletown, Conn., 1984), 7–8.

23. Ian Buruma, "Revenge in the Indies," *New York Review of Books,* Aug. 11, 1994, 30.

24. Spivak, "Three Women's Texts," 266.

6. WOMANIZING INDOCHINA: Fiction, Nation, and Cohabitation in Colonial Cambodia, 1890–1930

1. Throughout French rule (1863–1953), the term *Cambodgien* (Cambodian) was commonly used to denote the majority ethnic group in Cambodia, today known as Khmer. I have adopted this usage throughout this chapter.

2. Jules Michelet, *Jeanne d'Arc* (Paris, 1974), 151.

3. Isabelle Julia, "Daughters of the Century," in Julia, *La France: Images of Woman and Ideas of Nation, 1789–1989* (London, 1989), 90–91.

4. A. R. Lebel, *Histoire de la littérature coloniale en France* (Paris, 1931), 172.

5. Hugues le Roux, *Nos filles: Qu'en ferons-nous?* (Paris, 1898), 1, 211; Georges Hardy, *Ergaste ou le vocation coloniale* (Paris, 1929), 76; Roger Magraw, *France, 1815–1914: The Bourgeois Century* (London, 1983), 238–39: Peter Baugher, "The Contradiction of Colonialism: The French Experience in Indochina" (Ph.D. diss., Univ. of Wisconsin, 1989), 122–88.

6. Edward Said, "East Isn't East: The Impending End of the Age of Orientalism," *Times Literary Supplement*, Feb. 3, 1995, 5; Nicholas Thomas, *Colonialism's Culture: Anthropology, Travel, and Government* (Melbourne, 1994), 33–60.

7. C. Lavollée, "Le Tour du Monde," *Revue des Deux Mondes* (Paris, 1889): 906–17; Henri Mouhot, *Travels in Indo-China, Siam, Cambodia, and Laos* (Bangkok, 1986), 275–77.

8. Anthony Barrett, "Cambodia Will Never Disappear," *New Left Review* 180 (March–April, 1990), 101–25; Paul Doumer, *L'Indochine française (souvenirs)* (Paris, 1930), 290.

9. Doumer, *L'Indochine*, 9–26, 215.

10. Ibid., 13; Alain Corbin, *Women for Hire: Prostitution and Sexuality in France after 1850* (Cambridge, Mass., 1990), 331; Catherine Fouquet, *L'histoire des mères de moyen-âge à nos jours* (Paris, 1980), 138–78.

11. Anne-Marie Willis, *Illusions of Identity: The Art of Nation* (Sydney, 1993), 99; George Mosse, *The Nationalization of the Masses* (New York, 1974), 78; Asa Briggs, *Victorian Things* (London, 1988), 128; Donald Horne, *The Great Museum: The Re-Presentation of History* (London, 1984), 4.

12. Leonard Bell, *Colonial Constructs: European Images of Maori* (Melbourne, 1992), 70, 47–48, 150–52; Thomas, *Colonialism's Culture*, 112–13; Annie Coombes, *Reinventing Africa: Museums, Material Culture, and Popular Imagination* (New Haven, 1994), 89–105, 187–213; Anne McClintock, "Maidens, Maps, and Mines: King Solomon's Mines and the Reinvention of Patriarchy in Colonial South Africa," in *Women and Gender in South Africa to 1945*, ed. Cheryl Walker (Cape Town, 1990), 97–124; Doumer, *L'Indochine*, 269–70; George Groslier, *Danseuses cambodgiennes, anciennes et modernes* (Paris, 1913), 120.

13. George Groslier, "Les arts indigènes au Cambodge," *L'Indochine française: Receuil de notices rédigées à l'occasion du Xe Congrès de la Far Eastern Association of Tropical Medicine, Hanoi, 24–30 novembre 1938* (Hanoi, 1938), 161; Milton Osborne, *The French Presence in Cochinchina and*

Cambodia, 1859–1905 (Ithaca, N.Y., 1969), 257; *Sihanouk: Prince of Light, Prince of Darkness* (Sydney, 1994), 16; Elizabeth Becker, *When the War Was Over: The Voices of the Cambodian Revolution and Its People* (New York, 1986), 55; Ben Kiernan, *How Pol Pot Came to Power* (London, 1985), xi, 3–7.

14. Le Roux, *Nos filles* (Paris, 1898), 1, 211; E. Giret, "La Femme aux Colonies," *Revue Indochinoise* 117 (Jan. 14, 1901): 1.

15. Joseph Chailly-Bert, *L'émigration des femmes aux colonies* (Paris, 1896); Union Coloniale Française, Société Française d'Emigration des Femmes, 1–3, Archives d'outre-mer, Indochine, governor-general of Indochina (AOM INDO GGI) 7661.

16. Circular from André Lebon, minister of colonies, July 31, 1897, resident superior of Tonkin to GGI, Sept. 23, 1897, and note from Chenieux, premier bureau de Cochinchine, n.d., GGI to minister of colonies, n.d., Comtesse de Custine, president of the Society for the Emigration of Women, to GGI, Dec. 28, 1903, Governor-General Beau to Custine, March 22, 1904, AOM INDO GGI 7663.

17. Jean Ajalbert, *L'Indochine en peril* (Paris, 1906), 26; Eugène Pujarniscule, *Philoxène ou de la littérature coloniale* (Paris, 1931), 106–7, 155.

18. GGI, agence économique, "Renseignments sur les emplois privés ou administratifs en Indo-Chine," n.d. (c. early 1920s), 1, GGI, direction de l'instruction publique, "Situation des fonctionnaires de l'enseignement en Indochine," n.d. (c. late 1920s), 5, 7, GGI to minister of colonies, Dec. 9, 1927, AOM FM INDO NF 873; Harry Franck, *East of Siam: Ramblings in the Five Divisions of French Indo-China* (New York, 1926), 239; Société de Protection Maternelle et Infantile du Cambodge, AOM INDO Haut Commissariat au Cambodge (HCC) 13 (the society's statutes [*Statuts*] were published in Phnom Penh in 1927); Giret, "La Femme," 1; Janice Brownfoot, "Memsahibs in Colonial Malaya: A Study of European Wives in a British Colony and Protectorate, 1900–1940," in *The Incorporated Wife*, ed. Hilary Callan and Shirley Ardener (London, 1984), 191.

19. Ajalbert, *L'Indochine*, 31–32; Pierre Mille, *Sur la vaste terre* (Paris, 1906), 175–85.

20. Pierre Pasquier, "Rapport sur l'Indochine," *Compte rendu des travaux du Congrès colonial de Marseille*, 2 vols. (Marseille, 1906), 2:533.

21. Lagrillière-Beauclerc, *A travers l'Indochine: Etudes coloniales* (Paris, 1900), 134; Paul Bergue, "L'habitation européenne au Cambodge," *Revue Indochinoise* 7 (April 15, 1905): 490–99; Paul Igout, *Phnom Penh Then and Now* (Bangkok, 1993), 70, 137–38; Clotilde Chivas-Baron quoted in Baugher, "The Contradiction of Colonialism," 151; Marguerite Duras and

Michel Porte, *Les lieux de Marguerite Duras* (Paris, 1977), 56; Jean Ajalbert, *Ces phénomènes, artisans de l'empire* (Paris, 1941), 110.

22. Jean Marquet, *La France mondiale au XXé siècle, Indochine* (Paris, 1931), 175; Louis Malleret, *L'exotisme Indochinois dans la littérature française depuis 1860* (Paris, 1934), 224; Marguerite Duras, *The Sea Wall* (New York, 1985), 135–37.

23. "L'Exposition de l'Indochine" in *L'Illustration* (Paris), Sept. 1, 1900, 134–35; "L'état des esprits en Cochinchine," *Bulletin de la Comité de l'Asie Française,* Sept. 1906, 334, 253; Areno Iukanthor, *Destin de l'Empire* (Paris, 1935), 86–88; Captain Chan, report to GGI, July 1, 1906, 24–27, AOM INDO GGI 5881; Ajalbert, *Indochine,* 26–27.

24. Paul Russel Cravath, "Earth in Flower: An Historical and Descriptive Study of the Classical Dance Drama of Cambodia" (Ph.D. diss., Univ. of Hawaii, 1985), 173–74; *Les actualités diplomatiques et coloniales numéro spécial: l'Exposition de Hanoi en 1902* 1 (Sept. 1902): 35–38.

25. Jean Noury, *L'Indochine avant l'ouragan, 1900–1920* (Chartres, 1984), 156.

26. Taken from the Vietnamese for "little girl," *congaï* was a generic, derogatory term used in French Indochina to denote the Vietnamese, Cambodian, Laotian, Japanese, and Chinese concubines of Europeans. See Malleret, *L'exotisme,* 217 ff.; Charles Meyer, *La vie quotidienne des Français en Indochine* (Paris, 1985), 265 ff., 288.

27. Ajalbert, *Ces phénomènes,* 143–44; Malleret, *L'exotisme,* 217; David Spurr, *The Rhetoric of Empire: Colonial Discourse in Journalism, Travel Writing, and Imperial Administration* (Durham, N.C., 1993), 171.

28. Albert de Pouvourville, *Le cinquième bonheur* (Paris, 1922), and his *L'heure silencieuse* (Paris, 1926); Malleret, *L'exotisme;* Giret, "La Femme," 1; Ajalbert, *Ces phénomènes,* 169–71.

29. Meyer, *La vie quotidienne,* 268; Pujarniscle, *Philoxène,* 107.

30. Doumer, *L'Indochine,* 253–54; Jean Meyer et al., *Histoire de la France coloniale des origines à 1914* (Paris, 1990), 697–99; Patrice Moriat, *Les affaires politiques de l'Indochine (1895–1923): Les grands commis: du savoir au pouvoir* (Paris, 1995), 19–20.

31. Alain Forest, *Le Cambodge et la colonisation française: Histoire d'un colonisation sans heurts (1897–1920)* (Paris, 1980), 255.

32. M. E. Assaud, procureur-général, chef du Service Judiciaire en la Cochinchine et du Cambodge, "Confidential Circular," Saigon, Sept. 18, 1897, 1, Paul Doumer, "Confidential Circular," Saigon, Sept. 29, 1901, AOM INDO GGI 7770 procureur-général, chef du Service Judiciaire en Indo-Chine, circular, Saigon, Sept. 19, 1908, AOM INDO GGI 4680; GGI to minister of colonies, Nov. 7, 1910, Dec. 7, 1910, AOM FM INDO NF 76 (1).

33. "Les métis et l'oeuvre de la protection de l'enfance au Cambodge," *Revue Indochinoise*, Jan. 1913, 31; Champly, *The Road to Shanghai*, 83.

34. See, for example, Edouard Heckel and Cyprien Mandine, *L'enseignement colonial en France et à l'étranger* (Marseille, 1907), 44–45.

35. Malleret, *L'exotisme*, 41 ff.; Roland Meyer, *Cours de Cambodgien* (Paris, 1912); Meyer, *Saramani: Danseuse cambodgienne* (Paris, 1922); Meyer, *Cours de Laotien* (Paris, 1924); Meyer, *Indochine française: Le Laos* (Hanoi, 1931); Meyer, *Le propos du vieux colonial* (1952; rept., Paris, n.d.), back cover.

36. Meyer's work displays a much greater attempt to engage colonial society than that of Groslier, whose *Danseuses cambodgiennes, anciennes et modernes* (1913) lacked the depth and detail of *Saramani*. See Cravath, "Earth in Flower," 73–74.

37. Raphael Barquisseau, *Le roman colonial français* (Hanoi, 1926), 3.

38. Groslier to secretary-general, Hanoi, June 25, 1906, AOM INDO GGI 2397.

39. L. Forestier, "George Groslier: Prix de littérature coloniale 1929: *Le retour à l'argile*," *Extrême-Asie Revue Indochinoise Illustrée* 38 (Aug. 1929): 602.

40. Cravath, "Earth in Flower," 173–74; George Groslier, *A l'ombre d'Angkor* (Paris, 1916).

41. Albert Sarraut, *La mise en valeur des colonies françaises* (Paris, 1923), 104.

42. Groslier, "Les arts," 163; Groslier, *La route du plus fort* (Paris, 1925); Groslier, *Le retour*. See also Harriet Ponder, *Cambodian Glory* (London, 1936), 170–71.

43. Becker, *When the War*, 53–54; Marie Alexandrine Martin, *Cambodia: A Shattered Society* (Berkeley, Calif., 1994), 34; Alec Hargreaves, *The Colonial Experience in French Fiction* (London, 1981), 13–14.

44. Forestier, "George Groslier," 604.

45. For a discussion of portrayals of "good" colonial subjects as feminine, see David Henry Hwang, *M. Butterfly* (London, 1988), 99.

46. David Chandler, *A History of Cambodia* (Boulder, Colo., 1992), 156.

47. See Forest, *Le Cambodge*, 92, 117, 130, 146, 376–84; Tully, *Cambodia*, 149–76; Kiernan, *How Pol Pot*, 14.

7. SO CLOSE AND YET SO FAR: The Ambivalence of Dutch Colonial Rhetoric on Javanese Servants in Indonesia, 1900–1942

An earlier version of this essay appeared as "Orientalism and the Rhetoric of the Family: Javanese Servants in European Household Manuals and

Children's Fiction" in *Indonesia* 58 (Oct. 1994): 19–40 and is reprinted with the permission of the Cornell Southeast Asia Program.

1. Carol A. Breckenridge and Peter van der Veer, eds., *Orientalism and the Postcolonial Predicament: Perspectives on South Asia* (Philadelphia, 1993), 2.

2. K. Ballhatchet *Race, Sex, and Class under the Raj: Imperial Attitudes and Policies and Their Critics, 1793–1905* (London, 1980); for a Dutch version, see Rudy Kousbroek, "De Mems in de koloniale samenleving." *Deugd en Ondeugd: Jaarboek voor Vrouwengeschiedenis* 13 (1994): 149–62.

3. Edward Said, *Orientalism* (New York, 1979).

4. Ton Zwaan, "Familie, huwelijk en gezin in West-Europa: een introductie," in *Familie, huwelijk en gezin in West-Europa: Van Middeleeuwen tot moderne tijd*, ed. Ton Zwaan (Amsterdam/Heerlen, 1993), 28; Christiane Klapisch-Zuber, "Women Servants in Florence during the Fourteenth and Fifteenth Centuries," in *Women and Work in Preindustrial Europe*, ed. Barbara A. Hanawalt (Bloomington, Ind., 1986), 56–80.

5. Elsbeth Locher-Scholten, "Female Labor in Twentieth Century Java: European Notions—Indonesian Practice," in *Indonesian Women in Focus: Past and Present Notions*, ed. Elsbeth Locher-Scholten and Anke Niehof (Leiden, 1992), 77–79.

6. *Volkstelling 1930*, vol. 6, *Europese bevolkingsgroep* (Batavia, 1936), 23, 25, 40, 68, 70, 78, 79.

7. The sex ratio among Europeans changed considerably between 1880 and 1930: from 471 women per 1,000 men in 1880 to 636 per 1,000 in 1900 to 884 per 1,000 in 1930 (A. van Marle, "De groep der Europeanen," *Indonesië* 5 [1952]: 320–21).

8. Faye E. Dudden, *Serving Women: Household Service in Nineteenth Century America* (Middletown, Conn., 1983); Theresa M. McBride, *The Domestic Revolution: The Modernisation of the Household Service in England and France, 1820–1920* (London, 1976).

9. The many forms of Indonesian domestic service are illustrated in Arti Poerbani (pseud. A. P. Dajadiningrat), *Widijawati, het Javaansche meisje* (Amsterdam, 1948).

10. Jean Gelman Taylor, *The Social World of Batavia: European and Eurasian in Dutch Asia* (Madison, Wis., 1983).

11. M. Székely-Lulofs, *Onze bedienden in Indië* (Deventer, n.d.), 10; B. van Helsdingen-Schoevers, *De Europeesche vrouw in Indië* (Baarn, 1914), 32.

12. J. Kloppenburg-Versteegh, *Het leven van de Europeesche vrouw in Indië* (Deventer, 1913); C. J. Rutten-Pekelharing, *Waaraan moet ik denken? Wat moet ik doen? Wenken aan het Hollandsche meisje dat als huisvrouw naar Indië gaat* (Gorkum, 1927), 46–47.

13. Rutten-Pekelharing, *Waaraan moet ik denken?* 44–45; Ems I. H. van Soest, *De Hollandsche vrouw in Indië* (Deventer, n.d.), 96.

14. Deduced from *Volkstelling 1930*, vol. 8, *Overzicht voor Nederlandsch Indië* (Batavia, 1936), 126–27.

15. McBride, *Domestic Revolution*, 82–99; *Volkstelling 1930* 8:126–27; Locher-Scholten, "Female Labor," 96.

16. Deduced from *Volkstelling 1930* 8:94–95.

17. Kloppenburg-Versteegh, *Leven*; D. C. M. Bauduin, *Het Indische leven* (The Hague, 1927); Székely-Lulofs, *Bedienden*, 20; Bauduin, *Indische leven*, 67.

18. Shelly Errington, "Recasting Sex, Gender, and Power: A Theoretical and Regional Overview," in *Power and Difference: Gender in Island Southeast Asia*, ed. Jane M. Atkinson and Shelly Errington (Stanford, Calif., 1990), 5. Although researchers on Indonesian households accept this as a general pattern, no specific studies on the spatial organization of the Central Javanese household exist. On Madura, see Anke Niehof, "Women and Fertility in Madura, Indonesia" (Ph.D. diss., Leiden Univ., 1985), 215–16; concerning West Java, see R. Wessing, *Cosmology and Social Behavior in a West Javanese Settlement* (Athens, Ohio, 1978), 53–63.

19. This association started twenty years later than its Dutch sister association and ran a monthly *De Huisvrouw in Indië* (*De Huisvrouw in Indië* 7 [1938]: 72).

20. A. J. Resink-Wilkens, "Huishoudonderwijs voor het dessameisje," in *Indisch Vrouwenjaarboek 1936*, ed. M. A. E. van Lith–Van Schreven and J. H. Hooykaas–Van Leeuwen Boomkamp (Jogjakarta, 1936), 61–67; *De Huisvrouw in Indië* 5 (1936): 83, 7 (1938): 643.

21. Frances Gouda, *Dutch Culture Overseas: Colonial Practice in the Netherlands Indies, 1900–1942* (Amsterdam, 1995), 75–117.

22. Van Helsdingen-Schoevers, *Europeesche vrouw*, 32; *De Huisvrouw in Indië* 5 (1936): 700, 7 (1938): 518, 8 (1939): 618.

23. Székely-Lulofs, *Bedienden*, 22; see also Franke, "Personeel," 246.

24. For example, E. Breton de Nijs, *Vergeelde portretten: Uit een Indisch familiealbum* (Amsterdam, 1973); see also Ann L. Stoler, "Making Empire Respectable: The Politics of Race and Sexual Morality in 20th Century Colonial Cultures," *American Ethnologist* 16, 4 (1989): 26–51.

25. P. Peverelli, "De hygiëne van het gezin," in *Indisch Vrouwenjaarboek 1936*, ed. Van Lith–Van Schreven and Hooykaas–Van Leeuwen Boomkamp, 100–104, 149; Székely-Lulofs, *Bedienden*, 55.

26. Székely-Lulofs, *Bedienden*, 42. Fear of pollution was not an Indies monopoly. Similar patterns of behavior could be found in the relationship between Dutch mistresses and German housemaids in the prewar Nether-

lands; see Barbara Henkes, *Heimat in Holland: Duitse dienstmeisjes, 1920–1950* (Amsterdam, 1995), 80.

27. Kloppenburg-Versteegh was the most expressive in this respect. Babus used very special means to silence a child and get it to sleep: not only rocking it but even using opium "rubbed in on parts of the body decency prohibits to call by name" (*Leven*, 64–65). For a more balanced opinion, see *Indisch Vrouwenjaarboek*, 44, 230; see also Franke, "Indonesisch personeel," 247.

28. Székely-Lulofs, *Bedienden*, 35–36.

29. Kloppenburg-Versteegh, *Leven*, 54.

30. Ibid., 112; Rutten-Pekelharing, *Waaraan moet ik denken?* 50–51.

31. Van Helsdingen-Schoevers, *De Europeesche vrouw*, 25; Van Soest, *De Hollandsche vrouw*, 111.

32. Kloppenburg-Versteegh, *Leven*, 53; Van Helsdingen-Schoevers, *De Europeesche vrouw*, 32; Rutten-Pekelharing, *Waaraan moet ik denken?* 50.

33. Carol Z. Stearns and Peter N. Stearns, eds., *Emotion and Social Change: Towards a New Psychohistory* (New York, 1988), 7; Kloppenburg-Versteegh, *Leven*, 90, 91, 98. The same habitus is prescribed in children's fiction. Girls should not be choleric or hot-tempered.

34. Archive Koloniale School voor Meisjes en Vrouwen (Colonial School for Girls and Women), files 77, 78 and 86, Algemeen Rijksarchief (National Archives), The Hague.

35. Brochure 1923, ibid., file 77; Radiorede Ros Vrijman, July 19, 1938, ibid., file 81.

36. Radiorede Ros Vrijman, 19-7-1938, ibid., file 81; Brochure 1923, p. 12, and Vierde propagandaboekje 1927, ibid., file 77.

37. Brochure 1923, pp. 10, 12, and Derde propagandaboekje 1925, pp. 4, 16, ibid., file 77.

38. Brochure 1923, p. 9, ibid.

39. Joan W. Scott, "Gender, a Useful Category of Historical Analysis," *American Historical Review* 91, 5 (1986): 1054.

40. A journalist reminded his readers that servants rarely could be identified with the indigenous population in general (Melis Stoke, *Wat men in Indië moet doen en laten* [The Hague, 1939], 100). See also Kloppenburg-Versteegh, *Leven*, vi.

41. Albert Memmi has stressed the intimacy of this relationship as a reason behind the violence of servants toward their masters (A. Memmi, *Dominated Man: Notes towards a Portrait* [Boston, 1971], 178).

42. Székely-Lulofs, *Bedienden*; Franke, "Indonesisch personeel," 252.

43. L. Dasberg, *Het kinderboek als opvoeder: Twee eeuwen pedagogische normen en waarden in het historische kinderboek in Nederland* (Assen, 1981); Bob Dixon, *Catching Them Young*, vol. 1, *Sex, Race, and Class in Children's Fiction* (London, 1978), 48.

44. Dorothée Buur, *Indische jeugdliteratuur: Geannoteerde bibliografie van jeugdboeken over Nederlands-Indië en Indonesië* (Leiden, 1992); 21; J. H. Hooykaas–Van Leeuwen Boomkamp, "Inheemsche kinderboeken," in Van Lith–Van Schreven and Hooykaas–Van Leeuwen Boomkamp, *Indisch Vrouwenjaarboek*, 189–94.

45. The Protestant mission played an important role in popularizing the Indies in Holland by children's fiction about Indonesian children (Buur, *Indische jeugdliteratuur*, 17–20).

46. *Een weg tot volksontwikkeling (Openbare bibliotheken en leeszalen)*, Uitgave van de Commissie voor de Volkslectuur (Batavia, [c. 1920]).

47. Dasberg, *Kinderboek*, 182; Van der Horst–Van Doorn, *Kitty's leed en vreugde: Van Indisch meisjesleven* (Gouda, n.d.).

48. For example, M. C. van Zeggelen, *Dona Alve* (Amsterdam, 1928).

49. M. C. E. Ovink-Soer, *De Canneheuveltjes: Een verhaal uit het Indische kinderleven* (Gouda, 1912).

50. Ibid., 76.

51. Van Zeggelen, *Dona Alve*.

52. C. H. Sevenhuysen-Verhoeff, *Tussen sawah's en bergen* (Amersfoort, 1936), 38.

53. Tine Ophof-Sterk, *Een moeilijk jaar voor de Van Heerdentjes* (Weltevreden/Amersfoort, 1921), 198.

54. Ibid., 134.

55. M. J. van Marle-Hubregtse, *Ams houdt van Indië* (Deventer, 1941).

56. Ibid., 34.

57. Toni Morrison, *Playing in the Dark: Whiteness and the Literary Imagination* (Cambridge, Mass., 1992).

58. Van Marle-Hubregtse, *Ams*, 45, 58.

59. Ibid., 196.

60. See the advertisements for personnel, *De Huisvrouw in Indië* 5 (1936): 131.

61. Karel van Wolferen, *The Enigma of Japanese Power: People and Politics in a Stateless Nation* (New York, 1989); Laura Cooley, "Maintaining *Rukun* for Javanese Households and for the State," in *Women and Mediation in Indonesia*, ed. Sita van Bemmelen et al. (Leiden, 1992), 229–48.

8. ISLAM, GENDER, AND IDENTITIES IN THE MAKING OF FRENCH ALGERIA, 1830–1962

A different version of this essay appeared in L. Carl Brown and Matthew Gordon, eds., *Franco-Arab Encounters* (Beirut, 1997), 201–28. I express gratitude to the Virginia Foundation for the Humanities for a 1993 fellowship making the research for this article possible.

1. On Bugeaud, see Anthony T. Sullivan, *Thomas-Robert Bugeaud: France and Algeria, 1784–1849: Politics, Power, and the Good Society* (Hamden, Conn., 1983).

2. Hubertine Auclert, *Les femmes arabes en Algérie* (Paris, 1900), 146.

3. Women, whether European or indigenous, are notably absent in the substantial historical literature on French Algeria; the two standard histories, Charles-André Julien, *Histoire de l'Algérie contemporaine (1827–1871)* 1 (Paris, 1964), and Charles-Robert Ageron, *Histoire de l'Algérie contemporaine (1871–1954)* 2 (Paris, 1979), make virtually no reference to women. Jean Déjeux's *Femmes d'Algérie: Légendes, traditions, histoire, littérature* (Paris, 1987) and Marnia Lazreq's *The Eloquence of Silence: Algerian Women in Question* (New York, 1994) study Algerian women in the long *durée*.

4. Julia Clancy-Smith, *Rebel and Saint: Muslim Notables, Populist Protest, Colonial Encounters (Algeria and Tunisia, 1800–1904)* (Berkeley, Calif., 1994).

5. Surprisingly little recent historical research has been devoted to how French Algerian society came to be—within the larger, more complex matrix of its relations with the metropole and indigenous Muslim society. Algerian historians writing after independence have deliberately ignored settler society in their own research, while decrying its evils. David Prochaska's *Making Algeria French: Colonialism in Bône, 1870–1920* (Cambridge, Eng., 1990), and his "Reconstructing 'L'Algérie Française'" in *Connaissances du Maghreb: Sciences sociales et colonisation* (Paris, 1984), 65–78, are first-rate studies; the absence however, of any discussion of women and gender is regrettable.

6. Mahfoud Kaddache, *Histoire du nationalisme algérien, 1919–1951* (Alger, 1981).

7. In *Orientalism* (New York, 1979), Edward Said developed the notion of representation (1–28). Two founding texts for male gaze theory are John Berger's *Ways of Seeing* (New York, 1977) and Laura Mulvey's numerous works, particularly her collected essays, *Visual and Other Pleasures* (Bloomington, Ind., 1989). A reconsideration of Mulvey's thesis is Lorraine Gamman and Margaret Marshment, eds., *The Female Gaze: Women as Viewers of Popular Culture* (London, 1988). On colonial representations of Algeria,

see Jean-Robert Henry, ed., *Le Maghreb dans l'imaginaire français: La colonie, le désert, l'exil* (Aix-en-Provence, 1985), although women and gender are largely absent from this work.

8. The records of the Bureaux Arabes found in the Archives du Gouvernement Général de l'Algérie, Archives nationales, section d'outre-mer, Aix-en-Provence, H series, contain sporadic mention of Algerian Muslim women, usually about their role in resisting the French army.

9. Julia Clancy-Smith and Cynthia Gray-Ware Metcalf, "A Visit to a Tunisian Harem," *Journal of Maghrebi Studies* 1–2, 1 (Spring 1993): 43–49; Julia Clancy-Smith, "The Passionate Nomad Reconsidered: A European Woman in L'Algérie Française (Isabelle Eberhardt, 1877–1904)," in *Western Women and Imperialism: Complicity and Resistance*, ed. Nupur Chaudhuri and Margaret Strobel (Bloomington, Ind., 1992), 61–78.

10. Aside from Steven C. Hause's excellent biography, *Hubertine Auclert: The French Suffragette* (New Haven, 1987), there is little on Auclert; Edith Taieb, *La Citoyenne: Articles de 1881 à 1891* (Paris, 1982) is a collection of her articles.

11. This vast literature has hardly been studied for specific issues of women and gender in French North Africa; one recent analysis is Emily Apter's "Ethnographic Travesties: Colonial Realism, French Feminism, and the Case of Elissa Rhais," in *After Colonialism: Imperial Histories and Postcolonial Displacements*, ed. Gyan Prakash (Princeton, N.J., 1995), 299–325.

12. Laurence O. Michalak, "Popular French Perspectives on the Maghreb: Orientalist Painting of the Late 19th and Early 20th Centuries," in *Connaissances du Maghreb*, 47–63.

13. Malek Alloula, *The Colonial Harem*, trans. Myrna Godzich and Wlad Godzich (Manchester, Eng., 1986).

14. Ibid.; Berger, *Ways of Seeing*, 64.

15. Raoul Girardet, *Le temps des colonies* (Paris, 1979), 20–21; Sarah Graham-Brown, *Images of Women: The Portrayal of Women in Photography of the Middle East, 1860–1950* (New York, 1988).

16. Hector France, *Musk, Hashish, and Blood* (New York, n.d.).

17. For example, Alfred Baraudon, *Algérie et Tunisie: Récits de voyage et études* (Paris, 1893), 180–86. Lazreq, *Algerian Women*, 29–33, notes that the women of the Ouled Nail had been turned into sexual tourist attractions by the end of the century.

18. Webster's *Third International Dictionary of the English Language* contains the following definition of *Ouled Nail*: "An Arab prostitute and dancing girl of the North African cities usually dressed in brightly colored, bespangled costumes and ornamental often feathered headdress."

19. Philippe Jullian, *The Triumph of Art Nouveau: Paris Exposition, 1900* (New York, 1974); see also Zeyneb Çelik, *Displaying the Orient: The Architecture of Islam at Nineteenth-Century World's Fairs* (Berkeley, Calif., 1992).

20. Gaston Loth, *Le peuplement italien en Tunisie et en Algérie* (Paris, 1905); Jules Saurin, *Le peuplement français en Tunisie* (Paris, 1910).

21. On familial language and images in revolutionary politics, see Lynn Hunt, *The Family Romance of the French Revolution* (Berkeley, Calif., 1992).

22. Auclert, *Femmes*, 216–17.

23. The one notable exception to this was traveler and writer Isabelle Eberhardt (1877–1904). Cast as a licentious and thus dangerously rebellious European female, Eberhardt had numerous colonial Algerian male and female detractors, concerned with proper gender roles and behavior in front of the natives.

24. Julien, *Histoire* 1:297.

25. Edouard Adolphe Duchesne, *De la prostitution dans la ville d'Alger depuis la conquête* (Paris, 1853).

26. Ibid., 10.

27. In *Dutch Culture Overseas: Colonial Practice in the Netherlands Indies, 1900–1942* (Amsterdam, 1995), Frances Gouda notes that Dutch officials invoked the French Foreign Legion in Algeria, believed a den of iniquity due to rampant homosexuality, to argue for the Dutch army's use of native housekeepers and concubines in colonial barracks.

28. Duchesne, *Prostitution*, 44.

29. Ibid., 76.

30. Ibid., 70–75.

31. Ibid., 85.

32. Ibid., 70–75.

33. Ibid., 78.

34. Ibid., 82–83.

35. Ann Laura Stoler, "Rethinking Colonial Categories: European Communities and the Boundaries of Rule," *Comparative Studies in Society and History* 31, 1 (1989): 134–61; Stoler, "Carnal Knowledge and Imperial Power: Gender, Race, and Morality in Colonial Asia," in *Gender at the Crossroads of Knowledge: Feminist Anthropology in the Postmodern Era*, ed. Micaela di Leonardo (Berkeley, Calif., 1991), 51–101.

36. Vincent de Largeau, *Le Sahara algérien* (Paris, 1881), 222–26.

37. Allan Christelow, *Muslim Law Courts and the French Colonial State in Algeria* (Princeton, N.J., 1985), 86 n. 11.

38. Hause, *Auclert*, 140.

39. Among them, *Le Sahara algérien* (Paris, 1845) and *La vie arabe et la*

société musulmane (Paris, 1869). Daumas considered his investigation of women as "the natural complement to his earlier studies." See Augustin Bernard's biographical notice, *Revue Africaine* 56, 284 (1912): v-viii.

40. Eugène Daumas, "La femme arabe," *Revue Africaine* 56, 284 (1912): 1.

41. Rana Kabbani, *Europe's Myths of the Orient* (Bloomington, Ind., 1986); Dorothea M. Gallup, "The French Image of Algeria: Its Origin, Its Place in Colonial Ideology, Its Effect on Algerian Acculturation" (Ph.D. diss., Univ. of California, Los Angeles, 1973), 81–151.

42. For example, Louis Milliot, *Etude sur la condition de la femme musulmane au Maghreb (Maroc, Algérie, Tunisie)* (Paris, 1910).

43. Daumas, "La femme arabe," 2.

44. Ibid., 3.

45. Ibid., 1.

46. In mapping the cultural cartography of North African society, Daumas drew upon several cultural reference points. These were either New World Indians, less civilized than the Arabs, or European civilization, although he scarcely mentioned Western women. One of the few explicit allusions to European women is found in chap. 12, entitled "Woman and Love." Here Daumas discusses the impact of the segregation of the sexes upon Arab women, who are denied access to male company solely because of male jealousy. "Thus, entirely confined to feminine company, [Arab] women are ignorant of these refinements of deportment and language which distinguish European woman" (128).

47. Ibid., 34.

48. Ibid., 74.

49. Ibid., viii.

50. Milliot, *Etude*; Adrien Leclerc, "De la condition juridique de la femme musulmane en Algérie," *Congrès international de sociologie coloniale*, vol. 2, *Mémoires soumis au congrès* (Paris, 1901), 109–14.

51. François Leimdorfer's *Discours académique et colonisation: Thèmes de recherche sur l'Algérie pendant la période coloniale* (Paris, 1992) shows that after 1880 one of the most frequently studied questions was the condition of Arab women.

52. Julia Clancy-Smith, "In the Eye of the Beholder: The North African Sufi Orders and the Colonial Production of Knowledge, 1830–1900," *Africana Journal* 15 (1990): 220–57.

53. From the 1890s on, a huge number of works were published in France and Algeria on the question of assimilation; for example, Pierre Coeur, *L'Assimilation des indigènes musulmans* (Paris, 1890).

54. Octave Depont, "Aperçu sur l'administration des indigènes musul-

mans en Algérie," *Congrès international de sociologie coloniale*, vol. 2, *Mémoires soumis au congrès*, 89.

55. Hause, *Auclert*, 87–111; Steven C. Hause and Anne R. Kenney, *Women's Suffrage and Social Politics in the French Third Republic* (Princeton, N.J., 1984); Claire Goldberg Moses, *French Feminism in the 19th Century* (New York, 1984), 212–20; see also Jennifer Waelti-Walters and Steven C. Hause, *Feminisms of the Belle Epoque: A Historical and Literary Anthology* (Lincoln, Nebr., 1994).

56. Felicia Gordon, *The Integral Feminist: Madeleine Pelletier, 1874–1939: Feminism, Socialism, and Medicine* (Cambridge, Eng., 1990), 85.

57. Hause, *Auclert*, 132–48.

58. Auclert, *Femmes*, 3.

59. Patricia M. E. Lorcin, *Imperial Identities: Stereotyping, Prejudice, and Race in Colonial Algeria* (London, 1995), is the only recent study of race for French North Africa. The notion of a French Algerian race was preceded by several decades of colonial inquiry into the two indigenous "races" of Algeria—the Berbers and the Arabs; for example, Nicolas Auguste Pomel, *Des races indigènes de l'Algérie et du rôle que leur réservent leurs aptitudes* (Oran, 1871).

60. Julia Clancy-Smith, "Women of Modest Means: Migration, Identity, and Contraband in the 19th-Century Mediterranean World," paper delivered at the 18th International Congress of Historical Sciences, Montréal, Canada, 1995, 10.

61. Prochaska, *Making Algeria French*, 206–7.

62. Quoted in Ageron, *Histoire* 2:129.

63. Auclert, *Femmes*, 3.

64. Joan Wallach Scott, *Only Paradoxes to Offer: French Feminists and the Rights of Man* (Cambridge, Mass., 1996), 115–16.

65. Auclert, *Femmes*, 50.

66. Ibid., 138–44; Hause, *Auclert*, 142–43. Religion and gender were often invoked as reasons not to attempt to educate indigenous Algerian girls: for example, the comte de Caix de Saint-Aymour, *Questions algériennes: Arabes et Kabyles* (Paris, 1891), 255–56, invoked early age at marriage as an obstacle to educating Muslim girls.

67. Auclert, *Femmes*, 37–38.

68. Recent work emphasizes the dynamic whereby social causes and crusades in the European mother country were transposed to the colonies; for example, Antoinette M. Burton's "The White Woman's Burden: British Feminists and the 'Indian Woman,' 1865–1915," in Chaudhuri and Strobel, *Western Women*, 137–57.

69. This was by no means a novel strategy for Europeans writing on the Orient or Islam; Richard F. Burton (1821–1890) employed Arabian society as a device to criticize Victorian morality (Carroll McC. Pastner, "Englishmen in Arabia: Encounters with Middle Eastern Women," *Signs* 4, 21 [1978]: 309–23).

70. Auclert, *Femmes*, 49.

71. Ibid., 42–52.

72. Christelow, *Muslim Law Courts*, 124–28.

73. Ibid.; Jean-Paul Charnay, *La vie musulmane en Algérie d'après la jurisprudence de la première moitié du XXe siècle* (Paris, 1965).

74. Auclert, *Femmes*, 47.

75. Hause, *Auclert*, 143.

76. Marie Bugéja, *Nos soeurs musulmanes*, 2d ed. (Alger, 1931).

77. Hause, *Auclert*, 143.

78. Ageron, *Histoire* 2:118–33; Charles-Robert Ageron, *Les Algériens musulmans et la France (1871–1919)*, 2 vols. (Paris, 1968), particularly 2:1115–38. For example, the Algerian deputy, Sabatier, proposed in 1889 that those Muslims who had served under the French flag and wanted to be considered for individual naturalization had to renounce "buying their wives and selling their daughters" (cited in Ageron, *Les Algériens* 2:1116 n. 1).

79. M. Morand, *La famille musulmane* (Paris, 1903); Ageron, *Algériens* 2:981–1002.

80. Dalenda and Abdelhamid Largueche, *Marginales en terre d'Islam* (Tunis, 1992), 157; Tahar al-Haddad, *Notre femme, la législation islamique, et la société* (Tunis, 1931).

81. Charles D. Smith, *Islam and the Search for Social Order in Modern Egypt: A Biography of Muhammad Husayn Haykal* (Albany, 1983); Beth Baron, *The Women's Awakening in Egypt: Culture, Society, and the Press* (New Haven, 1994); John Ruedy, *Modern Algeria: The Origins and Development of a Nation* (Bloomington, Ind., 1992), 102.

82. E. G. Gautier, *Moeurs et coutumes des musulmans*, 2d ed. (Paris, 1949), 38. Among Gautier's numerous other works was *Un siècle de colonisation: Etudes au microscope* (Paris, 1930).

83. Louis Bertrand, *Devant L'Islam* (Paris, 1926), particularly "Notre Afrique," 127–75. See Lorcin, *Imperial Identities*, 196–213, for Bertrand's influence; David Prochaska, "History as Literature, Literature as History: Cagayous of Algiers," *American Historical Review* 101, 3 (June 1996): 671–711.

84. Gautier, *Moeurs*, 36–47.

85. Ruedy, *Algeria*, 139–44; Ageron, *Histoire* 2:449–66.

86. Cited in Philippe Lucas and Jean-Claude Vatin, *L'Algérie des anthro-*

pologues (Paris, 1982), 204. Viollette also wrote about "la femme indigène" in *L'Algérie vivra-t-elle?* (Paris, 1931).

9. CIVILIZING GENDER RELATIONS IN ALGERIA:
The Paradoxical Case of Marie Bugéja, 1919–39

1. Marie Bugéja to Governor-General Eugène Abel, Feb. 2, 1921, pp. 3–4, Administration locale des indigènes et personnel des communes mixtes (19H), Personnel file of Manuel Bugéja (Box 95), Archives du Gouvernement Général de l'Algérie, Archives nationales, section d'outre-mer, Aix-en-Provence (AGGA). Unless otherwise noted, all translations are my own.

Information in Bugéja's father's annual personnel reviews and her husband's memoirs indicates that Marie Bugéja (née Moisan) was born in either 1875 or 1877 (see ibid., 19H, box 146, for Pierre Marie Moisan's personnel file; see also Manuel Bugéja, *Souvenirs d'un fonctionnaire colonial* [Tangier, 1939], 92, 95). The date of her death, May 23, 1957, was noted in a review of her work by Dr. H. Marchand, "Deux défenseurs de la musulmane: Ferdinand Duchêne, Marie Bugéja," *Afrique* 267 (1957): 29. Marie Bugéja's mother was born in Algeria, and her father in Brittany. Marie married Manuel Bugéja on Aug. 31, 1895, and gave birth to their only child, a son, on June 24, 1896 (Manuel Bugéja, *Souvenirs*, 93–96). Bugéja is a Maltese name (see Marc Donato, *L'émigration des Maltais en Algérie au XIXème siècle* [Montpellier, 1985], 115).

2. Mirante to Abel, note 2269, Feb. 18, 1921, pp. 1–2, AGGA, 19H, box 95.

3. Charles-Robert Ageron, *Histoire de l'Algérie contemporaine*, vol. 2, *De l'insurrection de 1871 au déclenchement de la guerre de libération (1954)* (Paris, 1979), 274.

4. The Khaled faction's weekly newspaper *Ikdam* appeared from 1919 to 1923, when the colonial administration forced Emir Khaled into exile. On the Young Algerians movement, see Ruedy, *Modern Algeria*, 105–13, 129–33. See also Mahfoud Kaddache, *La vie politique à Alger de 1919 à 1939* (Alger, 1970), esp. 53–81; Charles-Robert Ageron, "Le mouvement jeune algérien," in *Etudes maghrébines: Mélanges*, ed. Charles-André Julien (Paris, 1964).

5. Mirante to Abel, note 2269, Feb. 18, 1921, p. 2, AGGA, 19H, box 95.

6. For earlier work focusing on the status of Algerian Muslim women, see, for example, Louis Milliot, *Etude sur la condition de la femme musulmane au Maghreb (Maroc, Algérie, Tunisie)* (Paris, 1910); Hubertine Auclert, *Les femmes arabes en Algérie* (Paris, 1900). I am grateful to Julia Clancy-Smith for suggesting these references. Of the sixty books written by

women living in Algeria during the interwar years, about one-third depicted the lives of indigenous Algerian women. See Jean Déjeux, "Elissa Rhaïs, conteuse algérienne (1876 – 1940)," in *Le Maghreb dans l'imaginaire français: La colonie, le désert, l'exil*, ed. Jean-Robert Henry et al. (Aix-en-Provence, 1985), 73. For literary analyses of colonial literature written by women about Algerian women, see Sakina Messaadi, *Les romancières coloniales et la femme colonisée: Contributions à une étude de la littérature coloniale en Algérie* (Alger, 1990); Denise Brahimi, *Femmes arabes et soeurs musulmanes* (Paris, 1984).

7. See Raymond F. Betts, *Assimilation and Association in French Colonial Theory, 1890 – 1914* (New York, 1961).

8. Bugéja published the following books between 1921 and 1939: *Nos soeurs musulmanes* (Paris, 1921); *Visions d'Algérie* (Alger, 1929); *Séduction orientale* (Alger, 1931); *Nos soeurs musulmanes*, 2d ed. (Alger, 1931); *Du vice à la vertu: Roman d'une Naïlia* (Paris, 1932); *Dans la tièdeur de la tente* (Alger, 1933); *Sous les rayons d'or* (Alger, 1934); *Femmes voilées, hommes . . . de même (récits et impressions de l'extrème Sud-Algérien)* (Alger, 1935); *Afrique, terre de légendes* (Alger, 1936); *Le feu du Maroc* (Tangier, 1937); *Enigme musulmane: Lettres à une Bretonne* (Tangier and Fez, 1938); *Coeur de Kabyle* (Tangier, 1939). By 1939 several journals and newspapers had published more than sixty of her articles and short fiction. The illustrated magazine *Terre d'Algérie*, which became *Terre d'Afrique* in 1921, published the lion's share of her descriptive travel pieces and short fiction. Thirteen of her public lectures appeared in the *Bulletin de la Société de Géographie d'Alger et de l'Afrique du Nord*. Various organizations in Algiers sponsored another five public talks which were not published. See Manuel Bugéja, *Souvenirs*, 187–90, for a list of Marie's publications. After 1939, Bugéja stopped publishing. In his 1957 review of her work, Dr. Henri-François Marchand speculated that Bugéja's precarious health forced her to "retire from literary life" ("Deux défenseurs de la musulmane," 29).

9. For a list of Bugéja's awards as of 1939, see Manuel Bugéja, *Souvenirs*, 187. Her name never appeared in *Afrique*, the organ of the Association des Ecrivains Algériens.

10. On erotic postcards as well as more general photography of indigenous peoples in North Africa and the Middle East, see Sarah Graham-Brown, *Images of Women: The Portrayal of Women in Photography of the Middle East, 1860 – 1950* (London, 1988); Malek Alloula, *The Colonial Harem* (Minneapolis, 1986).

11. Edward W. Said, *Orientalism* (New York, 1979). For an example of the broader view of Algerians in anthropology, see Mathéa Gaudry, *La*

femme chaouia de l'Aurès: Etude de sociologie berbère (Paris, 1929). For fiction, see, for example, Lucienne Favre, *Orientale 1930* (Paris, 1930). For reviews of colonial literature, see Roland Lebel, *Histoire de la littérature coloniale en France* (Paris, 1931); Jean Déjeux, *Bibliographie de la littérature "algerienne" des français* (Paris, 1978).

12. Cf. Judy Mabro, ed., *Veiled Half-Truths: Western Travellers' Perceptions of Middle Eastern Women* (London, 1991).

13. Bugéja, *Nos soeurs musulmanes*, 1st ed., 98. She gave no reference for the quoted phrase. All subsequent references are to this edition.

14. Bugéja, *Enigme musulmane*, 14.

15. Ageron, *Histoire de l'Algérie contemporaine*, 534; Fanny Colonna, "Un impact dérisoire," in *Instituteurs algériens, 1883–1939* (Paris, 1975), 49–63.

16. Alf Andrew Heggoy, "Algerian Women and the Right to Vote: Some Colonial Anomalies," *Muslim World* 64, 3 (July 1974): 233–34.

17. For the development of this idea as a useful tool in analyzing colonial societies, see Ann Laura Stoler, "Rethinking Colonial Categories: European Communities and the Boundaries of Rule," *Comparative Studies in Society and History* 31, 1 (Jan. 1989): 134–61.

18. Pierre Bourdieu, *The Algerians*, trans. Alan C. M. Ross (Boston, 1962). On the problems inherent in referring to Algerians as Muslims but not mentioning the Christianity of Europeans in Algeria, see Marnia Lazreg, "Feminism and Difference: The Perils of Writing as a Woman on Women in Algeria," in *Conflicts in Feminism*, ed. Marianne Hirsch and Evelyn Fox Keller (New York, 1990), esp. 329–31. On the construction of a distinct settler society, see David Prochaska, *Making Algeria French: Colonialism in Bône, 1870–1920* (Cambridge, 1990); Marc Baroli, *La vie quotidienne des français en Algérie, 1830–1914* (Paris, 1967).

19. On civil and political reform, see Ruedy, *Modern Algeria*, 110–13; Vincent Confer, *France and Algeria: The Problem of Civil and Political Reform, 1870–1920* (Syracuse, N.Y., 1966). The most comprehensive study of Algerian participation in the war effort is Gilbert Meynier, *L'Algérie révélée: La guerre de 1914–1918 et le premier quart du XXe siècle* (Geneva, 1981).

20. Alf Andrew Heggoy, "Cultural Disrespect: European and Algerian Views on Women in Colonial and Independent Algeria," *Muslim World* 62, 4 (1972): 325.

21. Bugéja reminisced about the trips with her father in *Enigme musulmane*, 51–52. When Bugéja was born, her father was a secretary at the sub–police station at Orléansville. He spent his career in more rural areas, primarily in Kabylia, and retired from the service on Dec. 31, 1899, as the administrator second class of the *commune mixte* of Guergour (AGGA,

19H, box 146). On the Bugéjas' courtship and wedding, see Manuel Bugéja, *Souvenirs*, 91–96. For an example of Bugéja's dinners with Algerians, see *Nos soeurs musulmanes*, 63–70.

22. Bugéja, "Excursion dans le Djurdjura des Beni-Kouffi," *Bulletin de la Société de Géographie d'Alger et de l'Afrique du Nord*, 1918, 97–116, quote on p. 104. The lecture took place on May 22, 1918, in the city hall of Algiers.

23. Bugéja, *Nos soeurs musulmanes*, 280. Frances Gouda explores the similar view of women held by the Dutch in Java and Bali in her "Teaching Indonesian Girls in Java and Bali, 1900–1942: Dutch Progressives, the Infatuation with 'Oriental' Refinement, and 'Western' Ideas about Proper Womanhood," *Women's History Review* 4, 1 (1995): 25–62.

24. Bugéja, "A travers l'Algérie: Impressions sur la femme musulmane," *Bulletin de la Société de Géographie d'Alger et de l'Afrique du Nord* (1919): 73.

25. Maria Vérone's review in a metropolitan journal, *Oeuvre*, May 11, 1922, quoted in Edmond Esquirol, preface to *Nos soeurs musulmanes*, 2d ed., 8–9.

26. Review of *Nos soeurs musulmanes* by Captain Peyronnet, *Bulletin de la Société de Géographie d'Alger et de l'Afrique du Nord*, 1921, 274–75.

27. Direction des Affaires Indigènes to secrétaire-général de Gouvernement, note 8558, July 13, 1921, pp. 4–5, AGGA, 19H, box 95.

28. Bugéja to Steeg, May 11, 1922, Mirante to Steeg, note 8047, May 27, 1922, ibid.

29. *Journal Officiel, Débats Parlementaires, Sénat*, March 21, 1935, 354.

30. Ibid., 356.

31. Ibid., March 22, 1935, 369.

32. My thanks to Bonnie G. Smith for suggesting the comparison with the criminal status of abortion in France in the 1920s and 1930s.

33. Bugéja, *Nos soeurs musulmanes*, 89–98. There is a growing body of literature on the problems of education and assimilation in Algeria. See, for example, Alf Andrew Heggoy, "Colonial Education in Algeria: Assimilation and Reaction," in *Education and the Colonial Experience*, ed. Philip G. Altbach and Gail P. Kelly, 2d ed., rev. (New York, 1991); Elsa M. Harik, "The Civilizing Mission of France in Algeria: The Schooling of a Native Population," in *The Politics of Education in Colonial Algeria and Kenya*, ed. Elsa M. Harik and Donald G. Schilling (Athens, Ohio, 1984).

34. Bourdieu, *The Algerians*, 97 n. 4.

35. Bugéja, *Nos soeurs musulmanes*, 272.

36. Stoler, "Rethinking Colonial Categories," esp. 154; Stoler, "Sexual Affronts and Racial Frontiers: European Identities and the Cultural Politics

of Exclusion in Colonial Southeast Asia," *Comparative Studies in Society and History* 34 (July 1992): 514–51.

37. Bugéja, *Enigme musulmane*, 150.

38. Ibid., 62.

39. Ibid., 150–51. On the significance of the veil in the Middle East and North Africa, see Leila Ahmed, "The Discourse of the Veil," in Ahmed, *Women and Gender in Islam* (New Haven, 1992), 144–68; Winifred Woodhull, "Unveiling Algeria," *Genders* 10 (Spring 1991): 112–31; Frantz Fanon, "Algeria Unveiled," in *A Dying Colonialism*, trans. Haakon Chevalier (New York, 1967).

40. Bugéja, *Enigme musulmane*, 190.

41. Heggoy, "Cultural Disrespect," 327–31; Jacques Berque, *French North Africa: The Maghrib between Two World Wars*, trans. Jean Stewart (London, 1967), 306–7.

42. Bugéja, *Nos soeurs musulmanes*, 99.

43. Fanon, "Algeria Unveiled"; Gouda, "Teaching Indonesian Girls," 28.

44. Bugéja, *Enigme musulmane*, 140.

45. Bugéja's perspective on the Congress and the reception of her report are recorded in her article, "Ce que fut le Congrès des Femmes Méditerranéennes," *Bulletin de la Société de Géographie d'Alger et de l'Afrique du Nord*, no. 131 (1932): 544–68.

46. On the uses of the modern woman in French discourse on women in the 1920s, see Mary Louise Roberts, *Civilization without Sexes: Reconstructing Gender in Postwar France, 1917–1927* (Chicago, 1994).

47. Bugéja, *Enigme musulman*, 154, 77.

48. Bugéja, *Nos soeurs musulmanes*, v.

49. I am indebted to Jan Lewis for helping me develop the descriptive term *civic wifehood and motherhood*.

50. Barbara Ramusack coined the term *maternal imperialist* in "Cultural Missionaries, Maternal Imperialists, Feminist Allies: British Women Activists in India, 1865–1945," in *Western Women and Imperialism: Complicity and Resistance*, ed. Nupur Chaudhuri and Margaret Strobel (Bloomington, Ind., 1992), 133. My discussion of Bugéja's maternalism is also influenced by Seth Koven and Sonya Michel's analysis of maternalism in the introduction to their edited volume, *Mothers of a New World: Maternalist Politics and the Origins of Welfare States* (New York, 1993).

51. Patricia Grimshaw, review of *Gender, Culture, and Empire: European Women in Colonial Nigeria*, by Helen Callaway, and *White Women in Fiji, 1835–1930: The Ruin of Empire?* by Claudia Knapman, *Gender and History* 1 (Spring 1989): 105.

52. Brahimi, *Femmes arabes*, 315.

53. Antoinette Burton, *Burdens of History: British Feminists, Indian Women, and Imperial Culture, 1865–1915* (Chapel Hill, N.C., 1994), 8–10.

54. See Herman Lebovics, *True France: The Wars over Cultural Identity, 1900–1945* (Ithaca, N.Y., 1992).

10. "IRRESISTIBLE SEDUCTIONS": Gendered Representations of Colonial Algeria around 1930

1. *L'Algérie: Album de planches* (Paris, 1931), 77. Unless otherwise noted, all translations from the French are mine.

2. Octave Depont, *L'Algérie du centenaire: L'oeuvre française de libération, de conquête morale, et d'évolution sociales des indigènes* (Paris, 1930).

3. Général Bonneval, "L'Algérie touristique," *Cahiers du Centenaire de l'Algérie* 7 (1930): 1. See also Ferdinand Duchêne, *Ceux d'Algérie: Types et coutumes* (Paris, 1929), 29.

4. Emily Apter, "Female Trouble in the Colonial Harem," *Differences* 4 (1992): 205–24.

5. Antoine Chollier, *Alger et sa région* (Grenoble, 1928), 14–17; Marcelle Vioux, "Visages d'Orient," *L'Illustration*, May 24, 1930.

6. Cf. Maurice Agulhon, *Marianne into Battle: Republican Imagery and Symbolism in France, 1789–1880* (Cambridge, Eng., 1981).

7. David Spurr, *The Rhetoric of Empire: Colonial Discourse in Journalism, Travel Writing, and Imperial Administration* (Durham, N.C., 1993), 7.

8. See further John Ruedy, *Modern Algeria: The Origins and Development of a Nation* (Bloomington, Ind., 1992).

9. Recent scholarship has analyzed many of the centenary events and initiatives of the organizers. See Nicolas Moll, "Le pouvoir coloniale et sa symbolique: Le centenaire de l'Algérie" (Mémoire de maîtrise, Université d'Aix-en-Provence, Institut d'Histoire des Pays d'Outre-Mer, 1989); Emanuelle Sibaud, "Les manifestations du centenaire de l'Algérie française en 1930" (Mémoire de maîtrise, Université de Paris I, 1989–90); Jacques Cantier, "Le gouverneur Bordes et l'Algérie du centenaire" (Mémoire de maîtrise d'histoire, Université de Toulouse-Mirail, 1989).

10. Thomas G. August, *The Selling of the Empire: British and French Imperialist Propaganda, 1890–1940* (Westport, Conn., 1985), 207.

11. "Documents annexes: Le discours de M. André Tardieu, 5 June 1929," *Cahiers du Centenaire de l'Algérie* 12 (1930): 53–54.

12. Bonneval, "L'Algérie touristique," 60. See further Jean-François Guilhaume, *Les mythes fondateurs de l'Algérie française* (Paris, 1992), 232.

13. *La Quinzaire Coloniale*, May 10, 1930.

14. Guilhaume, *Les mythes fondateurs*, 94.

15. F. Redon, *L'Algérie en 1930* (Alger, 1930), 73; *La Croix*, May 20, 1930.

16. E. F. Gautier, "L'évolution de l'Algérie," *Cahiers du Centenaire de l'Algérie* 3 (1930): 60.

17. Rebecca Stott, "The Dark Continent: Africa as Female Body in Haggard's Adventure Fiction," *Feminist Review* 32 (Summer 1989): 79. Cf. Mary Louise Pratt, *Imperial Eyes: Travel Writing and Transculturation* (London, 1992).

18. E. F. Gautier, *Un siècle de colonisation: Etudes au microscope* (Paris, 1930), 344; Pierre Deloncle, *La caravan aux éperons verts (mission Alger-Niger)* (Paris, 1927), 16.

19. Julien Franc, *La colonisation de la Mitidja* (Paris, 1928), vii.

20. Bonneval, "L'Algérie touristique," 11.

21. Jean Blottière, "Les productions algériennes," *Cahiers du Centenaire de l'Algérie* 9 (1930): 35.

22. Georges Rozet, *Algeria* (Paris, 1929), 142, 157; *La Quinzaine Coloniale*, Jan. 10, 1930.

23. Franc, *La colonisation*, vii-viii.

24. Ibid., 522.

25. Bonneval, "L'Algérie touristique," 5; Duchêne, *Ceux d'Algérie*, 12.

26. *La Dépêche Coloniale et Maritime*, March 30–31, 1930; Redon, *L'Algérie*, 133; *Le Monde Coloniale Illustré* 76 (Dec. 1929): 293.

27. Gautier, *Un siècle*, 302; Redon, *L'Algérie*, 67.

28. *Le Petit Parisien*, May 3, 1930.

29. Rozet, *Algeric*, 10–11.

30. *La Quinzaine Coloniale*, May 10, 1930.

31. Jean Mirante, "La France et les oeuvres indigènes en Algérie," *Cahiers du Centenaire de l'Algérie* 11 (1930), 22; Franc, *La colonisation*, 521–22, 701; Gautier, *Un siècle*, 238.

32. Christopher L. Miller, *Theories of Africans: Francophone Literature and Anthropology in Africa* (Chicago, 1990), 14.

33. Cf. Ruedy, *Modern Algeria*.

34. *Le Monde Colonial Illustré* 76 (Dec. 1929): 293; Felix Falck, *Guide de touriste en Algérie* (Paris, 1925), 19; Gautier, *Un siècle*, 235; Chollier, *Alger*, 11; Redon, *L'Algérie*, 11.

35. Redon, *L'Algérie*, 136.

36. Gautier, "L'évolution de l'Algérie," 12.

37. Rozet, *Algeria*, 29; Rozet, *L'Aurès, escalier du désert* (Alger, 1935).

38. Deloncle, *La caravan*, 71–72.

39. Homi Bhabha, "Of Mimicry and Man: The Ambivalence of Colonial Discourse," in Bhabha, *The Location of Culture* (London, 1994), 85–92.

40. Chollier, *Alger*, 9; *L'Illustration*, May 24, 1930.

41. *Panorama*, Oct. 1, 1930, 23; Deloncle, *La caravan*, 31.

42. *Le Matin*, Feb. 6, 1930.

43. *L'Illustration*, April 6, 1930.

44. Depont, *L'Algérie*, 218.

45. Duchêne, *Ceux d'Algérie*, 132. See also Chollier, *Alger*, 29, 42.

46. Edward Said, *Orientalism* (New York, 1978).

47. Rana Kabbani, *Imperial Fictions: Europe's Myths of the Orient* (London, 1994), 67.

48. Louis Lecoq, "Rues et foules d'Alger," *L'Illustration*, May 24, 1930.

49. Depont, *L'Algérie*, 210; Rozet, *Algeria*, 4, 6.

50. Gautier, *Un siècle*, 243.

51. For example, see *L'Algérie: Album*, 85.

52. Chollier, *Alger*, 76–77.

53. Mary Douglas, *Purity and Danger: An Analysis of Concepts of Pollution and Taboo* (London, 1966); Spurr, *The Rhetoric of Empire*, chap. 5.

54. Chollier, *Alger*, 77–89.

55. James Buzard, *The Beaten Track: European Tourism, Literature, and the Ways to Culture, 1800–1918* (Oxford, 1993), 208. Cf. Paul Greenhalgh, *Ephemeral Vistas: The Expositions Universelles, Great Exhibitions, and World's Fairs, 1851–1939* (Manchester, Eng., 1988); Timothy Mitchell, "Orientalism and the Exhibitionary Order," in *Colonialism and Culture*, ed. Nicholas B. Dirks (Ann Arbor, Mich., 1992), 289–318.

56. Frantz Fanon, "Algeria Unveiled," in *A Dying Colonialism*, trans. Haakon Chevalier (New York, 1965), 34–67. This essay has been extensively discussed by feminist and postcolonial scholars. For a recent critique, see Diana Fuss, "Interior Colonies: Frantz Fanon and the Politics of Identification," in *Identification Papers* (New York, 1995), 141–72.

57. Marnia Lazreg, *The Eloquence of Silence: Algerian Women in Question* (New York, 1994), 36–38; Lazreg, "Gender and Politics in Algeria: Unraveling the Religious Paradigm," *Signs* 15, 4 (1990): 759; Kadiatu Kanneh, "Feminism and the Colonial Body," in *The Post-Colonial Studies Reader*, ed. Bill Ashcroft, Gareth Griffiths, and Helen Tiffin (London, 1995), 346. See also Malek Alloula, *The Colonial Harem*, trans. Myrna Godzich and Wlad Godzich (Minneapolis, 1986); Sarah Graham-Brown, *Images of Women: The Portrayal of Women in Photography of the Middle East, 1860–1950* (New York, 1988); Irvin Cemil Schick, "Representing Middle Eastern Women: Feminism and Colonial Discourse," *Feminist Studies* 16 (Sum-

mer 1990): 345–8); Winifred Woodhull, "Unveiling Algeria," *Genders* 10 (Spring 1991): 117.

58. *Le Petit Parisien*, May 7, 13, 1930; *La République*, May 8, 11, 1930; *La Croix*, May 6, 13, 1930; *L'Illustration*, May 17, 1930.

59. Chollier, *Alger*, 80.

60. Lazreg, *The Eloquence of Silence*, 29–33; Lucien Raynaud, Henri Soulié, and Paul Picard, *Hygiène et pathologie nord-africaines, assistance médicale* (Paris, 1932), 184.

61. *L'Algérie: Album*, 212–13; Vioux, "Visages d'Orient"; Depont, *L'Algérie*, 219.

62. Deloncle, *La caravan*, 17, 19.

63. Chollier, *Alger*, 86–93.

64. Cf. Duchêne, *Ceux d'Algérie*.

65. Malek Chebel, "L'image de l'autochtone maghrébine," in *Images et colonies: Iconographie et propagande coloniale sur l'Afrique française de 1880 à 1962*, ed. Nicolas Bancel, Pascal Blanchard, and Laurent Gervereau (Paris, 1993), 272. "Scenes and types" was the label for a very popular series of postcards of colonized peoples, as well as a common phrase used in ethnographic studies.

66. Chollier, *Alger*, 29.

67. Mirante, "La France et les oeuvres indigènes," 34.

68. Augustin Berque, "Art antique et art musulman en Algérie," *Cahiers du Centenaire de l'Algérie* 6 (1930): 111.

69. Blottière, "Les productions algériennes," 70–71.

70. Berque, "Art antique et art musulman," 125.

71. Gautier, "L'evolution de L'Algérie," 74; Berque, "Art antique et art musulman," 125, 133.

72. Brian Spooner, "Weavers and Dealers: The Authenticity of an Oriental Carpet," in *The Social Life of Things: Commodities in Cultural Perspective*, ed. Arjun Appadurai (Cambridge, Eng., 1986), 222–23. On the notion of "traditional" arts and crafts when applied by European experts to practices in colonial or postcolonial settings, see Kwame Anthony Appiah, "Is the Post- in Postmodernism the Post- in Postcolonial?," *Critical Inquiry* 17, 2 (1991): 336–57.

73. Berque, "Art antique et art musulman," 133; Blottière, "Les productions algériennes," 71.

74. Spurr, *The Rhetoric of Empire*, 32.

75. *L'Illustration*, May 3, 1930.

76. I am indebted for this last insight to El-Arby En-Nachioui.

77. *La Dépêche Coloniale*, May 6, 1930.

78. Falck, *Guide*, 9; Rozet, *Algeria*, 11.

79. For examples of descriptions and illustrations of Arab men with medals, see Deloncle, *La caravan*, 16, 20; "Le Congrès de l'Union Fédérale des Anciens Combattants en Algérie," *L'Illustration*, May 3, 1930.

80. Chollier, *Alger*, 29, 42.

81. Kristin Ross, *Fast Cars, Clean Bodies: Decolonization and the Reordering of French Culture* (Cambridge, Mass., 1995), 124–25.

11. EMANCIPATING EACH OTHER: Dutch Colonial Missionaries' Encounter with Karo Women in Sumatra, 1900–1942

1. Masri Singarimbun, *Kinship, Descent, and Alliance among the Karo Batak* (Berkeley, Calif., 1975).

2. J. T. Cremer, cited in the NZG's *Extract Acten*, Sept. 20, 1889.

3. Rita Smith Kipp, "Conversion by Affiliation: The History of the Karo Batak Protestant Church," *American Ethnologist* 22 (1995): 868–82; Simon Rae, *Breath Becomes the Wind: Old and New in Karo Religion* (Dunedin, New Zealand, 1994), 96; Anthony Reid, *The Blood of the People: Revolution and the End of Traditional Rule in North Sumatra* (Kuala Lumpur, Malaysia, 1979), 70–73.

4. E. J. van den Berg, Notes of a Conference of Religion Teachers, held at Raya, Oct. 7, 1920. With the exception of a reference to a Memorie van Overgaven (n. 48), all the unpublished materials cited in this chapter can be found in the archive of the Nederlands Zendelinggenootschap, housed at the Hendrik Kraemer Instituut in Oegstgeest.

5. Rita Smith Kipp, *The Early Years of a Dutch Colonial Mission: The Karo Field* (Ann Arbor, Mich., 1993), 107–9.

6. J. H. Neumann, "Het jaar 1901 onder de Karo Bataks," *Mededeelingen NZG* 3 (1903): 40–42.

7. J. van Mujlwijk, Annual Report 1930, Sibolangit and Langkat. The wider colonial community, not just missionaries, attributed greater conservatism to women of the Indies than to men.

8. Board to Van Muylwijk, May 17, 1932, and H. Vuurmans, Annual Report 1938, Kabanjahe.

9. Board to Van Muylwijk, May 21, 1931, May 17, 1932; Vuurmans, Annual Report 1938.

10. E. J. van den Berg, "Jaarverslag over 1905 van den arbeid op de Hoog-

vlakte, zendingsressort Kaband-djahe," *Mededeelingen NZG* 50 (1906): 246 –56; J. H. Neumann, "Ressort Sibolangit: Het jaar 1906," ibid., 51 (1907): 59 –71.

11. See Kipp, *The Early Years*, 121–27, for an elaboration of this issue. Karo society was relatively egalitarian. There was little wealth disparity in traditional Karo life, and while headmanships devolved patrilineally in the lines of village founders, the position was usually a matter of dispute. There were no leaders whose purview extended beyond a single village in the highlands. In the lowlands, however, Karo headmen were part of Muslim sultanates and feared that conversion would compromise their position.

12. J. H. Meerwaldt, who worked with the Toba Batak, felt that women's volition in becoming Christian was usually preempted by their husbands' wishes, a situation he assumed prevailed over most of the Indies, rendering women "more passive than active" in matters of conversion (J. H. Meerwaldt, "De vrouw in de dienst der christelijke liefde op het terrein der zending," *Mededeelingen NZG* 48 [1905]: 436 – 46).

13. Van Muylwijk, Annual Reports 1929 and 1930.

14. Arie Kruyt, "De plaats die de Javaansche vrouw inneemt in de samenleving en in de christengemeente," *Mededeelingen NZG* 52 (1909): 318 – 35, 327; Jan K. Wijngaarden, "De zending onder de Karau-Bataks (Deli)," ibid., 38 (1894): 62 – 85.

15. Hendrik Kruyt, "Berichten van Br. H. C. Kruyt uit Deli," ibid., 34 (1890): 325 –31.

16. M. Karen Portier and Herman Slaats, "Women and the Division of Parental Land in Karo Society," in *Cultures and Societies of North Sumatra*, ed. Rainer Carle (Berlin, 1987), 303 – 8.

17. Rita Smith Kipp, "The Ideology of Kinship in Karo Batak Ritual" (Ph.D. diss., Univ. of Pittsburgh, 1976); Rita Smith Kipp, "The Thread of Three Colors," in *Art, Ritual, and Society in Indonesia*, ed. E. M. Bruner and J. O. Becker (Athens, Ohio, 1979), 62 –95.

18. Rita Smith Kipp, "Terms for Kith and Kin," *American Anthropologist* 86 (1984): 905 –26.

19. H. Vuurmans, Annual Report 1938, Kabanjahe.

20. Arie Kruyt, "De plaats die de Javaansche vrouw," 334 –35.

21. Ward Keeler, *Javanese Shadow Plays, Javanese Selves* (Princeton, N.J., 1987), 73.

22. Jan K. Wijngaarden, "Verslag omtrent de zending onder the Karau-Bataks over 1893," *Mededeelingen NZG* 38 (1894): 130 –83. Strictest avoidance applies between in-laws, specifically between husband's sister's husband and wife's brother's wife, husband's father and son's wife, and wife's

mother and daughter's husband, who may not speak to each other or even sit on the same plank of the floor. Real or classificatory brothers and sisters may speak, but should treat each other with great reserve and should not be alone together.

23. Neumann to Board, Dec. 9, 1900; J. H. Neumann, "Karo Batak zending: Verslag aangaande het zendingsressort Boeloeh-Awar," *Mededeelingen NZG* 43 (1901): 129–38.

24. Laurens Bodaan, Annual Report 1911.

25. Meint Joustra, Henri Guillaume, and J. H. Neumann, "Het jaar 1901 onder de Karo-bataks," *Maandberichten NZG* 1 (1903): 7–14.

26. J. H. Neumann, "Ressort Sibolangit"; J. H. Neumann, "Een Belangrijke Tijd," *Maandberichten NZG* 9 (1989): 132–33; J. P. Talens, "De hoogvlakte van Deli," ibid., 5 (1914): 69–76, 6 (1914): 87–90.

27. L. Bodaan, Annual Report 1916; Notes of a Conference, Deli zending, Feb. 14, 1919.

28. Meint Joustra, "Verslag van de zending onder de Karo-bataks, over het jaar 1895," *Mededeelingen NZG* 43 (1899): 325–38; J. H. Neumann, "Jaarverslag over het ressort Sibolangit," ibid., 47 (1903): 241.

29. Mary Margaret Steedly, "The Importance of Proper Names: Language and 'National Identity' in Karoland," *American Ethnologist* 23, 3 (1996): 447–74; Rita Smith Kipp, *Dissociated Identities: Ethnicity, Religion, and Class in an Indonesian Society* (Ann Arbor, Mich., 1993), 29.

30. Meint Joustra, "Verslag van de zending onder de Karo-Bataks, over het jaar 1895," *Mededeelingen NZG* 40 (1896): 220–44.

31. Rae, *Breath Becomes the Wind*, 29.

32. *Extract Acten NZG*, 1920, 93; Gezinus Smit, "De kweekschool te Raja (Deli), 9 Juni 1909–20 December 1920," *Maandberichten NZG* 7 (1921): 42–52.

33. Van Muylwijk to Board, Sept. 23, 1936.

34. Jan K. Wijngaarden, "Verslag omtrent de zending onder de Karau-Bataks over 1893," *Mededeelingen NZG* 35 (1894): 130–83; Neumann to Board, Aug. 3, 1902.

35. Rita Smith Kipp, "The Evangelical Uses of Leprosy," *Social Science and Medicine* 139, 2 (1994): 165–78.

36. Kipp, *The Early Years*, 143–46.

37. H. Pesik, "Uit de aanteekeningen der Minahassische onderwijzers over 1895," *Mededeelingen NZG* 40 (1896): 165–75.

38. Benjamin Wenas, "Van den Goeroe van Salaboelan, B. Wenas (Joustra): Vervolg van de aanteekeningen der Minahassische onderwijzers," ibid., 296–308.

39. Wenas, "Van den Goeroe."

40. Joustra, "Verslag van de zending," 237.

41. Van den Berg, "Jaarverslag over 1905"; E. J. van den Berg, "De zending op de Karo-Hoogvlakte in 1907," *Mededeelingen NZG* 52 (1908): 67–79; Van den Berg to Ginning, Jan. 15, 1908.

42. Van Muylwijk, Annual Report 1928; Van Muylwijk to Board, Dec. 12, 1925.

43. Board to Van Muylwijk, Dec. 1, 1927.

44. J. van Muylwijk, "Twaalf jaar in de Doesoen (Deli) (van begin 1923 tot einde 1934)," *Mededeelingen NZG* 80 (1936): 161–95.

45. *Extract Acten NZG*, 1928, 20.

46. Pieternella Wynekes, "Zr. P. Wynekes en het ziekenhuis te Sibolangit," *Maandberichten NZG* 8 (1928): 126–27.

47. J. van Muylwijk, "Geneest de Kranken," ibid., 8 (1928): 119–21; Van Muylwijk, "Twaalf jaar"; Wynekes, "Zr. P. Wynekes"; *Extract Acten NZG*, 1929, 122, and 1930, 130.

48. Van Muylwijk, Annual Report 1936.

49. Sandra Niessen, *Batak Cloth and Clothing: A Dynamic Indonesian Tradition* (Kuala Lumpur, Malaysia, 1993).

50. J. J. Smit-Liese, "Ook vrouwen en meisjes," *Nederlandsch Zendingsblad* 22, 10 (1939): 171–73.

51. G. Neumann-Bos, "C.M.C.M., Geen puzzle Meer," ibid., 170–71.

52. W. A. Smit, Annual Report 1937.

53. See Kipp, *Dissociated Identities*, 195, for a description of a Moria meeting.

54. G. Neumann-Bos, "C.M.C.M."

55. W. A. Smit to Conference, Dec. 5, 1938.

56. Vuurmans, Annual Report 1938, Kabanjahe.

57. W. A. Smit to Conference, Dec. 5, 1938.

58. Conference Notes 1939; Vuurmans, Annual Report 1938, Kabanjahe; W. A. Smit, Annual Report 1937.

59. W. A. Smit to Board, May 7, 1937.

60. Veronika Bennholdt-Thomsen, "Why Do Housewives Continue to Be Created in the Third World Too?" in *Women: the Last Colony*, ed. Maria Mies, Veronika Bennholdt-Thomas, and Claudia von Werlhof (London, 1988), 159–67.

61. Ingrid Rudie, *Visible Women in East Coast Malay Society* (Oslo, n.d.).

62. Kipp, *The Early Years*, 14.

63. For example, see Hendrik Kraemer, *The Christian Message in a Non-Christian World* (Grand Rapids, Mich., 1963), 323.

64. See, for example, Kipp, *The Early Years*, 137–38.

65. J. C. Neurdenburg, *Proeve eener handleiding bij het bespreken der zendingswetenschap* (Rotterdam, 1879).
66. Hendrik Kruyt, "Berichten van Br. H. C. Kruijt, te Bulo-Haur (Deli Tuwa)," *Mededeelingen NZG* 35 (1891): 43–74.
67. Dina Wijngaarden, "Letter," *Maandberichten NZG* 6 (1894): 90–93.
68. A. M. Brouwer, "The Preparation of Missionaries in Holland," *International Review of Missions* 12 (1912): 226–39.
69. A. Kruyt suggested that because gender segregation was not as rigid in the Indies as in many other colonial settings, the need for women missionaries was not felt as keenly (Kruyt, "De plaats die de Jaavansche vrouw").
70. Patricia R. Hill, *The World Their Household: The American Woman's Foreign Mission Movement and Cultural Transformation, 1870–1920* (Ann Arbor, Mich., 1985), 173.
71. *Extract Acten NZG*, 1936, 1937, 1938; Board to Deli Conference, Feb. 3, 1937.
72. Rita Smith Kipp, "Why Can't a Woman Be More Like Man? Bureaucratic Contradictions in the Dutch Missionary Society," in *Gendered Missions*, ed. Mary Huber and Nancy Lutkehaus (in press).

12. GOOD MOTHERS, MEDEAS, OR JEZEBELS: Feminine Imagery in Colonial and Anticolonial Rhetoric in the Dutch East Indies, 1900–1942

An earlier version of this chapter appeared as "The Gendered Rhetoric of Colonialism and Anti-Colonialism in Twentieth-Century Indonesia," in *Indonesia* 55 (April 1993): 1–22 and is reprinted with the permission of the Cornell Southeast Asia Program.

1. Hendrik Colijn, *Hoofdlijnen onzer koloniale politiek* (The Hague, 1932), 33–34; C. Snouck Hurgronje, *Colijn over Indië* (Amsterdam, 1928), 2–3.
2. Elsbeth Locher-Scholten, *Ethiek in fragmenten: Vijf studies over koloniaal denken en doen van Nederlanders in de Indonesische Archipel, 1877–1942* (Utrecht, 1981), 182–84.
3. As Lynn Hunt has argued in *The Family Romance of the French Revolution* (Berkeley, Calif., 1992), 8, 196.
4. *Handelingen van de Volksraad* (Proceedings of the People's Council, hereafter abbreviated as *HV*) (Batavia, 1918), second regular session, supplementary budget considerations, 9th meeting, Nov. 14, 1918, 159.
5. Helen Haste, *The Sexual Metaphor: Men, Women, and the Thinking That Makes the Difference* (Cambridge, Mass., 1994), 63.
6. *HV*, 1918, 159.

7. Ibid., 165.

8. Ibid., 163.

9. Ibid., 165.

10. M. B. van der Jagt, *Memoires van M. B. van der Jagt, Oud Gouverneur van Soerakarta* (The Hague, 1955), 299.

11. *Provinciaal Blad van Midden Java*, ser. D, no. 5, Dec. 30, 1939, 217.

12. J. J. B. Ostmeier, "Punten en Problemen: Eene proeve van studie over het Javaanse volkskarakter," *Insulinde* 2, 22 (Nov. 16, 1911): 3–5.

13. Frantz Fanon, *The Wretched of the Earth* (New York, 1963), 211.

14. Malek Alloula, *The Colonial Harem*, trans. Myrna and Wlad Godzich (Minneapolis, 1986), 3; Tan Malaka, *From Jail to Jail*, trans. Helen Jarvis, 3 vols. (Athens, Ohio, 1991), 1, 92. Tan Malaka referred to Georg Buchner's remark about the French Revolution: "The Revolution is like Saturn—it eats its own children."

15. Soetatmo Soeriokoesoemo, *Sabdo-Panditto-Ratoe: Het recht is van den wijze* (Weltevreden, Indonesia, 1920), 3, quoted by Takashi Shiraishi, "The Disputes between Tjipto Mangoenkoesoemo and Soetatmo Soeriok-oesoemo: Satria vs. Pandita," *Indonesia* 32 (Oct. 1981): 101.

16. H. B., "De Standaard over het 'Insulinde' Personeel," *Insulinde* 1, 15 (Aug. 1, 1910): 4–5.

17. *De Beweging* Algemeen Politiek Weekblad, 3, 7 (Feb. 12, 1921): 100.

18. Erle R. Dickover to the Secretary of State, Jan. 6, 1939, Military Intelligence Division, "Regional File," 1932–44, Netherlands East Indies, box 2631, Records of the War Department, General and Special Staffs, Record Group 165, National Archives, College Park, Md.

19. Ruth T. McVey, *The Rise of Indonesian Communism* (Ithaca, N.Y., 1965), 252.

20. *Indonesia Accuses! Soekarno's Defense Oration in the Political Trial of 1930*, trans. Roger K. Paget (Kuala Lumpur, 1975), 88.

21. Richard Cribb's interview with Wim Hendrix, Nov. 19, 1981, 3, "Texts of interviews conducted by the Australian historian R. Cribb with prominent Dutchmen and Indonesians about the period 1945–1950," Algemeen Rijksarchief (ARA), 2d Division, 2.22.06, Losse Aanwinsten na 1980, preliminary no. 188.

22. The postcard reads "Mother's Indonesia and Mother's India," which was most likely an awkward English translation of *Ibu Indonesia dan Ibu India*. See P. van Meel, *Getekend als koloniaal: Een relaas over de belevenissen van een KNIL-soldaat en de mensen die zijn leven deelden in de jaren 1930–1950* (Dordrecht, 1982), 98.

23. Van Meel, *Getekend als koloniaal*, 98.

24. *Het Indisch Nieuws* 2, 46 (Dec. 7, 1946): unpaged; John Coast, *Recruit to Revolution: Adventure and Politics in Indonesia* (London, 1952), 10.

25. Van Meel, *Getekend als koloniaal*, 98.

26. K'Tut Tantri, *Revolt in Paradise: One Woman's Fight for Freedom in Indonesia* (1960; rept., New York, 1989), 213.

27. Klaus Theweleit, *Male Fantasies*, vol. 1, *Women, Floods, Bodies, History*, trans. S. Conway (Minneapolis, 1987).

28. J. C. van Eerde, *Koloniale Volkenkunde*, pt. 1, "Omgang met inlanders," Bulletin no. 1, Ethnography Division, no. 1, Koninklijk Koloniaal Instituut (1914; rept., Amsterdam, 1928), 48.

29. G. L. Gonggrijp, *Brieven van opheffer aan de redactie van het Bataviaans Handelsblad*, 4th ed. (Maastricht, n.d.), 149; see also Rudy Kousbroek, *Het Oostindisch Kampsyndroom* (Amsterdam, 1992), 137.

30. Dr. Radjiman, in *HV*, 1918, 2d regular session, 171.

31. Ph. Coolhaas, "Ontstaan en groei," in *Wij gedenken . . . Gedenkboek van de vereniging van ambtenaren bij het binnenlands bestuur in Nederlands-Indië* (Utrecht, 1956), 62, 70; the Dutch words are *kinderlijk* and *kinderachtig*.

32. Hendrik Colijn, *Koloniale vraagstukken van heden en morgen* (Amsterdam, 1928), 34, quoted by Bernard Dahm, *Soekarno en de strijd om Indonesië's onafhankelijkheid* (Meppel, 1964), 341 n., 364.

33. Van der Jagt, *Memoires*, Appendix, 342; speech in the Volksraad, 2d regular session, Nov. 15, 1918.

34. J. S. Furnivall, *Netherlands India: A Study of Plural Economy* (Oxford, 1939), 389.

35. D. U. Stikker, ed., *Jhr. Mr. Dr. A. W. L. Tjarda van Starkenborch Stachouwer: Bijdragen tot een kenschets* (Rotterdam, 1978), 20.

36. D. H. Burger, "Het binnenlands bestuur op Java en Madoera," in *Wij gedenken*, 100.

37. Creutzberg's address to the *Indisch Genootschap* in the late 1920s, quoted in A. D. A. de Kat Angelino, *Colonial Policy*, 2 vols. (Chicago, 1931), 2:226; F. A. Volkers-Schippers, *Widoerileergang: Hoe men elementair naai- en huishoudonderricht kan geven aan de volksvrouw op Java* (Batavia, 1937), 5.

38. Jennifer and Paul Alexander, "Protecting Peasants from Capitalism: The Subordination of Javanese Traders by the Colonial State," *Comparative Studies in Society and History* 33, 2 (April 1991): 373.

39. The term *ernstige wil* was used in an explanatory memorandum to the Volksraad in 1925 regarding the proposed legislation to curtail women's work at night between 10 P.M. and 5 A.M. (see *HV*, 1925, 1st regular session,

subject 6, entry 3, Memorie van Toelichting, 7). H. E. B. Schmalhausen used *plichtgevoel* and *innerlijke aandrift* in *Over Java en de Javanen: Nagelaten geschriften* (Amsterdam, 1909), 49.

40. *HV*, 1918, 1st regular session, 5th meeting, June 19, 1918, 125.

41. Ibid., 1935–36, 1st regular session, 10th meeting, July 13, 1935, 192, 193.

42. Michael Adas, *Machines as the Measure of Men: Science, Technology, and Ideologies of Western Dominance* (Ithaca, N.Y., 1989), 304–5; for a thoughtful critique of the presumptions about the "mediating" role of the *nyai*, see Elsbeth Locher-Scholten, "The Nyai in Colonial Deli: A Case of Supposed Mediation," in *Indonesian Women and Mediation*, ed. Sita van Bemmelen, Madelon Djajadiningrat-Nieuwenhuis, Elsbeth Locher-Scholten, Elly Touwen-Bouwsma (Leiden, 1992), 265–80.

43. Emily S. Rosenberg, "Gender," in "A Round Table: Explaining the History of American Foreign Relations," *Journal of American History 77*, 1 (1990): 119. See also Jan Nederveen Pieterse, *Wit over zwart: Beelden van Afrika en zwarten in de westerse populaire cultuur* (Amsterdam, 1989), esp. chap. 5, "Kolonialisme en populaire cultuur," 76–101. Nationalist intellectuals in India too, advocated complex notions of modern womanhood; favoring female education so that Bengali mothers could provide a beneficial "cradle and nursery for the production of future citizens," on the one hand, they caricatured and vilified the educated woman who became independent, assertive, and disruptive of the patriarchal household, on the other. See Dipesh Chakrabarty, "Womanhood, Home, and the Domestic Order: Figures of the Modern in Bengali-Indian Colonial Thought," paper presented at Social Science Research Council conference on "Culture, Consciousness, and the Colonial State," Sussex, England, July 1989.

44. Terence Hawkes, *Shakespeare's Talking Animals: Language and Drama in Society* (London, 1973), 212; Stephen Greenblatt, *Marvelous Possessions: The Wonder of the New World* (Chicago, 1991), 86–118.

45. The Catholic priest and scholar of Javanese culture F. van Lith denounced this attitude in his article about "Het koloniaal onderwijscongres" which took place on April 24, 1924, in *Djawa* 4, 3 (Sept. 1924): 155.

46. Fanon, *The Wretched of the Earth*, 218–19.

47. Edward W. Said, "Representing the Colonized: Anthropology's Interlocutors," *Critical Inquiry* 15, 2 (Winter 1989): 210.

48. Clifford Geertz, *After the Fact: Two Countries, Four Decades, One Anthropologist* (Cambridge, Mass., 1995), 48.

49. Laura Cooley, "Maintaining *Rukun* for Javanese Households and for the State," in Van Bemmelen, *Women and Mediation*, 229–47.

50. Coast, *Recruit to Revolution*, 7.

13. TREKKING TO NEW GUINEA: Dutch Colonial Fantasies
of a Virgin Land, 1900–1940

1. Abbreviations employed are the following: *Handelingen Volksraad* (Proceedings of the People's Council): *HV*; *De Nieuw-Guineaer* (The New Guineaer): *DNG*; *Onze Toekomst* (Our future): *OT*; *Nederlandsch Indië* (Netherlands Indies): *NI*; *Tijdschrift Nieuw-Guinea* (New Guinea journal): *TNG*. A. A. Mussert, chairman of the Dutch National Socialist movement, 1935, quoted in A. Lijphart, *The Trauma of Decolonization: The Dutch and West New Guinea* (New Haven, 1966), 87.

2. Lijphart, *The Trauma of Decolonization*, 288; Hal Hill and Anna Weidemann, "Regional Development in Indonesia: Patterns and Issues," in *Unity and Diversity: Regional Economic Development in Indonesia since 1970*, ed. Hal Hill (Oxford, 1991), 7; Chris Manning and Michael Rumbiak, "Irian Jaya: Economic Change, Migrants, and Indigenous Welfare," ibid., 77–106.

3. See Sigmund Freud, "Medusa's Head," "Fetishism," and "Splitting of the Ego in the Defensive Process," in *Sexuality and the Psychology of Love*, ed. Philip Rieff (New York, 1963), 202–13. See also Victor N. Smirnoff, "The Fetishistic Transaction," in *Psychoanalysis in France*, ed. Serge Lebovici and Daniel Widlöcher (New York, 1980), 303–31; Jacques Derrida, *Spurs: Nietzsche's Styles*, trans. Barbara Harlow (Chicago, 1978).

4. Elsbeth Locher-Scholten, "Dutch Expansion in the Indonesian Archipelago around 1900 and the Imperialism Debate," *Journal of Southeast Asian Studies* 25, 1 (March 1994): 107; J. à Campo, "Een Maritiem BB. De Rol van de Koninklijke Paketvaart Maatschappij in de integratie van de koloniale staat," in *Imperialisme in de marge: De afronding van Nederlands-Indië*, ed. Dr. J. van Goor (Utrecht, 1985), 123–78.

5. P. E. Winkler, *Blank Nieuw-Guinea* (Utrecht, n.d.), 11.

6. The European population rose 167 percent between 1905 and 1930 (P. Drooglever, *De Vaderlandse Club, 1929–1942: Totoks en de Indische politiek* [Franeker, 1980], 5). Gender ratios in the European community went from 471.6 to 884.5 women per thousand men (R. Nieuwenhuys, *The Mirror of the Indies: A History of Dutch Colonial Literature* [Amherst, Mass., 1982], 201). A key factor in the rise of the *totok* community was the abolition of the Dutch monarch's control over the Indies. Before 1870, all Dutch persons who wished to enter the colony needed a passport from the king. See also Takashi Shiraishi, *An Age in Motion: Popular Radicalism in Java, 1912–1926* (Ithaca, N.Y., 1990); Tsuchiya Kenji, "Kartini's Image of the Javanese Landscape," *East Asian Cultural Studies* 25, 1–4 (1986): 59–86; and Tsuchiya Kenji, "Javanology and the Age of Ranggawarsita: An Introduction to Nine-

teenth Century Javanese Culture," in *Reading Southeast Asia* (Ithaca, N.Y., 1990), 75–109.

7. Drooglever, *De Vaderlandse Club*, 5. For data on the structure of the European community, see also Paul van der Veur, "Introduction to a Socio-Political Study of the Eurasians of Indonesia" (Ph.D. diss., Cornell Univ., 1955).

8. See Ann L. Stoler, "Making Empire Respectable: the Politics of Race and Sexual Morality in 20th Century Colonial Cultures," *American Ethnologist* 16, 4 (Nov. 1989): 636–39.

9. Henceforth, the terms "European" or *blijver* denote "legally European." I use the term *totok* for pure-blooded whites. On two very different sectors of the early colonial community, see Hanneke Ming, "Barracks Concubinage in the Indies," *Indonesia* 35 (April 1983): 65–94; J. Taylor, *The Social World of Batavia: European and Eurasian in Dutch Asia* (Madison, Wis., 1983).

10. See Pamela Pattynama, "Secrets and Danger: Interracial Sexuality in Louis Couperus's *The Hidden Force* and Dutch Colonial Culture around 1900," chap. 5 above; J. Furnivall, *Colonial Policy and Practice* (London, 1948), 217–76.

11. See Benedict Anderson, *Imagined Communities: Reflections on the Origin and Spread of Nationalism* (London, 1983); Shiraishi, *An Age in Motion*.

12. This trend was acknowledged with the passage of a new salary scheme that divided low-paying jobs for natives from high-paying jobs for European emigrants, leaving middle-level positions for "circles in the Netherlands Indies of relatively small numbers, whose general living standards call for the presence of an accordingly higher salary" (see Van der Veur, "Introduction to a Socio-Political Study," 253–60). As the training of natives improved, this relatively small group was gradually to be replaced by persons hired at the standard pay rate.

13. Ibid. On the Agrarian Act, which protected state control of colonial subjects and resources by inscribing rigid homologies between race, vocation, and land rights, see Daniel Lev, "Colonial Law and the Genesis of the Indonesian State," *Indonesia* 40 (1985): 57–74; Nancy Peluso, *Rich Forests, Poor People: Resource Control and Resistance in Java* (Berkeley, Calif., 1992); Stoler, *Capitalism and Confrontation in Sumatra's Plantation Belt, 1870–1979* (New Haven, 1985); Charles Zerner, *Community Rights, Customary Law, and the Law of Timber Concessions in Indonesia*, Document UTF/INS/ 065 (Jakarta, 1990).

14. K. Tsuchiya, *Democracy and Leadership: The Rise of the Taman Siswa Movement in Indonesia* (Honolulu, 1986).

15. Stoler, "Making Empire Respectable," 645.

16. See Stoler, *Capitalism and Confrontation*, 38–39, for a discussion of Dutch visions of *kolonisatie* (colonization) in Deli. The colonization of poor Javanese to the Outer Islands dated from 1902. Rudolf Mrazek describes how the Dutch called the camp at Boven Digoel an "isolation colony" (see Mrazek, *Sjahrir: Politics and Exile in Indonesia* [Ithaca, N.Y., 1994], 130).

17. The following account is drawn from Van der Veur, "Introduction to a Socio-Political Study," 351–69; Lijphart, *The Trauma of Decolonization*, 69–89; Drooglever, *De Vaderlandse Club*, 193–209.

18. Lijphart, *The Trauma of Decolonization*, 71. Busy promoting their own colonization project in Sumatra, the leaders of the Indo-European Union (IEV) were initially critical of A. Th. Schalk and his followers. The IEV finally came out in support of the New Guinea movement in 1933, more in defense of the maligned Indo-European colonists than out of any particular enthusiasm for the scheme (see *HV*, 1931–32, 873; ibid., 1933–34, 917; Van der Veur, "Introduction to a Socio-Political Study"). After much lobbying by the IEV and other right-wing associations, the societies were granted a share of the proceeds from the colonial lottery. Each colonist received a year's worth of aid from the crisis relief committees which relied on the societies to administer the funds. The KPM shipping line gave SIKNG and VKNG members free passage to New Guinea, fourth class. Few, if any colonists, were ever self-reliant. Most subsisted on the colonial dole.

19. On the Volksraad's mission, see S. L. van der Wal, *De Volksraad en de staatkundige ontwikkeling van Nederlands-Indië* (Groningen, 1965), 109. On the assembly's changing racial and political composition, see ibid., 95–120, 175–202.

20. Van der Veur, "Introduction to a Socio-Political Study," 229. Van der Veur argues that the IEV included one-fifth of the total Eurasian population in the Indies.

21. The Patriots Club (Vaderlandse Club, or VC) membership reached its peak in 1930. See Drooglever, *De Vaderlandse Club*, 348.

22. Van der Veur, "Introduction to a Socio-Political Study," 319. For an account of the changing stance of the National Socialist movement (National Socialistische Beweging, or NSB) on race, see M. C. van den Toorn, *Dietsch en volksch: Een verkenning van het taalgebruik der Nationaal-Socialisten in Nederland* (Groningen, 1975), 13. The first recruiters for the Indies branch of the NSB were Eurasians. As the decade progressed, they were gradually replaced by full-blooded Dutch men.

23. Winkler, *Blank Nieuw-Guinea*, 38.

24. See H. te Velde, *Gemeenschapszin en plichtsbesef: liberalisme en nationalisme in Nederland, 1870–1918* (Amsterdam, 1992), 151. Te Velde highlights the "sublimated eroticism" of Dutch nationalism at the turn of the century in his analysis of the pageantry that celebrated Queen Wilhelmina's inauguration. See also G. L. Mosse, *Nationalism and Sexuality: Middle-Class Morality and Sexual Norms in Modern Europe* (Madison, Wis., 1985).

25. Te Velde, *Gemeenschapszin en plichtsbesef*, 78, 151.

26. See Nieuwenhuys, *The Mirror of the Indies*, 205. Van der Veur quotes from a speech given by the IEV's longtime chairman, F. H. de Hoog, at the annual convention in 1934. "Have we members of the IEV organization really not always been fascists? Has the word of the General Committee and the chairman not always had more or less dictatorial power? . . . But this is exactly our greatest victory, that these fascist tendencies and these dictatorial powers existed within the IEV but were applied and exercised in such a way that you have never realized it yourselves" (Van der Veur, "Introduction to a Socio-Political Study," 232).

27. Klaus Theweleit, *Male Fantasies*, vol. 1, *Women, Floods, Bodies, History*, trans. S. Conway (Minneapolis, 1987).

28. Thamrin in *HV*, 1935–36, 182.

29. See Nieuwenhuys, *The Mirror of the Indies*; Pramoedya Ananta Toer, *Tempo doeloe: Antologi sastra Pra-Indonesia* (Jakarta, 1982).

30. "Waarom associatie," *DNG* 2, 4 (July 10, 1931): 3.

31. Ibid.; "De landbouw en andere mogelijkheden voor den Indo-Blijver," ibid., 2, 2 (May 10, 1931): 3. See also ibid., 4, 2 (May 1933): 3: "We Indos and Blijvers . . . may thank God that in these times New Guinea still exists for us. We live on in, through, and for our children, and most of us do not sufficiently sense this truth. Now our existence as a nation is at stake. . . . We want regeneration, and we are ready to start from the beginning. We want to be and remain an Indo-Blijver nation. But a nation needs land. And land is to be had in abundance in New Guinea; there is enough for every one of us."

32. See ibid., 1, 9 (Dec. 10, 1930): 4: "Toegepast historica" (Applied history) offers a satirical view of the founding of Holland by relating the early Batavians' history and character to that of the Indo-Blijvers. See also ibid., 2, 1 (April 10, 1931): 6: "Een lied uit 1930" (A ballad from 1930) describes the Indo's recognition "in father's fatherland" as the "noblest product" of the Indies. See also ibid., 5, 5 (Aug. 10, 1934): 4, and ibid., 5, 11a (Feb. 1, 1935): 3, for a discussion of "Indo Zionism," and ibid., 5, 11b (Feb. 16, 1935): 1, for a comparison of the Jews and the Indos.

33. Ibid., 2, 4 (July 10, 1931): 3.

34. Ibid., 2, 3 (July 10, 1931): 3; "Java en Nieuw-Guinea," ibid., 2, 5 (Aug. 10, 1931): 8; "Waar de landbouw bloeit, daar bloeit de staat," ibid., 1, 11 (Feb. 10, 1931): 13; "Java en Nieuw-Guinea," ibid., 2, 3 (June 10, 1931): 15.

35. Ibid., 4, 11 (Feb. 1934): 2–3; "Communisme," ibid., 1, 11 (Feb. 10, 1931): 2. For a somewhat different take on the relationship between waste and revolution, see Georges Bataille, "The Notion of Expenditure," in *Visions of Excess: Selected Writings, 1929–1939*, ed. Allan Stoekl (Minneapolis, 1985), 116–29.

36. "Waar de landbouw," *DNG* 2, 1 (April 10, 1931): 14. See also "Onze leidende principe," ibid., 3, 3 (June 1932): 6. An Indo pauper and a native peer through a window at wealthy *blijvers* enjoying themselves on the dance floor. Thoughts of revenge take shape in their minds. This piece was part of a bitter polemic against the VKNG, which attacked the SIKNG for including natives in their colony. The SIKNG called for the inclusion in the fatherland of "unrecognized Indo-Europeans," who were divided from their more fortunate brothers only by their lack of a Dutch name.

37. Which was emphatically absent in other versions of the fantasy. See "Verschilpunten tusschen de VKNG en SIKNG," ibid., 2, 2 (May 10, 1931): 7.

38. "Ondervinding meesteress," ibid., 1, 11 (Feb. 10, 1931): 4.

39. "De landbouw en andere mogelijkheden," ibid., 2, 9 (Dec. 10, 1931): 5; "De Indo en de Agr. Zaken," ibid., 3, 5 (Aug. 10, 1932): 14. See also ibid., 2, 9 (Dec. 10, 1931): 6: "Boar hunting for meat supplies" features a colonist in a T-shirt crouched beside a dead pig, his fellow colonists in a line behind him. Two bare-chested Papuan hunters stand at a respectful distance to the rear. Page 9 features a Papuan girl in Javanese native dress posing behind a clothesline. "Papuan beauty promoted to washer woman." The colonists not only needed Papuan labor; they also needed Papuan land. The SIKNG's new colonists got their farms by paying the local villagers to let them use their abandoned gardens.

40. "Het leven in de Papoea kampoeng Sam Sanggasse in Zuid Nieuw Guinea," ibid., 1, 11 (Feb. 10, 1931): 4.

41. "Eeuwige bezwaren," ibid., 1, 11 (Feb. 10, 1931): 8.

42. "Waarom associatie," ibid., 2, 4 (July 10, 1931): 5. See also ibid., 5, 7a (Oct. 1, 1934): 4.

43. J. H. Schijfsma, "Kolonisatie vrouw in Nieuw-Guinea," *Indisch Vrouwen Jaarboek*, 1936, 70, 68.

44. Ibid., 73.

45. "De politieke tendenz in onze beweging," *OT* 6, 53 (Oct. 19, 1933): 2.

46. See ibid., 8, 15 (April 11, 1935): 2; see also ibid., 8, 40 (Dec. 16, 1935): 1.

47. Winkler, *Blank Nieuw-Guinea*, 6, 55–56.

48. Ibid., 58.

49. Ibid., 21.

50. See the Dutch colonization newspaper, *De Kolonist* 1, 1 (Nov. 1933): 1.

51. The VC's program for New Guinea was shaped by its colonization study committees in the Indies and in Holland, which offered an expert assessment of New Guinea's potential. The membership of the Dutch study committee included three ex-governors of the Moluccas and two military officers; the chairman was L. H. W. van Sandick, a former governor of the Moluccas and East Sumatra and an ex-member of the Raad van Indie. Other members of the VC's study committee in Holland included: J. C. Brasser, a former KNIL colonel and a participant in the Mamberamo expedition and the Dutch-German Commission that set the border that divided the Indies from the German colony in New Guinea's northeast; V. A. Doeve, a former assistant resident at the disposal of the governor of the Moluccas and an ex-resident of Riouw; J. G. Larive, a former governor of the Moluccas; C. Poortman, a former resident of New Guinea and of Djambi; L. A. Snell, a participant in the Fransen Herderschee expedition to New Guinea's south coast and a former KNIL colonel; A. T. H. Winter, a retired professor and KNIL colonel and the VC's first chairman; with a special member in the Indies, Dr. H. B. Vrijburg, formerly the chief of Batavia's veterinary service and the founder of De Friesche Terp dairy farm in Pengalengan.

52. See Roep, *HV*, 1935–36, 62. Roep was a member of the Politiek Economisch Verbond who supported VC policy on New Guinea. For a similar view expressed by VC leaders, see *NI*, Sept. 15, 1935, 17, and May 15, 1934, 1.

53. *NI*, May 15, 1934, 6. See also Van Sandick, chairman of the Colonization Study Committee of the VC in Holland, in *HV*, 1935–36, 17.

54. *NI*, May 15, 1934, 1.

55. See Van Sandick, *HV*, 1935–36, 17.

56. *Ontwikkeling van en kolonisatie in Nieuw-Guinea, Rapport van de studiecommissie ingesteld door de Vaderlandsche Club in Nederland* (The Hague, 1934), 55.

57. W. K. H. Feuilletau de Bruyn, "De bevolking van Biak en het kolonisatievraagstuk van Noord Nieuw-Guinea," *TNG*, Dec. 15, 1936, 169. See Stoler, *Capitalism and Confrontation*, on the history of the penal sanction.

58. Feuilletau de Bruyn, *HV*, 1931–32, 1121. See also R. Tucker, ed., *The Marx Engels Reader* (New York, 1978), 734–60.

59. *OT* 6, 62 (Dec. 21, 1933): 4.

60. For a general discussion of the denial of "coevalness," see Johannes

Fabian, *Time and the Other: How Anthropology Makes Its Object* (New York, 1983), 1–37. In Australian New Guinea the Papuans' relegation to the Stone Age did not succeed in quelling racial fears (Stoler, "Making Empire Respectable," 641).

61. Van Sandick, the chairman of the VC's Colonization Study Committee, also belonged to the New Guinea Commission in Holland. The author of the VC's evolutionary portrait of Papuan land rights, Feuilletau de Bruyn, went on to edit *Tijdschrift Nieuw-Guinea*, a journal published throughout the 1940s and 1950s that featured articles from both sides of the island. He was also a prominent member of the New Guinea Study Circle in Amsterdam, which ran a library and a lecture series attended by retired officials and missionaries, businessmen, and prospective pioneers.

62. J. van Baal, *Ontglipt verleden* 2 (Franeker, 1989): 153.

63. See L. Spitzer, *Lives In Between: Assimilation and Marginality in Austria, Brazil, and West Africa, 1780–1945* (Cambridge, Eng., 1989), for a discussion of suicide, exile, and political activism as a way out for marginal figures who find their attempts to assimilate blocked by a dominant group.

64. Stoler, "Making Empire Respectable," 636.

65. See Mosse, *Nationalism and Sexuality*, 9.

66. See K. Portier, "Tussenstation 'Nieuw-Guinea,'" in *Het onbekend vaderland: De repatriering van Indische Nederlanders (1946–1964)*, ed. W. Willems and L. Lucassen (The Hague, 1994), 129–47, on the wave of Indo-European migration to New Guinea that followed Indonesian independence in Dec. 1949. Portier describes a shipload of would-be colonists dumping dining room sets, pianos, and automobiles into the bay after discovering that Manokwari's port had no jetty. All but a handful of the prewar colonists perished during Japan's invasion of New Guinea. Ironically, local Papuans saved a few of the VKNG settlers; see *OT* 13, 7 (July 1947).

67. Compare G. L. Tichelman, *NSB deportatie naar Oost en West* (Amsterdam, c. 1946), and Winkler, *Blank Nieuw-Guinea*. Tichelman's proposal would have given collaborators a choice between jail sentences and hard labor in New Guinea. Those who helped open land and roads would have received their own farms.

68. Portier, "Tussenstation 'Nieuw-Guinea,'" 143.

69. W. van Rooijen, "Toean Baroe, de nieuwe heer, Nieuw-Guinea, 1949–1962: Beleid, onderzoek en beeldvorming" (Ph.D. diss., Univ. of Amsterdam, 1989), 24–38.

70. For a description of the transmigration program in Irian Jaya, see Manning and Rumbiak, "Irian Jaya," 97–104. Indonesian fantasies concerning Irian Jaya call to mind Dutch dreams of New Guinea. For a breath-

less description of "the land of our exile," see I. F. M. Salim, *Vijftien jaar Boven Digoel: Concentratiekamp in Nieuw Guinea, bakermat van de Indonesische onafhankelijkheid* (Amsterdam, 1973), 35–37. The New Guinea portrayed is a sublimely maternal creature: "The gigantic island is itself surrounded by a number of neighboring islands, which nestle like children against the great maternal body."

71. Drooglever, *De Vaderlandse Club*, 203.

72. Quoted in Derrida, *Spurs*, 47.

CONTRIBUTORS

JEANNE M. BOWLAN is currently a doctoral candidate in modern European history at Rutgers University. Her dissertation is a study of the construction of gender norms in colonial Algeria after the First World War and is the larger in-progress study from which her chapter in this volume is drawn. Ms. Bowlan also presented parts of this essay to the 1993 Berkshire Conference on the History of Women. She recently completed extensive field and archival research in France on her dissertation.

JULIA CLANCY-SMITH is an Associate Professor of Modern Middle Eastern and North African History in the Department of History at the University of Arizona. Her first book, *Rebel and Saint: Muslim Notables, Populist Protest, Colonial Encounters (Algeria and Tunisia, 1800–1904)* (1994) has received three book awards. Clancy-Smith has published numerous articles on colonial North Africa and is currently working on a second scholarly monograph, entitled: "Displacements: Women, Migration, and Identities in the Nineteenth-Century Mediterranean World."

ALICE L. CONKLIN is an Assistant Professor of History at the University of Rochester, where she teaches modern French history, women's history, and the history of imperialism. She is the author of *A Mission to Civilize: The Republican Idea of Empire in France and West Africa, 1895–1930* (1997). Professor Conklin has also published "Democracy Rediscovered: The Advent of Association in French West Africa, 1914–1930" in *Cahiers d'Etudes Africaines*.

PENNY EDWARDS is a Commonwealth Fellow in the Department of History at Monash University in Australia, where she is completing a dissertation on the development of national and ethnic identity in colonial Cambodia. She earned degrees in Chinese studies and international relations from The School of Oriental and African Studies in London and Oxford University.

YAËL SIMPSON FLETCHER is a Ph.D. candidate in history at Emory University. She is completing a dissertation about immigrants, racial difference, and French national identity in Marseilles between 1919 and 1939. She has presented papers on the controversy over divorce during the Third Republic at meetings of the Berkshire Conference on the History of Women and the Society for French Historical Studies.

FRANCES GOUDA is an historian of modern Europe and colonialism in Southeast Asia and a Research Associate Professor in Women's Studies at George Washington University. She has recently published *Poverty and Political Culture: The Rhetoric of Social Welfare in the Netherlands and France, 1815–1854* (1995) and *Dutch Culture Overseas: Colonial Practice in the Netherlands Indies, 1900–1942* (1995), as well as a variety of articles on Dutch colonial ideology and practice. She is currently working on a Fulbright-sponsored project focusing on the United States, the Cold War, and the Indonesian struggle for independence, 1945–49.

JANET R. HORNE is an Associate Professor of French Literature, Language, and History in the Department of French of the University of Virginia. Her book, *La république sociale: Aux origines de l'état-providence*, will be published in Paris and in English in 1998 as *A Social Laboratory for Modern France: The Musée Social and the Rise of the Welfare State, 1890–1914*. She has written numerous articles, most recently, "Culture, History, and the Rhetoric of Reform at the 1889 Universal Exposition," in Robert Denommé and Roland Simon, eds., *The Unfinished Revolution: Notions of Culture in 19th and 20th Century France*.

RITA SMITH KIPP is Professor of Anthropology in the Department of Anthropology and Sociology at Kenyon College. She is the author of *The Early Years of the Dutch Colonial Mission: The Karo Field* (1990) and *Dissociated Identities: Ethnicity, Religion, and Class in an Indonesian Society* (1995). She has also published a wide range of articles, most recently, "Conversion by Affiliation: The History of the Karo Batak Protestant Church" in *American Ethnologist* (1995).

ELSBETH LOCHER-SCHOLTEN is an Associate Professor of History at the University of Utrecht in the Netherlands. She has written *Ethiek in fragmenten: Vijf studies over koloniaal denken en doen van Nederlanders in de Indonesische archipel, 1877–1942* (1981), and *Sumatraans sultanaat en koloniale staat: De relatie Djambi-Batavia (1830–1907) en het Nederlandse imperialisme* (1994). She is also a coeditor of several collections of essays on Indonesian women's history and the author of numerous articles focusing on historiography, gender, and the politics of culture in colonial Indonesia.

PAMELA PATTYNAMA is an Assistant Professor of Comparative Literature and Women's Studies at the University of Amsterdam in the Netherlands. She is the author of *Passages: Vrouwelijke adolescensie als verhaal en vertoog* (1992) and a coeditor of *Psychoanalyse en feminisme* (1993). She has also published in the fields of literary studies, photography, female adolescence, lesbian intertextuality, and interracial relations. The essay in this collection is part of a larger work devoted to narrative and visual representation, identity formation, and interracial sexuality in the literary history of the Dutch East Indies.

JEAN ELISABETH PEDERSEN is an Assistant Professor of History in the Humanities Department of the Eastman School of Music at the University of Rochester. She is currently working on a monograph entitled: "Legislating the Family: Republican Politics and Culture in France, 1870–1920." Her article "Regulating Abortion and Birth Control: Gender, Medicine, and Republican Politics in France" appeared in *French Historical Studies* (1996).

DANILYN FOX RUTHERFORD is an Assistant Professor of Anthropology at the University of Chicago. Her previous publications have focused on nationalism and cultural politics in contemporary Indonesia, such as "Of Birds and Gifts: Reviving Tradition on an Indonesian Frontier," in *Cultural Anthropology* (1996). She has coedited a volume devoted to Biak music in the Smithsonian/Folkways Records Music of Indonesia series.

INDEX

Italic page numbers refer to illustrations.